First World War
and Army of Occupation
War Diary
France, Belgium and Germany

61 DIVISION
Divisional Troops
Royal Army Medical Corps
2/2 South Midland Field Ambulance
4 September 1915 - 15 July 1919

WO95/3051/2

The Naval & Military Press Ltd
www.nmarchive.com
Published in association with The National Archives

Published by

The Naval & Military Press Ltd

Unit 10 Ridgewood Industrial Park,

Uckfield, East Sussex,

TN22 5QE England

Tel: +44 (0) 1825 749494

www.naval-military-press.com

www.nmarchive.com

This diary has been reprinted in facsimile from the original. Any imperfections are inevitably reproduced and the quality may fall short of modern type and cartographic standards.

Contents

Document type	Place/Title	Date From	Date To
Heading	2/2 South Midland Field Ambulance		
Heading	2-2nd Sth Midland Fld Amb. 1915 Sep-1919 July		
Heading	War Diary 2 Fd Amb 61 S.M.D Period Sept 1-Sept 30 1915		
War Diary	Oaklands Chelmsford	04/09/1915	06/09/1915
War Diary	Epping Camp	07/09/1915	30/09/1915
Heading	War Diary 2nd Field Amb 61 (S.M) Div. Period October 1-31 1915.		
War Diary	Epping Camp	07/10/1915	11/10/1915
War Diary	Chelmsford	12/10/1915	12/10/1915
War Diary	Hatfeed Period Chelmsford	13/10/1915	13/10/1915
War Diary	Chelmsford Epping	14/10/1915	14/10/1915
War Diary	Epping	19/10/1915	27/10/1915
War Diary	Chelmsford	29/10/1915	30/10/1915
Heading	War Diary 2nd Fd. Amb 61 (S Mid) Div Period 1st-30th Nov 1915		
War Diary	Oaklands Camp Chelmsford	01/11/1915	15/11/1915
Heading	War Diary Of 2. Fd Ambulance 61. S.M.D Period Dec 1-Dec 31 1915		
War Diary	Oaklands	01/12/1915	31/12/1915
Miscellaneous	Appendix 1 Routine Training		
Miscellaneous	Appendix II		
Miscellaneous	Scheme of field work Dec 14th 1915 in Little Waltham area Appendix III		
Miscellaneous	Appendix IV		
Heading	War Diary of 2nd Fd Amb 61. S.M Div From 1st Jan 1916 To 31 Jan 1916		
War Diary	Oaklands Chelmsford	01/01/1916	15/01/1916
War Diary	Oaklands	16/01/1916	16/01/1916
War Diary	Oaklands Hybridge	17/01/1916	17/01/1916
War Diary	Heybridge	18/01/1916	31/01/1916
Miscellaneous	Routine Training Appendix A		
Miscellaneous	Field Operation On 4/1/16. Appendix B	04/01/1916	04/01/1916
Miscellaneous	Scheme of Field Operations Carried out 11/1/16. Appendix C	11/01/1916	11/01/1916
Miscellaneous	Field Operation 25/1/16 Appendix D	25/01/1916	25/01/1916
Heading	War Diary 2/2 Fd Amb South Midland Period 25/5/16 To 31/5/16 Calonne-Sur-Lys 31/5/16		
War Diary	Perham-Down	23/05/1916	23/05/1916
War Diary	Southampton	24/05/1916	24/05/1916
War Diary	Havre	25/05/1916	26/05/1916
War Diary	Berguette	27/05/1916	27/05/1916
War Diary	Gonnehem	28/05/1916	30/05/1916
War Diary	Calonne Sur Lys	31/05/1916	31/05/1916
Miscellaneous	Appendix I War Diary 421 Fd Amb.		
Heading	War Diary 2/2 S. Mid Fd Amb 61 Div Period June 1-June 30 1916		
War Diary	Calonne Sur Lys	01/06/1916	10/06/1916
War Diary	Merville	11/06/1916	30/06/1916

Miscellaneous	Appendix I War Diary 421 Fd Amb 61 S.M Div Routine Duties		
Miscellaneous	Appendix II War Diary 2/2 S.Mid Fd Amb RAMC T.		
Miscellaneous	Appendix III War Diary 425 Fd Amb 61 Div	30/06/1916	30/06/1916
Heading	War Diary 2/2 S. Mid Fd Amb 61 Div From 1-31 July 1916 Vol III		
War Diary	Merville	01/07/1916	31/07/1916
Miscellaneous	Appendix I 2/2 Fd Amb RAMC T. 61Div		
Miscellaneous	Special Divisional Order	20/07/1916	20/07/1916
Miscellaneous	D.M.S No 1348	20/07/1916	20/07/1916
Heading	War Diary 2/2 Field Amb R.A.M.C.T 61 Div Period 1-31 Aug 1916 Volume IV		
War Diary	Lagorgue	01/08/1916	31/08/1916
Miscellaneous	App V O.C., 2/2nd F. Ambulance.	30/08/1916	30/08/1916
Miscellaneous	Appendix 2 O.C., 2/2nd F. Ambulance.	15/08/1916	15/08/1916
Miscellaneous	Appendix I War Diary of 2/2 Fd. Amb. 61 Divn		
Miscellaneous	Appendix 4 O.C 2/2 Fd Amb	28/08/1916	28/08/1916
Miscellaneous	Appendix 3 O.C 2/2 Fd Amb		
Miscellaneous	Summary of case at 2 Fd Amb 61Div For Period 1-31 Aug 1916	27/08/1916	27/08/1916
War Diary	War Diary 2/2 Sth Mid Fd Amb. Period 1-30 Sept 1916 Vol 5		
War Diary	Lagorgue	01/09/1916	30/09/1916
Miscellaneous	Appendix I War Diary 2/2 Fd Amb Divn		
Miscellaneous	Appendix II O.C 2/2 Fd Amb 61Divn	30/09/1916	30/09/1916
Heading	War Diary 2/2 S. Mid Fd Amb Vol VI Period 1-31 Oct 1916		
War Diary	Lagorgue	01/10/1916	27/10/1916
War Diary	Lagorgue Le Sart	28/10/1916	28/10/1916
War Diary	Le Sart	29/10/1916	31/10/1916
Miscellaneous	Bandages Dressing etc		
Heading	War Diary 2/2 S.M Fd Amb RAMC 2 Period 1-30 Nov 1916 Vol VII		
War Diary	Le Sart	01/11/1916	01/11/1916
War Diary	Le Sart To Busnes	02/11/1916	02/11/1916
War Diary	Busnes To Cauchy	03/11/1916	03/11/1916
War Diary	Cauchy To Rocourt	04/11/1916	04/11/1916
War Diary	Rocourt To Honval	05/11/1916	05/11/1916
War Diary	Honval To Villers L'Hopital	06/11/1916	06/11/1916
War Diary	Villers L'Hopital	07/11/1916	14/11/1916
War Diary	Vilers L'Hopital To Gorges	15/11/1916	15/11/1916
War Diary	Gorges To Pernois	16/11/1916	16/11/1916
War Diary	Pernois To Septonville	17/11/1916	17/11/1916
War Diary	Septenville To Warloy	18/11/1916	18/11/1916
War Diary	Warloy	19/11/1916	21/11/1916
War Diary	Vadencourt	22/11/1916	30/11/1916
Heading	War Diary 2/2 S.M Field Ambulance 61st Divn December 1916 Volume 8		
War Diary	Forceville	01/12/1916	31/12/1916
Heading	War Diary 2/2 S. Mid Fld Ambce R.A.M.C. (T.F.) Jan 1st-31st 1917 (inclusive)		
War Diary	Forceville	01/01/1917	15/01/1917
War Diary	Puchevillers	15/01/1917	17/01/1917
War Diary	Gezaincourt	17/01/1917	17/01/1917
War Diary	Le Plouy	18/01/1917	19/01/1917
War Diary	Domvast	19/01/1917	31/01/1917

Heading	War Diary 2/2 S. Mid Fld. Ambce R.A.M.C. (T.F.) Feb 1st-28th (Inclusive) 1917 Vol 10		
War Diary	Domvast	01/02/1917	04/02/1917
War Diary	Bussus-Bussue	04/02/1917	14/02/1917
War Diary	Wiencourt	15/02/1917	18/02/1917
War Diary	Vauvillers	18/02/1917	28/02/1917
Heading	War Diary 2/2 S. Mid Fld. Ambce R.A.M.C. (T.F) March 1st-31st Inclusive 1917		
War Diary	Vauvillers	01/03/1917	17/03/1917
War Diary	Herleville	17/03/1917	28/03/1917
War Diary	Athies	28/03/1917	31/03/1917
Heading	War Diary 2/2 S. Mid Fld. Ambce R.A.M.C. (T.F) April 1st-30th (inclusive) 1917 Vol-12		
War Diary	Athies Tertry	01/04/1917	11/04/1917
War Diary	Offoy	11/04/1917	21/04/1917
War Diary	Douilly	21/04/1917	30/04/1917
Heading	War Diary 2/2 S. Mid Fld. Ambce. R.A.M.C. (T.F.) May 1st-31st (Inclusive) 1917 Vol-13		
War Diary	Douilly	01/05/1917	15/05/1917
War Diary	Mesnil	15/05/1917	17/05/1917
War Diary	Wargnies	17/05/1917	21/05/1917
War Diary	Wargnies Bretel	21/05/1917	23/05/1917
War Diary	Ivergny	23/05/1917	24/05/1917
War Diary	Berneville	24/05/1917	31/05/1917
Heading	War Diary 2/2 S. Mid Fld. Ambce R.A.M.C.T.F June 1st-30th 1917 Vol-14		
War Diary	Berneville	01/06/1917	04/06/1917
War Diary	Arras	05/06/1917	10/06/1917
War Diary	Dainville	10/06/1917	23/06/1917
War Diary	Bachimont	23/06/1917	30/06/1917
Heading	War Diary 2/2 S. Mid Fld. Ambce R.A.M.C.T.F. July 1st-31st 1917 Vol-15		
Miscellaneous	Summary of medical War Diaries of 2/2nd S.M. F.A. 61st Division		
War Diary	Bachimont	01/07/1917	24/07/1917
War Diary	Sericourt	24/07/1917	26/07/1917
War Diary	Rubrouck	26/07/1917	31/07/1917
Heading	War Diary 2/2 S. Mid Fld. Ambce R.A.M.C. (T.F.) August 1st-31st 1917 Vol-16		
War Diary	Rubrouck	01/08/1917	15/08/1917
War Diary	Hillhoek	16/08/1917	31/08/1917
Miscellaneous	Summary Of Medical War Diaries Of 2/2nd S.M.F.A. 61st Div.		
War Diary	War Diary 2/2 S. Mid Fld. Ambce R.A.M.C. (T.F.) September 1st-30th (inclusive) 1917 Vol 17		
War Diary	Hillhoek	01/09/1917	14/09/1917
War Diary	Lee Camp L.0.6.9.2. Sheet 27.	15/09/1917	17/09/1917
War Diary	Eecke	17/09/1917	19/09/1917
War Diary	Berneville	19/09/1917	24/09/1917
War Diary	St. Nicholas	24/09/1917	30/09/1917
Miscellaneous	61st Div. 5th Corps 5th Army		
Heading	War Diary 2/2 S. Mid Fld Ambce R.A.M.C.T.F. October 1st-31st (inclusive) 1917 Volume-18		
War Diary	St. Nicholas Arras	01/10/1917	31/10/1917
Heading	War Diary 2/2 S. Mid Fld. Ambce R.A.M.C.T November 1st-30th 1917 Vol-19		

War Diary	St. Nicholas Arras	01/11/1917	29/11/1917
War Diary	Wanquetin	29/11/1917	30/11/1917
War Diary	Havrincourt Wood	30/11/1917	30/11/1917
Heading	War Diary 2/2 S. Mid Fld. Ambce R.A.M.C.T.F December 1st-31st 1917 Vol-20		
War Diary	Havrincourt Wood Fins	01/12/1917	03/12/1917
War Diary	Equancourt	03/12/1917	23/12/1917
War Diary	Sailly Le Sec	24/12/1917	30/12/1917
War Diary	Ignaucourt	30/12/1917	30/12/1917
War Diary	Le Quesnel	31/12/1917	31/12/1917
Heading	War Diary 2/2 S. Midland Field Ambulance R.A.M.C.T. January 1st-31st (inclusive) 1918 Volume 21		
War Diary	Le Quesnel	01/01/1918	06/01/1918
War Diary	Nesle	07/01/1918	09/01/1918
War Diary	Germaine	09/01/1918	14/01/1918
War Diary	Vaux	15/01/1918	31/01/1918
Heading	War Diary 2/2 S. Mid Fld. Ambce R.A.M.C. (T.F.) February 1st-28th (inclusive) 1918 Vol 22		
War Diary	Vaux	01/02/1918	22/02/1918
War Diary	Germaine	22/02/1918	25/02/1918
War Diary	Foreste	26/02/1918	28/02/1918
Heading	War Diary 2/2 S. Mid Fld. Ambce R.A.M.C.T. March 1st-31st 1918 Vol-23		
War Diary	Foreste	01/03/1918	22/03/1918
War Diary	Gruny	23/03/1918	23/03/1918
War Diary	Le Quesnoy	24/03/1918	26/03/1918
War Diary	Moreuil	26/03/1918	28/03/1918
War Diary	Oresmaux	28/03/1918	29/03/1918
War Diary	Dury	30/03/1918	31/03/1918
Heading	War Diary 2/2 S. Mid Fld. Ambce R.A.M.C.T April 1st-30th 1918 Vol-24		
War Diary	Dury	01/04/1918	04/04/1918
War Diary	Floxicourt	04/04/1918	11/04/1918
War Diary	Pierriere	12/04/1918	12/04/1918
War Diary	Guarbecque	12/04/1918	13/04/1918
War Diary	Molinghem	13/04/1918	30/04/1918
Heading	War Diary 2/2 S. Mid Fld. Ambce R.A.M.C.T May 1st-31st 1918 Vol-25		
War Diary	Molinghem	01/05/1918	31/05/1918
Heading	War Diary 2/2 S. Mid Fld. Ambce R.A.M.C.T June 1st-30th 1918 Vol-26		
War Diary	Molinghem	01/06/1918	11/07/1918
War Diary	Fontes	11/07/1918	21/07/1918
War Diary	W. Of Racquinghem	22/07/1918	31/07/1918
Heading	War Diary 2/2 S. Mid Fld. Ambce R.A.M.C.T August 1st-31st 1918 Vol-28		
War Diary	Lambres	01/08/1918	05/08/1918
War Diary	Steenbecque	06/08/1918	31/08/1918
Heading	War Diary 2/2 S. Mid Fld. Ambce R.A.M.C.T Sept 1st-31st 1918 Vol-29		
War Diary	Steenbecque	01/09/1918	17/09/1918
War Diary	Haverskerque	18/09/1918	30/09/1918
Heading	War Diary 2/2 S. Midland Fld. Ambce R.A.M.C.T October 1st-31st 1918 Vol-30		
War Diary	Steenbecque	01/10/1918	03/10/1918

War Diary	Molinghem	03/10/1918	06/10/1918
War Diary	Freshevillers	06/10/1918	09/10/1918
War Diary	Sheet 57c E.B.C 1 9	09/10/1918	18/10/1918
War Diary	Cantaing	18/10/1918	19/10/1918
War Diary	Cagnoncles	19/10/1918	23/10/1918
War Diary	St. Aubert	23/10/1918	25/10/1918
War Diary	Sheet 51 A P.30.b	26/10/1918	31/10/1918
Heading	War Diary 2/2 S. Mid Fld. Ambce R.A.M.C.T November 1st-30th 1918 Vol-31		
War Diary	Sheet 51a P.30.b	01/11/1918	02/11/1918
War Diary	Avesnes-Lez-Aubert	02/11/1918	05/11/1918
War Diary	Bermerain	05/11/1918	08/11/1918
War Diary	Sepmeries	08/11/1918	14/11/1918
War Diary	St Aubert	14/11/1918	15/11/1918
War Diary	Cambrai	15/11/1918	26/11/1918
War Diary	Mesnil-Domqueur	26/11/1918	30/11/1918
Heading	War Diary 2/2 S. Mid Fld. Ambce R.A.M.C.T December 1st-31st 1918 Vol-32		
War Diary	Mesnil-Domqueur	01/12/1918	08/12/1918
War Diary	Agenville	08/12/1918	31/12/1918
Heading	War Diary 2/2 S. Mid Fld. Ambulance R.A.M.C.T January 1st-31st Inclusive 1919 Vol-33		
War Diary	Agenville	01/01/1919	31/01/1919
Heading	War Diary 2/2 S. Mid Fld. Ambulance R.A.M.C.T February 1st To 28th Inclusive 1919 Vol-34		
War Diary	Agenville	01/02/1919	13/02/1919
War Diary	Yaucourt-Bussus	14/02/1919	28/02/1919
Heading	War Diary Vol-35 For March 1919 2/2 South Mid Field Amb		
War Diary	Yaucourt-Bussus	01/03/1919	31/03/1919
Heading	War Diary Vol-36 For April 1919 2/2 South Mid Field Ambulance		
War Diary	Yaucourt Bussus	01/04/1919	30/04/1919
Heading	War Diary Vol-37 For May 1919		
War Diary	Yaucourt Bussus	01/05/1919	31/05/1919
Heading	War Diary Vol-38 For June 1919		
War Diary	Yaucourt Bussus	01/06/1919	06/06/1919
War Diary	Abbeville	07/06/1919	30/06/1919
Heading	War Diary Vol-39 For July 1919		
War Diary	Abbeville	01/07/1919	15/07/1919

2/2 South Midland
Field Ambulance

61ST DIVISION

2-2ND STH MIDLD FLD AMB.

~~MAY 1916-DEC 1918~~

1915 SEP – 1919 JLY

2/2

War Diary. 2 Fd Amb 61 S M D

Period Sept 1 - Sept 20. 1915

Chelmsford - Epping

Epping Camp
1/10/15.

George N Gray
Lt Col RAMC.

Instructions regarding War Diaries and Intelligence Summaries are contained in F. S. Regs., Part II. and the Staff Manual respectively. Title pages will be prepared in manuscript.

WAR DIARY
or
INTELLIGENCE SUMMARY.
(Erase heading not required.)

Army Form C. 2118.

Hour, Date, Place	Summary of Events and Information	Remarks and references to Appendices
Oaklands Chelmsford Saty 4 Sept 1915	Lieut W J Craig reported for duty. A S C arrived, arrived to pack Stores preparatory to march for Epping Camp.	
Oaklands Chelmsford Monday Sept 6 1915	Unit proceeded by road to Epping. 9-15 – 4-30. No men fell out on march. No trouble with transport. On arrival unloaded wagons & arranged tents of duties.	
Epping Camp Tuesday 7 Sept 1915	Details of camp arranged, Officers round Stores tents, arranged with Regimental M.O's to undertake medical duties of Units which had no M.O. Air raid over camp at night. Whole unit called out by orderly, stood by for 1 hour 10–11 p.m. Men behaved well no sign of panic.	
Epping Camp Wed 8 Sept 1915	230 inoculations in morning. Zeppelins over camp again. Men stood by. Orders given to medical section to supply store men so that there was one man standing to each mule or horse.	
Epping Camp Friday Sept 10 1915	Brigadier General the Marquis of Salisbury inspected the Camp.	

Instructions regarding War Diaries and Intelligence Summaries are contained in F. S. Regs., Part II. and the Staff Manual respectively. Title pages will be prepared in manuscript.

WAR DIARY
or
INTELLIGENCE SUMMARY.
(Erase heading not required.)

Army Form C. 2118.

Hour, Date, Place	Summary of Events and Information	Remarks and references to Appendices
Epping Camp Saty Sept 11th 1915	All tents struck to air the ground. Air raid over camp 12.15 pm Explosive & incendiary bombs dropped in lines of R.F.A. & [illegible] Incendiary bombs burning in lines. All men turned out & fallen in. Details sent to transport to supply spare men to hold mules & horses. Arrangements made in medical inspection room for dressing any casualties. No harm done. Behaviour of whole unit exceedingly good under trying conditions.	
Epping Camp Sunday Sept 12 1915	Officer of R.E. from Witham over at 9.45 pm to make enquiries about raid. All men of unit on duty at the time paraded & questioned by officers. Whole unit paraded and instructed as to procedure should other raids occur.	
Epping Camp Thursday Sept 16 1915	Lieut J Bannerman reported for duty	
Epping Camp Friday Sept 24 1915	Unit took part in Brigade field day - medical arrangements made in accordance with the tactical scheme	

(73989) W4141—463. 400,000. 9/14. H.&J.Ltd. Forms/C. 2118/10.

Instructions regarding War Diaries and Intelligence Summaries are contained in F. S. Regs., Part II. and the Staff Manual respectively. Title pages will be prepared in manuscript.

WAR DIARY
or
INTELLIGENCE SUMMARY.
(Erase heading not required.)

Army Form C. 2118.

Hour, Date, Place	Summary of Events and Information	Remarks and references to Appendices
Epping Camp Wed Sept 29 1915	Major Warwick reported for duty. Unit paraded to hear address from representative of Minister of Munitions. Rolls of men available for such work prepared.	
Epping Camp Thursday Sept 30 1915.	Unit took part in Brigade operations, continuation of tactical scheme of previous Friday. Medical arrangements made for scheme	
Epping Camp. Period Sept 6-30 1915	Progressive work of the unit has proceeded during this period. The medical arrangements for 2/1 Wor. Bn, R.F.A. A.S.C. who have no medical officers attached have been performed by the unit. Field Hospital and V.A.D. Hospital have been supervised. During the earlier part of the period the weather was warm & dry, the last week of the month it was damp & cold. General health of camp has been good. A few venereal cases & a few cases of scabies. During last week a number of colds & rheumatic affections. The unit has supplied men for sanitary duty at the Hornfall Destructor in the Transport lines. These latter lines on our arrival were very unsatisfactory from a sanitary point of view, but have greatly improved. There have been a few casualties from accidents but not many. The behaviour of the whole unit during several periods of danger & tension has been [illegible]	

(73989) W4141—463. 400,000. 9/14. H.&J.Ltd. Forms/C. 2118/10.

Confidential

War Diary 2nd Field Amb 61 (S.M.) Div.

Period October 1 - 31 1915.

George W Craig
Lieut Col RAMC
O.C. 2nd Amb 61 S M D

Oaklands Camp
Chelmsford 3/XI/15

Instructions regarding War Diaries and Intelligence Summaries are contained in F. S. Regs., Part II. and the Staff Manual respectively. Title pages will be prepared in manuscript.

WAR DIARY
or
INTELLIGENCE SUMMARY.
(Erase heading not required.)

Army Form C. 2118.

Place	Date	Hour	Summary of Events and Information	Remarks and references to Appendices
Epping Camp	Oct 7/15		Surgeon General Culling visited the camp and inspected the sanitary condition of the whole camps of the Brigade	
Epping Camp	Oct 8/15		The unit took part in a Brigade field day. Dressing Station at Theydon Bois, advanced dressing station at the Hill, & then moved to Hobbs Cross.	
Epping	Oct 9 1915		Lieut J. Bannerman gazetted to the unit, dated 9 Sept 1915	
Epping	Oct 10 1915		Unit engaged in loading wagons for divisional operations.	
Epping	Oct 11 1915		Unit proceeded by road to Chelmsford, billeted at Crane court in assembly rooms.	
Chelmsford	Oct 12. 15		Proceeded in morning with Brigade Major to inspect site for bivouac at Hatfield Peverel. Unit proceeded to Hatfield Peverel by road in afternoon bivouacked in field at the Priory.	

T2134. Wt. W708—776. 500000. 4/15. Sir J. C. & S.

Instructions regarding War Diaries and Intelligence Summaries are contained in F. S. Regs., Part II. and the Staff Manual respectively. Title pages will be prepared in manuscript.

WAR DIARY
or
INTELLIGENCE SUMMARY.
(Erase heading not required.)

Army Form C. 2118.

Place	Date	Hour	Summary of Events and Information	Remarks and references to Appendices
Hatfield Peverel – Chelmsford	13 Oct. 15		Our Brigade in reserve. Inspected all the camps. A D M S 61 S M D & D D M S 3rd Army inspected camps. A D V S inspected transport. Unit returned by road to Chelmsford, very foggy after Boreham but transport did admirably. Unit reoccupied billets at Crane Court	
Chelmsford – Epping	14 Oct/15		Unit returned by road to camp at Epping. None of unit fell out. Halted, rest at [illegible] Heath.	
Epping	19 Oct/15		Unit took part in Brigade operations.	
Epping	22 Oct/15		28 recruits joined the unit from ad[illegible] [illegible]	
Epping	23 Oct/15		1 man joined 8th [illegible] for [illegible]	
Epping	27 Oct 15		Unit proceeded by road to Oaklands reoccupied huts [illegible] by [illegible]	
Chelmsford	29 Oct 15		3 recruits joined unit from [illegible]	

T2134. Wt. W708–776. 500000. 4/15. Sir J. C. & S.

Instructions regarding War Diaries and Intelligence Summaries are contained in F. S. Regs., Part II. and the Staff Manual respectively. Title pages will be prepared in manuscript.

WAR DIARY
or
INTELLIGENCE SUMMARY.
(Erase heading not required.)

Army Form C. 2118.

Place	Date	Hour	Summary of Events and Information	Remarks and references to Appendices
Chelmsford	30/X/15		proceeded to Danbury took over hospital there from 1st Fd Amb. Articles and beds & cots all taken over. Inspected the billeting arrangements for the orderlies.	

T2134. Wt. W708—776. 500000. 4/15. Sir J. C. & S.

Confidential.

War Diary. 2nd Fd. Amb 61.(S Mid.) Div.

Period 1st – 30th Nov 1915

Oaklands Camp.
Chelmsford
2/XII/XV.

George W Craig.
Lt Col RAMC T.
OC. 2nd Fd Amb 61 S M D

Instructions regarding War Diaries and Intelligence Summaries are contained in F. S. Regs., Part II. and the Staff Manual respectively. Title pages will be prepared in manuscript.

WAR DIARY
or
INTELLIGENCE SUMMARY.
(Erase heading not required.)

Army Form C. 2118.

Place	Date	Hour	Summary of Events and Information	Remarks and references to Appendices
Oaklands Camp Chelmsford	Nov 1. 1915		Field day with full transport, in Galleywood, Stock, Margaretting area. Regimental aid posts, advanced dressing station & dressing station opened, orders issued for a retirement	
	Nov 4th 1915		Unit took part in Brigade field day at Danbury. Advanced dressing station at Woodham Mortimer Hall, dressing station at MALDON. No actual casualties to attend to. A long march, none of the men of unit fell out.	
	Nov 10th 1915		53 recruits detailed to the unit from Birmingham bringing personnel up to strength	
	Nov 13 1915		Major Warwick transferred for duty from this unit to Provisional Bn at ROCHFORD.	
	Nov 15 1915		Chiropody class commenced.	

T2134. Wt. W708–776. 500000. 4/15. Sir J. C. & S.

Instructions regarding War Diaries and Intelligence Summaries are contained in F. S. Regs., Part II. and the Staff Manual respectively. Title pages will be prepared in manuscript.

WAR DIARY
or
INTELLIGENCE SUMMARY.
(Erase heading not required.)

Army Form C. 2118.

Place	Date	Hour	Summary of Events and Information	Remarks and references to Appendices
Oaklands Camp Chelmsford.			During the past month a number of recruits have been detailed to the unit which is now up to strength. As the men were quite untrained frequent recruit drills had to be imparted. The unit has been in charge of the hospital at Danbury where practical nursing is carried out by nursing orderlies. The Thresh Disinfector is also in charge of the unit and a large number of blankets and kits have been disinfected.	
			Every opportunity has been taken on field days to impress on all ranks the necessity for improvised work, and this has been carried out practically.	
			During the month the order for the transfer of the personnel of the transport of the unit to the Army Service Corps came out. With two exceptions the men were willing to transfer, and the necessary arrangements were made.	
			The training has been carried out in accordance with the general and special programme drawn up by the A.D.M.S.	
			One man was demobilized during the month	

T2134. Wt. W708–776. 500000. 4/15. Sir J. C. & S.

Confidential.

War Diary of

2. Fd Ambulance. 61. S M D

Period Dec 1 - Dec 31. 1915

George W Bray
Lt Col RAMC ?

Instructions regarding War Diaries and Intelligence Summaries are contained in F. S. Regs., Part II. and the Staff Manual respectively. Title pages will be prepared in manuscript.

WAR DIARY
or
INTELLIGENCE SUMMARY.
(Erase heading not required.)

Army Form C. 2118.

Place	Date	Hour	Summary of Events and Information	Remarks and references to Appendices
Dec 1. 1915	Oaklands		Routine Training (See Appendix i)	See appendix 1. G.W.C.
		3-30	Bathing parade.	
Dec. 2. 1915	Oaklands.		Routine training	G.W.C.
Dec 3. 1915	Oaklands.		Routine training.	
			One man released to munitions (Authority W.O letter 19 Gen No 5415-AG1.	
		11-1 PM.	Combined night alarm with 1st Fd Amb; wagons loaded at Stores, route march. WIDFORD - WRITTLE - CHELMSFORD.	Ref. O.S Map 30 Sc. 2m - 1in G.W.C.
Dec. 4th. 1915	Oaklands		General fatigues & cleaning of camp	G.W.C.
			Medical Inspection of unit	
Dec 5th. 1915	Oaklands.		Church Parade at Cathedral.	G.W.C.
			Inspection of transport by Col. Collis, O.C. 61 Div Train A.S.C	
Dec. 6. 1915	Oaklands.		Routine training.	G.W.C.

Instructions regarding War Diaries and Intelligence Summaries are contained in F. S. Regs., Part II. and the Staff Manual respectively. Title pages will be prepared in manuscript.

WAR DIARY
or
INTELLIGENCE SUMMARY.
(Erase heading not required.)

Army Form C. 2118.

Place	Date	Hour	Summary of Events and Information	Remarks and references to Appendices
Dec. 7 1915	Oaklands.		Routine training Bathing Parade Transfer of transport section to No 4 Coy. 61 Div train A.S.C. (Authority C.I. order 1662 d. 7/XII/XI. Examination of recruits for 5th rate of corps pay.	G. H. B.
Dec. 8 1915	Oaklands.		Field work in area GALLEYWOOD - WEST HANNINGFIELD - EAST HANNINGFIELD. GREAT BADDOW	Ref. OS Map 30 sc. 2 m - 1 inch appendix ii G. H. B.
Dec 9. 1915	Oaklands		Routine training. 5 men proceeded to Grove Park for examination for transfer to A.S.C. mechanical transport Lieut. J. H. Parsons proceeded on leave.	G. H. B.
Dec. 10th 1915	Oaklands.		Routine training One man transferred to 7 Prov. Bde Westcliff. Authority O/c Records P1729 d. 3/12/15	G. H. B.

Instructions regarding War Diaries and Intelligence Summaries are contained in F. S. Regs., Part II. and the Staff Manual respectively. Title pages will be prepared in manuscript.

WAR DIARY

or

INTELLIGENCE SUMMARY.

(Erase heading not required.)

Army Form C. 2118.

Place	Date	Hour	Summary of Events and Information	Remarks and references to Appendices
Dec 11th 1915	Oaklands.		Medical Inspection of Unit General fatigues & clearing of Camp. 10 men, detached from No 4 Coy 61 Div Train A.S.C. reported for duty.	GWB
Dec 12 1915	Oaklands.		Church Parade at Cathedral.	GWB
Dec 13. 1915	Oaklands.		Routine training. One man transferred to No 4 Coy. 61 Div Train A.S.C Inspection of remount cases at No 1 Coy A.S.C. ground.	GWB
Dec 14 1915	Oaklands.		Field work 9. AM to 4 PM in area CHIGNALL SMEALY, LITTLE WALTHAM.	Appendix iii Ref OS Map 30 GWB
Dec 15 1915	Oaklands		Routine training	GWB

T2134. Wt. W708–776. 500000. 4/15. Sir J. C. & S.

Instructions regarding War Diaries and Intelligence Summaries are contained in F. S. Regs., Part II. and the Staff Manual respectively. Title pages will be prepared in manuscript.

WAR DIARY
or
INTELLIGENCE SUMMARY.
(Erase heading not required.)

Army Form C. 2118.

Place	Date	Hour	Summary of Events and Information	Remarks and references to Appendices
Dec 16. 1915	Oaklands		Routine training	Ref. OS Map 30
		9. P.M.	Night march & packing of wagons. CHELMSFORD - BROOMFIELD - WRITTLE. CHELMSFORD.	G.H.C
Dec 17 1915	Oaklands.		Routine training.	
			Letter received calling special attention to Central Force order concerning Christmas Leave	G.H.C
Dec 18. 1915	Oaklands.		Medical inspection of unit	
			General fatigues & cleaning of camp.	G.H.C
			Bathing Parade.	
			Lieut Bannerman proceeded on detached duty as MO to 2/1. Ox & Bucks Bn.	G.H.C
Dec 19. 1915	Oaklands		Church Parade at St Johns Church	G.H.C
Dec 20. 1915	Oaklands		Routine training.	G.H.C
			Medical Board held by ADMS at Oaklands	

Instructions regarding War Diaries and Intelligence Summaries are contained in F. S. Regs., Part II. and the Staff Manual respectively. Title pages will be prepared in manuscript.

WAR DIARY
or
INTELLIGENCE SUMMARY.
(Erase heading not required.)

Army Form C. 2118.

Place	Date	Hour	Summary of Events and Information	Remarks and references to Appendices
Dec. 21 1915 Oaklands.			Routine training.	G.W.B.
Dec 22. 1915 Oaklands			Routine training Bathing parade.	G.W.B.
Dec 23. 15	Oaklands.		Routine training General fatigues & cleaning of camp. Men proceeded on Christmas leave	G.W.B.
Dec 24. 15	Oaklands.		Routine training.	G.W.B.
Dec 25. 15	Oaklands.		Christmas Church parade at St Johns Church. Inspection of huts which had been decorated, & award of prizes to best hut Visit to Danbury Hospital Visit to men's mess hut for Christmas dinner.	G.W.B.

T2134. Wt. W708–776. 500000. 4/15. Sir J. C. & S.

Instructions regarding War Diaries and Intelligence Summaries are contained in F. S. Regs., Part II. and the Staff Manual respectively. Title pages will be prepared in manuscript.

WAR DIARY
or
INTELLIGENCE SUMMARY.
(Erase heading not required.)

Army Form C. 2118.

Place	Date	Hour	Summary of Events and Information	Remarks and references to Appendices
Dec 26 1915	Oaklands.		Church parade at Cathedral Lieut Bond proceeded on leave of absence.	GWC.
Dec 27. 1915	Oaklands.		Routine training.	GWC
Dec 28. 1915	Oaklands		Routine training.	
Dec 29 1915	Oaklands		Routine training	
Dec 30. 1915	Oaklands.		Routine training. Orders received for Brigade field training on 31 Dec.	
Dec 31 1915	Oaklands		7.0. AM proceeded by route march to COLD NORTON. via GREAT BADDOW - SANDON DANBURY COMMON COCKCLARKS - Ambulance parked in field at Station. Hot meal served. Unit returned by road reaching camp 5-30 PM. A wet day, only 3 men, all recruits fell out on line of march.	Ref. O.S. Map 30 sc. 2 m - 1 inch Appendix IV GWC

Instructions regarding War Diaries and Intelligence Summaries are contained in F. S. Regs., Part II. and the Staff Manual respectively. Title pages will be prepared in manuscript.

WAR DIARY
or
INTELLIGENCE SUMMARY.
(Erase heading not required.)

Army Form C. 2118.

Place	Date	Hour	Summary of Events and Information	Remarks and references to Appendices
Dec 31. 1915 Oaklands.			Reported at Head Quarters LATCHINGDON for Conference.	G.W.C.
			Visited hospital at DANBURY.	
			Lieut W J Craig proceeded on leave.	

George W Craig Lt Col RAMC
OC 2 Fd Amb 61 SMD

Oaklands Camp
Chelmsford
Dec 31/15

T2134. Wt. W708–776. 500000. 4/15. Sir J. C. & S.

Appendix 1.

Subject Routine Training.

2. Fd Amb. 61. S M D

Oaklands Camp

Chelmsford

The routine training of the unit is carried out in accordance with the weekly training Programme submitted by A.D.M.S. Gr.S.M.D.

It comprises systematic training in all branches of the unit's work.

α. Physical Drill, daily.

β. Lectures
on surgical & medical work
on sanitation

γ. Demonstrations.
on contents of wagons & panniers.
on packing wagons
on extemporized first aid.
on building of bivouacs & shelters.
on sanitation
on use of water carts & sterilization of water

δ. Field work.
signalling
route marching & night marching.
erection of dressing stations.
collection & disposal of wounded.

ε. Practical instruction for nursing orderlies at Danbury Hospital & at Kenilworth.

Appendix ii

Outline of field work in GALLEYWOOD AREA

8/12/15

2nd Fd Amb G.S.M.D.

Ref. O.S. Map 30 SC 2m to 1 in

The advanced dressing station was opened in field at SHIP INN, the wounded were placed out CRONDON PARK - MOLEHILL COMMON.

Dressing station in field at Cross Roads ¼ mile W of first E in EASTHANNINGFIELD HALL

Appendix iii

Scheme of field work Dec 14 1915 in LITTLE WALTHAM area

2nd Fd Amb 61st Div

Ref. O.S Map 30. Sc 2 m ½ / in

The area beyond an imaginary line CHELMSFORD - BOYTON CROSS was to be cleared.

Advanced dressing Station was opened at CHIGNAL SMEALY, to which the casualties were brought by bearers.

Dressing Station at barn, at the Cross Roads at Church in LITTLE WALTHAM

Appendix IV

Tactical exercise held on Dec 31. 1915

182 Infy Bde Order no 30.

2 Fd Amb. 61. S M Div.
Oaklands Camp
Chelmsford

Ref. O.S. map 30. sc. 2^m to 1 inch.

The unit left camp in full marching order & proceeded by route march to COLD NORTON STATION.
The ambulance was parked in field at COLD NORTON STATION.

Intention. The position to be occupied, was a line ALTHORNE STATION, ALTHORNE BARNS LANGLING HALL - MARSH HOUSE.

Medical arrangements suggested for dealing with casualties in the area were.

Regimental Aid Posts — TYLE HALL.
LONDON HAYS.
in field at ALTHORNE BARNS.

Advanced Dressing Station. — SNOREHAM HALL.

Dressing Station. — in school at COLD NORTON

Headquarters 2nd Fd Amb. — in school at COLD NORTON.

It was understood that artillery fire could be neglected in the scheme, which influenced the selection of above positions.

Confidential

War Diary of

2nd Fd Amb 61 S M Div

From 1st Jany 1916 to 31 Jany 1916

George W Craig
Lt Col RAMC T
O.C. 2 Fd Amb 61 S M Div

Instructions regarding War Diaries and Intelligence Summaries are contained in F. S. Regs., Part II. and the Staff Manual respectively. Title pages will be prepared in manuscript.

WAR DIARY
or
INTELLIGENCE SUMMARY.
(Erase heading not required.)

Army Form C. 2118.

Place	Date	Hour	Summary of Events and Information	Remarks and references to Appendices
~~Oaklands~~ Chelmsford	1/1/16		Routine training	App A GWC
" "	2/1/16		Church Parade	GWC
"	3/1/16		Routine training. Lieut W J Craig granted 3 days leave of absence	GWC.
"	4/1/16		Field training by two sections. One section on road making at Oaklands.	App B GWC.
"	5/1/16		3 Sergeants reported for duty after attachment to 4 Coy ASC for instruction. Routine training	GWC
"	6/1/16		Routine training. Kit allowance granted to 33 recruits.	GWC
" "	7/1/16		Routine training. Lieut W J Craig reported for duty	GWC

Instructions regarding War Diaries and Intelligence Summaries are contained in F. S. Regs., Part II. and the Staff Manual respectively. Title pages will be prepared in manuscript.

WAR DIARY
or
INTELLIGENCE SUMMARY.
(Erase heading not required.)

Army Form C. 2118.

Place	Date	Hour	Summary of Events and Information	Remarks and references to Appendices
Oakland Chelmsford	8/1/16		Routine training. One man detached for water duty to 2/5 Glosters Bn	GHC
" "	9/1/16		Church Parade. One man discharged from unit under K.R. para 392 sub par XVI authority – medical board.	GHC.
" "	10/1/16		Routine training. N.C.O from 3/1 S M Fd Coy R.E reported for duty to supervise fatigue work on roads at huts	GHC
" "	11/1/16		Field training by B & C Sections, A Section left for road making.	App C GHC
" "	12/1/16		Routine training.	GHC
" "	13/1/16		Routine training	GHC
" "	14/1/16		Routine training. One man released from munition work reported for duty	GHC

Instructions regarding War Diaries and Intelligence Summaries are contained in F. S. Regs., Part II. and the Staff Manual respectively. Title pages will be prepared in manuscript.

WAR DIARY
or
INTELLIGENCE SUMMARY.
(Erase heading not required.)

Army Form C. 2118.

Place	Date	Hour	Summary of Events and Information	Remarks and references to Appendices
Oaklands			Orders received for move by unit to Heybridge.	
Chelmsford	15/1/16		Lieut J.H. Parsons proceeded to Heybridge to arrange billets for men.	G.W.C
			Routine training	
			One man transferred to Mechanical Transport A.S.C. authority W.O letter 115/A.S.C. 806 (Q.M.G.3)	
Oakland	16/1/16		Church Parade.	
			details engaged in packing wagons preparatory to move.	G.W.C
			Lieut Parsons at Heybridge again to complete billeting arrangements.	
Oaklands } Heybridge }	17/1/16		Unit proceeded by route march to Heybridge. Calling at Danbury Hospital, where hot dinner was awaiting the men. Reached Heybridge 4-0 P.M. Met by Lieut Parsons who took over and allotted the men to their billets. Lieut Groves R.A.M.C. reported for duty	G.W.C
Heybridge	18/1/16		Routine training. Fatigue work	
			Visit to V.A.D Hospital. 10 beds allotted to brigade for emergency cases.	G.W.C
" "	19/1/16		Routine training Fatigue work	G.W.C
			O.C attended lecture at R.A.M.C College on Gas Poisoning	

Instructions regarding War Diaries and Intelligence Summaries are contained in F. S. Regs., Part II. and the Staff Manual respectively. Title pages will be prepared in manuscript.

WAR DIARY
or
INTELLIGENCE SUMMARY.
(*Erase heading not required.*)

Army Form C. 2118.

Place	Date	Hour	Summary of Events and Information	Remarks and references to Appendices
Weybridge	20/1/16		Routine training.	GHG
" "	21/1/16		Routine training. A.D.M.S. 61 & S.M.O. visited Headquarters, giving instructions for Div San off to visit same & make report.	GHG
" "	22/1/16		Routine training. Capt Hulbert inspected Hosp & Advised that further accommodation be secured for dispensary & medical inspection room.	GHG
" "	23/1/16.		Church Parade at St Andrews Church Weybridge along with No 2 Coy A.S.C.	GHG
"	24/1/16		Routine training.	
			C Section took over nursing duties at Danbury Hospital, proceeding by route march.	GHG
			Lieut J H Parsons granted 7 days sick leave	
"	25/1/16		One man returned for duty with Provisional Bde.	
			Feed operations for whole unit. Fresh premises taken for dispensary & inspection room.	App D. GHG
			A.D.M.S. notified.	
"	26/1/16		Routine training. Capt Hulbert inspected new premises.	GHG
			Two men returned to duty from munition works.	

T2134. Wt. W708—776. 500000. 4/15. Sir J. C. & S.

Instructions regarding War Diaries and Intelligence Summaries are contained in F. S. Regs., Part II. and the Staff Manual respectively. Title pages will be prepared in manuscript.

WAR DIARY
or
INTELLIGENCE SUMMARY.
(Erase heading not required.)

Army Form C. 2118.

Place	Date	Hour	Summary of Events and Information	Remarks and references to Appendices
Heybridge	27/1/16		Routine training.	GWC
Heybridge	28/1/16		Routine training. Lieut Bowd granted 3 days leave of absence	GWC
" "	29/1/16		Routine training.	GWC
" "	30/1/16		Church Parade.	GWC
" "	31/1/16		Routine training one man reported for duty on expiry of period of demobilization	GWC

George W Craig
Lt Col Dames
OC 2 Idlawo 61 S MD

Heybridge 1/2/16

T2134. Wt. W708–776. 500000. 4/15. Sir J. C. & S.

Army Form C. 2118.

Instructions regarding War Diaries and Intelligence Summaries are contained in F. S. Regs., Part II. and the Staff Manual respectively. Title pages will be prepared in manuscript.

WAR DIARY
or
INTELLIGENCE SUMMARY.

(*Erase heading not required.*)

Place	Date	Hour	Summary of Events and Information	Remarks and references to Appendices

T2134. Wt. W708-776. 500000. 4/15. Sir J. C. & S.

Appendix "A"

Subject   Routine Training.

2nd Fd Amb 61 S M D

George W Craig
Lt Col RAMC

The Routine training of the unit is carried out in accordance with the weekly programme submitted from A D M S office. It comprises systematic training in all the departments of the work of the unit both theoretical & practical.

<u>The theory</u> includes. Lectures & demonstrations on
first aid
nursing
sanitation
gas poisoning.

<u>Demonstrations.</u> Water cart & sterilization
bandaging & application of splints.
erection of temporary shelters

<u>Field work.</u> Collection of wounded & disposal of same (by day & night)
night marches.
signalling.
Field cooking
Field sanitation.

<u>Nursing</u> Hospital work at Danbury.
Dressings at Medical Inspection Room
Treatment of Scabies cases.

During the first fortnight of the month the whole unit had been as far as possible, engaged in engineering & making roads round the huts at Oaklands, a supply of clinker and brushwood having been secured. A marked improvement was effected in the ground.

Appendix B.

Subject Field operations on 4/1/16

George W. Craig
Lt Col RAMC T
OC 2 Fd Amb 61 S M D

Ref. O.S. Map. 30. SC. 2 miles to 1 inch

An action was presumed to have taken place along line WRITTLE - OXNEY GREEN - NEWNEY GREEN (E. 2 & 3).
Regimental aid posts at OXNEY GREEN & NEWNEY GREEN.
Advanced dressing station in mission hall at HIGHWOOD QUARTER. (F 2)
Dressing station MILL GREEN (F 2)
Advantage was taken of the rough & very irregular ground on the heath at MILL GREEN, to practise the stretcher bearers in carrying wounded over very broken ground, in erecting shelters, and in dealing & removing patients from deep pits which served as trenches.
Field cooking was practised at MILL GREEN.

Appendix C.

Scheme of field operations carried out 11/1/16

George W. Craig
Lt Col RAMC
O.C. 2 Fd Amb 61 S M Div

Ref. O.S. Map 30. SC 2 m. to 1 inch

Imaginary line from SKREENS WOOD – RADLEY GREEN. E2.
advanced dressing station STONEHILL FARM. E2
dressing station MELBOURNE-FARM. E3.

Appendix D

Field operations 25/1/16

George McCraig
Lt Col RAMC T.

Ref. O.S. map 30. Sc. 2 miles – 1 inch.

~~Are~~ A landing had been effected but the invaders driven back from marshes ground

HARVEYS FARM – TOLLESBURY. E. 6 & 7.

Advanced dressing station TOLLESHUNT D'ARCY. D7.

dressing station GOLDHANGER E6.

The ground was very useful in accustoming the bearers to carry cases over different ground. A number of trenches were utilised to demonstrate the difficulties of dressing cases & removing them from the trenches.

61

61st Division

2/2 S M 2nd Amb

Vol 1

May 1916

CONFIDENTIAL

WAR DIARY

2/2 FD AMB. South Midland

Period

25/5/16 to 31/5/16

George W Craig [illegible]
OC 2/2 Fd Amb

CALONNE-SUR-LYS
31/5/16

Instructions regarding War Diaries and Intelligence Summaries are contained in F. S. Regs., Part II. and the Staff Manual respectively. Title pages will be prepared in manuscript.

WAR DIARY
or
INTELLIGENCE SUMMARY.
(Erase heading not required.)

Army Form C. 2118.

Place	Date	Hour	Summary of Events and Information	Remarks and references to Appendices
			Ref. O.S. Map 33 1/2" to mile	for 23/5/16
PERHAM - DOWN	23/5/16		Unit paraded at 7-15 AM to proceed by train from LUDGERSHALL. Transport and fatigue party under MAJOR FOSTER left camp at 6-30 AM. Wagons and horses entrained without any accident. Unit disentrained at SOUTHAMPTON. On arrival the unit was divided into two parties. One, 6 officers & 100 men under O.C. to embark on the CAESAREA, the remainder of the unit and all transport under MAJOR FOSTER embarked on AFRICAN PRINCE. CAESAREA was in collision with our escort at 12.30 midnight & the bows damaged and boat at once returned to SOUTHAMPTON	App. I G.H.C.
SOUTHAMPTON	24/5/16		Ship returned to dock and part of unit on board CAESAREA disembarked & remained on quay through the day. Embarked again at 6-0 PM.	G.H.C.
HAVRE	25/5/16		Arrived at HAVRE. Marched to another dock & rejoined transport & whole unit marched to camp no 2, SANVIC, & remained there for part of the day. There were no accidents to personnel, horses or wagons on the journey.	G.H.C.

Instructions regarding War Diaries and Intelligence Summaries are contained in F. S. Regs., Part II. and the Staff Manual respectively. Title pages will be prepared in manuscript.

WAR DIARY
or
INTELLIGENCE SUMMARY.

(Erase heading not required.)

Army Form C. 2118.

Place	Date	Hour	Summary of Events and Information	Remarks and references to Appendices
HAVRE	26/5/16		Unit paraded at 3-30 p.m. & proceeded by route march to point 6 for entraining. Arrived at Station at 6-0 P.M. & entrained. Train started 9.0 P.M.	[illegible]
BERGUETTE	27/5/16		Unit arrived here at 6.0 P.M. all wagons off train in 16 minutes, refreshment issued to men, route march to GONNEHEM, which was reached at 9-30 P.M. where unit was billeted for night	Ref. Map HAZEBROUCK 5A 1/100,000 [illegible]
GONNEHEM	28/5/16		Open air Church parade 11-0 A.M. Motor ambulances reported for duty. O.C. proceeded to BETHUNE under orders from A.D.M.S. 61 Div to make arrangements for attachment of unit to 33 DIV. for training.	[illegible]
GONNEHEM	29/5/16		A.D.M.S. 61 DIV (COL J. YOUNG T.D.) visited headquarters and notified that the ambulance proceed tomorrow by ROUTE MARCH TO CALONNE-SUR-LYS. O.C. proceeded to ST VENANT in afternoon for instruction from A.D.M.S.	[illegible]
GONNEHEM	30/5/16		CAPT. MARSHALL & 5 men left to supervise baths at GONNEHEM. Remainder of unit proceeded by road to CALONNE, took over hospital and billets from 107 F.D. AMB.	[illegible]

Instructions regarding War Diaries and Intelligence Summaries are contained in F. S. Regs., Part II. and the Staff Manual respectively. Title pages will be prepared in manuscript.

WAR DIARY
or
INTELLIGENCE SUMMARY.
(Erase heading not required.)

Army Form C. 2118.

Place	Date	Hour	Summary of Events and Information	Remarks and references to Appendices
CALONNE SUR LYS	31/5/16		General fatigues by unit. B Section detailed to Hospital. C Section to supervise baths and laundry arrangement. Incinerators & latrines built	R.C.

George W Craig
Lt Col RAMC
OC 2/2 Ld RAMC

CALONNE SUR LYS 31/5/16

WAR DIARY. 2/2 Fd Amb

Appendix I

Statement of personnel of unit on embarkation.

Officers. 10. LT COL G W CRAIG Officer commanding
MAJOR E C FOSTER
MAJOR A T WATERHOUSE
CAPT A D MOORE
" W J CRAIG
" J BANNERMAN
" B MARSHALL
" J F ROBINSON
" G WILKINSON
HON LIEUT E S BOND. QR.M.R.

Attached for Voyage. { REV G BROWN CTF (CE)
" J PERCY CTF (Wesleyan).

Other ranks. 220:

Horses. 56.

Wagons. 18.

George W Craig
Lt Col RAMC
2/2 Fd Amb.

61

Vol 2

June 1916

CONFIDENTIAL.

WAR DIARY

2/2. S. Mid Fd Amb. 61 Div.

Period June 1 - June 30. 1916

George W Craig
Lt Col RAMC.
O.C. 2/2 Fd Amb 61 Div

June 30th 1916

Instructions regarding War Diaries and Intelligence Summaries are contained in F. S. Regs., Part II. and the Staff Manual respectively. Title pages will be prepared in manuscript.

WAR DIARY
or
INTELLIGENCE SUMMARY.
(Erase heading not required.)

Army Form C. 2118.

Ref Sequence map 36A ~~Q 37 S 9~~ Q 32 C 3 ~~K 27 D 19~~ File

Place	Date	Hour	Summary of Events and Information	Remarks and references to Appendices
CALONNE SUR-LYS	June 1	1916	Fatigue work at Hospital, bathing at baths.	GHG
" "	June 2	1916	Instruction received for A sect to report at VIEILLE-CHAPELLE for instruction to O C 105 Fd Amb. O.C. proceeded to VIEILLE-CHAPELLE to make arrangements. Routine work.	GHG App I
" "	June 3	1916	A Section with complete personnel proceeded by route march to VIEILLE-CHAPELLE. Reporting to O C 105 Fd Amb, men arranged in billets. The details of the work of section are contained in App II. B & C Section routine work at Hospital & Bath. MAJOR E C FOSTER assumed command of the unit during absence of O.C.. B Section took on duty at Hospital	GHG App II
" "	June 4	1916	Church parade for unit in grounds near the Baths routine work. C B Section on duty at baths	GHG
" "	June 5	1916	routine duties, Drill for B & C Sections with GAS HELMET, all [illegible] MAJOR W J HOUSTEN D.A.D.M.S 61 DIV, Visited Hospital & Baths.	GHG

Instructions regarding War Diaries and Intelligence Summaries are contained in F. S. Regs., Part II. and the Staff Manual respectively. Title pages will be prepared in manuscript.

WAR DIARY
or
INTELLIGENCE SUMMARY.
(Erase heading not required.)

Army Form C. 2118.

Place	Date	Hour	Summary of Events and Information	Remarks and references to Appendices
			Ref Squared Map 36A Q. 3 D 5 3	
CALONNE SUR LYS	June 6	1916	routine duties.	GWC
" "	June 7	1916	COLONEL J YOUNG T D A.D.M.S 61 Div, inspected Hospital, baths & billets G.O.C 61 DIV. MAJOR GEN. COLIN MACKENZIE C.B visited hospital	GWC
" "	June 8	1916	Inspection of gas helmets, & lecture on gas attacks	GWC
" "	June 9	1916	Experimental alarm, two hours allowed for the unit to be packed and on the move. Owing to the absence of the whole of A Section personnel, the time was slightly exceeded, as the stores of A sect. had to be packed. All stores not to be ~~transported~~ taken, dumped at site behind hospital, according to secret orders received.	GWC
" "	June 10	1916	A Section returned from training, & reformed unit. Lt COL G.W CRAIG resumed command of the unit. Message received at 5-30 PM for unit to report at MERVILLE, and take over the XI CORPS REST STATION from 131 FD AMB. O C & MAJOR FOSTER proceeded to MERVILLE, to make preliminary arrangements	GWC

Army Form C. 2118.

WAR DIARY
or
INTELLIGENCE SUMMARY.
(Erase heading not required.)

Instructions regarding War Diaries and Intelligence Summaries are contained in F. S. Regs., Part II. and the Staff Manual respectively. Title pages will be prepared in manuscript.

Place	Date	Hour	Summary of Events and Information	Remarks and references to Appendices
			Ref Sequence map 36A K.29.D.1.9	
MERVILLE	June 11	1916	Whole unit proceeded to MERVILLE. OC, CAPT MOORE, LT BOND with some Clerks proceeded at 8-0 AM. Main body moved at 12-0 under MAJOR WATERHOUSE.	[illegible]
			CAPT WILKINSON & one horse ambulance wagon detailed to accompany 182 Infy BDE, by route march, on June 12.	
			CAPT ROBINSON with 9 men left at CALONNE to act as rear party until the hospital was handed over to incoming unit, and to continue work at the baths.	
			Unit took over XI Corps R.S. & Scabies hospital at REGNIER.LE.CLERQ	
" "	June 12	1916	CAPT WILKINSON reported for duty.	[illegible]
			details for various duties arranged.	
" "	June 13	1916	BRIG GENERAL H.C. HOLMAN, DA.QMG visited hospital	[illegible]
			MAJOR E.T POTTS-DSO DADMS XI CORPS visited hospital and announced preliminary arrangements for the requisitioning of CHATEAU DEMON, as a rest station for officers.	
			CAPT W.J CRAIG detailed for duty at divisional baths LAGORGUE, SERGT CRAMER & 23 OR [illegible] to LAGORGUE for temporary duty at the baths.	

2353 Wt. W2544/1454 700,000 5/15 D. D. & L. A.D.S.S. Forms/C. 2118.

Army Form C. 2118.

WAR DIARY
or
INTELLIGENCE SUMMARY.
(*Erase heading not required.*)

Instructions regarding War Diaries and Intelligence Summaries are contained in F. S. Regs., Part II. and the Staff Manual respectively. Title pages will be prepared in manuscript.

Ref Squared Map 36A K 29 D 1.9

Place	Date	Hour	Summary of Events and Information	Remarks and references to Appendices
MERVILLE	June 14. 1916		COL MORGAN ADMS 38 Div attended at CRS to examine 3 cases recommended for base. MAJOR A.T. WATERHOUSE detailed to act as MO i/c Officers Rest Station, requisition for house delivered by TOWN MAJOR. 2 men detailed to take possession. MAJOR POTTS DSO, DADMS XI CORPS visited hospital & CHATEAU.	GHC
"	June 15. 1916		COL J YOUNG ADMS 61 Div visited CRS, inspected buildings & visited skin hospital at REGNIER. Medical board on 3 cases. CAPT ROBINSON returned to duty having handed over at CALONNE	GHC
"	June 16. 1916		routine duties. MAJOR POTTS DSO DADMS XI CORPS visited Chateau & C.R.S.	GHC
"	June 17. 1916		routine duties	GHC
"	June 18. 1916		O.C. proceeded to HAZEBROUCK, for furnishing stores for Officers Rest Station	GHC
"	June 19. 1916		routine duties. fatigue party at work at Chateau.	GHC

2353 Wt. W2544/1454 700,000 5/15 D. D. & L. A.D.S.S. Forms/C 2118.

Instructions regarding War Diaries and Intelligence Summaries are contained in F. S. Regs., Part II. and the Staff Manual respectively. Title pages will be prepared in manuscript.

WAR DIARY
or
INTELLIGENCE SUMMARY.
(Erase heading not required.)

Army Form C. 2118.

Place	Date	Hour	Summary of Events and Information	Remarks and references to Appendices
			Ref squared map 36A K.29.D.1.4.	
MERVILLE	June 20	1916	Routine duties.	GMC
" "	June 21	1916	MAJOR POTTS DSO visited CRS & Skin hospital	GMC.
			COL. J YOUNG TD ADMS 61 DIV visited Chateau, hospital & Skin hospital	
" "	June 21		Wagon detailed to collect 1000 walking sticks from the forest at LA MOTTE and distribute to all CCS of 1st Army	
" "	June 22	1916	Instructions from DADMS XI Corps to admit cases to officers rest corps, applications for vacancies to be made by telegram to O.C. XI C.R.S.	GMC.
" "	June 23	1916	First application for admission to Officers Rest Station	GMC
			Lecture by CAPT CARPENTER RE on Gas, offensive & defensive at LA GORGUE. CAPT MARSHALL & two NCO's detailed to attend.	
" "	June 24	1916	COL FIRTH. DDMS XI CORPS, visited CRS & CHATEAU-DE-MON	GMC

2353 Wt. W2544/1454 700,000 5/15 D. D. & L. A.D.S.S. Forms/C. 2118.

Instructions regarding War Diaries and Intelligence Summaries are contained in F. S. Regs., Part II. and the Staff Manual respectively. Title pages will be prepared in manuscript.

WAR DIARY
or
INTELLIGENCE SUMMARY.
(*Erase heading not required.*)

Army Form C. 2118.

Place	Date	Hour	Summary of Events and Information	Remarks and references to Appendices
			Ref. squared map 36A ~~Q.3.D.5.3.~~ K.29.D.1.9 GHC	
MERVILLE	June 25/16		MAJOR HOYTEN DADMS 61 Div visited Rest Station and went round Church Service for Roman Catholics in church at MERVILLE 11-30 AM Church Service (C of E) in dining hall 15-0 p.m.	GHC
" "	June 26/16		COLONEL FIRTH DDMS XI. CORPS, MAJOR POTTS DSO DADMS XI Corps visited CRS & inspected stock depot at REGNIER-LE-CLERQ in morning COLONEL YOUNG T.D, ADMS 61 DIV. & Lt COL MARINDIN ~~DAQ~~ visited CRS, stock depot & officers rest station in afternoon	GHC
" "	June 27/16		Lecture in afternoon at HQRS 2/1st SM FD AMB by MAJOR FRANKAU OC 2 Lond CCS on relation of work at CCS to Field Ambulances	GHC
" "	June 28/16		Inspection of special cases at REGNIER, transfer of impetigo cases to CRS –	GHC
"	June 29/16		MAJOR POTTS DSO DADMS XI CORPS visited CRS & officers R.S. OC. at LAGORGUE re. Baths & laundry work. Salvage scheme for unit prepared	GHC

2353 Wt. W2544/1454 700,000 5/15 D. D. & L. A.D.S.S./Forms/C 2118.

Army Form C. 2118.

Instructions regarding War Diaries and Intelligence Summaries are contained in F. S. Regs., Part II. and the Staff Manual respectively. Title pages will be prepared in manuscript.

WAR DIARY
or
INTELLIGENCE SUMMARY.
(Erase heading not required.)

Ref. Sequence map 36^A
& K 29 D 19

Place	Date	Hour	Summary of Events and Information	Remarks and references to Appendices
MERVILLE	June 30/16		Claims officer to investigate claim for damage at rear of hospital	GHC
			Summary of cases attended to &c	App III

Geo. F. [illegible] Lt Col [illegible]
O.C. [illegible]
June 30th 1916

2353 Wt. W2544/1454 700,000 5/15 D. D. & L. A.D.S.S. Forms/C 2118.

Appendix I

War Diary 2/2 Fd Amb 61 S M Div

Routine Duties.

The routine duties of the unit referred to for brevity in the body of the diary have varied during the present month.

A. at CALONNE-SUR-LYS. June 1 - 10th

The unit as a Field Ambulance was in charge of a Field Ambulance Hospital and also superintended the Baths for troops, details of the bathing will be found in a separate appendix

B. at MERVILLE June 11th

The unit took over charge of the XI Corps Rest Station, provided for the care & treatment of convalescent cases, & men requiring slight dressings, transferred here from field ambulance hospitals.

A Corps Skin depot is also under charge of the unit. This situated at REGNIER-LE-CLERQ, has accommodation for 200 cases of Scabies & other skin affections.

An officer is detailed to superintend the XI corps baths in the town. This officer is also responsible for the town sanitation and has a daily visit to the Forest de NIEPPE, where a number of men are engaged at work in the forest.

The unit supplies chlorinated water to the Hospital Barges which halt here on the canal.

A Corps Rest Station has also been established for officers at the CHATEAU DEMON, in the town, this is supervised by an officer of the unit

An officer of the unit has also been detailed for work at the Divisional Baths & Laundry LAGORGUE

George W Craig
Lt Col RAMC T
OC 2/2 Fd Amb 61 Div

Appendix II

War Diary 2/2 S Mid Fd Amb R.A.M.C.

Report of work during the [illegible] [illegible] at 105 Fd Amb

VIELLE-CHAPELLE (Map 36A R 34.a 9.9)

The complete personnel of A Sect. including Lt Col G.W. CRAIG. CAPT MOORE, CAPT WILKINSON & LT & QR MR BOND proceeded by route march and reported to O.C. 105 Fd AMB on June 3rd arriving at 3-30 P.M. The men were accommodated in billets at H.Q.R. It was decided that the best method of instruction would be for the personnel of this unit to be divided into sections and temporarily absorbed into the other [illegible] unit

20 ~~[illegible]~~ NCOS & men at a time were detailed for the Advanced Dressing Station at ST VAAST (M 32 D 8.6) On ~~[illegible]~~ Sunday June 4th CAPT WILKINSON took up 20 men. At the advanced dressing station they assisted generally in the work of the various departments and all took their turn of duty in the dressing room. 2 men were detailed each day for work with the party at the aid post at FACTORY POST (S.9.D 1.7). CAPT MOORE took over from CAPT WILKINSON on June 7th. Those of the section who were not at the A.D.S. took their share of duty at the dressing station; the personnel of the departments [illegible] [illegible] instruction. Pack store keeper, orderly room clerks, clerk to QMaster, dressers, Hospital clerks, Incinerator orderlies & Sanitary Sergeant.

I was glad to notice that all the men of the section who were on duty in the A.D.S. behaved very well occasionally under fire them, [illegible] [illegible] circumstances and on the Monday evening June 5th two of the men who were also at the aid post did good work under fire. their first experience.

The officers, NCOS, & men of the 105th Fd Amb vied with each other in [illegible] on the help of their own experience and the lessons learned by all ranks were of the utmost value.

George W Craig
Lt Col R.A.M.C.
OC 2/2 Fd Amb 61(S.M.) Div

Appendix III
War Diary
2/2 S Mid Fd Amb 61 Div

Summary of Cases re treated 30/5/16 – 30/6/16

George W Craig
Lt Col RAMC (T)
OC 2/2 S M Fd Amb 61 Div

30/6/16

Cases admitted during month.

(GONNEHEM. May 28 – 29)	13	
CALONNE. May 30 – 10 June	11	taken over
	87	admitted
MERVILLE C.R.S. 11 June – 30 June	772	admitted
	147	taken over
REGNIER (scabies) 11 June – 30 June	411	admitted.
	120	taken over
Officers Rest Station. 24 June – 30 June.	3.	admitted

Total 1564

Dressings used June 11th June 30th

Bandages	151
Boric Lint.	$12\frac{1}{2}$ lbs
Plain lint	11 lbs
Cotton Wool.	$8\frac{1}{2}$ "
" Tissue	2 "
Gauze.	9 yds
Plaster	98 "
Sundries	2 boxes safety pins 9 triang band : 3 susp band

Admissions & Discharges. C R S

Date	C R S. ad.	disch. duty	disch. CCS	Scabies ad	dis duty	dis CCS	Officers Rs ad.	disch
June 11	39.	50.	6	12.				
" 12	31.	26.	5	10				
" 13	27.	29.	3	5.	1.			
" 14	37.	43.	3.	20.	14.			
" 15	41.	29.	3.	33.	5			
" 16	42.	26.	4	39	35.	35.		
" 17	38.	34.	0	2.	12.			
" 18	43	26	3	45	0.	0		
" 19	18	36.	1	20	0	0		
" 20	44	42.	4	38.	9.			
" 21	38.	46.	4	27.	2.			
" 22	58.	45.	8	26.	12			
" 23	32.	44	1	16	27.			
" 24	53.	47.	0	40.	25.		3.	
" 25	47.	45.	4.	13.	34			
" 26	38.	27.	3	23.	19.			
" 27	49.	54.	5	15	29.			
" 28	25	33.	4	5	16			
" 29	33.	46.	4	19	20			
" 30	39.	34.	1	3.	8.			
~~Daily Av.~~	772.	762.	66.	411	26.8	35	3.	
Daily Av.	38·6	38·1	3·3	20·5	13·4·			

Total admission 1186

Total discharged ~~1096~~ 1131.

Summary of Surgical & Medical Cases X / C R S

Date	Dressings	Medicine
June 11. 1916	99	48
" 12	128	68
" 13	112	75
" 14	120	80
" 15	120	82
" 16	125	75
" 17	135	85
" 18	122	88
" 19	130	92
" 20	130	79
" 21	138	85
" 22	145	76
" 23	160	88
" 24	130	89
" 25	130	92
" 26	168	98
" 27	148	100
" 28	138	80
" 29	117	74
" 30	135	75
Total	2630	1629
Daily average	131.5	81.4

Vaccinations for Impetigo

Cases treated 66

no. of inoculations 243.

Baths by unit

GONNEHEM

May 30 1916	235
" 31.	107.
June 1	478
" 2	250.
" 3	242.
" 6	629
" 8	601
" 9	146. Total 2688

CALONNE

June 1	220
" 2	103
" 3.	32
" 5	70
" 6	13
" 7	10
" 8	15
" 9	20
" 10	140
13	330
" 14	130 Total. 1083.

Total. 3771

Baths
MERVILLE

June 13 1916	342
" 14	385
" 15	377
" 16	380
" 17	220
" 19	208
" 20	326
" 21	84
" 22	148
" 23	81
" 24	62
" 25	nil
" 26	241
" 27	133
" 28	222
" 29	284
" 30	236
Total	3729
Daily Average	233

Total baths ~~10188~~ 7500
Daily average 214.

Confidential

61

Vol III

War Diary

2/2 S Mid Fd Amb 61 Div

From 1 – 31 July 1916.

July, 1916

Vol iii.

George W Craig Lt Col RAMC

OC 2/2 Fd Amb RAMC

61 Divn

Army Form C. 2118.

WAR DIARY
or
INTELLIGENCE SUMMARY.
(Erase heading not required.)

Instructions regarding War Diaries and Intelligence Summaries are contained in F. S. Regs., Part II. and the Staff Manual respectively. Title pages will be prepared in manuscript.

Place	Date	Hour	Summary of Events and Information	Remarks and references to Appendices
			Ref. Map 36 A 1/40,000 K. 29. D 1.9	
MERVILLE.	JULY 1. 1916		War Diary despatched for last month DADOS 61 DIV, inspected QRMR stores.	G.H.B
" "	JULY 2 "		Cinematograph entertainment at CRS, from the theatre at LA GORGUE much appreciated by the patients	G.H.B
" "	3/7/16		COL FIRTH DDMS, & MAJOR POTTS DSO called at CRS in morning. Indent on RCS completed for officers rest station	G.H.B
" "	4/7/16		Goods collected from ST OMER for chateau MAJOR POTTS in morning	G.H.B
" "	5/7/16		CAPT MIDDLETON RE re levels for draining ditch at back of CRS. New oven commenced in kitchen	G.H.B
"	6/7/16		Foden lorry disinfector despatched from REGNIER to BRAQUEMONT (DDMS XI Corps C/63/1)	G.H.B
	7/7/16		CPL GIBBS & 3 O.R sent to CALONNE SCHOOL as retaining party (DDMS XI Corps M 2/372 Q 4 G 14	G.H.B

Instructions regarding War Diaries and Intelligence Summaries are contained in F. S. Regs., Part II. and the Staff Manual respectively. Title pages will be prepared in manuscript.

WAR DIARY
or
INTELLIGENCE SUMMARY.
(Erase heading not required.)

Army Form C. 2118.

Place	Date	Hour	Summary of Events and Information	Remarks and references to Appendices
			Ref. Map 36A 1/40000 K.29 D1.9	
MERVILLE	8/7/16		CORP GIBBS came over in evening from CALONNE, Q4C14 with message from OC field ambulance about taking over buildings, sent him on to DDMS XI Corps for orders	G.H.B.
" "	9/7/16		detached party returned to unit from CALONNE Q4C14. COLONEL FIRTH DDMS XI Corps visited Rest Station	G.H.B.
" "	10/7/16		Lecture on the Navy at YMCA for patients at CRS	G.H.B.
"	11/7/16		message received from ADMS 61 DIV. CAPT MOORE & CAPT WILKINSON with 2 motor ambulances to report for duty to 2/3 F.D AMB at VIELLE CHAPELLE. meeting of OC'S field ambulances at ADMS office LAGORGUE L34 B.6.2	G.H.B.
"	12/7/16		MAJOR POTTS DSO DADMS XI CORPS, called at CRS	G.H.B.
"	13/7/16		ADMS 61 Div. & CAPT DAVISON visited CRS & ORS	G.H.B.

Instructions regarding War Diaries and Intelligence Summaries are contained in F. S. Regs., Part II. and the Staff Manual respectively. Title pages will be prepared in manuscript.

WAR DIARY
or
INTELLIGENCE SUMMARY.
(Erase heading not required.)

Army Form C. 2118.

Place	Date	Hour	Summary of Events and Information	Remarks and references to Appendices
			Ref Map 36A 1/40000 K 29 D 1.9	
MERVILLE	14/7/16		Concert for patients in evening, programme by A Section.	
			Instruction from DDMS to send wagons to PACAUT, to collect stores left by a field ambulance.	
			LT BOYERS detailed for collection. DDMS XI Corps & DADMS Visited CRS.	[illegible]
" "	15/7/16		Supplies from BRCS fetched for O.R.S from ST OMER.	
			Concert given by A Sect to patients at Skin depot REGNIER. K 36 D 8.8	[illegible]
" "	16/7/16		LT RIVERS over in morning from 1st 3d AMB for loan of first field dressings, 2 horse ambulances, stretcher carriers.	
			Were received from DDMS XI CORPS to hold two bearer divisions in readiness for a move.	[illegible]
			Men warned & preparations made.	
			Staff Capt. from C.E. XI CORPS to inspect floor in dining hall.	
			Order received 7.0 PM for 2 bearer divisions to report to [illegible] to O.C. 1st 3d Amb at LA GORGUE. L [illegible]	[illegible]
" "	17/7/16		CAPT BANNERMAN & CAPT. MARSHALL with two bearer subdivisions proceeded by [illegible] to LAGORGUE - 8.30 AM. Were to send MO to 3 posts in front. LT BOYERS sent from O.R.S. L 34 C 6.2	[illegible]

2353 Wt. W2544/1454 700,000 5/15 D. D. & L. A.D.S.S. Forms/C 2118.

Army Form C. 2118.

WAR DIARY
or
INTELLIGENCE SUMMARY.
(Erase heading not required.)

Instructions regarding War Diaries and Intelligence Summaries are contained in F. S. Regs., Part II. and the Staff Manual respectively. Title pages will be prepared in manuscript.

Place	Date	Hour	Summary of Events and Information	Remarks and references to Appendices
			Map Ref 36A 1/40,000 K 29.D.19	
MERVILLE	17/7/16		Wire from ADMS 61 Div. that all our detached men were returning to night CAPT MOORE, CAPT WILKINSON, CAPT BANNERMAN, CAPT MARSHALL and two bearer subdivisions returned for duty.	GWC
"	18/7/16		Changed billets for men of A Sect, with TOWN MAJOR. ADMS 61 DIV, & MAJOR MOXEY OC 3rd Fd Amb, MAJOR POTTS DSO DADMS XI CORPS visited CRS with orders for 2 bearer divisions to report for duty to morrow to 1 & 3 Fd Amb	GWC
"	19/7/16		36 B.6.2 CAPT MOORE, CAPT BANNERMAN took two bearer divisions to LAGORGUE for duty 21-0 PM wire from OC 1 Fd AMB to send all available motor ambulances	GWC
"	20/7/16		ADMS & MAJOR POTTS at CRS in afternoon CAPT MOORE, CAPT BANNERMAN and bearer division returned Message received from DDMS XI CORPS for communication to all ranks	GWC

Army Form C. 2118.

Instructions regarding War Diaries and Intelligence Summaries are contained in F. S. Regs., Part II. and the Staff Manual respectively. Title pages will be prepared in manuscript.

WAR DIARY
or
INTELLIGENCE SUMMARY.
(Erase heading not required.)

Place	Date	Hour	Summary of Events and Information	Remarks and references to Appendices
			Ref MAP 36A 1/40000 K 29 D 1.9.	
MERVILLE	21/7/16		MAJOR HOYTEN DADMS 61 DIV called to thank personally the bearers who had been detailed to work with him.	
			Special order from ADMS 61 DIV and from GOC XI CORPS.	GHB
			Whist drive in hall at night for patients	
			DDMS XI CORPS called at CRS.	
" "	22/7/16		drain at back of CRS completed.	
			MAJOR POTTS DADMS XI CORPS visited CRS	GHB
" "	23/7/16		routine duties	GHB
" "	24/7/16		routine duties	GHB
" "	25/7/16		5 bales of goods received for unit from Lady Mayoress of Birmingham	GHB
"	26/7/16		routine duties	GHB

2353 Wt. W2544/1454 700,000 5/15 D. D. & L. A.D.S.S. Forms/C. 2118.

Instructions regarding War Diaries and Intelligence Summaries are contained in F. S. Regs., Part II. and the Staff Manual respectively. Title pages will be prepared in manuscript.

WAR DIARY
or
INTELLIGENCE SUMMARY.
(Erase heading not required.)

Army Form C. 2118.

Place	Date	Hour	Summary of Events and Information	Remarks and references to Appendices
			Ref. Map 36A 1/40 000 K 29. D 1.9	
1 MERVILLE	27/7/16		Letter from DDMS XI CORPS, this unit to relieve 2/1 Fd Amb at LA GORGUE arrangements to be made for change by O.C. of the 2 units.	
"			Presentation of ribbons in Square by GEN. SIR C MONRO KCB GOC 1st ARMY	GHB
			CRS visited by G.O.C. 1st ARMY & GOC XI CORPS	
" "	28/7/16		DDMS XI CORPS, inspected CRS, & expressed himself pleased with the arrangements made by unit during their control here. Special order issued for notification of all concerned.	
			CAPT MOORE & 20 O.R. proceeded to LAVENTIE, to take over A.D.S from 1st Fd Amb	
			20 men from 1st Fd Amb reported here for instruction & remained here.	GHB
			MAJOR MACKIE. OC 2/1 Fd Amb came over to arrange for transfers.	
			Lecture to RAMC officers LA GORGUE by CAPT McNEE & COL GALLOWAY on "Pyrexia of unknown origin" L 34 B 6.2	
" "	29/7/16		CAPT BANNERMAN, CAPT WILKINSON & 50 O.R. to LA GORGUE	
			CAPT STOBIE, CAPT LANDER reported here for duty with 50 men.	GHB

Army Form C. 2118.

Instructions regarding War Diaries and Intelligence Summaries are contained in F. S. Regs., Part II. and the Staff Manual respectively. Title pages will be prepared in manuscript.

WAR DIARY
or
INTELLIGENCE SUMMARY.
(Erase heading not required.)

Place	Date	Hour	Summary of Events and Information	Remarks and references to Appendices
			Ref Map 36A 1/20 000 K 29. D. 1. 9	
MERVILLE	July 30 1916		Routine Duties	GWC
" "	July 31 - 1916		remainder of unit proceeded to LACOUTURE to take over from 1. Fd Amb reported arrival of unit to ADMS 61 Div	GWC
			George W Craig, Lt Col RAMC	
			OC 2/2 Fd Amb 61 (SM) Div	
			31/7/16	

War Diary
2/2 Fd Amb RAMC T 61 Div

Appendix I

Summary of work done during period July 1-31 1916

During the past month the unit has been responsible for the charge of XI Corps Rest Station.
This includes

1. The XI CRS at MERVILLE
2. The officers rest station at CHATEAU DEMON
3. The skin depot at REGNIER-LE-CLERQ
4. The corps baths at BRASSERIE ST ANTOINE
5. Daily attendance of a medical officer to see sick at CAUDESCURE where one orderly is always on duty
6. Supervision of the town sanitation of MERVILLE
7. Supply of water to all hospital barges which halt at MERVILLE

During the past month a large offensive ditch at the rear of the CRS has been effectively drained, & a better fall for the outlet secured

A new oven has been built in the kitchen

Closed box latrines have been substituted for the open pail system at CRS & at skin depot

A new boiler and incinerator have been built at REGNIER.
The pack store and clothing store at REGNIER have been enlarged.
The medical inspection room and bath room at REGNIER have been extended.

On two occasions during the month officers and bearer subdivisions have been attached for special duty to the 1st & 3rd Fd Amb 61 Divn. A special appendix gives details of their work.

George W. Craig, Lt Col RAMC
OC 2/3 Fd Amb 61 Div

Special Divisional order

The following message from G.O.C in C the British Armies in France is published for the information of all ranks.

"Please convey to the troops engaged night 19/20 my appreciation of their gallant effort and thorough preparation made for it. I wish them to realise that their enterprise has not been by any means in vain and that the gallantry with which they carried out the attack is fully recognised

Chief

I have much satisfaction in publishing the following message from the Corps Commander.

G.R. 39. 20/7/16

I wish to convey to all ranks of your division my appreciation of the gallant attack carried out yesterday by them. Although they were unable to consolidate the ground gained the effect on the enemy will be far-reaching and will prevent him from moving troops away from our front to the South. I wish you all in your next attack a more complete and permanent victory & that you may reap the full fruit of the energy and skill displayed by all Commanders & their staffs in the execution of their task

R Haking

Lieut Genl

Commanding XI Corps.

The division has not only fought gallantly but all ranks of every arm and service have been carried out in the most exemplary and devoted manner, working day and night, an amount of labour which has highly tested their endurance & discipline, and merits my unqualified praise.

Colin Mackenzie
Major General
Commanding 61 Divn

Headquarters
July 20 1916

Copies of Special orders issued

O.C 2/2 Fd Amb

The D.D.M.S X I Corps has asked me to convey to all ranks his appreciation of the excellent work which they have done during the past twenty four hours. Will you please let this be known to all your officers NCOS & men

James Young Col

20 7/16

ADMS 61 DN

O.C 2/2 Fd Amb

Will you please convey to the officers, NCOS & men of your unit temporarily attached for duty with the 1st & 3rd Fd Amb, my appreciation of the excellent work they did and the very great assistance they were to me and to the units to which they were attached. All ranks were most keen and assiduous in the performance of their various duties.

James Young Col.
ADMS 61 DN

20 7/16

DMS No 1348 20 July 1916

The following extract from a report made by the Inspector of Catering BEF d 16/7/16 is forwarded for information

"All casualty clearing stations and field ambulances have excellent catering arrangements.
A certain quantity of rations have to be kept in hand in these units for emergency purposes, but all through there is a very considerable underdrawal

W. W. Pike
Surg. General D.M.S.

HQrs
1st Army.

Ref map 36 S.W

War Diary
2/2 Fd Amb 61 Div

CAPT R.D MOORE with CAPT BANNERMAN, 3 NCOS and 72 stretcher bearers proceeded on July 19th to LAGORGUE, reporting at HQrs 1st Fd Amb at 9-45 AM. CAPT BANNERMAN & one bearer sub-division remaining here, the other with CAPT MOORE proceeded to 3rd Fd Amb.
CAPT MOORE was attached to the Divisional Theatre LAGORGUE which had been extemporized as a collecting station on July 16. L.34 b.6.2 (map 36.a N.E).
During the night 468 cases passed through here.
The station was closed at 12 noon, on July 20th.
The bearers returned to MERVILLE at 7-45 PM on July 20th.

The bearer subdivision of B section proceeded to RED HOUSE (M.6 d.2.0) dressing station at 16-30 PM, & proceeded thence to RAP at JOCKS LODGE at 17.0 PM. at 9 PM till 5 AM next morning there were at work collecting wounded from RAP and in the front trench with trench stretchers

a detachment of C section bearers at work between HUGOUMONT RAP (M ~~6.D.2.0~~ 12.C.3.4) & JOCKS LODGE (N.7 b.4.4)

Admissions & Discharges C R S

Date	C.R.S. ad.	C.R.S. Discharge duty	C.R.S. Discharge CCS	Stand depot ad.	Stand depot disch duty	Stand depot disch CCS	Officers R S ad	Officers R S dis.
July 1	23.	14.	6.	16	20		1	
" 2	16.	7.	3.	23.	13.		1.	
3	23.	23.	6	18	3.	54	6	
4	28	13.	9.	14.	10		0	1 duty
5	22.	16.	10	10.	13.		1	3 CCS
6	21.	10	4	19.	9.	1	1	1 duty
7	25	18	7	17	11.	2	2.	
8	9	10	3	7	8		2	1 CCS
9	13.	24.	5	14	8		2.	1 duty 1 CCS.
10	15	10.	12	21.	12		0	1 duty
11	3.	7	1	51.	14.	28	3.	1 duty
12	4	11	7	20	14		0	0
13	17.	6	4	25.	10		0	1 duty
14	66	19.	5	22.	14		2.	0.
15	24	8	10	19.	9.		0	0
16	45.	7	7.	7	12	25	0	0
17	33.	14	5	8	8		3.	2 duty. 3 CCS
18	34	17	8	38.	8	1	3	2 duty.
19	66.	7	3	23.	7		2	1 CCS
20	15.	39.	16	9	17.		0	1 CCS
21	46	17	22	34	25	29	2.	2 duty
22	48	2.	10	29	6		0	1 CCS
23	34	21	9.	21	3		4	1 CCS
24.	54	51	8	17	3		3	1 duty
	684.	371.	180	479	257	140.	38.	{13 duty 12 CCS

date	CRS ad.	CRS duty	CRS CCS	Shen depot ad.	Shen depot duty	Shen depot CCS	Officers ad	Officers duty	Officers CCS
25	20.	28.	4.	22.	23	28	1	0	5
26	17	21.	9	13.	10		2.	1	0
27	34.	8	5.	7	8	7.	0	2	0
28	26.	30	6.	25	28		0	0	0
29	27	12.	5.	26	25	1	0.	0	1
30	21.	6	4	35	9	–	1	1	–
31.									
	684.	371.	180.	479.	257.	140	38	13.	12.
	829	476	213	607	360	176	42	17	18

Summary of Dressings & Medicine July 1916

July	Dressings	Medicine
1	115	69
2	93	65
3	118	65
4	123	65
5	117	72
6	112	84
7	113	83
8	120	64
9	91	59
10	82	57
11	82	61
12	82	55
13	81	50
14	86	49
15	129	73
16	79	70
17	116	85
18	125	106
19	97	110
20	124	116
21	140	120
22	145	130
23	139	136
24	136	130
25	145	126
26	180	120
	2970	1220

July	Surgical	Medical
	2970	1220
27	160	133
28	165	127
29	153	125
30	160	120
31		
	3608	1725

Summary of dressings used

bandages	275
boric lint	24 3/4 lbs
lint	7 lbs
cotton wool	11 1/4 lbs
gauze	82 yds (3 3/4 packets)
plaster	170 yds (17 reels)
cellular tissue	10 lbs
safety pins	3 tins
triang. bandage	6
suspension bandage	3

Confidential

Aug 1916.

Vol 4

War Diary

(S.M.)
2/2 Field Amb. R.A.M.C.T.
51 Div.

Period 1–31 Aug. 1916

Volume. IV

George W. Craig
Lt Col R.A.M.C.T.
O.C. 2/2 Fd Amb. 51 Div

Sept 1. 1916.

Army Form C. 2118.

Instructions regarding War Diaries and Intelligence Summaries are contained in F. S. Regs., Part II. and the Staff Manual respectively. Title pages will be prepared in manuscript.

WAR DIARY
or
INTELLIGENCE SUMMARY.
(Erase heading not required.)

HQrs 2/2 Fd Amb. Ref OS Map 36 A N.E = L.34.b.6.2

Place	Date	Hour	Summary of Events and Information	Remarks and references to Appendices
LAGORGUE	1/8/1916		details busy with fatigues, completing carpenter work left unfinished by our predecessors.	
			OC up to A.D.S. LAVENTIE (G 34 C 42). fatigues busy filling sandbags for further protection of steel dug out	G.H.B.
			routine work	App I
" "	2/8/16		COL J YOUNG T.D. ADMS 61 Div called at HQs in morning and inspected premises. box latrines brought back from MERVILLE (K.29.D.1.9), tin latrines from here exchanged	G.H.B.
" "	3/8/16		OC to A.D.S. LAVENTIE a few cases brought in during night	G.H.B.
" "	4/8/16		ADMS called at HQRS in morning.	G.H.B.
" "	5/8/16		MAJOR WATERHOUSE relief for LAVENTIE (G 34 C 42). CAPT BANNERMAN returned to HQRS for duty. 183 BDE Sports in afternoon on ASC grounds	G.H.B.

2353 Wt. W2544/1454 700,000 5/15 D. D. & L. A.D.S.S. Forms/C. 2118.

Instructions regarding War Diaries and Intelligence Summaries are contained in F. S. Regs., Part II. and the Staff Manual respectively. Title pages will be prepared in manuscript.

WAR DIARY
or
INTELLIGENCE SUMMARY.
(*Erase heading not required.*)

Army Form C. 2118.

Place	Date	Hour	Summary of Events and Information	Remarks and references to Appendices
			Ref O.S. Map 36A N.E. HQRS 2/2 Fd Amb = L.G 34 b 6 2	
LA GORGUE	6/8/16		Church parade in transport field in front of hospital OC attended Church parade in GRAND PLACE BETHUNE, in commemoration of second anniversary of declaration of war. GEN. SIR C. MONRO. K.C.B. gave an address.	G.H.B.
" "	7/8/16		CAPT MOORE returned to HQRS for duty CAPT ROBINSON took up relief duties to ADS (G 34 C 42). OC up to A.D.S	G.H.B.
" "	8/8/16		COL YOUNG. TD ADMS 61 Div visited hospital. MAJOR-GEN COLIN MACKENZIE CB GOC 61 Div, visited HQRS, inspected the mess and talked to the wounded patients COL R.H. FIRTH DDMS XI CORPS MAJOR POTTS D-A-DMS XI CORPS inspected hospital in afternoon OC up to A.D.S in morning.	G.H.B.
" "	9/8/16		CAPT DAVISON called in morning re tank for washing water, and alterations in pumping arrangements [illegible] from hospital OC & CAPT MOORE up to bayonet fighting school in afternoon to inspect & report to ADMS 61 Div	G.H.B.

2353 Wt. W2544/1454 700,000 5/15 D. D. & L. A.D.S.S. Forms/C. 2118.

Instructions regarding War Diaries and Intelligence Summaries are contained in F. S. Regs., Part II. and the Staff Manual respectively. Title pages will be prepared in manuscript.

WAR DIARY
or
INTELLIGENCE SUMMARY.
(Erase heading not required.)

Army Form C. 2118.

Ref. O.S. map 36A N.E.
HQRS 2/2 Fd. Amb = L.34 B.6.2.
A.D.S at LAVENTIE. G.34 C.4.2.

Place	Date	Hour	Summary of Events and Information	Remarks and references to Appendices
LA GORGUE	10/8/16		CAPT BANNERMAN detailed as M.O. to attend daily at 9. A.M. to attend at bayonet fighting school; urine pit completed.	GWC
" "	11/8/16		SERGT HICKMAN detailed to attend for instruction at Divisional gas defence school. OC up to A.D.S in afternoon. A.D.M.S. called.	GWC
" "	12/8/16		CAPT B MARSHALL up to A.D.S for duty	GWC
" "	13/8/16		routine work. Church parade in morning in transport field	GWC
" "	14/8/16		A.D.M.S. called in morning. CAPT ROBINSON reported for duty from A.D.S. OC at A.D.S in afternoon. COL. C. WALLACE C.M.G. consulting surgeon to 1. ARMY lectured to medical officers on "GAS GANGRENE". LIEUT. O'BRIEN R.A.M.C. attached for instruction to unit.	GWC
" "	15/8/16		OC up to A.D.S with A.D.M.S., consultation re sandbags for steel shelter; report from D.G.O. of SGT. HICKMAN	GWC App ii GWC
" "	16/8/16		routine work	GWC

2353 Wt. W2544/1454 700,000 5/15 D. D. & L. A.D.S.S. Forms/C. 2118.

WAR DIARY
or
INTELLIGENCE SUMMARY.
(Erase heading not required.)

Army Form C. 2118.

Instructions regarding War Diaries and Intelligence Summaries are contained in F. S. Regs., Part II. and the Staff Manual respectively. Title pages will be prepared in manuscript.

Ref OS Map 36A N E
HQRS 2/2 Fd Amb = L 34 B 6 2
ADS at LAVENTIE = G 34 C 4 2

Place	Date	Hour	Summary of Events and Information	Remarks and references to Appendices
LA GORGUE	17/8/16		LIEUT Y QR MR E S BOND proceeded on special leave for 7 days (Authority D H Q)	
			OC to ADS in afternoon.	
			CAPT LOGAN, RAMC lectured to medical officers of division on music gas poisoning	GHG
"	18/8/16		routine duties, message from 184 Bde ref medical arrangements for to morrow OC up to ADS to see	GHG
			MAJOR WATERHOUSE	
"	19/8/16		MAJOR FOSTER detailed for duty at ADS to be moved to RED HOUSE (M 6 d 2 0) if needed.	
			LT MEENAN ~~at~~ RAP close to JOCKS LODGE (N 7 b 4 4). Two MO's at RED HOUSE (M 6 d 2 0)	GHG
			12 stretcher bearers sent up to report to MAJOR FOSTER & detailed to RED HOUSE 3 squads to (N 7 b 4 4)	
			3 in reserve at M 6 d 2 0 till required	
			3 motor ambulances sent up to RED HOUSE	
			20 casualties evacuated from us during night. 2 MAC cars sent for	
"	20/8/16		COL J YOUNG TO called in morning to see casualty list	GHG
			COL FIRTH DDMS XI CORPS called at HdQrs in afternoon	

2353 Wt. W2544/1454 700,000 5/15 D. D. & L. A.D.S.S. Forms/C. 2118.

Army Form C. 2118.

WAR DIARY
or
INTELLIGENCE SUMMARY.
(Erase heading not required.)

Instructions regarding War Diaries and Intelligence Summaries are contained in F. S. Regs., Part II. and the Staff Manual respectively. Title pages will be prepared in manuscript.

Ref O.S. Map 36^A NE
HQRS 2/2 Fd Amb = L34 B 6 2
ADS at LAVENTIE = G 34 C 4 2

Place	Date	Hour	Summary of Events and Information	Remarks and references to Appendices
LA GORGUE	21/8/16		LT O'BRIEN detailed for duty at A.D.S. CAPT MARSHALL returned for duty at HQRS	GWC
" "	22/8/16		SGT EDGINTON detailed to attend course of instruction at Divisional Gas Defence School	GWC
" "	23/8/16		CAPT MOORE, SGT. DOLPHIN, & CORPL OLDROYD, detailed to attend course of instruction in Physical Exercise ADMS 61 Div up to hospital in morning. OC up to ADS.	GWC
" "	24/8/16		Routine duties COL WALLACE CMG called in reference to possible transfer of CAPT ROBINSON as Surgeon to a CCS.	GWC
" "	25/8/16		CAPT GIBSON RAMC attended here with mobile X ray outfit to examine two cases. OC up to ADS at LAVENTIE	GWC
" "	26/8/16		COL HARRISON OC ASC 61 Div inspected transport of unit, and expressed himself as satisfied with the condition of horses, wagons, harness & shoeing	GWC

Instructions regarding War Diaries and Intelligence Summaries are contained in F. S. Regs., Part II. and the Staff Manual respectively. Title pages will be prepared in manuscript.

WAR DIARY
or
INTELLIGENCE SUMMARY.
(Erase heading not required.)

Army Form C. 2118.

Ref. O.S. Map 36^A NE
HQrs. 2/3rd Amb = L. 34. B 6 2
A.D.S. at LAVENTIE = G 34 C 4 2

Place	Date	Hour	Summary of Events and Information	Remarks and references to Appendices
LAGORGUE	26/8/16		Instructions from ADMS to detail M.O to attend to 182 MGS (R.2 central)	[illegible]
			Report received from Divn for officers report on 2408 SGT EDGINTON W.J.	App 3.
			MAJOR FOSTER & CAPT ROBINSON proceeded to ADS LAVENTIE	
			MAJOR WATERHOUSE & LT O'BRIEN returned for duty to HQRS	
			LIEUT QRMR E.S BOND returned to duty from leave	
"	27/8/16		330 blankets returned to DADOS	
			9 pair H.D horses sent with drivers and harness to [illegible] A Coy ASC	[illegible]
"	28/8/16		APM 61 Divn called to inquire into a case	[illegible]
			Routine work	
"	29/8/16		Report on inspection of transport by Lt COL HARRISON OC 61 Divn Train	[illegible]
"	30/8/16		Up to ADS with ADMS & on from there to find site for possible R.A.P.	
			CAPT NELIGAN Surgical specialist 7 CCS lectured to medical officers of division	[illegible]
"	~~31/8~~			

Army Form C. 2118.

Instructions regarding War Diaries and Intelligence Summaries are contained in F. S. Regs., Part II. and the Staff Manual respectively. Title pages will be prepared in manuscript.

WAR DIARY
or
INTELLIGENCE SUMMARY.
(Erase heading not required.)

Ref OS map 36a NE
HQrs 2 Fd Amb = L 34 B 6.2
ADS at LAVENTIE = G 34 C 4.2

Place	Date	Hour	Summary of Events and Information	Remarks and references to Appendices
LA GORGUE	31/8/16		OC up to ADS in afternoon with re work. Report on physical training course	GMcC App 5

George McCrae Lt Col RAMC T
OC 2 Fd Amb 61 Divn

L 34 B 6.2
Aug 31st 1916

2353 Wt. W2544/1454 700,000 5/15 D. D. & L. A.D.S.S. Forms/C. 2118.

War Diary   App. V

A.D.M.S.
No. 461M/16
Recd
Sent 30-8-16
61st (S.M.) Division

O.C.,
2/2nd F. Ambulance.

Herewith report on four days course Physical Training, 23rd - 27th inst. for your information:-

Capt. Moore,	Fair
Sergt. Dolphin.	Very fair
Corpl. Oldroyd.	Good.

James Young
Colonel,
A.D.M.S. 61st Division.

30/8/16.

George W Craig
Lt Col RAMC
OC 2/2 Fd Amb 61 Div

[illegible]

Appendix 2. War Diary

A. D. M. S. – No. 62 M/16 Recd ... Sent 15.8.16 61st (S.M.) Division

O.C.,
2/2nd F. Ambulance.

The following extract from report of D.G.O. 61st Division in connection with course held Aug. 11 - 14th is forwarded for your information:-

"2/2nd F. Amb. Sergt. Heckman. Very fair.
"This N.C.O. should be capable of giving useful
"elementary instruction in his Unit but is
"not good enough to be termed 'Instructor'".

James Young

Colonel,
A.D.M.S. 61st Division

15/8/16.

George W Bruce
Lt Col RAMC
OC 2/2 Fd Amb 61 Divn

Appendix I

War Diary of 2/2 Fd. Amb 61 Div

Routine work. The unit has headquarters and hospital accommodation at LA GORGUE (Ref L34B62)

Advanced dressing station at LAVENTIE (G34C43)

STEEL SHELTER is the limit under ordinary conditions for wheeled traffic. 2 orderlies are on duty there

The civil population of LA GORGUE attend daily as outpatients at the LABOUR HOSPITAL, and an MO from the unit attends to them

A medical officer of the unit also attends daily at

1 The BAYONET FIGHTING School

2 The 182 Bde Machine Gun section

3 daily sick parade at HQrs.

One MO is attached temporarily to 1/4 Gloucesters Bn

One " " " " " " 2/5 R War Regt

The dentist attends weekly at the unit HQrs

Men returned from XI Corps Rest Station, & T U men found fit for duty are returned to their units by the Fd Amb

George McCrae Lt Col RAMC
OC 2/2 Fd Amb

Appendix 4. War Diary

O.C 2/2 Fd Amb

The following remarks are the result of the inspection of your transport by Lt Col Harrison O.C Divnl Train

Horses H.D Good a bit fat. Tails might be cleaner
Shoeing good

Riders. Good every effort should be made to give these animals regular exercise. They are fat in some cases.

Harness. Good. breeching on a little high, in some cases requires repair. This is in hand. Line chains required.

Vehicles excellent well greased & clean.

The whole Field ambulance Transport generally speaking, up to standard

James Young Col
ADMS 61 Divn

28/8/16

George W Craig
O.C 2/2 Fd Amb 61 Divn

War Diary Appendix 3 C.41

OC 2/2. Fd Amb

Following extract from Divisional Gas Officers report on NCO'S who attended his instructional classes is forwarded for information

No 2408 Sgt W J Edgerton Very good

All possible use should be made of this NCO in giving instruction in the use & care of helmets & in making up sprayer solution &c

James Young
Col.
ADMS 61 Divn

George W Craig
Lt Col RAMC ?

OC 2/2 Fd Amb 61 Divn

Summary of cases at 2 Fd Amb 61 Div
for period 1-31 Aug 1916

Sick 808 }
Wounded 260 } admissions total 1068

Transferred to CCS 491
" C.R.S 465
Died 7
Returned to duty 105

Seen at medical inspection room 838

Civilians attended at Labour Hospital 360

George W Craig
LtCol RAMC
2/2 Fd Amb 61 Divn

Report on the Divisional Baths & Laundry
June 13th – Aug 12th 1916

During this period of sixty days 77509 men were bathed and a change of clean and mended underclothing given to each. The cost per man was .465 francs. The wages of the women employed at the laundry accounted for .413 francs of this. The remaining .052 being made up by materials local purchase etc.

The laundry & mending room worked for 52 days.

The laundry worked 260150 garments.

A daily average of 107 women were employed & the work done was 46 articles per woman per day.

In the mending room 46 women were employed daily & 78750 articles were mended. A daily average per woman of 29 articles.

A daily average of 153 women were employed & 6516.88 articles dealt with & an average cost of ·09 francs per garment.

O i/c Div Baths & Laundry
26.8.16

(Sd) W. J. Long
Capt R.A.M.C.T.
O.C. Baths & Laundry

		average per day
Number of men bathed	77509	1291.813
at Baths & Laundry	39096	651.6
at Sub Baths	38413	640.21

Maximum bathed in one day at Baths & Laundry 1320 Aug 7th.

Washing.

No of articles Washed	260150
average per day	5002.88
No of Women employed	5568
average per day	107.07
Average work per Women per day	46.72 articles

Menders

No of articles mended	78780
Average per day	1515.00
No of Women employed	2671
average per day	51.36
Average work per Women per day	29.53 articles

II

No of articles dealt with per day 6516.88
No of women employed per day 158.13
Wages paid to women fr 32033.2
Cost per garment (wages only) ·094.

Total cost of running the baths & laundry (see wages, materials & local purchases) fr 36103.35

Total cost of washing & giving a clean change to each man ·465 fr.

Labour Corps.	Laundry	Civilians.
121	113	126

From 31st July — 27 Aug. Total 360 patients

Dressings disposed of.

Bandages (3 in 5)	20 rolls.
" triangular	1.
Boric Lint	1 lb 6 ozs.
Plain "	4 ozs.
Cyan Gauze	2 yards
Jaconet	1 yard
Cotton wool	1 lb.
Pins	20

1 length of Fibre for Splints (fracture box)
1 tube of Catgut.

Ointments & Lotions disposed of.

Methylated Spirits	9 pts.
Boric Acid Sol (Sat)	1 Gall.
Carbolic Acid (1 : 20)	2½ pts
Lead & opium Lotion	2 ounces
Ung. Hydrag. Ammon	7 ozs
Ung. Sulphur	4 ozs.
Ung. Boric	4 ozs.
Ung. Hydr Ox. flav	1 oz.
Asepto Soap	1 tablet
Anaesthetic Ethyl Chloride	½ tube.

Drugs disposed of

Mist Expect	1 pt.
" Alb	1 pt.
" Bismuth	1 pt.
" Tonicus	1 pt.
Aspirin Tablets (10 gr)	72.
No. 9 "	8.
" 13 "	4.
Hydrag Cum Creta Tab (2 gr)	14.
Atrophine (Eye Drops)	1 oz
Tincture of Iodine	2 ozs.

Prescriptions dispensed as above.

August 27th/1916.

George W Craig
Lt Col RAMC
O.C. 2/2 Fd Amb 6 Divn

Sept. 1916

61st Div

Vol 5

CONFIDENTIAL

WAR DIARY.

2/2. Sth Mid Fd Amb

Period 1-30 Sept. 1916 Vol. 5.

George W Craig
Lt Col RAMC T.
O.C. 2/2 S. Mid Fd Amb.

30/9/16

Instructions regarding War Diaries and Intelligence Summaries are contained in F. S. Regs., Part II. and the Staff Manual respectively. Title pages will be prepared in manuscript.

WAR DIARY
or
INTELLIGENCE SUMMARY.
(Erase heading not required.)

Army Form C. 2118.

Place	Date	Hour	Summary of Events and Information	Remarks and references to Appendices
			Ref MAP 36A NE. HQRS of unit LAGORGUE = L34B62 ADS at LAVENTIE = G34C63	
LA GORGUE	1/9/16		3 NCOs detailed for instruction in detection of lice at Corps laundry	
			COL RAFIRTH DDMS XI Corps called at HQRS. Report received from Physical Training course	GMG
" "	2/9/16		CAPT McNEE 3 MOBILE LABY called re any case of diarrhoea in hospital	GMG
" "	3/9/16		COL YOUNG TD ADMS 61 Div inspected hospital in morning	GMG
"	4/9/16		O.C at ADS in morning Routine work	GMG
" "	5/9/16		MAJOR GEN COLIN MACKENZIE CB visited hospital in afternoon	GMG
	6/9/16		OC at ADMS office to arrange details for duty at Corps Laundry	GMG
	7/9/16		OC's attendance at ADMS office in afternoon re reduction of number of medical officers in unit	GMG

Instructions regarding War Diaries and Intelligence Summaries are contained in F. S. Regs., Part II. and the Staff Manual respectively. Title pages will be prepared in manuscript.

WAR DIARY
or
INTELLIGENCE SUMMARY.
(Erase heading not required.)

Army Form C. 2118.

Place	Date	Hour	Summary of Events and Information — Map Ref. 36A N.E	Remarks and references to Appendices
			HQRS of unit LA GORGUE = L34 B62 ADS at LAVENTIE = G34 C63.	
LA GORGUE	8/9/16		Stores for hospital from BRCS LT DUNN no 3 Mobile Laboratory gave demonstration to MO's of division on Typhoid, Para typhoid & Dysentery	GHG
" "	9/9/16		3 NCO's detailed to baths for detection of lice ADMS 61 Div called at Hospital: OC over to 1/2 London CCS with MAJOR BALL SSO	GHG
" "	10/9/16		Church parade in morning. Church service in ward for patients in evening At ADMS office 10 AM with OC 2/3 Fd Amb to discuss sanitary inspection of allotted area by an MO from each ambulance. CAPT MARSHALL detailed for the work.	GHG
" "	11/9/16		CAPT MOORE MAJOR WATERHOUSE to ADS for duty OC to ADS in afternoon.	GHG
" "	12/9/16		routine duty	GHG

2353 Wt. W2544/1454 700,000 5/15 D. D. & L. A.D.S.S./Forms/C. 2118.

Instructions regarding War Diaries and Intelligence Summaries are contained in F. S. Regs., Part II. and the Staff Manual respectively. Title pages will be prepared in manuscript.

WAR DIARY
or
INTELLIGENCE SUMMARY.
(Erase heading not required.)

Army Form C. 2118.

Map Ref. 36A N.E.

Place	Date	Hour	Summary of Events and Information (HQRS of unit LA GORGUE L.34 B 6.2; A.D.S at LAVENTIE G.34 C 6.3)	Remarks and references to Appendices
LA GORGUE	13/9/16		COL C WALLACE CMG Consulting Surgeon 1st ARMY called to see CAPT ROBINSON ref transfer to CCS. Report received from OC Physical course for 1 officer and 2 NCOS.	[illegible]
"	14/9/16		OC up to ADS. Routine work	[illegible]
"	15/9/16		Note from ADMS 61 Div that DMS 1st ARMY would inspect Unit. Order received for CAPT J F ROBINSON to report for duty to No 6 CCS BARLIN.	[illegible]
"	16/9/16		SURGEON GENERAL [illegible] DMS ARMY inspected HQRS of unit, and ADS at LAVENTIE. CAPT WILKINSON struck off strength of unit on attachment to 2/7 R WAR REGT	[illegible] ADMS [illegible]
"	17/9/16		CAPT BANNERMAN reported for duty from 2/4 Gloucester Regt (ADMS C R 28/M/16). Drawn in [illegible] for patients	[illegible]
"	18/9/16		CAPT ROBINSON reported for duty to CCS BARLIN and struck off strength of unit	DMS [illegible]
"	19/9/16		OC up to ADS. Support in dug out completed, and sand bag shelter in front of door commenced. Down to CRE to see about timber for horse standings.	[illegible]

Army Form C. 2118.

Instructions regarding War Diaries and Intelligence Summaries are contained in F. S. Regs., Part II. and the Staff Manual respectively. Title pages will be prepared in manuscript.

WAR DIARY
or
INTELLIGENCE SUMMARY.
(Erase heading not required.)

Map Ref. 36A NE
HQRS of unit: LA GORGUE L34 B62
ADS at LAVENTIE G34 C63

Place	Date	Hour	Summary of Events and Information	Remarks and references to Appendices
LA GORGUE	20/9/16		routine work	GWC
" "	21/9/16		CAPT BANNERMAN proceeded on 7 days leave COL J YOUNG ADMS 61 Div called and went round hospital LT COL MARINDIN called at hospital to introduce his successor LT COL SINGLETON	GWC
" "	22/9/16		routine work OC up to A.D.S. Sand bagging in front of door of steel shelter completed	GWC
" "	23/9/16		routine work	GWC
" "	24/9/16		O.C up to ADS at LAVENTIE. R.E started to erect motor to work pump in yard at HQRS	GWC
" "	25/9/16		CAPT DAVISON O.C 61 Div San Sect went round hospital ADMS 61 Div round in morning. ~~CAPT~~ MAJOR FOSTER & LT O BRIEN proceeded to A.D.S to relieve MAJOR WATERHOUSE & CAPT MOORE	GWC

Instructions regarding War Diaries and Intelligence Summaries are contained in F. S. Regs., Part II. and the Staff Manual respectively. Title pages will be prepared in manuscript.

WAR DIARY
or
INTELLIGENCE SUMMARY.
(Erase heading not required.)

Army Form C. 2118.

Ref Map 36A N.E.
HQRS of unit LA GORGUE L34 B62
ADS at LAVENTIE G34 C 33

Place	Date	Hour	Summary of Events and Information	Remarks and references to Appendices
LA GORGUE	26/9/16		COL YOUNG ADMS 61 DIV up to HQRS in morning. Opening of YMCA hut at LA GORGUE by LT GEN. SIR C ANDERSON KCB. Unit supplied concert party. Work commenced on kitchen floor, re-heating & building new oven	G.F.G.
"	27/9/16		O.C. down to ADMS office of arrangement for this unit to fetch and accommodate for night drafts arriving late at railway station. Motor engine for pumping from well in yard of HQRS completed	G.F.G.
"	28/9/16		LT O'BRIEN attached as M.O. for relief to 2/1 BUCKS BN.	G.F.G.
"	29/9/16		Routine work	G.F.G.
"	30/9/16		CAPT BANNERMAN reported for duty on return from leave. LT ANDERSON RAMC reported for attachment to the unit	G.F.G.

L. 34. B 62
30/9/16

George F. Gray
Lt Col RAMC T
Cmdg 2/1st ... [illegible]

2353 Wt. W2544/1454 700,000 5/15 D. D. & L. A.D.S.S. Forms/C 2118.

War Diary

2/2 Fd Amb 61 Div

Appendix I

The routine work of the unit during the past month has comprised the following duties.

Hospital at Headquarters LAGORGUE
Advanced dressing station at LAVENTIE,
outpatients & morning sick of detached units daily at HQRS
daily attendance of M.O at Labour Corps Hospital for attendance on civilians.
daily visit by M.O. to outlying units R.F.C. R.E labour corps, Divisional school of Instruction & Bayonet fighting school.
Sanitary inspections by M.O. of billet area in conjunction with DADMS
one medical officer supplied to take charge of the Divisional baths and laundry.
N.C.O in charge of sub baths at LAVENTIE
Supervision of water supply by pump at HQRs for regimental water carts which are filled from tanks
Horse r driver for Street sweeper
Horse r driver for cart for watering streets
Sanitary supervision of divisional canteen theatre.
orderly in charge of divisional library at canteen
Dental surgeon attends weekly at Headquarters

George W Craig Lt RAMC

War Diary Appendix II

2/2 Fd Amb. 6 Div.

Summary of Admissions for month Sept.

Sept	Adm Offic	Adm OR.	CCS O	CCS OR.	CRS O	CRS OR	Died O	Died OR	Duty O	Duty OR	Scabies O	Scabies OR	Ague
1	2	35	–	10	1	14	–	–	–	4	–	9	4
2	2	25	1	13	–	24	–	–	–	5	–	–	–
3	2	19	1	4	–	14	–	–	–	5	–	2	–
4	–	13	2	–	2	5	–	–	–	5	–	–	–
5	3	18	2	9	–	5	–	–	–	5	–	6	1
6	2	13	3	5	–	15	–	–	–	3	–	1	–
7	4	18	–	11	1	2	–	–	–	8	–	4	–
8	3	30	4	6	–	7	–	–	–	5	–	5	–
9	1	23	1	12	1	13	–	–	–	7	–	4	–
10	1	21	–	8	1	3	–	–	–	2	–	–	1
11	1	26	1	7	–	9	–	–	–	4	–	5	–
12	1	18	–	7	–	10	–	–	–	7	–	–	–
13	2	21	1	–	2	12	–	1	–	–	–	–	–
14	–	25	–	7	1	7	–	–	–	2	–	2	2
15	3	19	2	13	1	31	–	–	–	–	–	–	–
16	–	19	–	2	–	–	–	–	–	1	–	–	–
17	2	21	1	12	–	–	–	–	–	1	–	1	3
18	–	20	1	4	–	7	–	–	–	–	–	10	–
19	2	23	–	6	–	11	–	–	–	5	–	6	–
20	2	11	2	15	1	2	–	–	–	14	1	1	–
21	–	24	1	6	1	10	–	–	–	7	–	3	–
22	–	28	–	3	–	3	–	–	–	3	–	4	–
23	–	23	–	28	–	17	–	–	–	8	–	4	2
	33	493	23	188	12	221		1		101	1	61	13

S.	adm.		CCS.		CRS		Died		Duty.		Scabies		Arques.
	O	OR	O	OR	O	OR	O	OR	O	OR	O	OR	
	33	493	23	188	12	221	–	1	–	101	1	61	13
24	1	25	1	5	1	14	–	–	–	3		5	–
25	–	19	–	6	–	19	–	–	–	2		2	–
26	1	26	–	4	–	–	–	1	–	4		4	–
27	1	16	1	8	–	2	–	–	–	3		1	–
28	1	14	1	3	–	7	–	–	–	1		1	–
29	–	23	–	7	1	7	–	–	–	7		1	–
30	3	29	–	17	–	11	–	–	–	5		2	–
	40	645	26	238	14	281		2		126	1	83	13
		685		264		295		2		126		84	13

Daily average

22·8	8·8	9·8	·06	4.	2·6.

Outpatients & morning sick 644

Chiropody cases 106

George W [illegible]
Lt Col RAMC [illegible]
2/2 [illegible]

30/9/16

Labour Corps.	Laundry	Civilians
93	42	190.
		Total 325.

13 persons examined for enrolment in Labour Corps.

George W Craig
Lt Col RAMC T.
2/2 Fd Amb 61 Divn

30/9/16

For month ending Sept 28th. 1916.

Dressings		Drugs Ointments etc	
Rolls 3inch Bandages	48	Methylated Spirits	8 pts
Boric Lint	lbs 4½	Sol Acid Carbolic (1–20)	4
Hospital Lint	" 1½	" " Boric (sat)	3
Cyan Gauze	yds 6	Lotio Plumbi	6 ozs
Surgical Gauze	" 1	Mist Expect	1 pt
Jaconet	" 2	Mist alb	1½ "
Cotton Wool	lbs 1½	Mist Bismuth	½ "
adhesive plaster	reels 1	No 9 tablets	12
Silk Catgut	yds 1	" 13 "	6
Belladonna plaster	6" x 4"	Aspirins 5 gr.	20
		Tinct Iodine	2 oz
		Caustic	1 stick
		Boric Ung.	1 lb 2 ozs
		Zinc "	4 ozs
		Ung Opthalmicum	2 ozs
		1 tube Atrophine Sulp	

Drugs etc continued.

Ung. Hyd Ox Flav	1 oz
Tablet of Asepto Soap	1
Lin Terebinth.	½ pt
Lin Saponis.	6 ozs.

30 prescriptions made up at Dispensary.

George W Gray
Lt Col RAMC
2/2 Fd Amb 61 Dn

30/9/15

Confidential

Oct/16

61st Division

Vol 6

140/1-7/88

War Diary.

42 S. Mid Fd Amb.

VOL. VI

Period 1-31 Oct. 1916

George W Craig
Lt Col RAMC T
OC. 42 S Mid Fd. Amb.

1/XI/XVI.

1

Instructions regarding War Diaries and Intelligence Summaries are contained in F. S. Regs., Part II. and the Staff Manual respectively. Title pages will be prepared in manuscript.

WAR DIARY
or
INTELLIGENCE SUMMARY.
(Erase heading not required.)

Army Form C. 2118.

Place	Date	Hour	Summary of Events and Information	Remarks and references to Appendices
			Ref. Map 36^A^ N.E. HQRS of unit LA GORGUE – L 3A 3 6 2 ADS at LAVENTIE G 21 C 6 3	
LA GORGUE	1/10/16		CAPT. MARSHALL transferred to 1/3 Fd Amb & struck off strength of unit	
			LT C.B.C. ANDERSON detailed to ADS for duty. CAPT BANNERMAN reported for temporary duty to 1/1 BUCKS Bn	G.H.6
			LT D.J. O'BRIEN admitted to 1/2 London CCS and struck off strength of unit	
			Wounded German prisoner brought in to HQRS 11.15 pm	
"	2/10/16		Wounded prisoner transferred to 1/2 London CCS.	G.H.6
			MAJOR GENERAL COLIN MACKENZIE C.B. called & went round HQrs with a Russian officer.	
			Stores received from BRCS.	
"	3/10/16		COL R.H. FIRTH DDMS XI Corps, MAJOR POTTS DSO called and went round HQRS.	G.H.6
			Advice note from LADY MAYORESS BIRMINGHAM FUND re dispatch of food for unit	
"	4/10/16		LT C.B.C. ANDERSON detailed to 2/4 R. Berks Regt for temporary duty ([illegible]) to take up duties.	G.H.6

2353 Wt. W2544/1454 700,000 5/15 D. D. & L. A.D.S.S. Forms/C. 2118.

Instructions regarding War Diaries and Intelligence Summaries are contained in F. S. Regs., Part II. and the Staff Manual respectively. Title pages will be prepared in manuscript.

WAR DIARY
or
INTELLIGENCE SUMMARY.
(Erase heading not required.)

Army Form C. 2118.

Place	Date	Hour	Summary of Events and Information	Remarks and references to Appendices
			Ref Map 36A NE H.Qrs of Unit LA GORGUE. L34 B6.2 ADS at LAVENTIE = G 34 C 6 3	
LA GORGUE	5/X/16		LT ANDERSON reported to unit for duty. routine duties	GWC
" "	6/X/16.		OC left ADS in morning. 15 men detailed as fatigue party to MERVILLE, 10 to NOUVEAU MONDE MAJOR FRANKAU OC 1/2 London CCS, lectured to officers on WAR SURGERY. SURGEON GENERAL PIKE DMS 1 ARMY called at HQRS and went round hospital.	GWC
" "	7/X/16		Stores for hospital from RRCS.	GWC
" "	8/X/16		New suggestion for utilizing ground sheet as stretcher by means of portable handles attached to eyelet holes of waterproof sheet. Experimented with them and came to conclusion that they would be useful but that it would be an improvement if some sort of sling could be attached to take some of the weight on the bearers shoulder (Circular DMS 1st army 13/18)	GWC
" "	9/X/16		MAJOR WATERHOUSE & CAPT MOORE to LAVENTIE. Vice MAJOR FOSTER & LT ANDERSON CAPT BANNERMAN reported for duty from 1/1 BUCKS BN.	GWC

Instructions regarding War Diaries and Intelligence Summaries are contained in F. S. Regs., Part II. and the Staff Manual respectively. Title pages will be prepared in manuscript.

WAR DIARY
or
INTELLIGENCE SUMMARY.
(Erase heading not required.)

Army Form C. 2118.

Ref Map 36 NE
HQRS of unit LAGORGUE L32 B22
ADS at LAVENTIE G34 C63

Place	Date	Hour	Summary of Events and Information	Remarks and references to Appendices
LAGORGUE	9/X/16		CAPT BANNERMAN, SGT EDGINTON attended at Div Gas School for demonstration on new box respirator. [illegible] brought from flying corps buried with [illegible]	[illegible]
"	10/X/16		Meeting of OCs Fd Amb at ADMS office in afternoon. Instructions as to inspection of equipment re	[illegible]
"	11/X/16		OC to ADS. MAJOR SYLVESTER 1/2 London CCS visited HQrs routine duties.	[illegible]
"	12/X/16		CAPT BANNERMAN reported for duty to DAC. MAJOR WATERHOUSE for duty to ADS	[illegible]
"	13/X/16		CAPT DAVISON OC Sany Sect & CAPT PARKINSON ADMS 1st Army called & inspected sanitary arrangements at HQRS. Model of stove made from oil drum by PTE DUCKHOUSE, specimen asked for for OC Sany Sect. Meeting of O'sC field ambulances at ADMS Office. CAPT GILL reported for duty.	[illegible]

2353 Wt. W2544/1454 700,000 5/15 D. D. & L. A.D.S.S./Forms/C. 2118.

Instructions regarding War Diaries and Intelligence Summaries are contained in F. S. Regs., Part II. and the Staff Manual respectively. Title pages will be prepared in manuscript.

WAR DIARY
or
INTELLIGENCE SUMMARY.
(*Erase heading not required.*)

Army Form C. 2118.

Map Ref. 36^A NE

Place	Date	Hour	Summary of Events and Information	Remarks and references to Appendices
			HQRS. LAGORGUE. L 34. B 6.2.	
			A.DS at LAVENTIE. G 34 C.6.3.	
LAGORGUE	14/X/16		OC up to ADS	
			LT COL SINGLETON DSO AAQMG 61 DIV called and went round hospital	[illegible]
"	15/X/16		CAPT ANDERSON reported for duty to 2/4 GLOSTER BN.	
			MAJOR GENERAL C MACKENZIE C.B. called and went round wards	[illegible]
"	16/X/16		routine work	[illegible]
"	17/X/16		MAJOR FOSTER proceeded on leave of absence, leaving OC only medical officer available	[illegible]
"	18/X/16		routine duties. PTE FRANKUM granted 7 days special leave	[illegible]
"	19/X/16		Conference of OSC Fd Amb at ADMS office. Unit to be inspected by ADMS 61 Div to morrow	[illegible]
			CAPT McNEE called to see 3 case of diarrhoea. CAPT MARSHALL reported for temporary duty	[illegible]
"	20/X/16		ADMS 61 Div inspected unit at 11 A.M.	

Army Form C. 2118.

Instructions regarding War Diaries and Intelligence Summaries are contained in F. S. Regs., Part II. and the Staff Manual respectively. Title pages will be prepared in manuscript.

WAR DIARY
or
INTELLIGENCE SUMMARY.
(Erase heading not required.)

Map Ref. 36A NE
HQRS LA GORGUE L 34 B 6 2
ADS at LAVENTIE G 34 C 6 3

Place	Date	Hour	Summary of Events and Information	Remarks and references to Appendices
LA GORGUE	21/X/16		Lecture to medical officers by COL C WALLACE. CMG on military abdominal surgery.	[illegible]
" "	22/X/16		CAPT MACNEA 3 Motor Laby called to see cases.	
			CAPT THOMPSON 5th DIV 2/3 London field ambulance called [illegible]	[illegible]
" "	23/X/16		Routine duties	[illegible]
" "	24/X/16		Routine duties	[illegible]
" "	25/X/16		Lt COL FRENCH O.C. 2/3 LONDON F.A. called [illegible]	[illegible]
			COL FIRTH DDMS XI CORPS called at HQRS [illegible]	
			CAPT [illegible] returned to unit for permanent duty	
" "	31/X/16		CAPT THOMPSON [illegible] to ADS to take over.	[illegible]
			CAPT BANNERMAN & LE CAPT [illegible] for [illegible]	

Army Form C. 2118.

WAR DIARY
or
INTELLIGENCE SUMMARY.
(*Erase heading not required.*)

Instructions regarding War Diaries and Intelligence Summaries are contained in F. S. Regs., Part II. and the Staff Manual respectively. Title pages will be prepared in manuscript.

Ref MAP 36A NE
HQRS LA GORGUE L 31 B 6 2.
ADS at LAVENTIE G 34 C 6 3

Place	Date	Hour	Summary of Events and Information	Remarks and references to Appendices
LA GORGUE	27/X/16		2/3 London Fd Amb took over from the unit. COL BROWN ADMS 56 DIV, COL YOUNG ADMS 61 Div called at HQRS. GAS demonstration with new box respirators, lachrymatory fumes in room. 2 ambulance wagons detailed to follow 182 Infy BDE.	G.W.C
" " } LE SART }	28/X/16		Unit moved by route march to LE SART. MAJOR FOSTER & CAPT BANNERMAN met us. Men had tea & were conducted to billets. Ambulance wagon detailed to follow 182 Infy Bde (DCLI). ADMS 61 Div, HQrs 182 Infy Bde notified of arrival of headquarters. Fall-in-out state ordered.	G.W.C Map ref K.27.d [illegible]
LE SART	29/X/16		Routine duties. Inspection of billets & quarters.	G.W.C
" "	30/X/16		COL YOUNG ADMS 61 Div called at HQR in morning. Route march in afternoon.	G.W.C
" "	31/X/16		Route march morning and afternoon. Medical inspection in morning.	G.W.C

31/X/16

G W Craig
Lt Col RAMC
OC 2/2 S Mid Fd Amb

2353 Wt. W2544/1454 700,000 5/15 D. D. & L. A.D.S.S. Forms/C. 2118.

Bandages Dressings etc

Bandages	60 Rolls
Boric Lint	2 lbs
Hospital Lint	1 "
Cotton Wool	3 "
Cyan Gauze	6 yds
Jaconet	1 "

Drugs Medicines etc.

Methylated Spirit	5 pts
Sol Acid Carbolic (1-40)	4 "
Sol Acid Boric (sat)	2 "
Mist Bismuth	1 "
Mist Alba	1 "
Ung Acid Boric	1 lb 12 oz
Ung Hyd Dil	2 "
Sol Hydrogen Perox	4 "
Tinct Iodine	4 "
Asepto Soap	1 Tablet
Atrophine Sulphate	1 Tube
Pill. Asperin	50
" Mag.	12

War Diary 2/2 S Mid Fd Amb

During the period 1-31 Oct

600 cases were admitted to the field ambulance.

G W Craig Lt Col
O.C. 2/2 S M Fd Amb

1/XI/16

War Diary 2/2 S Mid Fd Amb
Routine Duties

During the period 1–27 Oct 1916 the routine duties of the unit comprised:

Attention to casualties at H.Qrs LAGORGUE & at ADS LAVENTIE
Attendance on casual sick out patients at HQRS
Attendance on civilians at Labour Hospital.
Pumping of water to fill tanks at HQRS
Distribution to ASC dumps of TO men, hospital cases & drafts returning to duty.
Visit by MO's to outlying units RFC RE
School of instruction & Bayonet fighting school
One medical officer supplied to take charge of Divisional bath & laundry
NCO in charge of Sub bath at LAVENTIE
Horse & driver supplied to Div Sanitary Section for road sweeper & for water cart for [illegible]

[illegible]
Lt Col RAMC
OC 2/2 S M Fd Amb
31/X/16

Nov. 1916

61st Divn.

Vol 7

CONFIDENTIAL

WAR DIARY.

2/2. S.M. Fd Amb. R.A.M.C.

VOL. VII.

Period 1-30-Nov. 1916

George W. Craig
Lt. Col. R.A.M.C.
O.C. 2/2. S.M. Fd Amb R.A.M.C.

30/XI/16

Instructions regarding War Diaries and Intelligence Summaries are contained in F. S. Regs., Part II. and the Staff Manual respectively. Title pages will be prepared in manuscript.

WAR DIARY
or
INTELLIGENCE SUMMARY.
(Erase heading not required.)

Army Form C. 2118.

Place	Date	Hour	Summary of Events and Information Ref MAP HAZEBROUCK 5th 1/100000	Remarks and references to Appendices
LE SART	NOV 1	1916	Unit out for route march in morning, wagons packed in afternoon. SGT CRANER and detached party returned from CALONNE, where baths had been closed down. GOC 182 Infy BDE, called in morning.	[illegible]
LESART TO BUSNES	NOV 2	1916	CAPT BANNERMAN & SGT OAKES left at 7-30 AM to arrange billets for night. Unit proceeded by route march. LESART-STEENWERQUE-ST VENANT-ROBECQ to farm at Canal near BUSNES. pouring wet all the way. arrived at billets at 12-30 noon	[illegible]
BUSNES TO CAUCHY	NOV 3	1916	CAPT BANNERMAN & SGT OAKES proceeded to RAIMBERT to meet Staff Captain re billets. Unit proceeded by route march. BUSNES-LILLERS-BURBURE-RAIMBERT-CAUCHY. Still raining and roads very muddy. ambulances very busy bringing in cases from neighbouring billets, & evacuating to CCS.	[illegible]
CAUCHY TO ROCOURT	NOV 4	1916	CAPT BANNERMAN & SGT OAKES reported for billeting duties. Unit proceeded by route march. AUCHEL-CAUCHY-FLORINGHEM-PERNES-VALHUON-LATHIEULOYE-ROCOURT.	[illegible]

2353 Wt. W2544/1454 700,000 5/15 D. D. & L. A.D.S.S./Forms/C. 2118.

Instructions regarding War Diaries and Intelligence Summaries are contained in F. S. Regs., Part II. and the Staff Manual respectively. Title pages will be prepared in manuscript.

WAR DIARY
or
INTELLIGENCE SUMMARY.
(Erase heading not required.)

Army Form C. 2118.

Place	Date	Hour	Summary of Events and Information	Remarks and references to Appendices
			Ref MAP HAZEBROUCK 5A 1/100000 } LENS XI 1/100000 }	
CAUCHY TO ROCOURT	NOV 4	1916	Haversack rations carried. 3/4 hour halt in mid day for lunch. Cars again busy at night bringing in cases.	GWB
ROCOURT TO HONVAL	NOV 5	1916	billeting party on ahead to arrange billets at HONVAL. Unit proceeded by route march, route Cross roads ½ mile S of E in MONCHY BRETON – Road junction ½ m. N of U in LE HAUT BARLET FM. road junction ¼ m. SW of 1st T in TINCQUETTE – AVERDOINGT – MAIZIERES – MAGNICOURT HOUVIN – HONVAL. Unit passed MAJOR GENERAL COLIN MACKENZIE CB on march. Extremely windy day and the wind undoubtedly increased the numbers of men who fell out.	GWB
HONVAL to VILLERS L'HÔPITAL	NOV 6	1916	Unit proceeded by route march HONVAL – FREVENT – BONNIERES – VILLERS L'HOPITAL. Very wet and cold on march. CAPT BANNERMAN on ahead to billet One horse ambulance detailed to follow 1/5 DCLI. CAPT VICKERS reported for duty vice CAPT MARSHALL detailed to STATIONARY HOSPITAL ABBEVILLE	GWB
VILLERS L'HOPITAL	NOV. 7.	1916	G.O.C. 182 Bde called in morning. COL YOUNG ADMS 61 DIV called in afternoon	GWB

Instructions regarding War Diaries and Intelligence Summaries are contained in F. S. Regs., Part II. and the Staff Manual respectively. Title pages will be prepared in manuscript.

WAR DIARY
or
INTELLIGENCE SUMMARY.
(Erase heading not required.)

Army Form C. 2118.

Place	Date	Hour	Summary of Events and Information Ref. Map Lens x 1/100,000	Remarks and references to Appendices
VILLERS L'HOPITAL	NOV 8	1916	Cold and very wet. busy bringing in cases from units of Bde.	G.h.G
" "	NOV 9.	1916	baths arranged for unit at barn behind cook house worked quite satisfactorily	G.h.G
" "	NOV 10	1916	Orders received from ADMS 61 Divn for CAPT MARSHALL to report for duty to ABBEVILLE called at ADV DEP MS for supplies at DOULLENS.	G.h.G
" "	NOV 11	1916	CAPT MARSHALL left unit to report for duty at ABBEVILLE, unit out for route march in morning	G.h.G
" "	NOV 12th	1916	Church parade in field at 10 O'C ADMS 61 DIV called, orders for bearer division of each section to report at ADMS office 12 noon for duty. CAPT BANNERMAN, CAPT VICKERS, LT ANDERSON [illegible] MAJOR CRICK, and senior chaplain of the division called.	G.h.G
" "	NOV 13	1916		
" "	NOV 14	1916	Orders received at 8.30 p.m. that the unit would move tomorrow wagons all cleaned. Col YOUNG TO ADMS 61 DIV called.	G.h.G

2353 Wt. W2544/1454 700,000 5/15 D. D. & L. A.D.S.S./Forms/C. 2118.

Instructions regarding War Diaries and Intelligence Summaries are contained in F. S. Regs., Part II. and the Staff Manual respectively. Title pages will be prepared in manuscript.

WAR DIARY
or
INTELLIGENCE SUMMARY.
(Erase heading not required.)

Army Form C. 2118.

Place	Date	Hour	Summary of Events and Information — Ref MAP XI. LENS. 1/100,000	Remarks and references to Appendices
VILLERS L'HOPITAL to GORGES.	NOV. 15	1916	Unit proceeded by route march VILLERS L'HOPITAL – FROHEN-LE-GRAND. FROHEN LE PETIT – MEILLARD – BERNAVILLE – GORGES where it billeted for night. One horse ambulance wagon detailed to follow 2nd column from BONNIERES. Bitterly cold on march, one very awkward hill to climb but transport did remarkably well. CAPT CRAIG detailed for temporary duty as MO to 2/6 R War Regt.	G.W.C
GORGES to PERNOIS	NOV 16	1916	Unit proceeded by route march GORGES – BERNAVILLE – BERNEUIL – DOMART – ST LEGER – PERNOIS. LT BONDON ahead to billet	G.W.C
PERNOIS to SEPTENVILLE	NOV 17	1916	Unit proceeded by route march SEPTENVILLE – HALLOY – HAVERNAS – NAOURS – TOLMAS – SEPTENVILLE. LT BOND on ahead to billet. Very stiff hill but transport did well, no hitch or breakdown	G.W.C
SEPTENVILLE to WARLOY	NOV 18	1916	Unit proceeded by route march SEPTENVILLE – RUBEMPRE – HÉRISSART – CONTAY – WARLOY. To camp next to PRISONERS OF WAR CAMP. Order received for SERG COLLIER to proceed with 5 motor ambulances to BOUZINCOURT. Bitterly cold march, sleet then rain, roads very muddy. Got meal for men, then prepared for 2/3rd FD AMB who came in late. Wire from CAPT BANNERMAN that no casualties had occurred with our bearer division. MAPS fetched from ADMS office	G.W.C

2353 Wt. W2544/1454 700,000 5/15 D. D. & L. A.D.S.S. Forms/C. 2118.

Army Form C. 2118.

WAR DIARY
or
INTELLIGENCE SUMMARY.
(Erase heading not required.)

Instructions regarding War Diaries and Intelligence Summaries are contained in F. S. Regs., Part II. and the Staff Manual respectively. Title pages will be prepared in manuscript.

Place	Date	Hour	Summary of Events and Information Ref map LENS XI 1/100 000	Remarks and references to Appendices
WARLOY.	NOV 19th	1916	Message received that the unit would not march to day. Church parades. Made arrangements for bathing the men. SGT COLLIER returned with 5 motor ambulances from MAC to which he had been attached for duty	SMG
WARLOY	NOV 20	1916	Orders received to move with 18 2 Infy BDE to morrow to ALBERT. CAPT BANNERMAN, CAPT VICKERS LT ANDERSON and bearer subdivisions returned, no casualties. Left orders for CAPT CRAIG to report to HQRS 18 Divn at ALBERT to arrange for taking over Divisional Baths. CAPT VICKERS detailed for medical duty with 2/8 Roy WAR. Regt. Orders received from ADMS 61 DIV to proceed to morrow morning to take over II Corps Rest Station at VADENCOURT.	SMG
WARLOY	NOV 21	1916	OC, QR.MR. F.S. BOND, Q M S SGT FOSS & Clerks proceeded at 9.0 AM to take over II Corps Rest Station at VADENCOURT from 57 FD AMB. MAJOR FOSTER brought up B Section with complete equipment MAJOR WATERHOUSE bringing on remainder of unit at 11.0 AM. Unit accommodated in tents at the Rest Station and commenced to take over.	SMG
VADENCOURT	22/XI/16		Busy taking over from 57th Fd Amb. MAJOR WATERHOUSE proceeded on leave	SMG

2353 Wt. W2544/1454 700,000 5/15 D. D. & L. A.D.S.S. Forms/C. 2118.

Army Form C. 2118.

Instructions regarding War Diaries and Intelligence Summaries are contained in F. S. Regs., Part II. and the Staff Manual respectively. Title pages will be prepared in manuscript.

WAR DIARY
or
INTELLIGENCE SUMMARY.
(Erase heading not required.)

Place	Date	Hour	Summary of Events and Information	Remarks and references to Appendices
			Ref Map LENS XI 1/100 000	
VADENCOURT	23/XI/16		52nd Fd Amb left. CAPT BANNERMAN reported for duty to 61 Divn Supply column	GB 6
" "	24/XI/16		SGT CRANER & 20 OR detailed for temporary duty at WARLOY with 1/2 SM Fd Amb	GB 6
" "	25/XI/16		routine duties	GB 6
" "	26/XI/16		routine duties	GB 6
" "	27/XI/16		over to ADMS 61 Div in morning with MAJOR FOSTER, orders to move to FORCEVILLE over to FORCEVILLE with ADMS and arranged to take over from Highland Fd Amb. CAPT VICKERS reported for duty from 4 E R War Regt.	GB 6
" "	28/XI/16		MAJOR FOSTER, QR & LT BOND & 20 OR over to FORCEVILLE to take over from Highland Fd Amb	GB 6
" "	29/XI/16		routine duties	GB 6

2353 Wt. W2544/1454 700,000 5/15 D. D. & L. A.D.S.S. Forms/C. 2118.

WAR DIARY
or
INTELLIGENCE SUMMARY.
(Erase heading not required.)

Instructions regarding War Diaries and Intelligence Summaries are contained in F. S. Regs., Part II. and the Staff Manual respectively. Title pages will be prepared in manuscript.

Army Form C. 2118.

Ref MAP LENS XI [illegible]

Place	Date	Hour	Summary of Events and Information	Remarks and references to Appendices
VADENCOURT	30/11/16		over to ADMS 61 Divn morning, orders to evacuate all cases from VADENCOURT dividing them between VARENNES (2/3 Fd Amb) & FORCEVILLE. over to FORCEVILLE & VARENNES to make arrangements. OC MAC called [illegible] for [illegible] at 7.0 AM to move patients.	[illegible]

George [illegible] Craig
Lt Col RAMC
OC 2/2 SM Fd Amb RAMC
30/11/16.

2353 Wt. W2544/1454 700,000 5/15 D. D. & L. A.D.S.S. Forms/C 2118.

Dec 1911

61st Div

140/900

Confidential

Vol 8

War Diary

2/2 SM Field Ambulance 61st Div

December 1916

Volume 8.

Army Form C. 2118.

WAR DIARY
or
INTELLIGENCE SUMMARY.
(Erase heading not required.)

Instructions regarding War Diaries and Intelligence Summaries are contained in F. S. Regs., Part II. and the Staff Manual respectively. Title pages will be prepared in manuscript.

Forceville
Map reference. Sheet 57D. P21 c 7.9

Place	Date	Hour	Summary of Events and Information	Remarks and references to Appendices
Forceville	1/12/16	22 hrs	The main body of this ambulance marched today from Vadencourt to Forceville to join the advance party. Sgt. [illegible] reported with 20 men from 2/[illegible] [illegible] where the party had been on detached duty. [illegible]	
"	2/12/16	21 hrs	Routine duties.	
"	3/12/16	22 hrs	Routine duties. [illegible] O.C. 2/2 S.M.F.A. [illegible] [illegible] sick.	
"	4/12/16	[illegible]	Major [illegible] acting O.C. [illegible] duties.	
"	5.12.16	22 hrs	Routine duties. This village was shelled [illegible] [illegible] Capt. R.D. Moore & [illegible] [illegible]	
"	6.12.16	22 hrs.	Routine duties. The hospital was visited today by D.M.S. Army and D.D.M.S. IV Corps.	
"	7.12.16	21 hrs	One Corporal and 29 men detached to assist 2/3 S.M.F.A. Lt. Anderson detached to act as Regimental M.O. 2/5 Gloucester Reg.	
"	8.12.16	21 hrs	Major Waterhouse reported for duty on returning from leave.	

2353 Wt. W2544/1454 700,000 5/15 D. D. & L. A.D.S.S. Forms/C. 2118.

Army Form C. 2118.

Instructions regarding War Diaries and Intelligence Summaries are contained in F. S. Regs., Part II. and the Staff Manual respectively. Title pages will be prepared in manuscript.

WAR DIARY
or
INTELLIGENCE SUMMARY.
(Erase heading not required.)

Place	Date	Hour	Summary of Events and Information Forceville Sheet 57D. P 21 c. 7-9	Remarks and references to Appendices
Forceville	9.12.16	21hrs.	Capt. Bannerman rejoins from detached duty with 61st Div. Train A.S.C.	E.C.F.
"	10.12.16	22hrs.	Routine duties. Considerable difficulty in obtaining certain supplies, wood etc.	E.C.F.
"	11.12.16	20hrs.	Routine duties. Wood for building now being received in adequate quantities.	E.C.F.
"	12.12.16	21hrs.	Routine duties.	E.C.F.
"	13.12.16	22hrs.	Routine duties. Visit of D.D.M.S. IV Corps.	E.C.F.
	14.12.16	20hrs.	Routine duties	E.C.F.
	15.12.16	20hrs	Routine duties.	E.C.F.
	16.12.16		Routine duties. S. Maj. Plaistow proceeds on leave.	E.C.F.
	17.12.16		Capt. Craig reported for duty with this ambulance, rejoining from 61st Divisional baths.	E.C.F.
	18.12.16		Routine duties.	E.C.F.
	19.12.16		Capt. Bannerman reports for duty rejoining from 2/1 S.M. F. Amb.	E.C.F.
	20.12.16		Routine duties	E.C.F.
	21.12.16		Routine duties	E.C.F.
	22.12.16		Hon. Lt. + Q.M. Bond admitted + transferred to No. 4 C.C.S.	E.C.F.
	23.12.16		Capt. Vickers proceeded to join 2/5 Warwick Reg. on temporary duty.	E.C.F.
	24.12.16		Capt. Moore proceeds on leave.	E.C.F.

2353 Wt. W2544/1454 700,000 5/15 D. D. & L. A.D.S.S. Forms/C. 2118.

Army Form C. 2118.

Instructions regarding War Diaries and Intelligence Summaries are contained in F. S. Regs., Part II. and the Staff Manual respectively. Title pages will be prepared in manuscript.

WAR DIARY
or
INTELLIGENCE SUMMARY.
(Erase heading not required.)

Forceville Sheet 57D. P 21 c.7.9

Place	Date	Hour	Summary of Events and Information	Remarks and references to Appendices
Forceville	25.12.16	21.0	Lt. Anderson rejoins for duty from 2/5 Gloucester Regt.	E.C.F.
"	26.12.16	20.0	Routine Duties.	E.C.F.
"	27.12.16	21.0	Routine Duties. Clayton apparatus used for first time.	E.C.F.
"	28.12.16	22.0	Routine Duties. Red Cross stores received to assist equipment of hospital	E.C.F.
"	29.12.16	20.0	Routine duties.	E.C.F.
"	30.12.16	21.0	Routine Duties. New baths opened for treatment of patients.	E.C.F.
"	31.12.16	20.0	Routine Duties. New dining hall opened for patients. The supply of hot water for patients is still inadequate owing to the fact that the necessary Soyer stoves have not yet arrived.	
			Lt. Anderson struck off the strength on transfer to I Corps.	E.C.F.

E. C. Foster
Major RAMC
for O.C. 2/2 S. M. F. Amb.

2353 Wt. W2544/1454 700,000 5/15 D. D. & L. A.D.S.S./Forms/C. 2118.

Jan. 1917

61st Div

140/941

Vol 9

CONFIDENTIAL

S

WAR DIARY

2/2 S. MID. FLD. AMBCE.
RAMC (T.F.)

VOL. 9.

JAN. 1st. – 31st. 1917 (inclusive)

Instructions regarding War Diaries and Intelligence Summaries are contained in F. S. Regs., Part II. and the Staff Manual respectively. Title pages will be prepared in manuscript.

WAR DIARY

~~or~~

~~INTELLIGENCE SUMMARY.~~

(*Erase heading not required.*)

Army Form C. 2118.

Place	Date	Hour	Summary of Events and Information FORCEVILLE P21. C. 7. 9 Sheet 57 D	Remarks and references to Appendices
FORCEVILLE	1.1.17	21.0	Patients in Hospital 300. The following new undertakings have been opened and are now in working order though not complete to the last detail. 1. Officers' Ward. 2. Baths. 3. Laundry 4. Drying room. 5 Open air drying ground. 6 Patients dining and recreation room. 7. Clayton disinfecting room. 8 New latrines (it is hoped to institute a new system of latrine accommodation throughout, the system in vogue when the ambulance arrived on Dec 1st. 1916 being considered unsatisfactory) 9. New incinerator. In addition, many months accumulation of manure has been removed from the hospital premises and billets. A system of drainage for the baths and general waterlogged condition of the ground has been instituted, new urine pits and sump pits for ablution benches have been dug. The accommodation for patients has been increased by 88 by means of the erection of tents.	
FORCEVILLE	2.1.17	20.0	Routine duties Lt. FAIRFAX joined for duty.	
"	3.1.17	22.0	Routine duties	

2353 Wt. W2544/1454 700,000 5/15 D. D. & L. A.D.S.S./Forms/C. 2118.

1

Instructions regarding War Diaries and Intelligence Summaries are contained in F. S. Regs., Part II. and the Staff Manual respectively. Title pages will be prepared in manuscript.

WAR DIARY

~~or~~

~~INTELLIGENCE SUMMARY.~~

(Erase heading not required.)

Army Form C. 2118.

Place	Date	Hour	Summary of Events and Information	Remarks and references to Appendices
FORCEVILLE	4/1/17		LT. COL. H. N. BURROUGHES. R.A.M.C(T.F) 2/1 S. M. Fld. Ambce, 61st. Division arrived to assume Command of 2/2 Fld. Amb. vice LT. COL. G. W. CRAIG R.A.M.C(T.F) evacuated sick 7. 12. 16. Authority D.M.S. Fifth Army P3/54d./31·12·16. Routine Work	HWB
	5/1/17		Inquiry was held by D.D.M.S. IV Corps in the presence of A.D.M.S & D.A.D.M.S 61st Division & O.C. of Unit into the mistakes made in the transfer of patients as shown in A.&D. books on the handing over by 54th. Fld. Ambce. to this Unit of CORPS REST STATION at VADENCOURT on Nov. 22nd. 1916. Evidence was given by MAJOR E.C. FOSTER, MAJOR A.T. WATERHOUSE, CAPT J. BANNERMAN, Q.M.S. FOSS and SGT JONES. D.M.S. Fifth Army visited Hospital. Routine Work.	HWB
	6/1/17		Inspection of Hospital, all premises and billets by O.C. Certain alterations decided upon. CAPT R.D. MOORE, CPL. C.E. MOSS, PTE T.L. EVETTS returned from leave. CAPT. J. BANNERMAN assumed the duties of Acting. Q.M. vice LIEUT E.S. BOWD evacuated sick 23. 12. 16. SGT MAJOR H. JACKSON, PTE F.W. BUSBY, PTE H. RUSSELL and DR. J. BRYAN proceeded on leave. Routine Work.	HWB
	7/1/17		Visit of A.D.M.S. 61st. Div. and DIV. SANIT. OFFICER. Materials drawn for beginning alterations. O.C. visited Fld. Ambce. workshop to discuss certain defects in the Ambce. Cars with O.C. Div. Supply Column. Routine Work.	HWB

2353 Wt. W2544/1454 700,000 5/15 D. D. & L. A.D.S.S./Forms/C. 2118.

Instructions regarding War Diaries and Intelligence Summaries are contained in F. S. Regs., Part II. and the Staff Manual respectively. Title pages will be prepared in manuscript.

WAR DIARY
~~or~~
~~INTELLIGENCE SUMMARY.~~
(Erase heading not required.)

Army Form C. 2118.

Place	Date	Hour	Summary of Events and Information	Remarks and references to Appendices
FORCEVILLE	8/1/17		C.R.E. sent a man to repair roof of hospital. SGT. SLIM - 61st. DIV. SANIT. SECT. reported for duty with Unit. PTE. C. C. PARTON - 61st. D.S.C. reported for duty vice PTE. ELLIOT evacuated sick. CAPT. J. BANNERMAN. RAMC(T.F) proceeded for temporary duty with the 2/5 R. WARWICKS. CAPT. V. C. W. VICKERS R.A.M.C(T.C) permanently attached to 2/8 R. WARWICKS and struck off strength of Unit. CAPT. W. J. F. CRAIG RAMC(T.F) assumed the duties of Acting Q.M. vice CAPT. J. BANNERMAN. RAMC(T.F) who proceeded for temporary duty with 2/5 R. WARWICKS. Construction of new cookhouse begun. Levelling of area of new latrines begun. LIEUT. D. MORRISON R.A.M.C(T.C) reported for Duty. Routine work.	[illegible]
	9/1/17		O.C. visited D.D.M.S. IV Corps. Improvements and alterations continued. Routine work.	[illegible]
	10/1/17		PTE. SELBY A.F. evacuated to No. 11 C.C.S. and struck off strength. CAPT. W. J. F. CRAIG R.A.M.C.T.F. and one motor ambulance proceeded for temporary duty with 2/1 S. M. F. AMB. Two horsed ambulances proceeded for temporary duty with 2/3 S. M. F. AMB. One Ford Car proceeded for temporary duty A.D.M.S. 61st DIV. Five tons of stores arrived for repairing the Hospital grounds. Improvements and alterations continued. Routine work.	[illegible]
	11/1/17		PTES. LUMLEY, PAGE, WILSON W.H., POWELL, MAYO, reported for duty and taken	[illegible]

3

WAR DIARY
~~or~~
~~INTELLIGENCE SUMMARY~~
(Erase heading not required.)

Army Form C. 2118.

Instructions regarding War Diaries and Intelligence Summaries are contained in F. S. Regs., Part II. and the Staff Manual respectively. Title pages will be prepared in manuscript.

Place	Date	Hour	Summary of Events and Information	Remarks and references to Appendices
FORCEVILLE	11/1/17		on strength of Unit. D.D.M.S IV CORPS visited Hospital and inspected alterations. CAPT. W.J.F. CRAIG R.A.M.C.T.F. and one motor ambulance returned from 2/1 S.M.F.AMB. Ford Car returned from A.D.M.S. 61st. Div. PTE. MILLER W.J. transferred to IV Corps Rest Station. Improvements and alterations continued. Routine work.	Hord
	12/1/17		C.O. visited A.D.M.S. 61st. Div. L'CPLS. ALDER, PLANT, RIDOUT proceeded for duty at 61st. DIV. BATHS. MARTINSART. Two horsed ambulances returned from 2/3 S.M.F.AMB. Improvements and alterations continued. SGT. SLIM returned to 61st. DIV. SANIT. SECT. Routine work	Hord
	13/1/17		LIEUT. E.S. BOWD. R.A.M.C.T.F. struck off strength of Unit. One Siddeley Deasy Car returned from workshop. MAJOR A.T. WATERHOUSE R.A.M.C.T.F. proceeded to ETAPLES for dental treatment. SGT. RAMSEY, DR. WAGSTAFFE, PTES AUGHTIE and HAYES proceeded on leave. PTE. FREEMAN H.W. proceeded as ration orderly with No 3 Coy. A.S.C. 61st. Div. Train vice PTE AUGHTIE on leave. One G.S. Waggon with two horses returned from No 3 Coy A.S.C. 61st. Div. Train. Routine work.	Hord
	14/1/17		DDMS IV Corps visited Hospital. Advance Party of 55 FLD. AMBCE. R.A.M.C. arrived to take over. Packing of Waggons. Two horses arrived from No 3 Coy A.S.C. 61st. D.T. Routine work.	Hord

2353 Wt. W2544/1454 700,000 5/15 D. D. & L. A.D.S.S./Forms/C. 2118.

4.

Instructions regarding War Diaries and Intelligence Summaries are contained in F. S. Regs., Part II. and the Staff Manual respectively. Title pages will be prepared in manuscript.

WAR DIARY

~~or~~

~~INTELLIGENCE SUMMARY.~~

(Erase heading not required.)

Army Form C. 2118.

Place	Date	Hour	Summary of Events and Information	Remarks and references to Appendices
FORCEVILLE	15/1/17		55th FLD. AMBCE. R.A.M.C. relieved the Unit at 9.0 am. Under orders received from 184 Inf. Bde. the Unit with waggons packed and transport complete moved off at 11.30 a.m. Maps LENS & ABBEVILLE 1/100,000 - Route FORCEVILLE - VARENNES - HARPONVILLE -	
PUCHEVILLERS			TOUTENCOURT - PUCHEVILLERS. Time of arrival 3.30 pm. All men billeted and transport parked at 4.0 pm. Casualties dealt with during the march 5. Cases evacuated to C.C.S. --- NIL. Hospital hut opened for the reception of sick.	Hord
	16/1/17		The Unit rested for the day at PUCHEVILLERS. Sick were received and treated in Hospital Hut. STF. SGT. CUMMINGS and SGT. ROBERTS returned from Leave. General fatigue work. Cases evacuated to C.C.S. 19.	Hord
	17/1/17		Under orders received from 184 Inf. Bde. the Unit with waggons packed and transport complete moved off at 10.45 am. Route - PUCHEVILLERS - VAL-DE-MAISON -	
GEZAINCOURT			BEAUVAL - GEZAINCOURT. Time of arrival 4.50 pm. All men billeted and transport parked. Hospital hut opened for the reception of Sick. One Siddeley Deasy Car sent to 61st. D.S.C. Ordnance Workshops - Axle trouble. Maltese Cart was run into by lorry and sustained two cracked shafts. Load transferred to a R.F.C. lorry and cart proceeded empty. Casualties dealt with during the march 6. Cases evacuated to C.C.S. 19. CAPT. J. BANNERMAN R.A.M.C.T. reported for duty.	Hord

2353 Wt. W2544/1454 700,000 5/15 D. D. & L. A.D.S.S./Forms/C. 2118.

5.

Instructions regarding War Diaries and Intelligence Summaries are contained in F. S. Regs., Part II. and the Staff Manual respectively. Title pages will be prepared in manuscript.

WAR DIARY

or

~~INTELLIGENCE SUMMARY.~~

(Erase heading not required.)

Army Form C. 2118.

Place	Date	Hour	Summary of Events and Information	Remarks and references to Appendices
LE PLOUY.	18/7		Under orders received from 184 Inf. Bde. the Unit less transport marched at 9.18 am. Route - LONGUEVILLETTE - FIENVILLERS - BERNAVILLE - LONGVILLERS - LE PLOUY. Time of arrival 4.15 pm. Owing to bad roads the Transport under CAPT. R.D. MOORE marched with Brigaded Transport - Route - HEM - FIENVILLERS - thence as Unit. Time of arrival 5.10 pm. All men billeted and transport parked. One Siddeley Deasy Car sent to 61st. D.S.C. Ordnance Workshops. 'Axle trouble'. Casualties dealt with during the march 13. Cases evacuated to C.C.S. 7. Hospital Hut opened for the reception of sick. PTE HUDSON E.G. evacuated to No. 39 C.C.S.	HMS.
DOMVAST.	19/7		PTE. CURETON F. evacuated to 2/1 S.M. C.C.S. and struck off strength of Unit. Under orders received from 184 Inf. Bde. the Unit with waggons packed and transport less 2 horsed ambulances moved off at 9.40 am. Route - ST. RIQUIER - HELLENCOURT - DOMVAST. Time of arrival 1.30 pm. Two horsed ambulances followed A.S.C. of 184 Bde. and rejoined Unit at DOMVAST. All men billeted and transport parked. Casualties dealt with on the march 1. Cases evacuated to C.C.S. 1. Empty house taken over as Hospital. 15 patients admitted.	HMS.

6

Instructions regarding War Diaries and Intelligence Summaries are contained in F. S. Regs., Part II. and the Staff Manual respectively. Title pages will be prepared in manuscript.

WAR DIARY

~~or~~

~~INTELLIGENCE SUMMARY.~~

(*Erase heading not required.*)

Army Form C. 2118.

Place	Date	Hour	Summary of Events and Information	Remarks and references to Appendices
DOMVAST.	20/7		O.C. went in lorry provided by Division to draw Red Cross material for furnishing officers' ward, returning at 5·0 pm. Officers' ward opened. Number of patients in hospital – Officers 1. Other Ranks 22. Hospital marquee erected for which no flooring was available. CAPT. W.J.F. CRAIG R.A.M.C.T. SGT. HICKMAN F. & PTE CHAPMAN F. proceeded on Leave. CAPT. A.T.I. MACDONALD R.A.M.C.T.C. reported for duty and taken on strength vice LIEUT. D. MORRISON R.A.M.C.T.C. transferred to A.D.M.S. Hospital Train and struck off strength of Unit. SGT. MAJ. JACKSON H.C. PTES. BUSBY F.W. RUSSELL H. & DR. BRYAN J. returned from Leave. Routine Work.	[illegible]
	21/7		Constructional work for improvement of hospital and billets decided upon. Necessary materials indented for. A second Hospital Marquee erected. Routine work.	[illegible]
	22/7		'C' Section removed from Hospital Duties for Drill and Kit Inspections for the week. A.D.M.S. 61st. Division visited Hospital. CAPT. W.K. CAMPBELL R.A.M.C. reported for duty and taken on strength of Unit. Routine work.	[illegible]
	23/7		Soak pits for urinals and ablution benches dug. Materials drawn from R.E.s for constructional work. PTE. MAYO H.M. transferred to No. 2. STAT. Hospital and struck off strength of Unit. Routine work.	[illegible]

2353 Wt. W2544/1454 700,000 5/15 D. D. & L. A.D.S.S./Forms/C. 2118.

Army Form C. 2118.

Instructions regarding War Diaries and Intelligence Summaries are contained in F. S. Regs., Part II. and the Staff Manual respectively. Title pages will be prepared in manuscript.

WAR DIARY
or
~~INTELLIGENCE SUMMARY.~~

(Erase heading not required.)

Place	Date	Hour	Summary of Events and Information	Remarks and references to Appendices
DOMVAST	24/1/17		Erection of meat store and pantry for hospital begun. MAJOR A.T. WATERHOUSE R.A.M.C.T. reported for duty. PTE. ALDIS E. proceeded to 61st. DIV. Concert Party. Routine work.	H.W.S.
	25/1/17		Constructional work continued. Deasy. Car - leaky radiator - sent to 61st. D.S.C. Ordnance workshops leaving two Deasys and one Ford Car. CAPT. H. H. FAIRFAX R.A.M.C.T.C. reported for duty. PTES. MANTON A.J. & AUSTIN E.H. reported for duty and taken on strength of Unit. PTE. HUDSON E.G. reported for duty. PTE. ALVA F. transferred to No. 2 Stationary Hospital and struck off strength. Routine work.	H.W.S.
	26/1/17		Hospital pantry completed. CAPT. W.K. CAMPBELL R.A.M.C. transferred to D.D.M.S. II Corps and struck off strength of Unit. SGT. RAMSEY J.B. PTES. AUGHTIE D. & HAYES J.F. and DR. WAGSTAFFE F. returned from leave. PTE MILLER W.J. reported for duty. Hospital Routine work. Throughout the week severe frost with bright sunshine during the day has prevailed.	H.W.S.
	27/1/17		Constructional work continued. A.D.M.S. 61st. Div. visited Hospital. One Deasy Car returned from workshops. O.C. visited A.D.M.S. 61st. Div. PTES CARTER & MITCHELL proceeded to 61st. D.S.C. for test. Hospital Routine work.	H.W.S.

2353 Wt. W2544/1454 700,000 5/15 D. D. & L. A.D.S.S./Forms/C. 2118.

8

Instructions regarding War Diaries and Intelligence Summaries are contained in F. S. Regs., Part II. and the Staff Manual respectively. Title pages will be prepared in manuscript.

WAR DIARY

~~or~~

~~INTELLIGENCE SUMMARY.~~

(Erase heading not required.)

Army Form C. 2118.

Place	Date	Hour	Summary of Events and Information	Remarks and references to Appendices
DOMVAST.	28/1/17		D.D.M.S. IV. Corps visited Hospital. Constructional work continued. Routine work.	
	29/1/17		Constructional work continued. St. SGT STOBART T.L. proceeded to MONTREUIL for test for Commission in A.S.C. PTE HOUGHTON J.D.R. evacuated to No. 2 Stationary Hospital and struck off strength. 'B' Section removed from Hospital Duties for Drill and Kit Inspections for the week. PTE. LOVELESS W.H. transferred to 61st. Div. Rest. Station. LIEUT. H.H. FAIRFAX R.A.M.C.T.C. proceeded for temporary duty with 2/5 Glosters. Erection of scullery and ablution benches begun. Routine work.	[illegible]
	30/1/17		Constructional work continued. O.C. made an inspection of all billets. One Deasy Car No. 6 returned from workshop. SGT. ROBERTS proceeded to G.O.C. Artillery for interview for Commission. Routine work.	[illegible]
	31/1/17		Constructional work continued. SGT. MATHIAS J.K. evacuated to No. 2 Stationary Hospital. PTE LOVELESS W.H. reported for duty. Deasy Car No. 18 returned from workshop. Routine work.	[illegible]

2/2nd SOUTH MIDLAND FIELD AMBULANCE R.A.M.C. No. Date

[illegible]

Feb. 1917

61st Div

140/1974

61

CONFIDENTIAL

Vol 10

WAR DIARY

2/2 S. MID. FLD. AMBCE
R.A.M.C. (T.F.)

FEB 1st. — 28th. (Inclusive)
1917

VOL:-10

Army Form C. 2118.

Instructions regarding War Diaries and Intelligence Summaries are contained in F. S. Regs., Part II. and the Staff Manual respectively. Title pages will be prepared in manuscript.

WAR DIARY
~~or~~
~~INTELLIGENCE SUMMARY.~~
(Erase heading not required.)

Place	Date	Hour	Summary of Events and Information	Remarks and references to Appendices
DOMVAST	1 2/17		Constructional work continued. Scullery and ablution benches completed. D.D.M.S. IV CORPS visited Hospital. CAPT. W.J.F. CRAIG R.A.M.C.(T.F.) returned from leave. Number of cases evacuated to C.C.S. 46. O.C. visited A.D.M.S. 61st. Division. Routine work.	
	2 2/17		Constructional work continued. Meat stores completed. O.C. visited A.D.M.S. 61st. Division. 'B' Section resumed hospital duties and fatigues. Number of cases evacuated to C.C.S. 2 officers - 55 O. Ranks. Routine work.	
	3 2/17		Constructional work continued. Canvas screens around latrines completed. Inspection of Hospital made by LIEUT. GENERAL SIR. C.L. WOOLLCOMBE, K.C.B. Commanding IV Corps accompanied by D.D.M.S. IV Corps and A.D.M.S. 61st. Division. Advanced party - 1 Officer & 4 O. Ranks - of 3/1 H. FLD. AMBCE. arrived to relieve Unit. Packing of waggons & General fatigues. Number of cases evacuated to C.C.S. - 1 Officer 23 O. Ranks.	
	4 2/17		MAJOR E.C. FOSTER R.A.M.C.(T.F.) proceeded for temporary duty with IV CORPS SCHOOL. Under orders received from 183rd. Inf. Bde. the Unit with waggons packed and transport complete - less two horsed ambulances, marched off at 10.0 am. Route - ST. RIQUIER,	
BUSSUS-BUSSUE.			BUSSUS-BUSSUE. Time of arrival 2.0 pm. All men billeted and transport parked	

2353 Wt. W2544/1454 700,000 5/15 D. D. & L. A.D.S.S. Forms/C. 2118.

Army Form C. 2118.

Instructions regarding War Diaries and Intelligence Summaries are contained in F. S. Regs., Part II. and the Staff Manual respectively. Title pages will be prepared in manuscript.

WAR DIARY
~~or~~
~~INTELLIGENCE SUMMARY.~~

(Erase heading not required.)

Place	Date	Hour	Summary of Events and Information	Remarks and references to Appendices
BUSSUS-BUSSUE	4 2/17		Hospital opened in school for reception of sick. Two horsed ambulances proceeded with Battalions of 2/4 and 2/6 Glosters, rejoining Unit at BUSSUS-BUSSUE. Casualties dealt with on the march 1 Officer. 24 O. Ranks. Cases evacuated to C.C.S. 1 Officer 41 O. Ranks. Cases evacuated to 1/2 H. FLD. AMBCE. 40. O. Ranks. Whole of patients were evacuated less 4 who accompanied Unit and were received into Hospital. DR. THOMPSON J. A.S.C. attached evacuated to 1/2 H. FLD. AMBCE. CAPT. A.T.I. MACDONALD R.A.M.C.(T.C.) proceeded for temporary duty with 308 Bde. R.F.A. Two Daimler Cars reported for duty vice two Siddeley Deasys sent to 61st. D.S.C. M.T. A.S.C.	HMB
	5 2/17		Sick were received and treated. Cleaning of Billets, Hospital and areas adjoining same. General Fatigues. SGT. HICKMAN F. and PTE. CHAPMAN F. returned from leave after being detained in Rest Camp Base for 4 days. Two Daimler Cars reported for duty vice 3 Siddeley Deasys sent to 61st. D.S.C. M.T. A.S.C.	HMB
	6 2/17		PTE. BARKER evacuated to New Zealand Stationary Hospital and struck off strength. L'CPL. PLANT returned from 61st. DIV. BATHS. Sick were received and treated. General Fatigues. Attention was drawn to the cleaning of harness by Horse Transport.	HMB

Army Form C. 2118.

Instructions regarding War Diaries and Intelligence Summaries are contained in F. S. Regs., Part II. and the Staff Manual respectively. Title pages will be prepared in manuscript.

WAR DIARY
~~or~~
~~INTELLIGENCE SUMMARY.~~

(Erase heading not required.)

Place	Date	Hour	Summary of Events and Information	Remarks and references to Appendices
BUSSUS-BUSSUE.	7/2/17		PTE. HARRISON H.W. proceeded to 5th Field Survey Coy. for test. DR. WAGSTAFFE A.S.C. attached evacuated to New Zealand Stationary Hospital and struck off strength. Sick were received and treated. General Fatigues.	
	8/2/17		O.C. visited A.D.M.S. 61st. Division. B+C. Sections - Company Drill and Route March. General Hospital Fatigues.	
	9/2/17		SGT MATHIAS + PTE. HOUGHTON reported for duty. Routine work and fatigues.	
	10/2/17		General Hospital Fatigues.	
	11/2/17		General Hospital Fatigues. Under orders from A.D.M.S 61st. Division the Hospital was closed at 6.0 pm. All patients were evacuated to New Zealand Stationary Hospital and 2/1 S. Mid. Fld. Ambce. PTES. HOUGHTON, PORTMAN + BEDFORDE. evacuated to New Zealand Stat. Hosp. and struck off strength. DR. BRYAN J. A.S.C. attached evacuated to 2/1 S. Mid. Fld. Ambce. PTES. CARTER + MITCHELL reported for duty. SGT. MATHIAS +1 man proceeded with lorry containing portion of unit equipment to WIENCOURT.	
	12/2/17		O.C. inspected all ranks. Special attention was drawn to the necessity for cleanliness of all clothing + equipment. SGT. OAKES reported at AILLY and proceeded	

Instructions regarding War Diaries and Intelligence Summaries are contained in F. S. Regs., Part II. and the Staff Manual respectively. Title pages will be prepared in manuscript.

WAR DIARY
or
INTELLIGENCE SUMMARY.
(Erase heading not required.)

Army Form C. 2118.

Place	Date	Hour	Summary of Events and Information	Remarks and references to Appendices
BUSSUS-BUSSUE	12 2/17		with 183rd. Inf. Bde. billeting party. The transport with waggons packed together with SGTS. BIRKBY + CRANER with 14 O. Ranks moved under the command of MAJOR A.T. WATERHOUSE R.A.M.C.(T.F.) at 9.0 am. Route AILLY, + ST. SAUVEUR CAPT. A.T.I. MACDONALD R.A.M.C.(T.C) reported from 308 Bde. R.F.A. PTES. SEWARD F. and GILKES S.T. reported for duty and taken on strength of Unit. PTE. WILTSHIRE evacuated to 2/1 S. Mid. Fld. Ambce. thence to C.C.S. and struck off strength of Unit. Cases evacuated to 2/1 S. Mid. Fld. Ambce. – 6. Routine work.	H.W.B.
	13 2/17		All ranks paraded in full marching order and were inspected by O.C. DR. BRYAN A.S.C. attached reported for duty. CAPT. W.H. BELL R.A.M.C.(T.C.) reported for duty and taken on strength of unit. Transport moved from ST. SAUVEUR to AUBIGNY. One Daimler car proceeded for temporary duty with 307 Bde. R.F.A. General Fatigues.	H.W.B.
	14 2/17		Two Daimler Cars proceeded for temporary duty with Divisional Headquarters. PTE. NEWTON. J. evacuated to 2/1 S. Mid. Fld. Ambce. Motor Ambulances under SGT. COLLIER proceeded by road to WIENCOURT via AMIENS and MARCELCAVE Horse transport moved from AUBIGNY to WIENCOURT arriving complete at 11.30 am. Under orders from 183rd. Inf. Bde. the Unit less transport moved at	H.W.B.

Army Form C. 2118.

Instructions regarding War Diaries and Intelligence Summaries are contained in F. S. Regs., Part II. and the Staff Manual respectively. Title pages will be prepared in manuscript.

WAR DIARY

~~or~~

~~INTELLIGENCE SUMMARY.~~

(Erase heading not required.)

Place	Date	Hour	Summary of Events and Information	Remarks and references to Appendices
BUSSUS-BUSSUE	14 2/17		11·30 am. Route - AILLY-le-haut-CLOCHER, + PONT REMY STATION. Time of arrival 2·45 pm. Falling out Casualties NIL. Entrained at 7·0 pm. Arrived at MARCEL CAVE and detrained at 1·45 am. (Feb. 15/17) and proceeded by march route to	
WIEN'COURT.	15 2/17		WIENCOURT arriving at 2·30 am. (Feb. 15/17) The Unit stationed at WIENCOURT. O.C. visited A.D.M.S. 61st. Division. Sick reported from 183rd. Inf. Bde. and were treated or evacuated to C.C.S. One Daimler Car reported for duty from 307 Bde. R.F.A. CAPT. C.O.T. YOUNG R.A.M.C.(S.R.) reported for duty and taken on strength of Unit. General Fatigues.	
	16 2/17		O.C. visited ADVANCED DRESSING STATION at SANITAS to arrange taking over from FRENCH. General Fatigues.	
	17 2/17		O.C. visited A.D.S. at DENIÉCOURT and Relay Posts in trenches, making arrangements for taking over with the M.O. 124th R.I. of the French Army. Portion of transport taking rations + equipment proceeded to VAUVILLERS under command of CAPT. W. J. F. CRAIG. R.A.M.C. (T.F.). One car with driver and orderly from 2/1 S. M. Fld. Ambce. reported for duty. Motor cycle returned from A.D.M.S. 61st. Division. SGT. ROBERTS proceeded to ENGLAND for Commission. DR. THOMPSON reported for duty	

2353 Wt. W2544/1454 700,000 5/15 D. D. & L. A.D.S.S./Forms/C. 2118.

Instructions regarding War Diaries and Intelligence Summaries are contained in F. S. Regs., Part II. and the Staff Manual respectively. Title pages will be prepared in manuscript.

WAR DIARY
~~or~~
~~INTELLIGENCE~~ SUMMARY.
(Erase heading not required.)

Army Form C. 2118.

Place	Date	Hour	Summary of Events and Information	Remarks and references to Appendices
WIENCOURT	17 2/17		L'SGT. DOLPHIN transferred to 2/3 S. Mid. Fd. Ambce. At 6.30pm. CAPT. J. BANNERMAN, STF. SGT. MARTIN, SGT CRANER and 26 O. Ranks proceeded for duty at DENIÉCOURT. (A.D.S.) and HERLEVILLE (A.D.S.) One Daimler Car stationed at ESTREES. General fatigues.	[illegible]
	18 2/17		At 6.0 am. CAPT W.H. BELL RA.M.C(T.C), STF. SGT. CUMMINGS, SGT. BIRKBY and 30 O. Ranks proceeded for duty at SANITAS (A.D.S). Under orders received from A.D.M.S. 61.st Div. the Unit with remaining portion of transport moved off at 9.0 am. Route GUILLAUCOURT, HARBONNIÈRES,	
VAUVILLERS			VAUVILLERS. Time of arrival 11.0 am. Falling out returns NIL. All men billeted, General fatigues. Cleaning of billets and areas adjoining same. PTE. HOUGHTON reported for duty and taken on the strength of the Unit. MAJOR A.T. WATER-HOUSE R.A.M.C.(T.F) proceeded for duty at HERLEVILLE (A.D.S). SGT. HICKMAN and 7. O. Ranks proceeded for duty at TOUR CARRÉ and LIHONS. Headquarters of Ambulance stationed at ~~xx~~ VAUVILLERS. MAJOR A.T. WATERHOUSE R.A.M.C(T.F) and 11 O. Ranks stationed at HERLEVILLE., CAPT. J. BANNERMAN RAMC (T.F) and 17 O. Ranks at DENIÉCOURT., CAPT. W.H. BELL R.A.M.C(T.C) and 22 O. Ranks	[illegible]

2353 Wt. W2544/1454 700,000 5/15 D. D. & L. A.D.S.S./Forms/C. 2118.

Instructions regarding War Diaries and Intelligence Summaries are contained in F. S. Regs., Part II. and the Staff Manual respectively. Title pages will be prepared in manuscript.

WAR DIARY
~~or~~
~~INTELLIGENCE~~ SUMMARY.
(Erase heading not required.)

Army Form C. 2118.

Place	Date	Hour	Summary of Events and Information	Remarks and references to Appendices
VAUVILLERS	18 2/17		at SANITAS. Two Daimler Cars stationed at HERLEVILLE, after dusk one proceeds for duty at SANITAS. Ford Car stationed at TOUR CARRÉ after dusk proceeds for duty at LIHONS. After dusk car at ESTREES proceeds for duty at DENIÉCOURT.	Hol
	19 2/17		DR. FREEBURY reported for duty and taken on strength of Unit. General fatigues. Headquarters moved to premises vacated by FRENCH GROUPE BRANCARDIER DIVISIONNAIRE. In accordance with orders from A.D.M.S 61st. Division all sick and wounded from the Trenches except ① Cases unfit for transport ② Cases of an urgent or infectious nature - are being sent direct to 2/3 S.M.F. Ambce, no notification being made in A.&D. Books of this Unit. O.C. visited A.D.S. DENIECOURT to inspect. CAPT. R.D. MOORE R.A.M.C(T.F.) visited Relay Posts at TOUR CARRÉ and LIHONS to inspect. Trenches - Routine work.	Hol
	20 2/17		SGT. DOLPHIN reported for duty. O.C. visited HERLEVILLE and SANITAS A.D.S. Trenches - Routine work - Headquarters - Routine work and fatigues.	Hol
	21 2/17		PTE HARRISON H.W. reported for duty. O.C. visited SANITAS A.D.S. and ABLAINCOURT TRENCH. Trenches - Routine work - Headquarters - Routine work and fatigues	Hol
	22 2/17		D.A.D.M.S. 61st Division visited H.Qrs. of Unit. CPL. GIBBS and a party of	Hol

Army Form C. 2118.

Instructions regarding War Diaries and Intelligence Summaries are contained in F. S. Regs., Part II. and the Staff Manual respectively. Title pages will be prepared in manuscript.

WAR DIARY
or
~~INTELLIGENCE SUMMARY.~~
(Erase heading not required.)

Place	Date	Hour	Summary of Events and Information	Remarks and references to Appendices
VAUVILLERS	22 2/17		5 men proceeded for duty at SANITAS A.D.S. Baths and hospital opened for use of unit. SGT. DOGGETT H. proceeded for duty at DENIÉCOURT vice CPL. CHATTAWAY returned sick. Trenches - Routine work. Headquarters - Routine work and fatigues.	HWB
	23 2/17		A party of 1 N.C.O. and 11 men proceeded for temporary duty at TOUR CARRÉ. CPL. MOSS with motor bicycle proceeded for duty at HERLEVILLE (Advanced H. Qrs.) PTES. CARTWRIGHT and NEALE evacuated to 2/3 S. Mid. Fld. Ambce. - 'shell gas poisoning' - thence to C.C.S. and struck off strength of Unit. PTE. EVANS W. transferred to 2/3 S. Mid. Fld. Ambce. Motor bicycle sent to 61st. D.S.C. Ordnance Workshops for repairs. PTES MACFARLANE and DIKE returned from trenches suffering from effect of gas shells, and admitted into Hospital. Trenches - Routine work. Headquarters - Routine work and fatigues.	HWB
	24 2/17		O.C. visited DENIÉCOURT and LEFT BDE. H. Qrs. D.A.D.M.S. 61st. Division visited H.Qrs. of Unit. PTES SMITH A (1902) and BRAZIER J. transferred to 2/3 S. Mid. Fld. Ambce. Trenches - Routine work. Headquarters - Routine work and fatigues.	HWB
	25 2/17		Trenches - Routine work. Headquarters. - Routine work and fatigues.	HWB

A5834 Wt. W4973/M687 750,000 8/16 D. D. & L. Ltd. Forms/C.2118/13.

Instructions regarding War Diaries and Intelligence Summaries are contained in F. S. Regs., Part II. and the Staff Manual respectively. Title pages will be prepared in manuscript.

WAR DIARY
or
~~INTELLIGENCE SUMMARY.~~
(Erase heading not required.)

Army Form C. 2118.

Place	Date	Hour	Summary of Events and Information	Remarks and references to Appendices
VAUVILLERS	26/2/17		CAPT. W.J.F. CRAIG R.A.M.C.(T.F.) appointed Town Major of VAUVILLERS. PTE. MARTIN proceeded for duty at Transportation Depot - BOULOGNE - Authority D.A.G. Base. Capt. C.O.J. YOUNG R.A.M.C.(S.R) proceeded for temporary duty with 306 Bde. R.F.A. O.C. visited TOUR CARRE. Trenches-Routine Work - H.Qrs. Routine Work and Fatigues.	[illegible]
	27/2/17		PTE CURETON reported for duty and taken on strength of Unit. D.D.M.S. IV CORPS visited Headquarters. G.O.C. 61st. Division visited Headquarters. Trenches - Routine Work. Headquarters - Routine Work and Fatigues.	[illegible]
	28/2/17		Trenches - Routine Work. Headquarters - Routine Work and Fatigues	[illegible]

[illegible signature]

2353 Wt. W2544/1454 700,000 5/15 D. D. & L. A.D.S.S./Forms/C. 2118.

Mar. 1917

61st Div.

Vol XI

140/2042

S

CONFIDENTIAL

WAR DIARY

2/2 S. MID. FLD. AMBCE.
R.A.M.C(T.F)

March 1st. — 31st. inclusive
1917

VOL.-- II

Instructions regarding War Diaries and Intelligence Summaries are contained in F. S. Regs., Part II. and the Staff Manual respectively. Title pages will be prepared in manuscript.

WAR DIARY
~~or~~
~~INTELLIGENCE SUMMARY.~~
(Erase heading not required.)

Army Form C. 2118.

Place	Date	Hour	Summary of Events and Information	Remarks and references to Appendices
VAUVILLERS	1/3/17		A party of 14 men proceeded for stretcher work between Relay Posts and DENIÉCOURT A.D.S. PTES. SMITH A. (1902) & BRAZIER J returned for duty. CAPT. A.T.I. MACDONALD R.A.M.C.(T.C) proceeded for duty at DENIÉCOURT A.D.S. CAPT. C.O.J. YOUNG R.A.M.C.(S.R.) returned for duty. Trenches - Routine work. Headquarters Routine work & fatigues.	HNS.
	2/3/17		O.C. visited A.D.M.S. 61st. Division. CAPT. H. H. FAIRFAX R.A.M.C(T.C) reported for duty. CAPT. J. BANNERMAN R.A.M.C(T.F) returned from DENIÉCOURT A.D.S. Trenches - Routine work. Headquarters - Routine work and fatigues.	HNS.
	3/3/17		Two Cars from 2/1 S. Mid. Fld. Ambce. reported for duty. Two Cars proceeded to 61st. D.S.C. Ord. Workshops for repairs. CAPT. R.D. MOORE R.A.M.C(T.F) attended demonstration by A.D.M.S. 1st. Division on French method of treatment of Trench Foot. D.D.M.S. IV Corps visited Headquarters and proceeded with O.C. to DENIÉCOURT A.D.S. D.A.D.M.S. 61st. Div. visited H.Qrs. CAPT. C.O.J. YOUNG R.A.M.C. (S.R.) proceeded for duty at SANITAS vice CAPT. W. H. BELL R.A.M.C(T.C) returned. Trenches - Routine work. Headquarters - Routine work and fatigues.	HNS.
	4/3/17		CAPT. R.D. MOORE R.A.M.C(T.F.) proceeded for duty at HERLEVILLE vice	HNS.

2353 Wt. W2544/1454 700,000 5/15 D. D. & L. A.D.S.S. Forms/C. 2118.

Army Form C. 2118.

Instructions regarding War Diaries and Intelligence Summaries are contained in F. S. Regs., Part II. and the Staff Manual respectively. Title pages will be prepared in manuscript.

WAR DIARY
or
~~INTELLIGENCE~~ SUMMARY.
(Erase heading not required.)

Place	Date	Hour	Summary of Events and Information	Remarks and references to Appendices
VAUVILLERS	4 3/17		MAJOR A.T. WATERHOUSE R.A.M.C.(T.F.) returned to Headquarters. PTE NEWMAN F.J. returned from trenches suffering from effect of gas shell poisoning and admitted into Hospital. Trenches - Routine work. Headquarters Routine work + fatigues.	HWS
	5 3/17		O.C. visited SANITAS A.D.S. to inspect. PTES COX G. + ANDREWS J. returned from trenches sick and admitted into Hospital. CPL. DOLMAN A.V. and 5 men proceeded for duty at DENIÉCOURT A.D.S. One Daimler Car reported for duty from 61st. D.S.C. Ordnance Workshop. Trenches - Routine work. Headquarters - Routine work and fatigues.	HWS
	6 3/17		Acting A.D.M.S. 61st. Div. + O.C. visited DENIÉCOURT and SANITAS Advanced Dressing Stations, and HERLEVILLE. CAPT. W.J.F. CRAIG R.A.M.C.(T.F.) and batman proceeded for duty to IV CORPS. H.QRS. CAPT. J. BANNERMAN R.A.M.C.(T.F.) commenced duties as Town Major of VAUVILLERS. SGT. CRANER F proceeded for duty at TOUR CARRÉ vice SGT. HICKMAN F returned to H.Qrs. CPL GIBBS + 5 men returned for duty. One ambulance reported for duty from 61st. D.S.C. Ord. Workshops. ST. SGT. CUMMINGS T. proceeded for duty at HERLEVILLE vice ST. SGT. MARTIN R.P. returned to H.Qrs. PTES. DENNY J., DOANE A.,	HWS

Instructions regarding War Diaries and Intelligence Summaries are contained in F. S. Regs., Part II. and the Staff Manual respectively. Title pages will be prepared in manuscript.

WAR DIARY
or
~~INTELLIGENCE SUMMARY.~~

(*Erase heading not required.*)

Army Form C. 2118.

Place	Date	Hour	Summary of Events and Information	Remarks and references to Appendices
VAUVILLERS	6/3/17		HOLBROOK W. A., HONKS R. W., KIDMAN T. F., KING C. E., & MOSELEY H. A., reported for duty and taken on strength of Unit. Trenches - Routine work. Headquarters - Routine work and fatigues.	[illegible]
	7/3/17		Trenches - Routine work. Headquarters. - Routine work and fatigues. Latrines at Headquarters for use of Unit completed.	[illegible]
	8/3/17		Trenches - Routine work. Headquarters - Routine work and fatigues. Construction of Ablution Benches for use of Unit commenced at Headquarters.	[illegible]
	9/3/17		CAPT. H. H. FAIRFAX R.A.M.C. (T.C.) and 9 men proceeded for duty at LIHONS to take over A. D. S. from 35th Division, with 2 men stationed at TOUR CARRÉ and men at relay posts, VALLEY POST and TRIANGLE WOOD. One Daimler Car reported for duty from 61st. D.S.C. Ord. Workshops. Trenches - Routine work. Headquarters - Routine work and fatigues. Ablution Shelter completed.	[illegible]
	10/3/17		PTE. NEWMAN F discharged to duty. L'CPL. PLANT G. reported for duty. Trenches - Routine work. Headquarters - Routine work and fatigues. Duck boards laid at H. Qrs. at rear of men's billet. Soakage pit adjoining ablution shelter commenced.	[illegible]

Instructions regarding War Diaries and Intelligence Summaries are contained in F. S. Regs., Part II. and the Staff Manual respectively. Title pages will be prepared in manuscript.

WAR DIARY
or
~~INTELLIGENCE SUMMARY~~.
(Erase heading not required.)

Army Form C. 2118.

Place	Date	Hour	Summary of Events and Information	Remarks and references to Appendices
VAUVILLERS	11 3/17		Adrian hut taken over from the French, and in use as Quartermaster's Stores, was inspected by man by order of C.R.E. 61st. Div. (Authority D.R.O. 874 dated 28 2/17). PTE WILTSHIRE reported for duty and taken on strength of Unit. SGT. ROBERTS E.F. officially struck off strength from day he proceeded to England for Commission. (Authority - O/c R.A.M.C. Section G.H.Q.). CPL. GIBBS proceeded for duty at SANITAS A.D.S. vice L'CPL. DAVIS returned to H. Qrs. Trenches - Routine work. Headquarters - Routine work and fatigues.	HWS
	12 3/17		O.C. visited LIHONS and SANITAS Advanced Dressing Stations. PTE BARGUSS evacuated to No. 38 C.C.S. and struck off strength of Unit. Ford Car from 2/1 S. M. Fld. Ambce reported for duty. PTE COX G. discharged to duty. Trenches - Routine work. Headquarters - Routine work and fatigues.	HWS
	13 3/17		A.D.M.S. 61st. Division visited Headquarters.	HWS
	14 3/17		Trenches - Routine work. Headquarters - Routine work and fatigues.	HWS
	15 3/17		MAJOR A.T. WATERHOUSE R.A.M.C.(T.F.) assumed Command of the Unit during the temporary absence of LT. COL. H.N. BURROUGHES RAMC(T.F.) proceeded on leave. CPL CHATTAWAY W.J. proceeded for duty at DENIECOURT A.D.S. vice CPL. DOLMAN A.V. returned to H. Qrs.	A.T. Waterhouse Major RAMC

Instructions regarding War Diaries and Intelligence Summaries are contained in F. S. Regs., Part II. and the Staff Manual respectively. Title pages will be prepared in manuscript.

WAR DIARY ~~or~~ ~~INTELLIGENCE SUMMARY~~.

(*Erase heading not required.*)

Army Form C. 2118.

Place	Date	Hour	Summary of Events and Information	Remarks and references to Appendices
VAUVILLERS	15 3/17		PTE. EVANS W. reported for duty from hospital. L'CPL. VIGURS returned from SANITAS A.D.S.. One Daimler Car returned to 2/1 S. Mid. Fld. Ambce. Trenches - Routine work Headquarters - Routine work and fatigues.	[illegible]
	16 3/17		MAJOR A.T. WATERHOUSE R.A.M.C.(T.F.) accompanied by SGT. MAJOR JACKSON H.C. visited HERLEVILLE, SANITAS, VERMANDOVILLERS, SERPENTINE TRENCH and VERDUN POST to inspect. Trenches - Routine work. Headquarters - Routine work and fatigues.	[illegible]
	17 3/17		SGT. EDGINTON proceeded for duty at HERLEVILLE A.D.S. vice SGT. BIRKBY returned to Headquarters. One Daimler Car and Ford Car returned to 2/1 S. Mid. Fld. Ambce. A party of 90 men proceeded for duty at DENIECOURT and SANITAS Advanced Dressing Stations. CAPT. W. H. BELL R.A.M.C.(T.C) proceeded for duty at SANITAS A.D.S vice CAPT. C.O.T. YOUNG R.A.M.C.(S.R.) returned to Headquarters. Under orders received from A.D.M.S. 61st. Division MAJOR A.T. WATERHOUSE R.A.M.C.(T.F.), SGT. MAJOR JACKSON,	
HERLEVILLE			2 Sergts & 6 O.R. proceeded to HERLEVILLE and established Headquarters. PTES EVANS W. & ANDREWS J. evacuated to 2/3 S. Mid. Fld. Ambce. Trenches - Routine work - Headquarters - Fatigues.	[illegible]
	18 3/17		Remaining portion of personnel and equipment of Unit arrived at HERLEVILLE	[illegible]

2353 Wt. W2544/1454 700,000 5/15 D. D. & L. A.D.S.S. Forms/C. 2118.

Instructions regarding War Diaries and Intelligence Summaries are contained in F. S. Regs., Part II. and the Staff Manual respectively. Title pages will be prepared in manuscript.

WAR DIARY
~~or~~
~~INTELLIGENCE SUMMARY.~~
(Erase heading not required.)

Army Form C. 2118.

MAP - ROSIERES - COMBINED

Place	Date	Hour	Summary of Events and Information	Remarks and references to Appendices
HERLEVILLE	18/3/17		PTES HARRISON & GILKES, DR. BRYAN & DR. PARSONS evacuated to 2/3 S. Mid. Fld. Ambce. CAPT. J. BANNERMAN RAMC(T.F.) vacated duties as Town Major at VAUVILLERS and proceeded for duty at SANITAS A.D.S. vice CAPT. W. H. BELL RAMC(T.C) who proceeded with a party and established an A.D.S. at ABLAINCOURT. CAPT. C.O.J. YOUNG R.A.M.C.(S.R) with a party proceeded for duty at T.8.C.4.8. (rear of SUGAR FACTORY) and established an A.D.S. Trenches - Routine work. H.Qrs. Fatigues.	A.T.W.
	19/3/17		Unit headquarters stationed at HERLEVILLE. PTES HARRISON & ANDREWS evacuated to C.C.S. and struck off strength. A.D.M.S. 61st. Div. visited headquarters. CAPT. H.H. FAIRFAX RAMC(T.C) and party were relieved by 2/1 S.M. Fld. Ambce, at LIHONS, and proceeded for duty at SANITAS A.D.S. T.21.d.9.9. MARCHELEPOT was occupied preparatory to making it an A.D.S. MAJOR A.T. WATERHOUSE RAMC(T.F.) inspected ABLAINCOURT A.D.S. and road between VERMANDOVILLERS and CHAULNES. Trenches - Routine work. H.Qrs. Fatigues.	A.T.W.
	20/3/17		MAJOR A.T. WATERHOUSE RAMC(T.F) accompanied by SGT. MAJOR JACKSON H.C. visited DENIECOURT and SUGAR FACTORY. A.D.M.S. 61st. Division visited H.Qrs. T.8.C.4.8. (rear of SUGAR FACTORY) A.D.S. closed. CAPT C.O.J. YOUNG RAMC. (S.R.) with a	A.T.W.

Instructions regarding War Diaries and Intelligence Summaries are contained in F. S. Regs., Part II. and the Staff Manual respectively. Title pages will be prepared in manuscript.

WAR DIARY
~~or~~
~~INTELLIGENCE~~ SUMMARY.
(*Erase heading not required.*)

Army Form C. 2118.

MAP - ROSIERES - COMBINED

Place	Date	Hour	Summary of Events and Information	Remarks and references to Appendices
HERLEVILLE	20 3/17		party of men established an A.D.S. at T.21.d.9.9. MARCHELEPOT with Relay Posts at T.28.b.8.8. MARCHELEPOT and T.30.d.3.4. LICOURT. DR. COWLEY evacuated to 2/3 S. Mid. Fld. Ambce. PTE GILKES & DR. BRYAN J transferred to C.C.S. and struck off strength. CAPT. H.H. FAIRFAX RAMC(T.C) proceeded for duty at MARCHELEPOT A.D.S. Trenches - Routine work. H.Qrs. Fatigues	H.W.
	21 3/17		DR. PARSONS reported for duty from 2/3 S. Mid. Fld. Ambce. CAPT R.D. MOORE R.A.M.C(T.F) visited VERMANDOVILLERS, DENIECOURT and MARCHELEPOT. PTE SEWARD F. evacuated to 2/3 S. Mid Fld. Ambce. PTE EVANS W. transferred to C.C.S. and struck off strength. Trenches - Routine work. - H.Qrs. Fatigues.	H.W.
	22 3/17		MAJOR A.T. WATERHOUSE R.A.M.C(T.F) accompanied by SGT MAJOR PLAISTOW visited SANITAS, DENIECOURT and MARCHELEPOT Advanced Dressing Stations. S.MAJOR JACKSON H.C. visited ABLAINCOURT A.D.S. Trenches - Routine work. Headquarters Fatigues.	H.W.
	23 3/17		DR COWLEY reported for duty. PTE SEWARD F. transferred to C.C.S. and struck off strength of unit. Trenches - Routine work. Headquarters - Fatigues.	H.W.
	24 3/17		CAPT. R.D. MOORE R.A.M.C(T.F) visited ABLAINCOURT and SANITAS Advanced	H.W.

2353 Wt. W2544/1454 700,000 5/15 D. D. & L. A.D.S.S./Forms/C. 2118.

Instructions regarding War Diaries and Intelligence Summaries are contained in F. S. Regs., Part II. and the Staff Manual respectively. Title pages will be prepared in manuscript.

WAR DIARY
or
~~INTELLIGENCE SUMMARY.~~

(Erase heading not required.)

Army Form C. 2118.

Place	Date	Hour	Summary of Events and Information	Remarks and references to Appendices
HERLEVILLE	24 3/17		Dressing Stations to inspect. LT. COL. H.N. BURROUGHES R.A.M.C.(T.F) returned from leave and assumed Command of the Unit. CAPT. R.D. MOORE R.A.M.C.(T.F) proceeded for duty at SANITAS A.D.S. Trenches - Routine work. H.Qrs. Fatigues.	F.H. [illegible] Major RAMC
	25 3/17		O.C., CAPT. R.D. MOORE RAMC(T.F) and SGT. MAJOR JACKSON H.C. visited SANITAS, DENIECOURT and MARCHELEPOT Advanced Dressing Stations to inspect. PTE. PAGE evacuated to 2/3 S. Mid. Fld. Ambce. Trenches Routine work. H.Qrs. Fatigues.	HNB
	26 3/17		PTES. BANNISTER W.F., BROWN T.L. and EVANS E.O. reported for duty and taken on strength of Unit. One horsed ambulance returned to H.Qrs. Five G.S. waggons loaded with stores and equipment proceeded to MARCHELEPOT. Contents of same were dumped in dugouts close to A.D.S. H.Qrs. Fatigues.	HNB
	27 3/17		O.C. accompanied by D.A.D.M.S. 61st. Division visited ATHIES, MONTECOURT, and TERTRY for locating sites for Headquarters and Advanced Dressing Station. CAPT. C.O.T. YOUNG R.A.M.C.(S.R), CAPT. W.H. BELL R.A.M.C.(T.C) and CAPT. H.H. FAIRFAX R.A.M.C.(T.C.) proceeded to ATHIES ~~[illegible]~~ with 40. O. Ranks as an advanced party. A.D.S. at SANITAS closed and CAPT. R.D. MOORE R.A.M.C.(T.F) and CAPT. J. BANNERMAN R.A.M.C.(T.F) and party proceeded to MARCHELEPOT A.D.S.	HNB

Instructions regarding War Diaries and Intelligence Summaries are contained in F. S. Regs., Part II. and the Staff Manual respectively. Title pages will be prepared in manuscript.

WAR DIARY
or
~~INTELLIGENCE SUMMARY.~~
(Erase heading not required.)

Army Form C. 2118.

Place	Date	Hour	Summary of Events and Information	Remarks and references to Appendices
HERLEVILLE	28/3/17		Under orders received from A.D.M.S. 61st Division; the Unit with remaining portion of transport under command of MAJOR A.T. WATERHOUSE R.A.M.C.(T.F.) moved off at 10.0 am. Route FOUCAUCOURT, DENIECOURT, MARCHELEPOT, ST. CRIST, ENNEMAIN, ATHIES arriving at 6.30 pm. Falling out Casualties NIL. All men billeted and transport parked. Room opened for reception of sick. A.D.S. at DENIECOURT closed and CAPT. A.T.I. MACDONALD R.A.M.C.(T.C.) and party joined Unit as it was passing through DENIECOURT. At MARCHELEPOT, MAJOR A.T. WATERHOUSE R.A.M.C.(T.F.) stayed for duty and CAPT A.T.I. MACDONALD	[illegible]
ATHIES			R.A.M.C.(T.C.) brought Unit on to ATHIES. Unit is quartered in ruined foundry. Accommodation everywhere bad owing to the destructive efforts of the retiring enemy. CAPT. W.H. BELL R.A.M.C.(T.C.) and 13 O. Ranks proceeded to TERTRY to open an A.D.S. Motor transport arrived complete at ATHIES. [illegible]	[illegible]
	29/3/17		PTE PAGE transferred to C.C.S. and struck off strength. 3 Operating Tents and 4 Bell Tents erected for reception of sick and wounded. Improvement of existing accommodation in ruined house. Officers' ward opened. One Daimler Car - one Ford Car and one Water cart with horses stationed at TERTRY. Weather very wet.	[illegible]

2353 Wt. W2544/1454 700,000 5/15 D. D. & L. A.D.S.S./Forms/C. 2118.

Instructions regarding War Diaries and Intelligence Summaries are contained in F. S. Regs., Part II. and the Staff Manual respectively. Title pages will be prepared in manuscript.

WAR DIARY
or
~~INTELLIGENCE SUMMARY.~~
(Erase heading not required.)

Army Form C. 2118.

MAP. 62.C.

Place	Date	Hour	Summary of Events and Information	Remarks and references to Appendices
ATHIES	29 3/17		Roads heavy and waterlogged in places. H.Qrs. General Fatigues.	HWB
	30 3/17		CAPT. C.O.J. YOUNG R.A.M.C(S.R), CAPT. H. H. FAIRFAX R.A.M.C(T.C) with 60 other ranks and 3 horsed ambulances proceeded to form temporary Advanced Dressing Station for the attack on SOYECOURT village.— CAPT. C.O.J. YOUNG. R.A.M.C(S.R) & 30 bearers stationed in VRAIGNES WOOD - MAP. REF. Q.27.b.9.6. CAPT. H. H. FAIRFAX R.A.M.C.T.C. & 30 bearers stationed in POEUILLY village Map Ref. Q.28.b.8.2. Three horsed ambulances stationed at Q.26.d.2.7 to evacuate cases as far as mine crater situated at P.30.d.2.7. Six motor ambulances of which two were provided by 2/3 S.M. Fd. Ambce. stationed at mine crater at P.30.d.2.7 for evacuating cases to 2/1 Fd. Ambce. BETHENCOURT. Total number of cases evacuated 11. 2500 PTE WARD P.W. promoted to the rank of Lance Corporal to take effect from 14 3/17.	HWB
	31 3/17.		Under orders received from A.D.M.S. 61st. Division CAPT. W. H. BELL R.A.M.C(T.C) and 6. O.Ranks reopened Advanced Dressing Station at POEUILLY. CAPT. J. BANNERMAN R.A.M.C(T.F) & 20. O. Ranks proceeded to TERTRY. 12 O. Ranks were sent from TERTRY to reinforce CAPT W. H. BELL	HWBrumaghes Lt Col

61st Div.

140/...

Vol 12

CONFIDENTIAL

S WAR DIARY

2/2 S. MID. FLD. AMBCE.
R.A.M.C. (T.F.)

April 1st. - 30th. (Inclusive)
1917

VOL. - 12

Instructions regarding War Diaries and Intelligence Summaries are contained in F. S. Regs., Part II. and the Staff Manual respectively. Title pages will be prepared in manuscript.

WAR DIARY
or
INTELLIGENCE SUMMARY.
(Erase heading not required.)

Army Form C. 2118.

Place	Date	Hour	Summary of Events and Information	Remarks and references to Appendices
ATHIES.	1/4/17		Under orders received from A.D.M.S. 61st. Div. the remaining personnel and equipment together with transport moved under the command of MAJOR A.T. WATERHOUSE R.A.M.C.(T.F) at 9.30 am. Route MONTECOURT, TERTRY.	
TERTRY.			Time of arrival 11.30 am. Falling out casualties NIL. All men billeted and transport parked. 1 Marquee, 2 Operating Tents, and 4 Bell Tents were erected for the reception of sick and wounded. On receipt of 61st. Div. R.A.M.C Operation Order No. 20 the following dispositions were made. CAPT. T. BANNERMAN R.A.M.C.(T.F), CAPT C.O.J. YOUNG R.A.M.C.(S.R), C Section Bearer Sub-division and 4 O. Ranks of 'B' Section proceeded for duty to VERMAND. CAPT. R.D. MOORE R.A.M.C.(T.F), 'B' Bearer Sub-division and 6 O. Ranks proceeded by march route to join CAPT. W.H. BELL'S party at POEUILLY. Both parties proceeded to form Advanced Dressing Stations at (Map reference)- R.26.c.2.2 and Q.29.c.1.5. (Map 62.c). 2 Daimler Cars from 2/1 S. Mid. Fld. Ambce. and 1 Daimler from 2/3 S. Mid. Fld. Ambce. reported for temporary duty.	AWB
	2/4/17		2 Marquees and 4 Bell Tents erected for the reception of sick and wounded. No. of Casualties admitted to Hospital and evacuated to 2/1 S. Mid. Fld. Ambce. 4. Officers 74. O. Ranks. 9 GERMANS. 1 Daimler Car returned to 2/1 S. Mid. Fld. Ambce. and 1 to 2/3 S. Mid. Fld. Ambce.	AWB

A5834 Wt. W4973/M687 750,000 8/16 D. D. & L. Ltd. Forms/C.2118/13.

Instructions regarding War Diaries and Intelligence Summaries are contained in F. S. Regs., Part II. and the Staff Manual respectively. Title pages will be prepared in manuscript.

WAR DIARY
or
~~INTELLIGENCE SUMMARY.~~
(*Erase heading not required.*)

Army Form C. 2118.

Place	Date	Hour	Summary of Events and Information	Remarks and references to Appendices
TERTRY	3/4/17		STF. SGT. STOBART T.L. granted commission and struck off strength of unit. O.C. visited VERMAND and POEUILLY Advanced Dressing Stations. [illegible] sent to 61st. D.S.C. Ord. W'shop. 4 Officers, 39 O. Ranks and 1 GERMAN admitted to hospital and evacuated to 2/1 S. Mid. Fd. Ambce.	H.W.L.
	4/4/17		D.A.D.M.S. 61st. Div. visited H.Qrs. and hospital. O.C. visited [illegible] Division. L'CPL WALKER & DR. WHITE discharged from hospital to duty. PTE COCKSWORTH proceeded for duty with 61st. D.S.C. and ceased to be attached to this unit. CAPT. W.T.F. CRAIG R.A.M.C.(T.F.) and [illegible] reported for duty from IV Corps Baths and Laundry.	H.W.L.
	5/4/17		O.C. visited VERMAND A.D.S. then to [illegible] to [illegible] arrangements with Medical Officer 2/5 Gloucesters.	H.W.L.
	6/4/17		Hospital cleared for reception of wounded. [illegible] 61st. Division visited H.Qrs. PTE. W. [illegible] D. transferred to [illegible] Heavy Battery R.G.A. and struck off strength. L'CPL. [illegible] returned from line and admitted into Hospital. CAPT. W.T.F. CRAIG R.A.M.C.(T.F.) proceeded for duty at VERMAND A.D.S. Shelter erected [illegible] for reception of walking cases.	H.W.L.

A5834 Wt W4973/M687 750,000 8/16 D. D. & L. Ltd. Forms/C.2118/13.

Instructions regarding War Diaries and Intelligence Summaries are contained in F. S. Regs., Part II. and the Staff Manual respectively. Title pages will be prepared in manuscript.

WAR DIARY
or
~~INTELLIGENCE SUMMARY.~~
(Erase heading not required.)

Army Form C. 2118.

Place	Date	Hour	Summary of Events and Information	Remarks and references to Appendices
TERTRY.	7 4/17		Casualties admitted to Hospital and evacuated to 2/1 S. Mid. Fld. Ambce. 61st. Division – wounded 7 Officers 52 O. Ranks. Sick 31 O. Ranks. 59th. Division – wounded 2 " 32 " . Construction of new cookhouse in Hospital Area commenced. One Daimler Car returned to 2/1 S. Mid. Fld. Ambce.	Hwb.
	8 4/17		L'CPL. ALDER, PTES. DEAN, NICHOLLS W. A. & RIDOUT reported for duty from 61st. Div. Baths. Car No. 7 with driver and orderly proceeded to 61st. D.S.C. Ord. W'shops. Car No. 6 with driver and orderly proceeded for temporary duty with 2/3 S. Mid. Fld. Ambce. New cookhouse in Hospital area completed.	Hwb.
	9 4/17		O.C. accompanied by A.D.M.S. 35th. Division inspected Hospital thence on to VERMAND and POEUILLY Advanced Dressing Stations, preparatory to being relieved by 105th. Fld. Ambce. Car No. 7 reported for duty from 61st. D.S.C. Ord. W'shops.	Hwb.
	10 4/17		SGT. MARTLE W. CPLS. BERRY E.J., LOVELL W.T. and PTES. SHEPPERD L.W. and HUMPHREYS H. reported for duty and taken on strength of Unit. Under orders received from A.D.M.S. 61st. Div., CAPT. W.H. BELL R.A.M.C.(T.C.) SGT. GREGORY and 8 O. Ranks with 3 G.S. Waggons loaded with stores and equipment proceeded to OFFOY as an advanced party. CPL. CHATTAWAY and 10 O.Ranks proceeded for temporary duty to 36 C.C.S. at CAYEUX.	Hwb.

Instructions regarding War Diaries and Intelligence Summaries are contained in F. S. Regs., Part II. and the Staff Manual respectively. Title pages will be prepared in manuscript.

WAR DIARY
or
~~INTELLIGENCE SUMMARY.~~
(Erase heading not required.)

Army Form C. 2118.

Place	Date	Hour	Summary of Events and Information	Remarks and references to Appendices
TERTRY.	10/4/17		CAPT. W. J. F. CRAIG R.A.M.C.(T.F.) proceeded for duty at HARBONNIERES. 1 Officer & 6 O.Ranks of 105th. Fld. Ambce. arrived as Advanced Party of the relieving ambce. Car No. 6 returned from 2/3 S. Mid. Fld. Ambce.	[illegible]
OFFOY.	11/4/17		The Ambulance was relieved by 105th. Fld. Ambce. Under orders received from A.D.M.S. 61st. Div., portion of ambce. stationed at H.Qrs. with remaining portion of stores and equipment moved at 12.30pm. under command of MAJOR A. T. WATERHOUSE R.A.M.C.(T.F.) Route - MERAUCOURT, MONCHY LAGACHE, FLEZ, GUIZANCOURT, CROIX MOLIGNAUX, MATIGNY and OFFOY. Time of arrival 4.30pm. Falling out casualties NIL. All men billeted and transport parked. Hospital opened for reception of sick. Parties from Advanced Dressing Stations at VERMAND and POEUILLY were relieved by 105th. Fld. Ambce. and proceeded by march route to OFFOY under command of CAPT. J. BANNERMAN R.A.M.C.(T.F.) and CAPT. R. D. MOORE R.A.M.C.(T.F.) respectively. CAPT. H. A. FAIRFAX R.A.M.C.(T.C.) proceeded on special leave. Pte. ARKELL A. admitted to 105th. Fld. Ambce.	[illegible]
	12/4/17		No. 2357 PTE. PORTMAN L. reported for duty and taken on the strength vice No. 2508 PTE. HUMPHREYS H. transferred to 2/1 S. Mid. Fld. Ambce and struck off strength. PTE HUNT A.E. reported for duty and taken on strength of Unit. Ford Car and motor bicycle proceeded to 61st. D.S.C. Ord. Workshops	[illegible]

A5834 Wt. W4973/M687 750,000 8/16 D. D. & L. Ltd. Forms/C.2118/13.

Army Form C. 2118.

Instructions regarding War Diaries and Intelligence Summaries are contained in F. S. Regs., Part II. and the Staff Manual respectively. Title pages will be prepared in manuscript.

WAR DIARY

~~or~~

~~INTELLIGENCE SUMMARY.~~

(*Erase heading not required.*)

Place	Date	Hour	Summary of Events and Information	Remarks and references to Appendices
OFFOY	12 4/17		Lce. CPL. VIGURS E.N. discharged to duty.	HWS
	13 4/17		No. 2650 PTE. SHEPPERD L.W. transferred to 2/3 S. Mid. Fld. Ambce. and struck off strength. Three Operating Tents, ~~and~~ two Marquees, and five Bell Tents erected for the reception of sick. PTE COOPER R. reported for duty. D.A.D.M.S. 61st. Div. visited hospital. PTE. ARKELL A. evacuated to 107th. Fld. Ambce. and struck off strength.	HWS
	14 4/17		A.D.M.S. 61st. Div. and O.C. made an inspection of Hospital. Two Daimler Cars proceeded for duty to 107th. Fld. Ambce.	HWS
	15 4/17		Parade of all Ranks and an inspection by A.D.M.S. 61st. Divn. PTE. THORNTON C.W. proceeded for test at Photographic Section No. 7 Squadron R.F.C. Motor bicycle and Ford Car returned from 61st. D.S.C. Ord. W'shops.	HWS
	16 4/17		T4/248773 DR. HOUSE G.W. reported for duty and taken on strength. Two Daimler Cars returned from 107th. Fld. Ambulance. CPL. CHATTAWAY W.T. promoted to acting rank of Sergeant Dispenser. PTE. THORNTON C.W. taken on strength of No. 7 Squadron R.F.C. and struck off strength of this Unit. SGT. HARTLE W. transferred to 2/1 S. Mid. Fld. Ambce and struck off strength.	HWS
	17 4/17.		CAPT. C.O.J. YOUNG R.A.M.C. (S.R.) proceeded for temporary duty to 2/5 Glosters.	HWS

A5834 Wt. W4973/M687 750,000 8/16 D. D. & L. Ltd. Forms/C.2118/13.

Instructions regarding War Diaries and Intelligence Summaries are contained in F. S. Regs., Part II. and the Staff Manual respectively. Title pages will be prepared in manuscript.

WAR DIARY
~~or~~
~~INTELLIGENCE~~ ~~SUMMARY.~~
(Erase heading not required.)

Army Form C. 2118.

Place	Date	Hour	Summary of Events and Information	Remarks and references to Appendices
OFFOY	17/4/17		Ford Car sent to 61st. D.S.C. Ord. W'shops. DR. TRING R.T. No. 4 Coy. A.S.C, attached, appointed Acting Rank of Sergeant.	H.W.
	18/4/17		SGT. OAKES R.T. proceeded on leave. CAPT. J. BANNERMAN R.A.M.C. (T.F) proceeded for temporary duty with 2/6 R. Warwicks. CAPT. R. D. MOORE R.A.M.C.(T.F) proceeded for temporary duty with 2/8 Worcesters. PTE. ROOK. F.S. - M.T. A.S.C. with Ford Car No. 29119 reported for duty and taken on strength of Unit. Ford Car No. 18 returned from 61st. D.S.C. Ord' W'shops.	H.W.
	19/4/17		O.C. accompanied by SGT. MAJOR. JACKSON H. C. visited H.Qrs. of 2/3 S. Mid Fld. Ambce. at DOUILLY preparatory to relieving 2/3 Fld. Ambce.	H.W.
	20/4/17		One Daimler Car proceeded for temporary duty with 2/3 S. Mid. Fld. Ambce. Advanced Party - 1 Officer & 21 O. Ranks of Relieving Ambce. (92nd. Fld. Ambce) arrived. CAPT. W. H. BELL R.A.M.C(T.C) & 21 O. Ranks together with two G. S. waggons proceeded as an Advanced Party to DOUILLY to relieve 2/3 S. Mid. Fld. Ambce.	H.W.
	21/4/17		The Unit was relieved by 92nd. Fld. Ambce. Under orders received from 61st. Division the Unit together with Transport moved at 8.0 a.m.	
DOUILLY			Route - TOULLE, DOUILLY. Time of arrival 9.30 a.m. Relief of 2/3 S. Mid. Fld. Ambce. complete by 10.0 a.m. No. of patients taken over - 18.	H.W.

A5834 Wt. W4973/M687 750,000 8/16 D. D. & L. Ltd. Forms/C.2118/13.

Army Form C. 2118.

Instructions regarding War Diaries and Intelligence Summaries are contained in F. S. Regs., Part II. and the Staff Manual respectively. Title pages will be prepared in manuscript.

WAR DIARY

~~or~~

~~INTELLIGENCE SUMMARY.~~

(*Erase heading not required.*)

Place	Date	Hour	Summary of Events and Information	Remarks and references to Appendices
DOUILLY	21 4/17		CAPT. C.O.J. YOUNG R.A.M.C.(S.R.) reported for duty from 2/5 Glosters.	HmB
	22 4/17		PTE. WILLIAMS with motor bicycle proceeded for temporary duty with A.D.M.S 61st. Divn. CAPT. A.T.I. MACDONALD R.A.M.C.(T.C.) evacuated sick to 91st. Fld. Ambce. 2 Marquees and 3 Operating Tents erected for reception of sick.	HmB
	23 4/17		L'CPL. ALDER, PTES. NICHOLLS W.A., RIDOUT, BUSBY, water cart with driver and water duty orderly proceeded to 2/3 S. Mid. Fld. Ambce. for temporary duty at the Trench Foot Baths, Billet No. 27 GERMAINE.	HmB
	24 4/17		Ford Car, No. 18 returned for duty from 61st. D.S.C. Ord. Workshops. DR. COWLEY, No 4 Coy. A.S.C. attached admitted to Hospital and transferred to Corps Rest Station. CAPT. H. H. FAIRFAX R.A.M.C.(T.C.) returned from leave.	HmB
	25 4/17		ST. SGT. MARTIN R.P. proceeded on leave to ENGLAND. DR. BROWN, No. 4 Coy. A.S.C. attached transferred sick to Corps Rest Station.	HmB
	26 4/17		SGT. CHATTAWAY W.J. and 10 men reported for duty from 36 C.C.S. Room in ruined house opened as extra hospital accommodation for 24 patients.	HmB
	27 4/17		DR COWLEY reported for duty from Corps Rest Station.	HmB
	28 4/17		No. M2/153802 PTE. PACK G.A. tried by Field General Court Martial under Army Act Section 11 on the charge of "Neglecting to obey Fourth Army Standing Order No. 230 in that he did on April 14th 1917 drive a motor ambulance	HmB

Instructions regarding War Diaries and Intelligence Summaries are contained in F. S. Regs., Part II, and the Staff Manual respectively. Title pages will be prepared in manuscript.

WAR DIARY

~~or~~

~~INTELLIGENCE SUMMARY.~~

(Erase heading not required.)

Army Form C. 2118.

Place	Date	Hour	Summary of Events and Information	Remarks and references to Appendices
DOUILLY	28/4/17		on the road between MESNIL and NESLE at an excessive speed.	[illegible]
	29/4/17		DR. BROWN evacuated from Corps Rest Station to C.C.S. and struck off strength.	
			CAPT. W.H. BELL R.A.M.C.(T.C) proceeded for temporary duty with 2/8 R. Warwicks	[illegible]
	30/4/17		A.D.M.S. 61st Division visited Hospital. D.D.M.S. IX Corps inspected Headquarters and hospital.	
				[illegible]

[illegible]
Lt. Col. R.A.M.C. T.

A5834 Wt W4973/M687 750,000 8/16 D. D. & L. Ltd. Forms/C.2118/13.

61st Div 140/2161 Medical

May 1917 Vol. 13

S

CONFIDENTIAL

WAR DIARY

2/2 S. MID. FLD. AMBCE.
R.A.M.C. (T.F.)

VOL - 13

May 1st. - 31st. (inclusive)
1917

Instructions regarding War Diaries and Intelligence Summaries are contained in F. S. Regs., Part II. and the Staff Manual respectively. Title pages will be prepared in manuscript.

WAR DIARY
~~or~~
~~INTELLIGENCE SUMMARY.~~

(Erase heading not required.)

Army Form C. 2118.

Place	Date	Hour	Summary of Events and Information	Remarks and references to Appendices
DOUILLY	1/5/17		MAJOR A. T. WATERHOUSE R.A.M.C.(T.F.) assumed command of the Unit vice LT. COL. H.N. BURROUGHES R.A.M.C.(T.F.) who proceeded on leave to PARIS. DR. THOMPSON, No. 4 Coy. A.S.C. attached, admitted to Hospital and evacuated to Corps Rest Station. No. 201676 L/Cpl. DUNN 2/7 Worcesters reported for course of Chiropody. PTE THORNTON C.W. retaken on strength of Unit – Authority IV Corps. 1846 A. dated 30/4/17.	ATW
	2/5/17		CAPT. J. BANNERMAN R.A.M.C.(T.F.) reported for duty. SGT. OAKES R.T. returned from leave. Bathing accommodation constructed for use of personnel of Unit enabling each man to have a bath at least once a week.	ATW
	3/5/17		Routine work.	ATW
	4/5/17		A.D.M.S. 61st. Division visited Hospital. CAPT. C.O.T. YOUNG R.A.M.C. (S.R.) awarded the MILITARY CROSS under authority granted by HIS MAJESTY THE KING.	ATW
	5/5/17		PTE HOLBROOK admitted to Hospital and evacuated to No. [illegible] C.C.S. and struck off strength. CAPT. C.O.T. YOUNG R.A.M.C.(S.R.), SGT. [illegible] and [illegible] men together with G.S. Waggon proceeded on temporary duty at ETREILLERS. CAPT. A.T.I. MACDONALD R.A.M.C.(T.F.) returned from Hospital and reported for duty. LT. COL. H.N. BURROUGHES R.A.M.C. (T.F.) returned from leave and assumed Command of the Unit.	[illegible]

A5834 Wt. W4973/M687 750,000 8/16 D. D. & L. Ltd. Forms/C.2118/13.

Army Form C. 2118.

WAR DIARY
or
~~INTELLIGENCE SUMMARY.~~
(Erase heading not required.)

Instructions regarding War Diaries and Intelligence Summaries are contained in F. S. Regs., Part II. and the Staff Manual respectively. Title pages will be prepared in manuscript.

Place	Date	Hour	Summary of Events and Information	Remarks and references to Appendices
DOUILLY	5/5/17		Construction of new premises as Orderly Room and Dispensary commenced.	H.W.B.
	6/5/17		Daimler Car No. 6 sent to 61st. D.S.C. Ord. W'shops. PTE. WILTSHIRE reported for duty and taken on the strength of the Unit. CAPT. C.O.T. YOUNG R.A.M.C.(S.R) and SGT. DOGGETT reported for duty.	H.W.B.
	7/5/17		PTE. WILSON H.W. admitted to Hospital and evacuated to No. 21 C.C.S. and struck off strength.	H.W.B.
	8/5/17		Daimler Car No. 6 reported for duty. PTE. FRANKUM, water cart-driver-orderly and 2 horses reported for duty from Trench Foot Baths at GERMAINE.	H.W.B.
	9/5/17		ST. SGT. MARTIN R.P. returned from leave. CAPT. C.O.T. YOUNG R.A.M.C (S.R) proceeded for temporary duty with 2/4 Glosters.	H.W.B.
	10/5/17		PTE. APPS H. and PTE. WILLIAMS W.J. proceeded on leave to ENGLAND. CPL. MOSS proceeded for temporary duty with A.D.M.S. 61st. Divn.	H.W.B.
	11/5/17		A.D.M.S 61st. Divn. visited Hospital. CPL. MOSS reported for duty from A.D.M.S 61st. Divn. PTE. SMITH T. transferred from 2/1st. S. Mid. Fld. Ambce. and taken on strength of this Unit. - Transfer to date from 31/3/17. CAPT. A.T.I. MACDONALD R.A.M.C.(T.C) detailed as Sanitary Adviser to the Town Major of DOUILLY.	H.W.B.

Instructions regarding War Diaries and Intelligence Summaries are contained in F. S. Regs., Part II. and the Staff Manual respectively. Title pages will be prepared in manuscript.

WAR DIARY
~~or~~
~~INTELLIGENCE SUMMARY.~~
(Erase heading not required.)

Army Form C. 2118.

Place	Date	Hour	Summary of Events and Information	Remarks and references to Appendices
DOULLY	12/5/17		No. 201989 L/CPL. KING H. G. 2/4 Ox. & Bucks. L. I. reported for course of Chiropody. PTE. PUGH A. R. admitted to Hospital and transferred to 21 C.C.S. and struck off strength. 6 men returned from Trench Foot Bath – GERMAINE and reported for duty.	H.D.
"	13/5/17		Car No. 18 proceeded to 61st. D.S.C. [illegible] workshops.	H.D.
	14/5/17		PTE. AUGHTIE D. proceeded for water duty with 2/4 R. Berks and struck off strength of Unit. CAPT. A. T. I. MACDONALD R.A.M.C.(T.C.) and 11 – O. Ranks proceeded to MESNIL as an advanced party preparatory to Relieving 2/1 S. Mid. Fld. Ambce.	H.D.
	15/5/17		Under orders received from 183rd Inf. Bde. the Unit with transport complete moved at 8.45 a.m. – Route – MATIGNY – Y – [illegible] – MESNIL. Time of arrival 12.45 p.m. Hospital opened for the reception of sick. PTE. THOMPSON J. transferred ~~[illegible]~~ from Corps Rest Station and struck off strength. PTE BROCKHOUSE H. proceeded for temporary duty as runner to 183rd. Inf. Bde. Headquarters.	H.D.
MESNIL.	16/5/17		Unit stationed at MESNIL. PTE GRIFFITHS A. transferred to 21 C.C.S. and struck off strength. Horsed Ambulance proceeded for temporary duty with 306 Bde. R. G. A.	H.D.

A5834 Wt. W4973/M687 750,000 8/16 D. D. & L. Ltd. Forms/C.2118/13.

Army Form C. 2118.

WAR DIARY
or
~~INTELLIGENCE~~ SUMMARY.
(Erase heading not required.)

Instructions regarding War Diaries and Intelligence Summaries are contained in F. S. Regs., Part II. and the Staff Manual respectively. Title pages will be prepared in manuscript.

Place	Date	Hour	Summary of Events and Information	Remarks and references to Appendices
MESNIL	17/5/17		Under orders received from 182nd. Inf. Bde. the Unit less Horse Transport moved at 5.40 am. and entrained at NESLE at 7.15 am. - arrived and detrained at LONGEAU at 9.30 am; thence proceeded by march route to	
WARGNIES			WARGNIES - Route - AMIENS, FLESSELLES and NAOURS. Time of arrival 5.15 pm. Hospital opened for reception of sick. Horse Transport moved by march route under command of MAJOR A.T. WATERHOUSE R.A.M.C.(T.F.) at 8.0 am. PTES. ADAWAY and OSLAND proceeded on leave to ENGLAND.	HWl
	18/5/17		A.D.M.S. 61st. Div. visited H.Qrs. CAPT. H. S. PEMBERTON R.A.M.C. (S.R.) reported for duty and taken on the strength of the Unit.	HWl
	19/5/17		Lecture and demonstration on the Box Respirator given by Divisional Gas Officer. PTE BUSBY F.W. reported for duty from Div. Baths.	HWl
	20/5/17		CAPT. H.H. FAIRFAX R.A.M.C.(T.C.) proceeded for duty with 2/5 R. Warwicks and struck off strength vice CAPT. G.L. WILKINSON R.A.M.C.(T.F.) who reported for duty and taken on strength. Daimler Car No. 6 with driver - Dr. CAMPBELL - proceeded to 61st. D.S.C. Ord. Workshops thence to Base, and struck off strength thus causing one car deficient in Establishment. Horse Transport arrived complete 12.0 (noon). and rejoined Unit. CAPT. W. J. F. CRAIG R.A.M.C.(T.F.) reported for duty from HARBONNIERES.	HWl
	21/5/17		Under orders received from 183rd I. Bde. the Unit with Transport moved	HWl

A5834 Wt. W4973/M687 750,000 8/16 D. D. & L. Ltd. Forms/C.2118/13.

Instructions regarding War Diaries and Intelligence Summaries are contained in F. S. Regs., Part II. and the Staff Manual respectively. Title pages will be prepared in manuscript.

WAR DIARY
or
INTELLIGENCE SUMMARY.
(*Erase heading not required.*)

Army Form C. 2118.

Place	Date	Hour	Summary of Events and Information	Remarks and references to Appendices
WARGNIES BRETEL.	21/5/17		at 5.50 am. Route NAOURS, TALMAS, BEAUVAL, GEZAINCOURT, BRETEL. Time of arrival 12.30 pm. Falling out casualties NIL. Room opened as hospital for reception of sick.	[illegible]
	22/5/17		PTES WARNES and GOURLAY proceeded on leave to England. PTE. HAYES J.S. proceeded for water duty with 184 M.G.C. and struck off strength of Unit. PTE. DAVIES S.C.E. transferred to [illegible] and struck off strength. Motor Ambulance proceeded for temporary duty with [illegible] 61st. Div. Artillery.	[illegible]
IVERGNY.	23/5/17		Under orders received from 182nd. Infy. Bde the Unit with transport moved at 7.15 am. Route - HAUTE-VISÉE, BOUQUE MAISON, LE SOUICH, IVERGNY. Owing to slippery state of road on steep hill into DOULLENS, one horsed ambulance wagon skidded and fell into ditch. Remainder of transport halted while ambulance wagon was drawn out by [illegible] horses. [illegible] then resumed march independently. Time of arrival of [illegible] 11.45 am. Falling out Casualties NIL. Unit opened as hospital for reception of sick. Horse Transport arrived at 2.0 pm.	[illegible]
	24/5/17		Under orders received from 182nd. Inf. Bde the R.A.M.C personnel embussed at 9.0 am. and proceeded via LE SOUICH, LUCHEUX, HUMBERCOURT, LA BELLE VUE, LARBRET and debussed at LE BAC DU SUD.	

Instructions regarding War Diaries and Intelligence Summaries are contained in F. S. Regs., Part II. and the Staff Manual respectively. Title pages will be prepared in manuscript.

WAR DIARY
or
~~INTELLIGENCE SUMMARY.~~

(Erase heading not required.)

Army Form C. 2118.

Place	Date	Hour	Summary of Events and Information	Remarks and references to Appendices
BERNEVILLE	24/5/17		Time of arrival 12.0 (noon). Thence the Unit proceeded by March Route via BEAUMETZ arriving at BERNEVILLE at 3.0 pm. Falling out Casualties NIL. School opened as Hospital for reception of sick. The Horse Transport under Command of MAJOR A.T. WATERHOUSE R.A.M.C(T.F.) moved with 182nd. Inf. Bde. Transport at 10.21 am. The Transport arrived complete at 6.15 pm. thus rejoining Unit at BERNEVILLE. PTE BRAKE F.E. admitted to Hospital and evacuated to No3 STATIONARY HOSPITAL and struck off strength.	HWB.
	25/5/17		CAPT. G.L. WILKINSON R.A.M.C(T.F.) proceeded for temporary duty with 306 Bde R.F.A. PTES APPS H. & WILLIAMS W.J. returned from leave and reported for duty.	HWB.
	26/5/17		CAPT. C.O.J. YOUNG R.A.M.C(S.R) reported for duty from 2/4 Glosters. CPL. LUCAS J. reported for duty and taken on strength.	HWB.
	27/5/17		A.D.M.S. 61st Division visited Hospital and H.Qrs. PTE. BARTLETT F. admitted to Hosp. and evacuated to No. 37 C.C.S. and struck off strength. Car No. 10 proceeded to 61st. D.S.C. Ord. Workshops.	HWB.
	28/5/17		A fatigue party of 1 Sgt. & 19 men proceeded to G 20. a. 1.5. (Map 51.B.) for stacking manure dump. A.D.M.S. 61st Divn. visited H.Qrs.	HWB.
	29/5/17		CAPT. W.J.F. CRAIG R.A.M.C(T.F.), 1 Sgt. & 19 O.Ranks. proceeded as a fatigue party to G.20. a. 1.5. (Map 51.B.) CAPT. J. BANNERMAN R.A.M.C.(T.F.)	HWB.

A5834 Wt. W4973/M687 750,000 8/16 D. D. & L. Ltd. Forms/C.2118/13.

Army Form C. 2118.

Instructions regarding War Diaries and Intelligence Summaries are contained in F. S. Regs., Part II. and the Staff Manual respectively. Title pages will be prepared in manuscript.

WAR DIARY
or
~~INTELLIGENCE SUMMARY.~~
(Erase heading not required.)

Place	Date	Hour	Summary of Events and Information	Remarks and references to Appendices
BERNEVILLE	29/5/17		proceeded on leave. LT. COL. G. W. CRAIG R.A.M.C(T.F) reported and taken on supernumerary strength pending orders.	[illegible]
	30/5/17		A.D.M.S. [illegible] Div. visited H.Qrs. CAPT. A.T.I. MACDONALD R.A.M.C.(T.C), CAPT. C.O.T. YOUNG R.A.M.C (S.R) and 36 O.Rank. together with portion of equipment and water cart proceeded to HOPITAL ST. JEAN ARRAS as an Advanced Party preparatory to relieving 49th. Fld. Amb. A party consisting of 1 Sgt. & 19 men proceeded to C. 30. a. 1. 5. (Map 51 B.) [illegible] reported for duty from workshops.	[illegible]
	31/5/17		O.C. accompanied by Sgt. MAJOR JACKSON M.C [illegible] HOPITAL ST. JEAN ARRAS. PTE W. ROSS with car No. [illegible] reported for M.T. and taken on strength.	[illegible]

[illegible signature]
Lt Col
OC [illegible]

A5834 Wt. W4973/M687 750,000 8/16 D. D. & L. Ltd. Forms/C.2118/13.

June 1917. 8

5

140/2230 MEDICAL

Vol. 14

CONFIDENTIAL

WAR DIARY

2/2 S. MID. FLD. AMBCE.

R.A.M.C.T.F.

June 1st. — 30th.

1917

VOL - 14

Army Form C. 2118.

Instructions regarding War Diaries and Intelligence Summaries are contained in F. S. Regs., Part II. and the Staff Manual respectively. Title pages will be prepared in manuscript.

WAR DIARY
or
~~INTELLIGENCE SUMMARY.~~
(*Erase heading not required.*)

Place	Date	Hour	Summary of Events and Information	Remarks and references to Appendices
BERNEVILLE ARRAS.	1 6/17.		Under orders received from A.D.M.S. 61st. Divn. the remaining portion of personnel of Ambulance and transport moved at 7.30 a.m. Route - WARLUS - thence by dry weather track to ARRAS. Time of arrival 10.0 a.m. Main Dressing Station at HÔPITAL ST. JEAN - RUE ST. AUBERT - taken over from 49th Fd. Ambce. CAPT. G.L. WILKINSON R.A.M.C.(T.F.) reported for duty from 306 Bde. R.F.A. MAJOR E.C. FOSTER R.A.M.C.(T.F.) attached IV Corps. Infy. Schools struck off strength to take effect from 31 5/17. Authority G. A.Q. Third Army letter OB/1444 dated 31 5/17. Car No. 10 with driver and orderly proceeded for temporary duty with 2/1 S. Mid. Fd. Ambce. PTES OSLAND & ADAWAY reported from leave.	H.M.S.
	2 6/17.		A.D.M.S. 61st. Divn. visited Hospital. LT. COL. G.W. CRAIG R.A.M.C.(T.F.) proceeded for duty at DAINVILLE and struck off supernumerary strength. ARRAS bombed by hostile aircraft during the night.	H.M.S.
	3 6/17.		PTES. OLDNALL F.T., OWEN G., GLOVER H., CHAMBERLAIN R., & CHESTERS L., reported for duty and taken on strength of Unit. A.D.M.S. 61st. Divn. visited Hospital. ARRAS again bombarded by aircraft at night.	H.M.S.
	4 6/17.		L/CPL. DUNN 2/7 Worcesters returned to his Unit as fit to take up duties as Chiropodist. CAPT. R.C. COATSWORTH R.A.M.C.(T.F.) and PTE. BEDFORD E. reported for duty and taken on the strength. Aircraft bombardment at night repeated.	H.M.S.

A5834 Wt W4973/M687 750,000 8/16 D. D. & L. Ltd. Forms/C.2118/13.

Instructions regarding War Diaries and Intelligence Summaries are contained in F. S. Regs., Part II. and the Staff Manual respectively. Title pages will be prepared in manuscript.

WAR DIARY
~~or~~
~~INTELLIGENCE SUMMARY.~~
(Erase heading not required.)

Army Form C. 2118.

Place	Date	Hour	Summary of Events and Information	Remarks and references to Appendices
ARRAS.	5 6/17		D.D.M.S. VI Corps visited Hospital. Night bombardment by aircraft for the 4th night in succession.	Hons
	6 6/17		SGT. FOSS No 4 Coy. A.S.C. attached proceeded on leave to England. A.D.M.S 61st. Divn. visited Hospital. Owing to the repeated night bombardments an order was issued by Town Major to the effect that all ranks were to sleep in cellars. This was done and accommodation for 50 patients in cellars was prepared and used. A cellar dressing room was also installed & used. There was no night bombardment. Under orders from A.D.M.S 61st. Divn. accommodation was provided for 50 patients at CONVENT-du-SACRAMENT-RUE D'AMIENS, Medical Officer i/c CAPT. R.C. COATSWORTH R.A.M.C.(T.F.)	Hons
	7 6/17		PTES. WARNES and GOURLAY returned from leave. PTE. KIMBERLEY J.C. reported for duty and taken on the strength. A.D.M.S 61st. Divn. visited Hospital.	Hons
	8 6/17		PTES. DAVIES S.C.E. & BRAKE F.E. reported for duty & taken on the strength.	Hons
	9 6/17		CAPT. C.O.J. YOUNG. R.A.M.C.(S.R.) proceeded for temporary duty to VI Corps Rest Station. LIEUT. O. BASTABLE - HON. LIEUT. & Q.M.B. reported for duty and taken on the strength. PTE. L.C. HUBAND & PTE. EDGINGTON B.T. evacuated to C.C.S. and struck off strength. Advance Party of 2/1 London Fld. Ambce. arrived.	Hons
	10 6/17		Unit was relieved by 2/1 London Fld. Ambce. 56th Division. Under orders	

Instructions regarding War Diaries and Intelligence Summaries are contained in F. S. Regs., Part II. and the Staff Manual respectively. Title pages will be prepared in manuscript.

WAR DIARY ~~or~~ ~~INTELLIGENCE SUMMARY.~~

(Erase heading not required.)

Army Form C. 2118.

Place	Date	Hour	Summary of Events and Information	Remarks and references to Appendices
ARRAS.	10/7/17		received from 182nd. Inf. Bde. portion of Transport moved at 1.30pm. and arrived at DAINVILLE at 3.0pm. followed by Personnel and remainder of transport who left at 4.10pm. and arrived at DAINVILLE at 5.45pm.	
DAINVILLE			School opened as hospital for reception of sick. CAPT. R. C. COATSWORTH RA.M.C(T.F) proceeded for duty with 1/5 D.C.L.I. Car reported for duty from 2/1 S. Mid. Fld. Ambce.	[illegible]
	11/7/17		Car No. 7 with driver proceeded to 61st. D.S.C. Sid. Workshops. No. 437258 PTE. KIMBERLEY J. C. & No. 448053 PTE. CHESTERS L. transferred to 2/3 S. Mid. Fld. Ambce. and struck off strength. CAPT. J. BANNERMAN RAMC (T.F) reported from leave. Horsed ambulance with driver and orderly reported for duty from 306 Bde. R.F.A. CAPT. W. J. F. CRAIG R.A.M.C(T.F) proceeded for temporary duty to 61st. Div. Baths. A fatigue party proceeded to G.30. a. 0. 4. (Sheet 51 b.) for stacking manure dump.	[illegible]
	12/7/17		PTES. CLARKE J.K., KIMBERLEY C.H.W., CARTER G., & DR. TEALE P. J. transferred sick to VI Corps Rest Station. A fatigue party proceeded to G.30. a. 0. 4. (Sheet 51.b.) for stacking manure dump.	[illegible]
	13/7/17		SGT. MATHIAS J. K. transferred to VI Corps Rest Station. A fatigue party proceeded to G.30. a. 0. 4. (Sheet 51 b.) for stacking manure dump.	[illegible]

A5834 Wt. W4973/M687 750,000 8/16 D. D. & L. Ltd. Forms/C.2118/13.

Instructions regarding War Diaries and Intelligence Summaries are contained in F. S. Regs., Part II. and the Staff Manual respectively. Title pages will be prepared in manuscript.

WAR DIARY
or
INTELLIGENCE SUMMARY.
(Erase heading not required.)

Army Form C. 2118.

Place	Date	Hour	Summary of Events and Information	Remarks and references to Appendices
DAINVILLE	14/6/17		CAPT. J. BANNERMAN R.A.M.C.(T.F.) proceeded for temporary duty with 2/6 R. Warwicks. SGT. OAKES R.J. evacuated sick to VI Corps Rest Station. T4/248889 Dr. LEE C.R. No 4 Coy. A.S.C. attached permanently attached to IV Corps Schools and struck off strength to take effect from 21/5/17. PTE. TONKS J. proceeded on leave to England.	HWS
	15/6/17		CPL. CREFFIELD E.F. No 4 Coy. A.S.C. attached reported from leave. T4/248944 DR. MALINSKI G. No 4 Coy A.S.C. attached evacuated sick to CCS & struck off strength.	HWS
	16/6/17		Under orders received from D.D.M.S. VI Corps St. SGT. CUMMINGS T. and a party of 30 men proceeded by Lorry to ST. NICHOLAS and struck Church Army Marquee. SGT. MATHIAS J.K. reported for duty from VI Corps Rest Station. T1/1896 Dr. BAKER P. & T4/248799 DR. SPRINGHAM S. No 4 Coy. A.S.C. reported for duty and taken on the strength. PTE KIMBERLEY C.H.W. reported for duty from VI Corps Rest Station. Car No. 18 with driver proceeded to Divl. D.S.C. Ord. Workshops.	HWS
	17/6/17		Routine Work.	HWS
	18/6/17		Routine Work.	HWS
	19/6/17		DR. TEALE P.J. No 4 Coy. A.S.C. attached & PTE CLARKE J.K. reported for duty from VI Corps Rest Station. DR. GEORGE K. No. 4. Coy. A.S.C. attached & PTE. BYARD C. transferred sick to VI Corps Rest Station. CAPT. W.H. BELL R.A.M.C.(T.C.) reported for duty from 2/8 R. Warwicks. PTE. CARTER G. reported for duty from VI Corps Rest Station.	HWS

A5834 Wt. W4973/M687 750,000 8/16 D. D. & L. Ltd. Forms/C.2118/13.

Army Form C. 2118.

WAR DIARY
or
~~INTELLIGENCE SUMMARY.~~
(Erase heading not required.)

Instructions regarding War Diaries and Intelligence Summaries are contained in F. S. Regs., Part II. and the Staff Manual respectively. Title pages will be prepared in manuscript.

Place	Date	Hour	Summary of Events and Information	Remarks and references to Appendices
DAINVILLE	19/6/17		CAPT. C. O. J. YOUNG R.A.M.C.(S.R.) appointed acting D.A.D.M.S. VI Corps during the absence of that officer on leave.	[illegible]
	20/6/17		SGT. DAKES R.J. reported for duty from VI Corps Rest Station. CAPT. W. H. BELL R.A.M.C.T.C. transferred to 306 Bde. R.F.A. and struck off strength. CAPT. R. C. COATSWORTH R.A.M.C.T.C. transferred to 1/5 D.C.L.I. and struck off strength. Pte. GRAY G.W. No. 4 Coy. A.S.C. attached evacuated sick to VI Corps Rest Station.	[illegible]
	21/6/17		Dr. SMITH W.T. No. 4 Coy. A.S.C. attached evacuated sick to VI Corps [illegible]. 4 drivers & 8 mules reported for temporary duty with [illegible].	[illegible]
	22/6/17		Under orders received from 183rd. Infy. Bde. the Transport complete under command of MAJOR A.T. WATERHOUSE R.A.M.C.T.F. together with 4 N.C.O's & 10 men of R.A.M.C. personnel moved by march route at 3.45 a.m. Route – WARLUS, WANQUETIN, HAUTEVILLE, AVESNES-LE-COMTE, LIENCOURT, LE CAUROY and REBREUVIETTE. Time of arrival 2-0 p.m. Dr. TEALE R.T. No. 4 Coy. A.S.C. attached admitted to Hospital.	[illegible]
	23/6/17		Under orders received from 182nd. Inf. Bde. the ambulance moved at [illegible] by march route along WARLUS – DAINVILLE ROAD. The unit embussed at L.32. [illegible] (Sheet 51 C) at 9.0 a.m. and arrived at BEAUMONT at [illegible].	
BEAUMONT			Rooms in Chateau opened as Hospital wards for (a) Officers (b) Other Ranks.	[illegible]

A5834 W: W4973/M687 750,000 8/16 D. D. & L. Ltd. Forms/C.2118/13.

Army Form C. 2118.

Instructions regarding War Diaries and Intelligence Summaries are contained in F. S. Regs., Part II. and the Staff Manual respectively. Title pages will be prepared in manuscript.

WAR DIARY
or
~~INTELLIGENCE SUMMARY.~~
(Erase heading not required.)

Place	Date	Hour	Summary of Events and Information	Remarks and references to Appendices
BACHIMONT.	23/6/17		Horse Transport moved from REBREUVIETTE at 6.15 am. Route FRÉVENT, LIGNY-SUR-CANCHE, VACQUERIE-LE-BOUCQ, ROUGEFAY, BACHIMONT. Time of arrival 11.30 am.	H.D.
	24/6/17		4 Drivers & 8 mules attached for the move returned to 182nd. Inf. Bde. H.Qrs. A.D.M.S. 61st. Divn. visited Hospital. Ford Car No. A. 24343 evacuated from 61st. D.S.C. Ord. workshops to Base & struck off strength.	H.D.
	25/6/17		M/303369 PTE. ROSS W. 61st. Divn. Supply Col. M.T. A.S.C. attached returned to 61st. D.S.C. and struck off strength. Driver of Ford Car No. A. 24343 reported for duty from workshop. B Section withdrawn from Hospital duties for drill & kit inspections under Section Commander for the week. Four men detailed to help French farmers on the land.	H.D.
	26/6/17		T4/248881 DR. BRYAN J. No 4 Coy. A.S.C. attached reported for duty and taken on the strength. T4/248899 DR. TEALE P.J. No 4 Coy. A.S.C. attached discharged from hospital. T4/248863 DR SMITH W.T. No 4 Coy. A.S.C. attached evacuated to C.C.S. and struck off strength. No. 437465 PTE. BYARD C.E. evacuated to C.C.S. and struck off strength.	H.D.
	27/6/17		DR. GEORGE K. No 4 Coy A.S.C. attached & PTE. DERRICK C.F. reported for duty from VI Corps Rest Station. CAPT. W.J.F. CRAIG R.A.M.C.T.F. reported for duty from 61st. Divn. Baths. CAPT. CORNELIUS R.A.M.C.(S.R.) reported	H.D.

A5834 Wt. W4973/M687 750,000 8/16 D. D. & L. Ltd. Forms/C.2118/13.

Instructions regarding War Diaries and Intelligence Summaries are contained in F. S. Regs., Part II. and the Staff Manual respectively. Title pages will be prepared in manuscript.

WAR DIARY

or

~~INTELLIGENCE SUMMARY.~~

(Erase heading not required.)

Army Form C. 2118.

Place	Date	Hour	Summary of Events and Information	Remarks and references to Appendices
BACHIMONT	27/6/17		for duty and taken on the strength.	
	28/6/17		MAJOR A.T. WATERHOUSE R.A.M.C.T.F. and PTE. WILLIAMS C. proceeded on leave to England. CAPT. CORNELIUS R.A.M.C.(S.R.) posted to 2/8 [illegible] and struck off strength. L'CPL. ALDER P.W. reported for duty from 61st Divn. Baths. No. 437081 PTE. FREEMAN G. evacuated to C.C.S. and struck off strength. PTE TONKS J. reported from leave.	[illegible]
	29/6/17		L'CPL. ALDER P.W. proceeded to ENGLAND for commission. L'CPL. [illegible] J. admitted to hospital & evacuated to C.C.S. and struck off strength. CAPT. J. BANNERMAN R.A.M.C.T.F. reported for duty from 2/3 [illegible]	[illegible]
	30/6/17		A.D.M.S. & D.A.D.M.S. 61st Divn. inspected hospital. Examination for 2nd & 3rd Class Nursing Orderlies held by O.C. [illegible]	

[illegible]

[illegible]

O.C. 2/3 [illegible]

A5834 Wt W4973/M687 750,000 8/16 D. D. & L. Ltd. Forms/C.2118/13.

9

140/2298

MEDICAL

Vol 15

CONFIDENTIAL
WAR DIARY

July 1917

2/2 S. Mid. Fd. Ambce.
R.A.M.C.T.F.

July 1st. — 31st.
1917.

VOL 15

B.E.F.

SUMMARY OF MEDICAL WAR DIARIES OF 2/2nd S.M. F.A. 61st Div.

8th Corps. 5th ARMY.

19th Corps from Aug. 15th.

5th Corps from 15th Sept.

To 17th Corps. 3rd ARMY from 18th Sept.

Western Front Operations -"July - November 1917."

Officer Commanding - Lt.Col. H.N. Burroughs (T).

SUMMARISED UNDER THE FOLLOWING HEADINGS:-

Phase "D" 1. Passchendaele Operations, "July - Nov. 1917".

(a) - Operations commencing 1/7/17.

(b) - Operations commencing 1/10/17.

Canadians attacked Passchemdaele, Oct 30th.
Canadians took Passchendaele, Nov.6th.

2/2nd S.M. F.A. 61st Div. 8th Corps. 5th ARMY.

O.C. - Lt.Col. H.N. Burroughs (T).

Unit transferred to 19th Corps. WESTERN FRONT.
July - Aug. 1917.

PHASE "D" 1. Passchendaele Operations, July-Nov.1917.

(a) - Operations commencing 1/7/17.

Headquarters at RUBROUCK.

July 26th. Moves and Transfer. Unit arrived in 8th Corps area from 6th Corps. 1st ARMY.

2/2nd (S.M) F.A. 61st Div. 8th Corps. 5th ARMY.

O.C. - Lt.Col. H.N. Burroughs (T).

Unit transferred to 19th Corps. WESTERN FRONT.
July - Aug. 1917.

PHASE "D" 1. Passchendaele Operations, July-Nov.1917.

(a) - Operations commencing 1/7/17.

Headquarters at RUBROUCK.

July 26th. Moves and Transfer.) Unit arrived in 8th Corps area from 6th Corps. 1st ARMY.

Army Form C. 2118.

Instructions regarding War Diaries and Intelligence Summaries are contained in F. S. Regs., Part II. and the Staff Manual respectively. Title pages will be prepared in manuscript.

WAR DIARY
or
INTELLIGENCE SUMMARY
(Erase heading not required.)

Place	Date	Hour	Summary of Events and Information	Remarks and references to Appendices
BACHIMONT	1·7·17		T4/248864 Dr· GRAY G·W· No·4 Coy· A·S·C· attached reported for duty from VI Corps Rest Station·	HWB
"	2·7·17		A Section withdrawn from hospital duties for drill and kit inspections under Section Commander for the week· No·437401 Pte· HARWOOD F· EVACUATED sick to C·C·S· and struck off strength·	HWB
"	3·7·17		CAPT· A·T·I·MACDONALD R·A·M·C·T·C· reported from leave· No· 437401 Pte· HARWOOD F· reported for duty from C·C·S· and taken on strength of unit· CAPT· C·O·J·YOUNG R·A·M·C·S·R· REPORTED from detached duty from VI Corps· CAPT· W·J·F·CRAIG R·A·M·C·T·F: proceeded for temporary duty as M·O· i/c 2/4 Ox· & Bucks·L·I· Ford Car & Motor Bicycle sent to 61st· D·S·C· Ord· Workshop·	HWB
"	4·7·17		Ford Car reported for duty from Workshop·	HWB
"	5·7·17		Routine Work· Motor Bicycle reported for duty from Workshop·	HWB
"	6·7·17		No·M2/079033 Pte· MORTON K·M· M·T·A·S·C· attached with Ford Car No· A 9951 reported for duty and taken on the strength· One L·D· Horse transferred to 2/3 S·Mid·Fld·Ambce· and struck off strength· Pte· TRISTRAM B·J· evacuated to No· 6 Stationary Hospital and struck off strength·	HWB
"	7·7·17		Routine Work·	HWB
"	8·7·17		CAPT·C·O·J·YOUNG R·A·M·C·S·R· attached to 2/4 Royal Berks and struck off strength vice CAPT· C·H·ROBSON R·A·M·C·T·C· who reported for duty and was taken on the strength· No·TI/648 Dr·BERRY J·T· & No·T/32871 Dr· WHELON W· No 4 Coy A·S·C· attached reported for duty and taken on the strength· Daimler Car No·7 with driver and orderly proceeded for temporary duty with 61st· Divisional Artillery· No·437100 Pte· SMITH W·E· evacuated sick to C·C·S· and struck off strength·	HWB

Army Form C. 2118.

WAR DIARY
or
~~INTELLIGENCE SUMMARY~~
(Erase heading not required.)

Instructions regarding War Diaries and Intelligence Summaries are contained in F. S. Regs., Part II. and the Staff Manual respectively. Title pages will be prepared in manuscript.

Place	Date	Hour	Summary of Events and Information	Remarks and references to Appendices
BACHIMONT	9·7·17		C Section withdrawn from Hospital Duties for Drill and Kit Inspections under Section Commander for the week· Five men of A Section and four men of B Section detailed to help French Farmers on the land· M2/131222 Pte·ROGERS L·M·T·A·S·C·attached proceeded on leave to ENGLAND· No437350 Pte·ALDIS E· transferred to 61st·Divisional Employment Company and struck off strength·	
"	10·7·17		T4/248863 Dr·SMITH W·T· No·4 Coy·A·S·C· attached reported for duty and taken on the strength· No·437138 Sgt·DOGGETT H· reported for duty from leave· No·437361 Pte· FREEMAN H·W· reported from detached duty· Major A·T·WATERHOUSE R·A·M·C·T·F·and Capt· R·D·MOORE R·A·M·C·T·F· reported from leave·	
"	11·7·17		A·D·M·S· 61st·Division visited Hospital· No 437255 Pte·WILLIAMS C· reported from leave·	
"	12·7·17		LIEUT·COL·H·N·BURROUHGES R·A·M·C·T· proceeded on leave to England and Major A·T· WATERHOUSE R·A·M·C·T· assumed command of the Unit· T4/248886 Dr·FRANCE T·R· No·4 Coy· A·S·C· attached reported for duty and taken on the strength· 2·H·D·Horses received and taken on the strength·	
"	13·7·17		1·H·D· Horse returned for duty from 61st· Divisional Mobile Veterinary Section·	
"	14·7·17		Routine Work·	
"	15·7·17		Routine Work·	
"	16·7·17		No·439169 L'CPL·HURLEY W·R· reported for duty from 2/3 S·Mid·Fld·Amb· and taken on the strength· Two men reported from 2/6 Waricks· for a course of Chiropody· Daimler Ambulance with driver and orderly reported from temporary duty with Divisional Artillery· B Section withdrawn from Hospital duties for Drill and Kit Inspections under Section Commander for the week· 8 men detailed to help French Farmers on the land·	
"	17·7·17		Routine Work· Daimler Ambulance NO 19205 and Ford Car NO 29119 proceeded to 61st· Div· Supply Column Ord· Workshops· B Section paraded complete with Transport in ~~xxxx~~ order· to demonstrate to the Regimental M·O's· of the Brigade certain aspects of the work of Field Ambulances· The Section marched to a field below the Hospital, where they had	

Army Form C. 2118.

WAR DIARY
or
~~INTELLIGENCE SUMMARY.~~
(Erase heading not required.)

Instructions regarding War Diaries and Intelligence Summaries are contained in F. S. Regs., Part II. and the Staff Manual respectively. Title pages will be prepared in manuscript.

Place	Date	Hour	Summary of Events and Information	Remarks and references to Appendices
BACHIMONT	17.7.17		previously erected a shelter. The wagons were unloaded , sufficient equipment was unpacked to enable the men to fit up the shelter as an Advanced Dressing Station; to which men representing wounded were brought in on stretchers.	A.T.I.
"	18.7.17		Routine Work. Daimler Ambulance No 19205 and Ford Car No 29119 returned from 61st. Div. Supply Column Ord. Workshops. for duty.	A.T.I.
"	19.7.17		1.H.D.Horse transferred to 2/3 S.Mid.Fld.Amb. and struck off strength. Capt. A.T.I. MACDONALD R.A.M.C.T.C. attended Sick Parade at 184 M.G.Coy.	A.T.I.
"	20.7.17		Capt. C.O.J.YOUNG R.A.M.C.S.R. reported for duty from 2/4 Berks. and taken on the strength. Capt. A.T.I.MACDONALD R.A.M.C.T.C. proceeded for duty with 2/4 Berks. Capt. G.L.WILKINSON R.A.M.C.T.F. proceeded for temporary duty with 2/8 Worcesters.	A.T.I.
"	21.7.17		Capt.C.O.J.YOUNG R.A.M.C.S.R. detailed to attend daily at 184 M.G.Coy. as Medical Officer.	A.T.I.
"	22.7.17		Capt.J.BANNERMAN R.A.M.C.T.F. evacuated sick to No.6 Stationary Hospital FREVENT.	A.T.I.
"	23.7.17		T1/1896 Dr.BAKER P. No.4 Coy.A.S.C. attached returned to No.4 Coy. and struck off strength. No.437479 Pte.TIMMS B. No.439316 Pte.DIKE A.J. No.437387 Pte.GREEN A.C. No.437348 Sergt. CHATTAWAY W.J. & No.437491 Pte.JONES W. evacuated to No.6 Stationary Hospital FREVENT and struck off strength. Capt.C.O.J.YOUNG R.A.M.C.S.R. evacuated sick to No.6 Stationary Hospital FREVENT.	A.T.I.
" SERICOURT	24.7.17		Under orders received from 182 Infantry Brigade the Unit with Transport complete moved at 7.15.am. Route ROUGEFAY, VACQUERIE- le-Boucq, FREVENT, and SERICOURT. Time of arrival 11.45.am.All men billeted and Transport parked. Hospital opened for reception of sick. Lt.Col.H.N.BURROUGHES R.A.M.C.T.F. reported from leave and re-assumed command of the Unit.	A.T.I. Macdonald Major RAMC
"	25.7.17		Unit stationed at SERICOURT. No.437360 Pte FINDLAY F. & No.437161 Pte.PRITCHETT V.E.C. evacuated to No.6 Stationary Hospital FREVENT and Struck off strength. Under orders received from 182 Infantry Brigade the Transport moved complete at 10.15pm. to FREVENT STATION. ~~leaving~~ Ambulance Personnel proceeded to FREVENT STATION leaving SERICOURT by March Route at 11.50pm. The whole Unit with Transport ~~complete~~ complete entrained and	HNB

Instructions regarding War Diaries and Intelligence Summaries are contained in F. S. Regs., Part II. and the Staff Manual respectively. Title pages will be prepared in manuscript.

WAR DIARY
or
~~INTELLIGENCE SUMMARY.~~

(Erase heading not required.)

Army Form C. 2118.

Place	Date	Hour	Summary of Events and Information	Remarks and references to Appendices
RUBROUCK	26.7.17		LEFT FREVENT at 2.30.am., arriving and detraining at CASSEL STATION at 9.0.am. After detrainment the Unit moved by March Route to RUBROUCK via, WEMAERS - CAPPEL, and OEHTEZEELE, arriving at 1.0.pm. Hospital opened for the reception of sick. A.D.M.S. and D.A.D.M.S. 61 st. Division visited Headquarters.	HWS
"	27.7.17		T4/248888 Dr. GEORGE A. No.4 Coy. A.S.C. attached No.435290 Pte. SMITH T. No.437361 Pte. FREEMAN H.W. No.437520 Pte. SHEPPEY F. and No.437222 Pte. HIGGS C.R. proceeded on leave to ENGLAND. D.D.M.S. VIIIth. Corps visited Hospital.	HWS
"	28.7.17		No.437503 Pte. CRIPPS W. granted special leave of absence to ENGLAND. O.C. attended conference at A.D.M.S. Office.	HWS
"	29.7.17		No.437143 Pte. MAYES W.O. reported for duty and taken on the strength.	HWS
"	30.7.17		Routine Work.	HWS
"	31.7.17		Routine Work.	
			~~Routine Work.~~	

H. Simmonds
Lt.Col. RAMC
O.C. 2/2 S. Mid. Fd. Ambulance

A5834 Wt. W4973/M687 750,000 8/16 D. D. & L. Ltd. Forms/C.2118/13.

16 140/2364 MEDICAL

Aug. 1917 5

CONFIDENTIAL

Vol 16

WAR DIARY

2/2 S. Mid. Fld. Ambce.
R.A.M.C. (T.F.)

August 1st. — 31st. (inclusive)
1917.

VOL-16

Army Form C. 2118.

Instructions regarding War Diaries and Intelligence Summaries are contained in F. S. Regs., Part II. and the Staff Manual respectively. Title pages will be prepared in manuscript.

WAR DIARY
or
INTELLIGENCE SUMMARY.
(Erase heading not required.)

Place	Date	Hour	Summary of Events and Information	Remarks and references to Appendices
RUBROUCK	1.8.17.		CAPT.W.J.F.CRAIG.R.A.M.C.T.reported for duty from 2/4 Ox & BUCKS. 437484.PTE HUBAND.F 437447.PTE.BURTON W 436493 PTE DUBEIL A J reported for duty from leave. CAPT.G.L.WILKINSON R.A.M.C.T. reported for duty from 2/8/Worcesters. T4/248892 DR.NEWNAM.G. No. 4 Co A.S.C. attached evacuated to 2/3 Field Ambulance.	H.W.
"	2.8.17.		CAPT.H.S.PEMBERTON.R.A.M.C.(S.R.) proceeded for temporary duty as M.O.with 1/5.D.C.L.I. 437020 SGT GREGORY J reported from leave. Car No A24942 proceeded to Workshop for adjustment of Rear Axles & Rngine overhaul.	H.W.
"	3.8.17		A.D.M.S. visited Hospital. O.C. visited XV111 Corps Main Dressing Station. 437246 Pte GLOVER.H. evacuated to C.C.S. & struck off the strength. 437387 Pte GREEN A C reported for duty from C.C.S. & taken on the strength. 437414 Sgt EDGINTON W J 437368 PTE FELL A 437180 PTE MEREDITH J F 437308 PTE BLADON TH M2/167150 L.CPL BIGNELL A proceeded on leave.	H.W.
"	4.8.17		O.C. inspected Water Cart of 182 M.G.C. 437548 SGT CHATTAWAY W J 437479 PTE TIMMS B 439316 PTE DIKE A J 437491 PTE JONES W reported for duty from C.C.S. & taken on the strength. CAPT.W.J.F. CRAIG.R AM C T PROCEEDED for temporary duty with 2/7. R Warwicks.	H.W.
"	5.8.17		T4/248940 DR COWLEY A W J evacuated sick to C C S & struck of the strength. Car NO 24842 returned from Workshop. No.10 Car proceeded to Workshop with Driver & Orderly .Bay Gelding H.D.792 sent to 61 M.V.Section, thence to Base & struck off the strength.	H.W.
"	6.8.17		182 INFANTRY BRIGADE practice trench attack. Main Dressing & Advanced Dressing Station formed by C Section at Sheet 27 B 21 d 5.1 & B 26 d 4.8. respectively. 150 casualties wer dealt with. Water was carried to A D S by Pack Horse,carrying 6 Petrol Tins filled with water.	H.W.
"	7.8.17.		435581 PTE POWEL C. EVACUATED TO CCS and struck off strength. 437161 PTE PRITCHETT V E C reported for duty from C C S & taken on the strength. CAPT. H.S.PEMBERTON.R.A.M.C.(S.R.) reported from temporary duty with 1/5. D.C.LI. Routine Hospital Work.	H.W.

A5834 Wt. W4973/M687 750,000 8/16 D. D. & L. Ltd. Forms/C.2118/13.

Instructions regarding War Diaries and Intelligence Summaries are contained in F. S. Regs., Part II. and the Staff Manual respectively. Title pages will be prepared in manuscript.

WAR DIARY
or
INTELLIGENCE SUMMARY.
(Erase heading not required.)

Army Form C. 2118.

Place	Date	Hour	Summary of Events and Information	Remarks and references to Appendices
RUBROUCK	8.8.17.		437520 PTE SHEPPEY F 437222 PTE HIGGS C R 436290 PTE SMITH T 437361 PTE FREEMAN H W T4/24888 DR GEORGE A reported from leave of absence. Routine Hospital Work.	H.W.S.
"	9.8.17.		Under instructions from A.D.M.S. 61 Division a Medical Board assembled at Hqrs for the purpose of re-classifying P.B. Details in the immediate area. President O.C. Members:- CAPT.H.S.PEMBERTON.R.A.M.C.(S.R.) & CAPT.R.D.MOORE. R.A.M.C.T. Under orders from 182 Infantry Brigade the unit proceeded on a Route March. Dress F.S.Marching Order.437106 L.Sg DOLPHIN J REPORTED for duty from Cyclists' Base Depot & taken on the strength.	H.W.S.
"	10.8.17.		436503 PTE CRIPPS W reported for duty from Leave. Unit proceeded on a Route March,Dress F.S. Marching Order. Thresh Disinfector reported for the disinfecting of Hospital Blankets etc. 437235 SGT WHITEHOUSE T H 437467 PTE CURETON 437269 PTE MACFARLANE J H 437467 PTE WILTSHIRE D G proceeded on leave. Routine Hospital Work.	H.W.S.
"	11.8.17.		2 Men 2/6 R Warwicks rejoined their unit on the conclusion of the Chiropody Course. Under instructions from 182 Infantry Brigade 16 men from each of the :- 2/5 2/6 2/7 2/8 R.Warwicks reported for training as Stretcher Bearers. T4/248940 DR COWLEY A J No 4 A.S.C attached, reported for duty from C C S & is taken on the strength. No 10 Car reported for duty from Workshop. No.18 Car proceeded for temporary duty to A.D.M.S. Office.	H.W.S.
"	12.8.17.		10 Re-inforcements reported for duty & are taken on the strength. Routine Hospital Work.	H.W.S.
"	13.8.17		O.C. accompanied by the Q.M.R. & the Sgt.Major visited XIX C.R.S. Capt.C.H.ROBSON.R.A.M. (T.C.) 437101 PTE LOVELESS W H 437566 PTE EVANS E O 437582 PTE HUDSON E G 436390 PTE DAVIES S C E proceeded for duty at Divisional Depot Batt. at MERCKECHEM.	H.W.S.
"	14.8.17.		266187 PTE WEST.J 2/7 R WARWICKS reported for a course in Chiropody. Under orders from A.D.M.S 61 Division,advance partyof 15 N.C.Os & Men under CAPT H.S.PEMBERTON R.A.M.C. S.R. proceeded at 8.0.am. by cars to HILLHOEK to take over XIX C.R.S. A second party of 18 O.R proceeded by car at 11.30.am. & 4 G S Wagons 1 Water Cart & 1 Horse Ambulance Wagon under SGT.FOSS.A E to XIX C R S. 437468 L.CPL WARD F W 437013 S SGT MARTIN R P 437257 PTE CRACKNELL J 437459 PTE FLATTERY F S 437481 PTE CLARKE J K T4/248887 DR GUEST V N . A S C. attached, evacuated to 58 Gen Hospital & struck off the strength. Hospital closed at 12 noon.	H.W.S.

A5834 Wt. W4973/M687 750,000 8/16 D. D. & L. Ltd. Forms/C.2118/13.

Instructions regarding War Diaries and Intelligence Summaries are contained in F. S. Regs., Part II, and the Staff Manual respectively. Title pages will be prepared in manuscript.

WAR DIARY
or
INTELLIGENCE SUMMARY.
(Erase heading not required.)

Army Form C. 2118.

Place	Date	Hour	Summary of Events and Information	Remarks and references to Appendices
RUBROUCK	15.8.17.		Remainder of Transport under Major A T WATERHOUSE R A M C T proceeded by road leaving RUBROUCK at 6.0.am with 183 Infantry Brigade Transport, arriving at X1X C R S HILLOEK AT 5.30.pm. 35 N C O's & Men proceeded at 7.30.am under CAPT.GL. WILKINSON R.A.M.C.T. by Motor Ambulances to X1X C R S at HILLHOEK. C R S taken over from 110 Field Ambulance with 844 Patients at 4.0.pm. Remainder of personnel under CAPT R D MOORE R A M C T proceeded by March Route to ESQUELBECQ, entrained for HOPOUTRE & reported at X1X C R S at 8.0.pm. 20 N C O 's & Men 47 Field Amb. attached for duty. CAPT.J.L.WHATLEY.R.A.M.C. T.C. IS ~~xxxxx~~ attached for duty. 437414 SGT EDGINTON W J 437180 PTE MEREDITH J F 437308 PTE FELL A 437508 PTE BLADON T H & M2/167150 L.CPL BIGNELL A.(M.T. A.S.C.attached) reported from leave	A.W.
HILLHOEK	16.8.17		Under orders of D D M S X1X CORPS THE C R S is closed to admissions for 48 Hours. General fatigues in camp area, large quantity of salvage found & sorted. Erection of Tents & Bivouacs for R.A.M.C. personnel.	A.W.
"	17.8.17.		Under orders from A.D.M.S. 61 Division, B.Section Bearer Sub Division consisting of 34 N.C.O.'s & men were attached for duty to 2/3 Field Ambulance. T4/248817. Dr.WHEELER.A.H 4 Co. A.S.C. reported for duty & taken on the strength. D.M.S. FIFTH ARMY visited Rest Station. D.D.M.S. X1X Corps visited Rest Station ,also A.D.M.S. 16 Division.	A.W.
"	18.8.17.		Hospital Work Routine ,& Structional alterations were begun.	A.W.
"	19.8.17		Hospital Routine Work. 20 N.C.O' & men 47 FIELD AMBULANCE (attached for duty) rejoined their Unit. Car No. 9 reported for duty from Workshop.	A.W.
"	20.8.17.		Hospital Routine Work. X1X Corps Commander ,LT.GEN.H.E.WATTS.C.B. C.M.G. visited Rest station. CAPT.C.H.ROBSON R.A.M.C. T.C. & PTE DAVIES S.C.E. reported for duty from 61 DIVISIONAL DEPOT BATT. M2/L67360 Pte NETHERCOTT A M.T. A.S.C. attached, admitted to Hospital.	A.W.
"	21.8.17		Under instructions from D.D.M.S. X1X CORPS 322056 PTE GLASS N D 105137 PTE BOWER J E 100196 PTE GRIMSHAW T 322061 PTE HENDERSON C G proceeded for duty at X1X Corps RE- INF. DEPOT . 435335 PTE THORNTON C.W. attached 5th BRIGADE R.F.C. is transferred on probation to R.F.C. as PHOTOGRAPHER with effect from 6.8.17. under A.G.'s authority D/2333/760. 6.8.17. 437471 PTE BARTLETT F admitted to HOSPITAL. UNDER orders from A.D.M.S. 5 Horse Ambulances, 2 G.S.Wagons 3 Pack Horses 8 Drivers & 4 Motor Ambulances, carrying 3 Days	A.W.

Instructions regarding War Diaries and Intelligence Summaries are contained in F. S. Regs., Part II. and the Staff Manual respectively. Title pages will be prepared in manuscript.

WAR DIARY
or
INTELLIGENCE SUMMARY.
(Erase heading not required.)

Army Form C. 2118.

Place	Date	Hour	Summary of Events and Information	Remarks and references to Appendices
HILLHOEK	21.8.17.		Rations,proceeded for temporary duty with 2/1 FIELD AMBULANCE. 2 Motor Cycles attached to A.D.M.S. 437144 PTE OLDHALL F J wounded in action, evacuated to C C S & struck off the strength.	HWS
"	22.8.17.		CAPT.C H ROBSON R.A.M.C. T.C. proceeded for temporary duty with 2/1 FIELD AMBULANCE. CAPT.G.L.WILKINSON.R.A.M.C.T. proceeded for duty with 2/4/ GLOSTERS & struck off the strength CAPT.W.STOBIE.R.A.M.C.T. is attached for duty. A.D.M.S. 36 DIVISION visited C.R.S.	HWS
"	23.8.17.		437387 PTE GREEN.A.C. appointed 1st Class Nursing Orderly. 437452 PTE HARWOOD D W & 437520 PTE SHEPPEY T appointed 2nd Class Nursing Orderlies,437455 PTE STANFORD G.A.C. appointed 2nd Clerk,all with effect from 1.8.17. 437269 PTE MACFARLANE J H reported from Leave. 1 remount H D drawn from 61 Divisional Train. Under orders from A.D.M.S. 61 Division 2 BEARER SUB DIVISIONS CONSISTING OF 42 O.R. proceeded at 4.30.pm for duty with 2/3 FIELD AMBULANCE. MB/167360 PTE NETHERCOTT H M.T. ASC attached, discharged from Hospital; 437281 PTE ROBINSON L E 437383 PTE MATTHEWS D J Died of Wounds received in action.437263 SGT CRANER F 439169 L.CPL HURLEY W R 437454 PTE DOWD J E 437082 PTE SMITH A 437143 PTE MAYES W O 437390 PTE DAVIES S C E 437450 PTE TAYLOR A wounded in action,evacuated to C CS & struck off strength.	HWS
"	24.8.17.		2 DAIMLER CARS reported from detached duty with 2/1 FIELD AMBULANCE.437233 SGT WHITEHOUSE T.H. 437252 PTE CURETON F 437467 PTE WILTSHIRE D G reported for duty from leave. 437279 PT MITCHELL A J 437486 PTE GREEN W T admitted to hospital . 437471 PTE BARTLETT F discharged from hospital. Hospital Routine Work.	HWS
"	25.8.17		T4/248901 SGT TRING R J & T4/248885 DR EARL A E NO.4 CO A.S.C. attached , proceeded on leave . Under instructions from A.D.M.S. a Medical Board assembled, PRESIDENT MAJOR A T WATERHOUSE.R.A.M.C.T. MEMBERS:- CAPT R.D.MOORE R.A.M.C.T & CAPT A.J.WHATLEY R.A.M.C T.C. FOR THE purpose of classifying Class A men of H.T.& M.T. A.S.C. attached to this Unit. 435586 PTE PAYNE H 437507 PTE HARRIS R H C admitted to Hospital. 437180.PTE MEREDITH J F 437271.PTE MAYES J S 437466 PTE ROSCORLA A 437461 PTE TURNER N D 437458 PTE WILSON L Wounded in Action.	HWS
"	26.8.17		435581 PTE POWELL C reported for duty from C.C.S. and taken on the strength.	HWS

A5834 Wt. W4973/M687 750,000 8/16 D. D. & L. Ltd. Forms/C.2118/13.

Army Form C. 2118.

Instructions regarding War Diaries and Intelligence Summaries are contained in F. S. Regs., Part II. and the Staff Manual respectively. Title pages will be prepared in manuscript.

WAR DIARY or INTELLIGENCE SUMMARY.

(Erase heading not required.)

Place	Date	Hour	Summary of Events and Information	Remarks and references to Appendices
HILLHOEK	26.8.17		437507 Pte.HARRIS R.H. discharged from Hospital. Hospital Routine Work.	[initials]
"	27.8.17		437385 Pte.PAYNE A. 437180 Pte.MEREDITH J.F. 437271 Pte.MAYES J. 437466 Pte.ROSCORLA A. 437461 Pte.TURNER N.D. & 437458 Pte.WILSON L. discharged to Duty from Hospital. 437279 Pte.MITCHELL A. & 437486 Pte.GREEN W.T. discharged to Duty. T4/248895 Dr.OAKLEY C.J. A.S.C.attached admitted to Hospital. Routine Work.	[initials]
"	28.8.17		437521 Pte.FRANKUM J.F. admitted to Hospital "Gassed". 437213 L/Cpl.VIGURS E.N. admitted to Hospital & evacuated to C.C.S. & struck off strength. D.D.M.S. XIX Corps visited Rest Station. Hospital Routine Work.	[initials]
"	29.8.17		437441 Pte.O'LOUGHLIN L. & 437466 Pte.ROSCORLA A. appointed Sanitary Orderlies with pay. 437258 Sgt.MATHIAS J.R.L. 437370 L/Cpl.WALKER H. 437382 Pte.CARTER G. 322064 Pte. PETERSON 437218 Pte.JONES L. & 437510 Pte.MORRIS H. reported from 2/3 S.M.F.Amb. 6 Other Ranks proceeded for duty with 2/3 S.M.F.Amb. M2/113089 Pte.MULGROVE S. M.T.A.S.C. attached admitted to Hospital "Gassed". Under orders received from A.D.M.S. 61st.Divn. 4 R.Horses transferred to 61st.Divn.Artillery. Motor Bicycle & cyclist reported from duty with A.D.M.S. 61st.Divn. Motor Bicycle sent to Workshop with Broken Frame.	[initials]
"	30.8.17		437468 L/Cpl.WARDE W.& 437459 Pte.FLATTERY F.S. reported for duty from 58th.Scottish General Hospital & taken on the strength. Capt.STOBIE W. R.A.M.C.T.F. attached 2/5 R. Warwicks. 2 R.Horses transferred to 61st.Divn.Artillery. Motor Bicycle & Rider reported from Workshop. 51 O.Ranks of 2/1 S.M.F.Amb. bathed. 437388 Pte.Butler T.& 437499 Pte. HORTON B.J. reported as "MISSING" when on detached duty with 2/3 S.M.F.Amb. Authority A.D.M.S. 61st.Divn. 902M/17 dated 30.8.17.	[initials]
"	31.8.17		437478 Pte.WOODHEAD E. returned sick from 2/3 S.M.F.Amb. and admitted to Hospital. Hospital Routine Work.	

[signature] Lt Col. RAMC

B.E.F.

SUMMARY OF MEDICAL WAR DIARIES OF 2/2nd (S.M.) F.A. 61st Div.

5th Corps. 5th ARMY.

19th Corps from Aug. 15th.

5th Corps from 15th Sept.

To 17th Corps. 3rd ARMY from 18th Sept.

Western Front Operations -"July - November 1917."

Officer Commanding - Lt.Col. H.N. Burroughs (T).

SUMMARISED UNDER THE FOLLOWING HEADINGS:-

Phase "D" 1. Passchendaele Operations, "July - Nov. 1917"

(a) - Operations commencing 1/7/17.

(b) - Operations commencing 1/10/17.

Canadians attacked Passchendaele, Oct 30th.
Canadians took Passchendaele, Nov.6th.

Aug.	1st-14th.	Operations R.A.M.C. Routine and Training.
	15th.	Moves and Transfer. Unit transferred with 61st Div. to 19th Corps and moved to HILLHOEK.

2/2nd (S.M) F.A. 61st Div. 19th Corps. 5th ARMY. WESTERN FRONT. Aug-Sept./17

O.C. = Lt.Col. H.N. Burroughs (T).

To 5th Corps, from 15th Sept.

PHASE "D" 1. Passchendaele Operations, July - Nov. 1917.

(a) - Operations commencing 1/7/17.

	Headquarters at RUBROUCK.
Aug. 15th.	Moves and Transfer. Unit transferred with 61st Div. to 19th Corps and moved to HILLHOEK.
	Medical Arrangements. C.R.S. taken over from No. 110. F.A.
17th.	Moves. Detachment. "B" Section Br. S.D. to 2/3rd S.M. F.A.
21st.	Casualties R.A.M.C. 0 & 1 wounded.
23rd.	Moves. Detachment. 2 Br. S.D's to 2/3rd S.M. F.A.
	Casualties. R.A.M.C. 0 & 2 died of wounds. 0 & 7 wounded.
25th.	0 & 5 wounded.
28th.	Casualties R.A.M.C. Gas. 0 & 1 gassed.
30th.	Casualties R.A.M.C. 0 & 2 missing.
Sept. 7th.	Transfer. Unit transferred with 61st Div. to 5th Corps.

Aug. 1st-14th. Operations R.A.M.C. Routine and Training.

15th. Moves and Transfer. Unit transferred with 61st Div. to 19th Corps and moved to HILLHOEK.

2/2nd (S.M.) F.A. 61st Div. 19th Corps. 5th ARMY. WESTERN FRONT.

O.C. = Lt.Col. H.N. Burroughs (T). Aug.-Sept.1917

To 5th Corps, from 15th Sept.

PHASE "D" 1. Passchendaele Operations, July - Nov. 1917.

(a) - Operations commencing 1/7/17.

Headquarters at RUBROUCK.

Aug. 15th. Moves and Transfer. Unit transferred with 61st Div. to 19th Corps and moved to HILLHOEK.

Medical Arrangements. C.R.S. taken over from No. 110. F.A.

17th. Moves. Detachment. "B" Section Br. S.D. to 2/3rd S.M.) F.A.

21st. Casualties R.A.M.C. 0 & 1 wounded.

23rd. Moves. Detachment. 2 Br. S.D's to 2/3rd (S.M. F.A.

Casualties. R.A.M.C. 0 & 2 died of wounds. 0 & 7 wounded.

25th. 0 & 5 wounded.

28th. Casualties R.A.M.C. Gas. 0 & 1 gassed.

30th. Casualties R.A.M.C. 0 & 2 missing.

Sept. 7th. Transfer. Unit transferred with 61st Div. to 5th Corps.

MEDICAL

9

Vol 17

CONFIDENTIAL

WAR DIARY

2/2 S. Mid. Fd. Ambce.
R.A.M.C. (T.F.)

VOL - 17

September 1st. - 30th. (inclusive)
1917.

Instructions regarding War Diaries and Intelligence Summaries are contained in F. S. Regs., Part II. and the Staff Manual respectively. Title pages will be prepared in manuscript.

WAR DIARY
or
INTELLIGENCE SUMMARY.
(Erase heading not required.)

Army Form C. 2118.

Place	Date	Hour	Summary of Events and Information	Remarks and references to Appendices
HILLHOEK	I.9.I7		Capt.H.S.PEMBERTON R.A.M.C.S.R. proceeded for temporary duty to 2/3 S.Mid.Fld.Ambce. 437481 Pte.CLARKE J.K. & 437257 Pte.CRACKNELL J.L. reported for duty from C.C.S. and taken on the strength.6 H.D.horses;3 L.D.horses; 6 Drivers & 3 Ambulance Wagons reported from detached duty with 2/I S.Mid.FldAmbce.437483 Pte.NEWMAN F.J. admitted to Hospital and evacuated to C.C.S. and struck off strength. 437484 Pte.HUBAND F.P. admitted to Hospital.	HWB
"	2.9.I7		M2/113089 Pte MULGROVE S M.T. A S C attached Discharged to duty.322056 Pte GLASS N D evacuated to C C S & struck off Strength.	HWB
"	3.9.I7		437478 Pte WOODHEAD E W discharged from Hospital. Car No 10 with driver & orderly reported for duty from Workshop.437448 Pte Brockhouse A 437213 PTE SMITH A L & 439316 Pte DIKE A J reported from detached duty with 2/3 FIELD AMBULANCE.	HWB
"	4.9.I7		1 H D Horse drawn from No 3 Co.A S C & taken on the Strength. CAPT.H.S.PEMBERTON R.A.M.C SR reported from detached duty with 2/3 FIELD AMBULANCE.50929 PTE AGNEW A.10113 PTE FARRINGTON J 32267 PTE COATES A 201165 PTE LEATHER G 200704.PTE HAYES A 251998 PTE McNULTY E.251659 PTE DOHERTY M 49711 PTE CAFFREY J & 36131 PTE KENNEDY J reported for duty as Batmen with No 4 Co A S C attached.	HWB
"	5.9.I7		D.D.M.S. XIX CORPS visited REST STATION . CAPT.B.WALLACE R.A.M.C.(T.C.) reported for duty & taken on the strength. I.L.D. HORSE & 1 H D HORSE sent to 6I MOBILE VET.SECTION. 437020 SGT GREGORY J admitted to Hospital,evacuated to CCS & struck off strength. 437486 Pte GREEN W T 437457 PTE KIMBERLY C H W 437180 PTE MEREDITH J F & 437463 PTE HAYLOR B J returned sick from detached duty with 2/3 Field Ambulance. 437478 PTE WOODHEAD E W discharged from Hospital	HWB
"	6.9.I7		437484 PTE HUBAND F P discharged from Hospital .437466 PTE ROSCORLA A & M2/167659 PTE STEVENS H M.T. A.S.C attached, proceeded on Leave to ENGLAND.437487 PTE BURROWS W M & 437385 PTE PAYNE H returned from detached duty with 2/3 FIELD AMBULANCE. T4/248887 DR. GUEST V N NO.4 CO. A.S.C. attached, reported from C C S & taken on Strength. CAPT.DALE. WOOD. R.A.M.C.T. is attached for duty & rations.	HWB

A5834 Wt. W4973/M687 750,000 8/16 D. D. & L. Ltd. Forms/C.2118/13.

Instructions regarding War Diaries and Intelligence Summaries are contained in F. S. Regs., Part II. and the Staff Manual respectively. Title pages will be prepared in manuscript.

WAR DIARY
or
INTELLIGENCE SUMMARY.
(Erase heading not required.)

Army Form C. 2118.

Place	Date	Hour	Summary of Events and Information	Remarks and references to Appendices
HILLHOEK	7.9.17		Capt.J.L.WHATLEY R.A.M.C.T.C. & batman returned to 2/1/S.M.F.Amb. & struck off strength. T4/248896 Dr.RUBERY C.J. No.4 Coy.A.S.C. attached admitted to Hospital. A.D.M.S. 59th. Division visited Hospital. No.437531 Pte.FRANKUM J.W.discharged from Hospital.	H.W.
"	8.9.17		O.C. visited A.D.M.S.office. Capt.B.WALLACE B. R.A.M.C. proceeded to A.D.M.S. office for interview. No.437486 Pte.GREEN W.T. evacuated to C.C.S. & struck off strength. No.405104 Pte.CARNELL O.H.,No.390379 Pte.PARKIN J.,No.405500 Pte.LEE T.W.,No.405232 Pte. ANTHONY J.,No.388271 Pte.BARKER H.,& No.401058 Pte.GIBSON H.W. reported from the Base for Duty & taken on the strength. No.437487 Pte.BURROWS W.M. returned sick from detached duty with 2/3 S.M.F.Amb.& admitted to Hospital.	H.W.
"	9.9.17		Capt.B.WALLACE R.A.M.C. proceeded to Base & struck off strength. T4/248901 Sgt.TRING R.J. & T4/248885 Dr.EARL A.E. reported from leave. No.439570 Sgt.LOVELL W.T. proceeded for temporary duty with 2/3 S.M.F.Amb.vice No.437412 Sgt.Hickman F. returned. 8 men proceeded for temporary duty with 2/3 S.M.F.Amb.	H.W.
"	10.9.17		Capt.H.S.PEMBERTON R.A.M.C.S.R. proceeded to ENGLAND on duty & struck off strength. 1 H.D. horse returned for duty from 61st.Mobile Vet.Section. Lieut.E.V.WHITTAKER U.S.A.- M.O.R.C. reported for duty & taken on the strength. No.437531 Pte.FRANKUM J.W. discharged to duty.	H.W.
"	11.9.17		1 H.D. horse sent to 61st.Mobile Vet.Section. No.200714 Pte.HAYES A. 1/5 Manchesters attached transferred to 2/3 S.M.F.Amb. & struck off strength. 2 N.C.Os; proceeded for temporary duty with 2/3 S.M.F.Amb. No.437252 Pte.HOUGHTON J.D.R. evacuated to C.C.S. (Gassed in Action) & struck off strength.	H.W.
"	12.9.17		T4/248879 Dr.BAIDARO I; T1/648 Dr.BERRY J.T.;T4/248884 Dr.DODD F.;T4/248942 Dr.FREEBURY G. T4/248891 Dr.MILES W.;T4/248863 Dr.SMITH W.T.;T4/248899 DR.TEALE F.J.;& T1/38871 Dr. WHELAN W. No.4 Coy.A.S.C. attached proceeded to H.T.&.S.Depot & struck off strength. T4/036273 Dr.BLAND J.NO.4 Coy.A.S.C. attached reported for duty & taken on the strength.	H.W.
"	13.9.17		Capt.DALE WOOD R.A.M.C.T.C. & No.437342 Pte.RUSSELL H. proceeded for temporary duty with 2/3 S.M.F.Ambce.	H.W.

A5834 Wt.W4973/M687 750,000 8/16 D. D. & L. Ltd. Forms/C.2118/13.

Instructions regarding War Diaries and Intelligence Summaries are contained in F. S. Regs., Part II. and the Staff Manual respectively. Title pages will be prepared in manuscript.

WAR DIARY
or
INTELLIGENCE SUMMARY.
(Erase heading not required.)

Army Form C. 2118.

Place	Date	Hour	Summary of Events and Information	Remarks and references to Appendices
HILLHOEK	I4.9.I7		Advance Party of relieving Ambulance-2/2 North.Midland Field Ambulance- arrived to take over. Car No.I8 with driver & orderly reported from Workshop. No.437342 Pte.RUSSELL H. reported from detached duty with 2/3 S.M.F.Amb. T4/248896 Dr.RUBERY C.J.No.4 Coy.A.S.C. attached discharged to duty.	HWS
LEE CAMP. L.IO.c.9.2. Sheet 27.	I5.9.I7		The Ambulance was relieved by 2/2 North Midland Field Ambulance. Under orders received from I82 Infantry Brigade the Unit with Transport complete moved by March Route at I.30.pm. & arrived at L.IO.c.9.2. Sheet 27. at 2.30.pm. Operating Tent opened as Hospital for the reception of sick. No.437566 Pte.EVANS E.O.,No.437572 Pte.HUDSON E.G.,& No.437IOI Pte. LOVELESS W.H. reportedfromdetached duty with 6Ist.Divisional Depot Battalion. 23 N.C.Os;& Men reported from detached duty with 2/2 S.M.F.Ambce. Cars Nos.6 & 9 reported from detached duty.	HWS
"	I6.9.I7		Routine Work.	HWS
EECKE	I7.9.I7		Under orders received from I82 Infantry Brigade the U nit with Transport complete moved by March Route at 7.35.am.-Route:-HILLHOEK,ABEELE,STEENVOORDE,EECKE. location Sheet 27. Q.I9.a.3.6. Time of arrival-I2.0 noon. Falling out casualties NIL. Operating Tent erected as Hospital for reception of sick. No.4372I7 Pte.ARKELL A. evacuated to C.C.S. & struck off strength.	HWS
"	I8.9.I7		Car No.7 proceeded for temporary duty to A.D.M.S. Office. No.437305 Pte.GOURLAY W.J. & No.437385 Pte.PAYNE H. discharged from V Corps Rest Station & reported for duty.	HWS
~~ARRAS~~ BERNEVILLE	I9.9.I7		Under orders received from I82 Infantry Brigade the Horse Transport moved by March Route at II.I5.am. & entrained at CAESTRE STATION. Unit Personnel moved by March Route at I2.50.pm. & entrained at CAESTRE STATION. Time of Departure 3.5.pm. & arrived at ARRAS - 9.30.pm. The Unit with Transport detrained. Personnel proceeded by March Route to BERNEVILLE arriving at I2.I5.am.	HWS
"	20.9.I7		The Transport arrived at BERNEVILLE at 4.0.am. No.437466 Pte ROSCORLA A. & M2/I67659 Pte.STEVENS H.-M.T.A.S.C. attached reported from leave. No.4374II Sgt.OAKES R.J. proceeded to TANK DUMP,Advanced Dressing Station,for instruction with 5Ist.Fld.Ambce. No.437235 Sgt. WHITEHOUSE T.H. proceeded to L'ABBAYETTE, Advanced Dressing Station,fot instruction by 53rd.Fld.Ambce. O.C.,Major A.T.WATERHOUSE R.A.M.C.T.F.,& Capt.R.D.MOORE R.A.M.C.T.F. visited TANK DUMP & SUPPORT LINES.	HWS

Instructions regarding War Diaries and Intelligence Summaries are contained in F. S. Regs., Part II. and the Staff Manual respectively. Title pages will be prepared in manuscript.

WAR DIARY
or
INTELLIGENCE SUMMARY.
(Erase heading not required.)

Army Form C. 2118.

Place	Date	Hour	Summary of Events and Information	Remarks and references to Appendices
BERNEVILLE	21.9.17.		A party of 9 N C.Os & men proceeded as an Advance Party to Sheet 51B H.11.a.5.5 TANK DUMP Advanced Dressing Station preparatory to taking over. LT.QMR.O.BASTABLE visited TANK DUMP & Support Lines.	Hms
"	22.9.17.		Car No 7 reported from detached duty. An Advance Party proceeded to ST.NICHOLAS preparatory to relieving 51St Field Ambulance.	Hms
"	23.9.17.		No 437225 CPL DOLMAN.A.V.& 437209 Pte TONKS J proceeded on leave to ENGLAND. 437368 Pte FELL A evacuated to C C S & struck off strength .Advance Parties proceeded for duty to ST. NICHOLAS, Loading Post & TANK DUMP. Capt.R.D.MOORE.R.A.M.C.T. proceeded for duty to TANK DUMP Advanced Dressing Station.	Hms
" ST.NICHOLAS	24.9.17.		Under orders received from 182nd Infantry Brigade the remaining personnel of unit & transport moved by March Route at 9.30.am. Route - WARLUS?DAINVILLE,ARRAS,ST.NICHOLAS. Time of arrival 11.30.am. Hospital opened for the reception of sick.437032 Staff Sgt CUMMINGS T. 437361 Pte FREEMAN H W 437386 Pte PARKES G A C & 74599 Pte GAYLAND T evacuated to XVll Corps Rest Station. A party proceeded for duty to L'ABBAYETTE Advanced Dressing Station. Major A T Waterhouse R.A.M.C.T. proceeded to L'ABBAYETTE Advanced Dressing Station for duty The following Advanced Dressing Stations & Posts have been taken over for the clearing of Sick & Wounded from the Left Sector of the Divisional Front(GREENLAND HILL SECTOR) Sheet 51 B Advanced Dressing Station TANK DUMP H.11.a.5.5: Wheeled Stretcher Post on ATHIES-FAMPOUX Road at H.16.d 4.4. Inaddition to these,Field Ambulance Personnel are kept at R.A.P's. of right & left battalions in the front line of Left Sector-situated at H.6.c;3.8. and H.12.b.8.3. The method of evacuation is by carry from R.A.P.to A.D.S.at TANK DUMP, thence by wheeled stretcher or carry outside the trench to wheeled stretcher post at H.16.d;4.4.-thence by wheeled stretcher 400 yards down ATHIES-FAMPOUX ROAD-thence by car to Main Dressing Station (HOSPICE DES VIEILLARDS-ARRAS) calling on the way at ADVANCED POST at L'ABBAYETTE,H.14.b.7.1.	Hms
"	25.9.17.		437101 St.Sgt.MARTIN R.P. reported for duty from 58th.(Scottish) General Hospital and taken on the strength. Capt.C.H.ROBSON R.A.M.C.T.C. reported from detached duty with 2/3 S.M.F.Ambce. Lieut.E.V.WHITTAKER U.S.A.-M.O.R.C. proceeded for duty at TANK DUMP,A.D.S.	Hms

Instructions regarding War Diaries and Intelligence Summaries are contained in F. S. Regs., Part II. and the Staff Manual respectively. Title pages will be prepared in manuscript.

WAR DIARY

or

INTELLIGENCE SUMMARY.

(*Erase heading not required.*)

Army Form C. 2118.

Place	Date	Hour	Summary of Events and Information	Remarks and references to Appendices
ST.NICHOLAS	25.8.I7		No.437032 St.Sgt.CUMMINGS evacuated to Corps Rest Station.	HWB
"	26.9.I7		No.437IOI Pte.LOVELESS W.H. proceeded for temporary duty to 6Ist.Depot Battalion. No.437566 Pte.EVANS E.O. proceeded for temporary duty to 6Ist.Divisional Baths. 437470 Pte COOPER R. proceeded to Base Depot for Dental Treatment & struck off strength. O.C.went to inspect Advanced Water Reservoir at H IO.a; with a view to chlorinating the water there for consumption in the trenches. This scheme is not practicable as the reservoir is in an exposed position,is of 6000 gallons capacity & contains a varying quantity of water. No.437490 Pte.EDGINGTON B.J. reported for duty from Base & taken on the strength.	HWB
"	27.9.I7.		A.D.M.S. 6Ist.Division visited H.Qrs. O.C. visited Advanced Dressing Station at TANK DUMP D.D.M.S. XVII Corps visited Headquarters & inspected the billets & horse lines. O.C. & other officers visited the Divisional Theatre & were vastly entertained. I L.D. horse received from 6Ist.Divn.MoB.Vet. & taken on the strength. H.D.horse that was evacuated to 6Ist.Mobile Vet.Section II.9.I7. Destroyed & struck off strength.	HWB
"	28.9.I7.		Alterations & improvements to billets etc. continued. Routine Work. 437360 Pte.FINDLAY F.L. reported for duty from C.C.S. & taken on the strength.	HWB
"	29.9.I7.		T4/248882 Dr.BURLING E.J. reported for duty from Corps Rest Station. O.C. visited Advanced Medical Posts of the Right Sector of the Divisional Front with O.C. 2/I Field Ambulance.	HWB
"	30.9.I7.		No.323056 Pte.GLASS N.D. reported from C.C.S. & taken on the strength. No.32205I Pte. HENDERSON C.G.,I009I6 Pte.GRIMSHAW T.& I05I37 Pte.GOWER J.E. reported for duty from XIX Corps Re-inforcement Depot. No.437463 Pte.HAYLOR B.J. reported from leave. Sgt.Major JACKSON H.C. & Q.M.Sgt.FOSS S.E. visited ~~IX~~ L'ABBAYETTE & TANK DUMP Advanced Dressing Stations.	HWB

HWB[illegible]
Lt Col

A5834 Wt. W4973/M687 750,000 8/16 D. D. & L. Ltd. Forms/C.2118/13.

2/2nd (S.M) F.A. 61st Div. 5th Corps. 5th ARMY. WESTERN FRONT
Sept. 1917.

O.C. = Lt.Col. H.N. Burroughs (T).

Transfer. To 17th Corps, 3rd ARMY.

PHASE "D" 1. Passchendaele Operations, July-Nov. 1917.

(a) - Operations commencing 1/7/17.

Sept. 7th. Transfer. Unit transferred with 61st Div. to 5th Corps.

15th. Medical Arrangements. C.R.S. handed over to 2/2nd N.M.F.A.

Moves. To L.10.C.9.2. (Sheet 27).

17th. To EECKE.

18th. Transfer.) Unit transferred with 61st Div. to 17th
and Moves.) Corps, 3rd ARMY and moved to BERNEVILLE.

2/2nd (S.M) F.A. 61st Div. 5th Corps. 5th ARMY. WESTERN FRONT
Sept. 1917.

O.C. = Lt.Col. H.N. Burroughs (T).

Transfer. To 17th Corps, 3rd ARMY.

PHASE "D" 1. Passchendaele Operations, July-Nov. 1917.

(a) - Operations commencing 1/7/17.

Sept. 7th. Transfer. Unit transferred with 61st Div. to 5th Corps.

15th. Medical Arrangements. C.R.S. handed over to 2/2nd N.M.F.A.

Moves. To L.10.C.9.2. (Sheet 27).

17th. To EECKE.

18th. Transfer.) Unit transferred with 61st Div. to 17th
and Moves.) Corps, 3rd ARMY and moved to BERNEVILLE.

11

CONFIDENTIAL

WAR DIARY.

2/2. Sth Mid. Fld Ambce
R. A. M. C. T. F.

October 1st - 31st (inclusive).
1917

Volume - 18.

Instructions regarding War Diaries and Intelligence Summaries are contained in F. S. Regs., Part II. and the Staff Manual respectively. Title pages will be prepared in manuscript.

WAR DIARY
or
INTELLIGENCE SUMMARY.

(Erase heading not required.)

Army Form C. 2118.

Place	Date	Hour	Summary of Events and Information	Remarks and references to Appendices
ST.NICHOLAS ARRAS	I.IO.I7.		Capt.C.H.ROBSON R.A.M.C.T.C.,No.437348 Sgt.CHATTAWAY W.J.,437434 Sgt.BIRKBY L.,437364 Pte.SMITH E.,437460 Pte.DAVIES H.F.,437516 Pte.TAYLOR A.E., 437501 Pte.EKINS A.A. 437523 Pte.STANWELL L.G.,437336 Pte.HAWKINS W.A.,T4/248709 Dr.PORTSMOUTH J. No.4 Coy. A.S.C. attached & MB/099465 Pte.WEAVER J. M.T.A.S.C. attached proceeded on leave to ENGLAND. Lieut.E.V.WHITTAKER M.O.R.C.,U.S.A. proceeded for temporary duty to XVII Corps Reinforcement Camp. I.H.D. horse drawn from 2/I Fld.Ambce. & taken on the strength. O.C. Visited A.D.S.TANK DUMP and L'ABBAYETTE. No.437506 Pte.DEAN C.R. reported for duty from 6ist.Divn.Baths. No.437386 Pte.PARKES G.A.E. REPORTED for duty from C.R.S. I.H.D. horse drawn from No.3 Coy.A.S.C. & taken on the strength. I.H.D. horse sent to 6ist.Mobile Vet.Section.	[illegible]
"	2.IO.I7.		No.437032 St.Sgt.CUMMINGS T. & No.74599 Pte.GAYLAND T. reported for duty from C.R.S. O.C. visited Advanced Dressing Stations with two Surgeons of U.S.R. for instructional purposes.	[illegible]
"	3.IO.I7.		No.437255 Pte.WILLIAMS C. -"Wounded in Action " on Ist.inst. was transferred to C.R.S. O.C. visited A.D.S. TANK DUMP. I H.D. sent to 6ist.Mobile Vet.Section on I.IO.I7. evacuated to Base & struck off strength.	[illegible]
"	4.IO.I7.		Routine Work. No.437498 Pte.CALLANAN G.C. admitted to Hospital & evacuated to 2/3 Fld. Ambce.	[illegible]
"	5.IO.I7.		Routine Work. 437312 Pte.DURY W.H., 437107 Pte.NICHOLLS F.W.,437334 Pte.TAYLOR A.G. 437487 Pte.BURROWS W.M., 437075 Pte.RUSSON W.J.,T4/248882 Dr.BURLING E.J. No.4 Coy. A.S.C. attached & MB/079035 Pte.MORTON K.W .,M.T.A.S.C. attached granted leave of absence to ENGLAND.	[illegible]
"	6.IO.I7.		No.437109 Pte.GREW C. proceeded to Base Depot for"Dental Treatment" & struck off strength No.437225 Cpl.DOLMAN A.V. reported for duty from leave of absence.	[illegible]

Instructions regarding War Diaries and Intelligence Summaries are contained in F. S. Regs., Part II. and the Staff Manual respectively. Title pages will be prepared in manuscript.

WAR DIARY

~~or~~

~~INTELLIGENCE SUMMARY.~~

(Erase heading not required.)

Army Form C. 2118.

Place	Date	Hour	Summary of Events and Information	Remarks and references to Appendices
ST·NICHOLAS ARRAS·	7·IO·I7·		No·43709I Pte·COX·R· proceeded for course of Cookery to Third Army School of Cookery ALBERT· Water cart & orderly returned for duty from Workshop· 22 N·C·O's & Men proceeded on IO days leave of absence to England· No·437006 S·Maj·JACKSON H·C· proceeded on one month's leave of absence to England·. No·437326 Pte·RILEY A·J· proceeded for temporary duty to 6Ist·Divn·Workshops·	H.M.
"	8·IO·I7·		Routine Work· No·437294 Pte·COX G· evacuated sick to 2/3 Fld·Ambce·	H.M.
"	9·IO·I7·		Routine Work· D·D·M·S·XVII Corps visited Headquarters & Billets· O·C· visited AD·S· TANK DUMP· No·437282 Pte·BANNISTER W·J· reported for duty from XVII C·R·Station·	H.M.
"	IO·IO·I7·		Routine Work·	H.M.
"	II·IO·I7·		Car No·9 sent to Workshop for fitting of Heating Apparatus·No·43727I Pte·MAYES J·S· admitted to hospital & evacuated to 2/3 Fld·Ambce·	H.M.
"	I2·IO·I7·		No·43727I Pte·MAYES J·S·,437498 Pte·CALLANAN G·C· & 437294 Pte·COX G· reported for duty from 2/3 Fld·Ambce· Routine Work·	H.M.
"	I3·IO·I7·		M2/I67346 Pte·SCOTT E·R· M·T·A·S·C· attached reported for duty from C·R·Station·	H.M.
"	I4·IO·I7·		Lieut· & Q·Mr· O·BASTABLE R·A·M·C·T· & I3 Other Ranks proceeded on leave to England· Car No·9 reported for duty from Workshop·	H.M.
"	I5·IO·I7·		Routine Work· No·43736I Pte·FREEMAN H·W· evacuated from C·R·S· to C·C·S· & struck off the strength·	H.M.
"	I6·IO·I7·		Capt·C·H·ROBSON R·A·M·C·T·C· reported back from leave· Routine Work·	H.M.
"	I7·IO·I7·		6 Men returned from leave· Routine Work·	H.M.
"	I8·IO·I7·		D·M·S· Third Army accompanied by D·D·M·S·XVII Corps & acting A·D·M·S·6Ist·Division inspected the Headquarters of the Unit,Medical Inspection hut and Men's Billets and Horse Lines· A visit of inspection was then made to L'ABBAYETTE A·D·S·	H.M.

A5834 Wt.W4973/M687 750,000 8/16 D. D. & L. Ltd. Forms/C.2118/13.

Army Form C. 2118.

Instructions regarding War Diaries and Intelligence Summaries are contained in F. S. Regs., Part II. and the Staff Manual respectively. Title pages will be prepared in manuscript.

WAR DIARY
or
~~INTELLIGENCE SUMMARY~~
(Erase heading not required.)

Place	Date	Hour	Summary of Events and Information	Remarks and references to Appendices
ST·NICHOLAS ARRAS·	I8·I0·I7·		1 man reported from leave· Capt C·H·ROBSON·R·A·M·C· T·C· proceeded for duty to TANK DUMP A·D·S· vice Capt·R·D·MOORE R·A·M·C·T·who reported to headquarters·	H.W.B.
"	I9·I0·I7·		1 Motor Ambulance proceeded to Workshop· O·C· visited A·D·S· TANK DUMP & reconnoitred road from H·10 a 5·5 to H 17 b 6·0 with a view to evacuating cases at night by Ford Car	H.W.B.
"	20·I0·I7·		2 N·C·O·s & 3 men reported from leave· CAPT·L E BOLSTER R·A·M·C· T·C ,CAPT·R·N·WATSON R·A·M·C· T·C· & LIEUT·W·L·M·DAY·R·A·M·C· T·C· reported for duty and taken on,the strength· O·C· visited TANK DUMP & site of proposed new R·A·P· IN CALEDONIAN AVENUE H·6·d 5·6	H.W.B.
"	2I·I0·I7·		1 N·C·O· & 3men reported from leave· 1 N·C·O· & 11 men proceeded on leave to ENGLAND· O·C· visited TANK DUMP A·D·S· & L'ABBAYETTE A·D·S·	H.W.B.
"	22·I0·I7·		Capt·R·D·MOORE R·A·M·C·T· proceeded for duty to L'ABBAYETTE A·D·S· vice Major A·T· WATERHOUSE R·A·M·C·T· who returned to Hqrs· CAPT R·N·WATSON R·A·M·C·T·C· Proceeded to A·D·S· L'ABBAYETTE for instruction and duty· PTE HARWOOD F No43740I reported from leave	H.W.B.
"	23·I0·I7		Lieut W·L·M·Day proceeded for duty to A·D·S·TANK DUMP · Lt·Col H·N·BURROUGHES R·A·M·C·T PROCEEDED on leave to England and Major A·T·WATERHOUSE R·A·M·C·T·F· assumed command of the Unit· A·D·M·S· visited Hqrs· A·D·M·S· XVII Corps inspected transport and expressed his approval before leaving· O·C·visited L'ABBAYETTE and TANK DUMP A·D·S's· No437255 PteWILLIAMS C· reported for duty from C·R·S·· 1·H·D· evacuated to 6Ist·M·V·SECTION·	A.T.W.
"	24·I0·I7		O·C·Visited A·D·S's· No43550I PteAUSTIN E·H· reported for duty from 2/3·Fld Ambce· Capt R·D·MOORE R·A·M·C·T· PROCEEDED from A·D·S· L'ABBAYETTE to A·D·S· TANK DUMP·	A.T.W.
"	25·I0·I7		Capt C·H·ROBSON R·A·M·C·T·C· returned to Hqrs for duty from A·D·S· TANK DUMP· No43709I Pte Cox R· reported for duty from Course of Cookery at Third Army School of Cookery, ALBERT· No T4/248878 Dr ADAMS J· reported from leave· Lieut W·L·M·DAY R·A·M·C·T·C· reported for duty from A·D·S· TANK DUMP·	A.T.W.
"	26·I0·I7		A·D·M·S· 6Ist Div· visited Hqrs and Camp· O·C· visited A·D·S's· No 437334 Pte TAYLOR A·G admitted to hospital and evacuated to 2/3·Field Ambce·	A.T.W.

Instructions regarding War Diaries and Intelligence Summaries are contained in F. S. Regs., Part II. and the Staff Manual respectively. Title pages will be prepared in manuscript.

WAR DIARY

or

~~INTELLIGENCE SUMMARY~~

(Erase heading not required.)

Army Form C. 2118.

Place	Date	Hour	Summary of Events and Information	Remarks and references to Appendices
ST·NICHOLAS .ARRAS·	27·IO·I7·		Lieut &Q·Mr O·BASTABLE R·A·M·C·T· and IO·other ranks reported from leave· No439538 Pte BRAKE F·E· admitted to Hospital and evacuated to 2/3·Field Ambulance· ROUTINE.WORK·	A.T.W.
"	28·IO·I7·		Capt C·H·ROBSON R·A·M·C·T·C· proceeded to A·D·S· TANK DUMP vice Capt R·D·MOORE R·A·M·C·T who reported to Hqrs for duty· Capt L·E·BOLSTER R·A·M·C·T·C· proceeded to 2/5·Glosters for temporary duty· Capt R·D·MOORE R·A·M·C·T· & I2·Other Ranks proceeded on leave to England· ROUTINE.WORK·	A.T.W.
"	29·IO·I7·		No20II65 Pte LEATHER G· (I/5·Manchesters attached·) proceeded on leave to England· No437I38 Sgt DOGGETT H· & No390379 Pte PARKIN J· admitted to hospital & evacuated to 2/3·Fld Ambce·	A.T.W.
"	30·IO·I7·		8·men proceeded to H·6·d 5·5· to assist in constructing new R·A·P· No439538 Pte BRAKE F·E· & No437334 Pte TAYLOR A·G· reported for duty from 2/3/Fld Ambce: NoM2/I56597 Pte WILLIAMS.W REPORTED from detached duty with A·D·M·S· Office· No T4/248799 Dr SPRINGHAM S Admitted to hospital and evacuated to 2/3·Fld Ambce·.	A.T.W.
" "	31·IO·I7·		No437326 Pte RILEY A·H· reported from detached duty with 6Ist Div·Supply Column· No437212 L'Cpl VIGURS E·N· reported from Base for duty and taken on the strength· Capt L·E·BOLSTER R·A·M·C·T·C· reported from detached duty with 2/5th Glosters·	A.T.W.

A.T. Waterhouse Major RAMCT
Actg O.C. 2/2 South Midland
Field Ambulance

A5834 Wt. W4973/M687 750,000 8/16 D. D. & L. Ltd. Forms/C.2118/13.

Nov. 1917 17 CONFIDENTIAL Medical

140/2878

WAR DIARY Vol 19

2/2 S. Mid. Fd. Ambce
R.A.M.C.T.

November 1st. – 30th
(inclusive) 1917

VOL 19.

Army Form C. 2118.

Instructions regarding War Diaries and Intelligence Summaries are contained in F. S. Regs., Part II. and the Staff Manual respectively. Title pages will be prepared in manuscript.

WAR DIARY

~~or~~

~~INTELLIGENCE SUMMARY.~~

(Erase heading not required.)

Place	Date	Hour	Summary of Events and Information	Remarks and references to Appendices
ST·NICHOLAS ARRAS	I·II·I7·		Capt·L·E·BOLSTER R·A·M·C·T·C· proceeded to TANK DUMP for duty· A·D·M·S· visited H'Qrs O·C· visited Advanced Dressing Stations· No·43726I Sgt·JONES P·B· admitted to hospital whilst on leave in England 25·IO·I7·	
"	2·II·I7·		No·390379 Pte·PARKIN J· reported for duty from 2/3 S·M·F·Ambce· 8 Other Ranks reported from leave·	
"	3·II·I7·		No·435530 Cpl·LUCAS J· proceeded for temporary duty to Brigade Schools· I man reported from leave·	
"	4·II·I7·		Lieut·Col·H·N·BURROUGHES R·A·M·C·T·F· reported from leave and re-assumed command of the Unit·. 8 men proceeded on leave to England· I N·C·O· reported from leave·	
"	5·II·I7·		Capt·L·E·BOLSTER R·A·M·C·T·C· proceeded for temporary duty to I/5 D·C·L·I· T4/248828 Dr·HOWARD G·N· No·4 Coy·A·S·C· attached proceeded for temporary duty to 6Ist·D·S·C· No·390379 Pte·PARKIN J· admitted to Hospital & evacuated to C·C·S· and struck off strength· T4/248779 Dr·SPRINGHAM S·R· No·4 Coy·A·S·C·attached reported for duty from hospital·	
"	6·11·17·		Major A·T·WATERHOUSE R·A·M·C·T·F· & 6 men proceeded on leave to England· No·437016 L/Sgt· DOLPHIN J·D· admitted to Hospital & transferred to 2/3 S·Mid·Fld·Ambce·	
"	7·11·17·		Lieut·O·BASTABLE R·A·M·C·T·F·,St·Sergt·WHITEHOUSE T·H· and cooks attended a lecture at 2/3 Field Ambulance given by The Commandant Third Army School of Cookery·No·437016 L/Sgt· DOLPHIN J·D· evacuated to C·C·S· and struck off strength· No·437212 L/Cpl·VIGURS E·N· admitted to Hospital & transferred to 2/3 Field Ambulance·	
"	8·11·17·		No·437006 T/Sgt·Major JACKSON H·C· reported from leave· I·N·C·O· & 7 men proceeded on leave to England· O·C· visited TANK DUMP– New exit for A·D·S· into CABLE TRENCH planned·	
"	9·11·17·		1 N·C·O· & 8 men returned from leave· Routine Work·	

A5834 Wt W4973/M687 750,000 8/16 D. D. & L. Ltd. Forms/C.2118/13.

Instructions regarding War Diaries and Intelligence Summaries are contained in F. S. Regs., Part II. and the Staff Manual respectively. Title pages will be prepared in manuscript.

WAR DIARY

~~INTELLIGENCE SUMMARY~~

(Erase heading not required.)

Army Form C. 2118.

Place	Date	Hour	Summary of Events and Information	Remarks and references to Appendices
ST·NICHOLAS ARRAS·	10·11·17·		437261 Sgt·JONES P·B· posted to Southern Command for temporary Home Service & struck off strength to take effect from 29·10·17· No·437222 Pte·HIGGS C·R· "Wounded in Action" but remained on duty· No·437180 Pte·MEREDITH J·F· admitted to Hospital & evacuated to 2/3 S·M·Fld·Ambce·	[initials]
"	11·11·17·		Car No·44005 with driver & orderly proceeded to 61st·D·S·C·Workshops· No·437212 L/Cpl· VIGURS E·N· reported for duty from Hospital· No·437522 Pte·GORDON A·H· admitted to Hospital & evacuated to 2/3 S·M·Fld·Ambce·	[initials]
"	12·11·17·		Car No·10, having been hit by a shell fragment, proceeded to Workshop· No·437138 Sgt· DOGGETT H· reported for duty from XVII Corps Rest Station· Capt·R·D·MOORE R·A·M·C·T·F· & 1 man reported from leave·	[initials]
"	13·11·17·		No·201165. Pte·LEATHER G· 1/5 Manchesters attached admitted to Hospital & evacuated to 2/3 S·M·Fld·Ambce·	[initials]
"	14·11·17·		Capt·R·D·MOORE R·A·M·C·T·F· proceeded for duty to A·D·S· L'ABBAYETTE vice Capt·R·N· WATSON R·A·M·C·T·C· returned to Hqrs· Car No·44005 with driver & orderly returned from Workshop· Under instructions from A·D·M·S·61st·Division Lieut·W·L·M·DAY R·A·M·C·T·C· proceeded for temporary duty to 19 C·C·S· vice Capt·G·L·WILKINSON R·A·M·C·T·F· who proceeded to 61st·Divn·Depot Battn· vice Lieut·E·V·WHITAKER M·O·R·C·,U·S·A· who report- for duty with unit· No·437138 Sgt·DOGGETT H· evacuated to C·C·S· & struck off strength· No·201165 Pte·LEATHER G· 1/5 Manchesters attached evacuated to C·C·S· & struck off strength·	[initials]
"	15·11·17·		Capt·R·N·WATSON R·A·M·C·T·C· returned to England "Expiration of Contract" & struck off strength· No·T4/248828 Dr·HOWARD G·N· No·4 Coy·A·S·C·attached reported for duty from 61st·D·S·C·	[initials]
"	16·11·17·		No·437522 Pte·GORDON A·H· reported for duty from 2/3 S·M·Fld·Ambce· Routine Work·	[initials]
"	17·11·17·		10 men proceeded on leave to England· Routine Work·	[initials]

2353 Wt. W2544/1454 700,000 5/15 D. D. & L. A.D.S.S./Forms/C. 2118.

Instructions regarding War Diaries and Intelligence Summaries are contained in F. S. Regs., Part II. and the Staff Manual respectively. Title pages will be prepared in manuscript.

WAR DIARY

or

~~INTELLIGENCE SUMMARY~~

(Erase heading not required.)

Army Form C. 2118.

Place	Date	Hour	Summary of Events and Information	Remarks and references to Appendices
ST·NICHOLAS ARRAS	18·11·17		Lieut·E·V·WHITAKER M·O·R·C·,U·S·A· & 14 Other Ranks proceeded for temporary duty to No·3,C·C·S· No·543003 Sergt·DRYSDALE G·W· reported for duty & taken on the strength·	HWS
"	19·11·17		10 Men proceeded on leave to England· Routine Work·	
"	20·11·17·		No·437297 Pte·ENGLISH W·J· admitted to Hospital & evacuated to 2/3 S·M·Fld·Ambulance· Routine Work·	HWS
"	21·11·17·		Car No·9951 with driver sent to Workshop and returned for duty in the evening· Routine Work·	HWS
"	22·11·17·		7 Men reported from leave· Car No·29115 with driver sent to Workshop and returned for duty in the evening· Routine Work·	HWS
"	23·11·17		Routine Work·	HWS
"	24·11·17		Major A·T·WATERHOUSE R·A·M·C·T·F· & 6 Other Ranks reported from leave· 10 Other Ranks proceeded on leave to England· Capt·L·E·BOLSTER R·A·M·C·T·C· reported for duty from 1/5 D·C·L·I· Car No·24952 with driver proceeded to Workshop·	HWS
"	25·11·17·		No·437470 Pte·COOPER R· reported for duty & taken on the strength· Capt·L·E·BOLSTER R·A·M·C·T·C· proceeded for temporary duty to XVll Corps Rest Station·No·437490 L/Cpl· EDGINGTON B·J· proceeded for a "Course" at XVll Corps Gas School· Major A·T·WATERHOUSE R·A·M·C·T·F·proceeded for duty to L'ABBAYETTE,A·D·S· vice Capt·R·D·MOORE R·A·M·C·T·F· who proceeded for duty to TANK DUMP A·D·S·,vice Capt·C·H·ROBSON R·A·M·C·T·C· who reported to Hqrs for duty·Under instructions from A·D·M·S·61st·Division, Lieut·W·L·M·DAY R·A·M·C·T·C· & Capt·L·E·BOLSTER R·A·M·C·T·C· were transferred to 2/3 S·M·Fld·Ambulance & struck off strength· 1st·Lieut·B·J·GALLAGHER M·O·R·C·,U·S·A· & 1st·Lieut·R·J·ERICKSON M·O·R·C·,U·S·A· reported for duty & taken on the strength·	HWS

2353 Wt. W2544/1454 700,000 5/15 D. D. & L. A.D.S.S./Forms/C. 2118.

Instructions regarding War Diaries and Intelligence Summaries are contained in F. S. Regs., Part II. and the Staff Manual respectively. Title pages will be prepared in manuscript.

WAR DIARY

or

~~INTELLIGENCE SUMMARY~~.

(Erase heading not required.)

Army Form C. 2118.

Place	Date	Hour	Summary of Events and Information	Remarks and references to Appendices
ST NICHOLAS ARRAS	26·11·17		Car No 24942 with driver reported for duty from w'shop. No 437180 Pte MEREDITH J F & 437180 PTE ENGLISH W J reported for duty from Hospital.	HWS
"	27·11·17		Routine Work.	
"	28·11·17.		Advance Parties of relieving Field Ambulances (45th & 46th) arrived; Capt C.H.ROBSON. R.A.M.C. T.C. & batman proceeded for temporary duty to 2/4 GLOSTERS. 2 men proceeded on Leave.	HWS
" WANQUETIN	29·11·17		The unit was relieved by 45th & 46th Field Ambulances. Under instructions from A.D.M.S. 61 Division the unit with Transport complete moved at 10.0.am .Route-ARRAS-DAINVILLE-WARLUS-WANQUETIN. Time of arrival 1.30.pm. Falling Out Casualties-NIL.	HWS
" HAVRINCOURT.WOOD	30·11·17		Under Orders received from 182 Infantry Brigade the Ambulance less Transport moved at 6.45.am & arrived at BEAUMETZ-LES-LOGES Station at 8.0.am. Unit entrained & moved at 9.0 am. Detrained at BAPAUME at 10.30.am,thence proceeded by Bus & debussed at RUYAULCOURT, thence the unit proceeded by road to HAVRINCOURT WOOD . Time of arrival 6.0.pM. The Horse Transport under MAJOR A T WATERHOUSE R.A.M.C.T.MOVED with & under the Orders of 182 Infantry Brigade Transport.	HWS

H.W. ... Lt Col RAMC T.

14 CONFIDENTIAL Medical

Vol 20

Dec. 1917

WAR DIARY

2/2 S. Mid. Fd. Amb.
R.A.M.C.T.

VOL 20

Dec. 1st – 31st (inclusive)
1917

Instructions regarding War Diaries and Intelligence Summaries are contained in F. S. Regs., Part II. and the Staff Manual respectively. Title pages will be prepared in manuscript.

Army [illegible] C. 2118.

WAR DIARY
or
~~INTELLIGENCE SUMMARY.~~
(*Erase heading not required.*)

Place	Date	Hour	Summary of Events and Information	Remarks and references to Appendices
HAVRINCOURT WOOD. FINS.	1·12·17		The Unit moved by march route at 3·30·am· via METZ and arrived at FINS at 5·20·am· Horse Transport under MAJOR A/T·WATERHOUSE R·A·M·C·T·F· arrived at 11·0·am· No·437348 Sgt·CHATTAWAY W·J· & No·437475 Pte·ADAWAY G· admitted to Hospital & evacuated to 111 C·M·D·Station· Capt·C·H·ROBSON R·A·M·C·T·C· attached 2/4 Glosters "Killed in Action·"	[illegible]
"	2·12·17		Unders orders received from A·D·M·S·61st·Division Capt·R·D·MOORE R·A·M·C·T·F· & Lieut·R·J·ERICKSON M·O·R·C·,U·S·A· & 46 Other Ranks proceeded for temporary duty to 2/3 S·M·Fld·Ambce· Lieut·B·J·GALLAGHER M·O·R·C·,U·S·A·proceeded for temporary duty to 2/4 Glosters· 3 Other Ranks proceeded as clerks to 111 C·M·D·S· 24 Other Ranks proceeded for temporary duty to 2/3 S·M·Fld·AMBCE·	[illegible]
EQUANCOURT	3·12·17		No·437490 L/Cpl·EDGINGTON B·J· reported for duty from "Gas Course·" No·437368 Pte· FELL A·, & No·437109 Pte·GREW C· reported from Base & taken on the strength· 1 man reported from leave· Underx orders received from A·D·M·S· 61st·Division the remaining portion of Unit moved to EQUANCOURT, time of arrival 11·0·am· 7 Other Ranks proceeded for temporary duty to 2/3 S·M·Fld·Ambce· No·437508 Pte·BLADON T·H· reported as " MISSING"	[illegible]
"	4·12·17·		No·437459 Pte·FLATTERY F·S· reported sick from detached duty with 2/3 S·M·Fld·Ambce· & evacuated to 111 C·M·D·S·	[illegible]
"	5·12·17·		10 men reported from leave· 1 H·D·Horse sent to 61st·Mobile Vet·Section· No·437180 Pte·MEREDITH J·F· & No·251998 Pte·McNulty E· 1/6 Manchesters attached admitted to Hospital & evacuated to 111 C·M·D·S· No·439571 A/Sgt·DERRICK C·J·,No·74599 Pte·GAYLARD T·, No·437320 Pte·GARDNER A·, No·437471 Pte·BARTLETT F·, & No·437498 Pte·CALLANAN G·C· " Gassed" evacuated to C·C·S·& struck off strength· No·105137 Pte·GOWER J·E· " Wounded in Action", evacuated to C·C·S· & struck off strength· No·322056 Pte·GLASS N·D·evacuated to C·C·S· suffering from "Exhaustion" & struck off strength·No·437447 Pte·BURTON W· evacuated sick to C·C·S·& struck off strength·No437336 Pte·HAWKINS W·A·, & No·437386 Pte·PARKES G·A·E· admitted to Hospital & evacuated to C·R·S·	[illegible]
"	6·12·17·		No·437075 Pte·RUSSON W·J evacuated sick to C·C·S·& struck off strength· Routine Work· 10 mën proceeded for temporary duty to 2/3 S·M·Fld·Ambce·	[illegible]

2353 Wt. W2514/1454 700,000 5/15 D. D. & L. A.D.S.S./Forms/C. 2118.

Army [illegible]m C. 2118.

Instructions regarding War Diaries and Intelligence Summaries are contained in F. S. Regs., Part II. and the Staff Manual respectively. Title pages will be prepared in manuscript.

WAR DIARY
or
~~INTELLIGENCE SUMMARY.~~
(Erase heading not required.)

Place	Date	Hour	Summary of Events and Information	Remarks and references to Appendices
EQUANCOURT	7.12.17.	(S)	9 men reported from leave. 1 H.D.Horse evacuated to Base & struck off strength. No.437376 Pte.BUSHNELL G.H.,No.437564 Pte.CHAMBERLAIN R., No.439489 Pte.KIDMAN T.F., No.437257 Pte.CRACKNELL J.L. & No.405500 Pte.LEE T.W. " Gassed Shell " evacuated to C.C.S. & struck off strength.	
"	8.12.17.		No.437462 Pte.OSLAND H.J. admitted to Hospital"sick",evacuated to C.C.S. & struck off strength.No.437446 Pte.BRAZIER J.S., No.437461 Pte.TURNER N.D., No.437522 Pte.GORDON A.H., No.437496 Pte.CHAPMAN F., & No.437467 Pte.WILTSHIRE D.G. admitted to Hospital & evacuated to C.R.S.	
"	9.12.17.		22 N.C.O's & Men reported from detached duty with 2/3 S.M.Fld.Ambce. 1 Car with driver returned from Workshop. 10 N.C.O's & Men returned from leave. No.437475 Pte.ADAWAY G. reported for duty from C.R.S.	
"	10.12.17.		No.347348 Sgt.CHATTAWAY W.J. evacuated from C.R.S. to C.C.S. & struck off strength. Major A.T.WATERHOUSE R.A.M.C.T.F. proceeded for temporary duty to 2/3 S.M.Fld.Ambce. vice Capt.R.D.MOORE R.A.M.C.T.F. who reported to Hqrs.for duty. M2/113089 Pte. MULGROVE S.,M.T.A.S.C. attached admitted to Hospital & evacuated to C.R.S.	
"	11.12.17.		No.437258 Sgt.MATHIAS J.K. & No.437445 Pte.HERBERT V. admitted to Hospital & evacuated to C.R.S. 1 N.C.O. reported from detached duty with 2/2 S.M.Fld.Ambce. Major A.T.WATERHOUSE R.A.M.C.T.F. reported from detached duty with 2/3 S.M.Fld.Ambce. 7 men reported from leave.	
"	12.12.17.		437478 Pte.WOODHEAD E. admitted to Hospital & evacuated to C.R.S. 437446 Pte.BRAZIER J.S., 437461 Pte.TURNER N.D., 437496 Pte.CHAPMAN F., 437467 Pte.WILTSHIRE D.G., & 437522 Pte. GORDON A.H. discharged from C.R.S. & reported for duty. No.437271 Pte.MAYES J.S. admitted to Hospital & evacuated to C.R.S.	
"	13.12.17.		Routine Work.	
"	14.12.17.		17 N.C.O's & Men proceeded for temporary duty to 2/3 S.M.Fld.Ambce;vice 17 Other Ranks who reported from 2/3 S.M.Fld.Ambce. No.437462 Pte.OSLAND H.J. reported for duty from C.C.S. & taken on the strength. Car No.10 reported for duty from Workshop. 2 men reported	

2353 Wt. W2544/1454 700,000 5/15 D. D. & L. A.D.S.S./Forms/C. 2118.

Instructions regarding War Diaries and Intelligence Summaries are contained in F. S. Regs., Part II. and the Staff Manual respectively. Title pages will be prepared in manuscript.

WAR DIARY
or
~~INTELLIGENCE SUMMARY~~.
(Erase heading not required.)

Army Form C. 2118.

Place	Date	Hour	Summary of Events and Information	Remarks and references to Appendices
EQUANCOURT	14·12·17·		from leave·No·437233 Sgt·WHITEHOUSE T·H· & No·437521 Pte·FRANKUM J·H· admitted to Hospital & evacuated to C·R·S· T4/248 886 Dvr·FRANCE T·R· No·4 Coy·A·S·C· attached proceeded to R·A·Base Depot,HAVRE, for a test in signalling· T4/248828 Dvr·HOWARD G·N· No·4 Coy A·S·C· attached admitted to Hospital & evacuated to C·C·S· & struck off strength· 437336 Pte·HAWKINS W·A· reported for duty from C·R·S· 1 Car with driver & orderly reported from detached duty with 2/3 S·M·Fld·Ambce· No·437466 Pte·ROSCORLA A·, 437180 Pte·MEREDITH J·F·, & M2/113089 Pte·MULGROVE S·, M·T·A·S·C· attached evacuated from C·R·S· to C·C·S· & struck off strength·	[initials]
"	15·12·17·			
"	16·12·17·		No·437457 Pte·KIMBERLEY C·H·W· admitted to Hospital & evacuated to C·R·S· Lieut·B·J· GALLAGHER M·O·R·C·,U·S·A· reported from detached duty with 2/4 Glosters· 433530 Cpl· LUCAS J·, 437507 Pte·HARRIS R·H·C·, 437360 Pte·FINDLAY F·J· admitted to Hospital & evacuated to C·R·S·	[initials]
"	17·12·17·		No·437496 Pte·CHAPMAN F· admitted to Hospital & evacuated to C·R·S· 1 man reported from detached duty with 2/3 S·M·Fld·Ambce·	[initials]
"	18·12·17·		437521 Pte·FRANKUM J· reported for duty from C·R·S· 437517 Pte·HASSELL W·J· & 437282 Pte·BANNISTER W· evacuated sick to C·R·S·	[initials]
"	19·12·17·		437233 Sgt·WHITEHOUSE T·H·, &437258 Sgt·MATTHIAS J·K· reported for duty from C·R·S· 3 Clerks returned from detached duty at 111 C·M·D·Station· 22 Other Ranks, 3 Daimlers, 2 Fords with drivers & orderlies reported from detached duty with 2/3 S·M·Fld·Ambce·	[initials]
"	20·12·17·		Routine Work·	[initials]
"	21·12·17·		1 man proceeded on leave to England· Routine Work·	[initials]
"	22·12·17·		437517 Pte·HASSELL W·J· & 437282 Pte·BANNISTER W· reported for duty from C·R·S· Lieut·E·V·WHITAKER M·O·R·C·,U·S·A· & 13 Other Ranks reported from detached duty at No·3·C·C·S· Capt·G·L·WILKINSON R·A·M·C·T·F· reported from detached duty with 61st·Divn·Depot Battn· Lieut·R·J·ERICKSON M·O·R·C·,U·S·A· & 1 Daimler with driver & orderly reported from detached duty with 2/3 S·M·Fld·Ambce· 337290 Pte·HYATT G·A·,430039 Pte·GUEST W·H·, 363396 Pte·CONROY W·,431516 Pte·COOK H·,405432 Pte·PASHLEY G·A·,493492 Pte·COCKRANE W·J	[initials]

Instructions regarding War Diaries and Intelligence Summaries are contained in F. S. Regs., Part II. and the Staff Manual respectively. Title pages will be prepared in manuscript.

WAR DIARY or ~~INTELLIGENCE SUMMARY~~

(Erase heading not required.)

Army Form C. 2118.

Place	Date	Hour	Summary of Events and Information	Remarks and references to Appendices
EQUANCOURT	22·12·17		300105 Pte·NICHOL C·, 357310 Pte·DIXON W·E·,368046 Pte·FRENCH J·H·,& 368313 Pte·MORGAN J·, reported for duty from Base & taken on the strength·	Hon
"	23·12·17		Unders orders received from 182 Infantry Brigade the Transport under Major A·T·WATERHOUSE R·A·M·C·T·F· moved by march route at 7·15·am· The R·A·M·C· Personnel moved by march route at 11·30·am· & arrived at YTRES Station at 12·0·noon· After loading portion of Brigade Transport the Unit entrained & moved at 3·30·pm· & arrived & detrained at CORBIE at 9·45·pm· After unloading of transport the unit moved by march route & arrived at SAILLY-LE-SEC via VAUX at 2·30·pm·	Hon
SAILLY LE SEC·	24·12·17·		The Horse Transport under Major A·T·WATERHOUSE R·A·M·C·T·F· arrived complete at 4·0·pm· 1 N·C·O·proceeded on leave· 435581 PTE·POWELL C· & T4/248887 Dvr·GUEST V·N· evacuated to No·41 Stationary Hospital & struck off strength· Lieut·E·V·WHITTAKER M·O·R·C·,U·S·A· proceeded for temporary duty to 2/8 R·Warwicks·	Hon
"	25·12·17·		Routine Work· Hospital opened for retention of the sick of the Brigade·	Hon
"	26·12·17·		437470 Pte·COOPER R· evacuated sick to 41 Stationary Hospital & struck off strength· M2/156597 Pte·WILLIAMS W·J· M·T·A·S;C·attached admitted to Hospital·	Hon
"	27·12·17·		437525 Pte·STANWELL L·G· proceeded for temporary duty to 16th·Division Headquarters· 437252 Pte·CURETON F·H· proceeded to XV111 Corps Hqrs·Medical Inspection Room for temporary duty· T4/248887 Dvr·GUEST V·N· No·4 Coy·A·S·C· attached reported & for duty from 41 Stationary Hospital & taken on the strength· Lieut·R·J·ERICKSON M·O·R·C·,U·S·A· proceeded for temporary duty to 2/7 Worcesters·	Hon
"	28·12·17·		Capt·G·L·WILKINSON R·A·M·C·T·F· proceeded to 77 Labour Group & struck off strength·	Hon
"	29·12·17·		Lieut·B·J·GALLAGHER M·O·R·C·,U·S·A· granted leave of absence to PARIS· 6 Other Ranks proceeded on leave to England· XV111 Corps Dental Surgeon arrived & was attached to Unit for duty· Pte·WILLIAMS W·J· evacuated sick to 41 Stationary Hospital & struck off strength·	Hon
IGNAUCOURT	30·12·17		Under orders received from 182 Infantry Brigade the Unit with Transport complete moved by march route to 9·0·am· Route SAILLY LAURETTE,WARFUSEE-ABANCOURT,MARCELCAVE,IGNAUCOURT· Time of arrival of Personnel 1·15·pm· Transport arrived complete at 3·0·pm·	Hon

Instructions regarding War Diaries and Intelligence Summaries are contained in F. S. Regs., Part II. and the Staff Manual respectively. Title pages will be prepared in manuscript.

C. 2118.

WAR DIARY
or
~~INTELLIGENCE SUMMARY~~.
(Erase heading not required.)

Place	Date	Hour	Summary of Events and Information	Remarks and references to Appendices
LE QUESNEL	31/12.17.		Underx orders received from 182 Infantry Brigade the Unit with Transport complete moved by march route at 9.15.am. Route CAYEUX, BEAUCOURT, LE QUESNEL. Time of arrival 1.15.pm. A/Sgt. DERRICK C. reported from Base & taken on the strength.	HmB

H.M. Burroughes
Lt Col. RAMC

CONFIDENTIAL

MEDICAL

Vol. 21

WAR DIARY

2/2 South Midland Field Ambulance
R. A. M. C. T.

January 1st. – 31st (inclusive)
1918

VOLUME – 21

Army Form C. 2118.

WAR DIARY
or
~~INTELLIGENCE SUMMARY.~~
(Erase heading not required.)

Place	Date	Hour	Summary of Events and Information	Remarks and references to Appendices
LE QUESNEL	1·1·18·		437452 Pte·HARWOOD D·W· reported from detached duty at G·H·Q· Field Post Office· XV111 Corps Dental Surgeon returned to SAILLY-le-SEC and ceased to be attached for duty·	H.M.S.
"	2·1·18·		439517 Pte·HANKS R· & 435495 Pte·DOANE A·W· proceeded on leave to England· 405434 Pte·PASHLEY G·A· proceeded to No·7 Field Ambulance & struck off strength· T4/248878 Dvr·ADAMS J·, No·4 Coy·A·S·C·attached & 437441 Pte·O'LOUGHLIN P· admitted to Hospital & evacuated to 41 Stationary Hospital & struck off strength· 437271 Pte·MAYES J·S· having joined Cyclists Base Depot is struck off the strength to take effect from 21·12·17· 437523 Pte·STANWELL L·G· reported for duty from 16th·Division Headquarters· 437101 Pte·LOVELESS W·H· reported from detached duty with 61st·Division Depot Battalion·	H.M.S.
"	3·1·18·		437491 Pte·JONES W· proceeded to PERONNE for Class arranged for Water Duty men· 437463 Pte·HAYLOR B?J? admitted to Hospital & evacuated to 41 Stationary Hospital & struck off strength· Car No·18 with driver proceeded for temporary duty to XV111 Corps Dental Surgeon· 437494 Pte·HUNT L·V· proceeded for temporary duty as Medical Orderly to the 182 M·G·C· Lieut·B·J·GALLAGHER M·O·R·C·,U·S·A· reported from leave to PARIS· T4/248886 Dvr·FRANCE T·R· No·4 Coy·A·S·C· attached transferred to Royal Field Artillery & struck off strength to take effect from 26·12·17·	H.M.S.
"	4·1·18·		Lieut·E·V·WHITAKER M·O·R·C·,U·S·A· posted as Medical Officer to 2/8 R·Warwicks & struck off strength· The Unit complete less motor transport was inspected by A·D·M·S·61st·Division· There were present on parade:- R·A·M·C·) 4 Officers;)118 Other Ranks· — A·S·C·} H·T·} 33 Other Ranks· — Horses 42; Vehicles 16 The Ambulance paraded in line; weather bitterly cold but fine· There were 4 inches of snow· The A·D·M·S· expressed himself as fully satisfied with the appearance of the men and transport·	H.M.S.
"	5·1·18·		437467 Pte·WILTSHIRE D·G· & T4/248864 Dvr·GRAY W·G· No·4 Coy·A·S·C· attached evacuated to 41 Stationary Hospital & struck off strength· 435164 Pte·HUBAND L·C· reported for duty from No·7 Field Ambulance & taken on the strength· 437489 Pte·CALLANAN G·C·,493571 Pte·FREDERICKS A·, & 364429 Pte·JONES R· reported for duty from Base & taken on the strength· 493492 Pte·COCKRANE W·J·, 439538 Pte·BRAKE F·E·, & 437225 Cpl·DOLMAN A·V· admitted to Hospital & evacuated to 41 Stationary Hospital & struck off strength·	H.M.S.

A5834 Wt. W4973/M687 750,000 8/16 D. D. & L. Ltd. Forms/C.2118/13.

Army Form C. 2118.

...ctions regarding War Diaries and Intelligence Summaries are contained in F. S. Regs., Part II. and the Staff Manual respectively. Title pages will be prepared in manuscript.

WAR DIARY
or
~~INTELLIGENCE SUMMARY.~~
(Erase heading not required.)

Place	Date	Hour	Summary of Events and Information	Remarks and references to Appendices
LE QUESNEL	6·1·18·		Lieut·B·J·GALLIAGHER M·O·R·C·,U·S·A· posted to 2/5 Glosters as Medical Officer & struck off strength vice Capt·W·SPEEDY R·A·M·C· who reported for duty and taken on the strength· M2/156597 Pte·WILLIAMS W·J· M·T·A·S·C· attached reported from 41 stationary Hospital & taken on the strength·	
NESLE	7·1·18·		Under orders received from 182 Infantry Brigade the Unit with Transport complete moved by march route at 9·0·am· Route- BOUCHOIR,ROYE,RETHONVILLERS,NESLE· Time of arrival 6·5·pm· Distance 17 miles· Condition of the roads was very bad owing to melting snow & later to a fresh fall of snow· There was a halt from 12·30·pm· to 1·30·pm; during which two Soyer Stoves were brought into use & an issue of hot tea & rum was made· Extra transport of 3 G·S·Wagons & 1 Motor Lorry was provided· 437312 Pte·DURY W·H· was admitted to Hospital & evacuated to 41 Stationary Hospital & struck off strength· 437491 Pte· JONES W· reported for duty from Water duty Class·	
"	8·1·18·		Capt·W·SPEEDY R·A·M·C· proceeded to England & struck off strength· One H·D·horse drawn from Divisional Train & taken on the strength·	
"	9·1·18·		Under orders received from 182 Infantry Brigade the Unit with Transport complete moved by march route·The starting point should have been passed at 10·40·am· but owing to delays of units in advance the actual time of passing starting point was 11·30·am· This delay was regrettable as the day was very cold & men & horses were kept waiting for this long period·Route VOYENNES,MATIGNY,DOUILLY,GERMAINE· Time of arrival 6·15·pm· Length of march about 13 miles· A halt was made from 1·30·pm·to 2·30·pm· & as on the 7th· inst an issue of hot rum and milk was made· There was a heavy snowstorm during the afternoon· Extra transport of 6 G·S·Wagons was provided & little difficulty was experienced except on one hill entering DOUILLY, where accurate driving was essential owing to the slippery surface & the excessive camber· All wagons came up the hill successfully though they had to pass other transport in difficulties·	
GERMAINE				
"	10·1·18·		437516 Pte·HASSELL W·T· & 437357 Pte·KEELING H· proceeded for temporary duty to 2/6 R· Warwicks as Water Duty men· 437470 Pte·COOPER R· reported for duty from 41 Stationary Hospital & taken on the strength· Commanding Officer & Major A·T·WATERHOUSE R·A·M·C·T· with 3 Bearer Sergeants proceeded on reconnaiscence of the French Aid Posts,in order to prepare for relief· 8 Other Ranks sent to 2/8 Warwicks for duty at their R·A·P·	

A5834 Wt. W4973/M687 750,000 8/16 D. D. & L. Ltd. Forms/C.2118/13.

Instructions regarding War Diaries and Intelligence Summaries are contained in F. S. Regs., Part II. and the Staff Manual respectively. Title pages will be prepared in manuscript.

WAR DIARY

or

~~INTELLIGENCE SUMMARY.~~

(*Erase heading not required.*)

Army Form C. 2118.

Place	Date	Hour	Summary of Events and Information	Remarks and references to Appendices
GERMAINE	11·1·18·		437494 Pte·HUNT L·V· reported from detached duty with 182 M·G·C· 251998 Pte·McNULTY E· 1/6 Manchesters attached evacuated sick to England & struck off strength· The following posts were taken over from the French to which parties were sent for duty for evacuation of sick & wounded from the Line·:- SAVY,A·D·S·, Sheet 62 C· X·29·c·6·5·, Dressing Station,BOIS de SAVY,Sheet 62 B,S·20·a;5·1·, Dressing Station,Sunken Road,North of HOLNON,Sheet 62 B·,S·2·a·9·4· Relay Posts also established in BOYAN BRETON & in Quarry, Sheet 62 B·, S·21·a·8·3· One car is stationed at A·D·S·SAVY, one at Dressing Station BOIS de SAVY, and one at Sunken Road,North of HOLNON· 4 Other Ranks sent to 2/7 Warwicks for duty at their R·A·P·	[illegible]
"	12·1·18·		Headquarters & Transport Lines of Unit moved into GERMAINE Village,Sheet 66 D·,E·17·b;3·8· Ford Car No·18 reported from detached duty with Dental Surgeon XV111 Corps·	[illegible]
"	13·1·18·		Ford Car No·18 sent to Workshop· M2/113089 Pte·MULGROVE S·,M·T·A·S·C· attached reported for duty from Base & taken on the strength· 368313 Pte·MORGAN J· admitted to Hospital & evacuated to 61st·Division Main Dressing Station·	[illegible]
"	14·1·18·		Car No·18 with driver & orderly reported from Workshop· 6 men reported from leave·	[illegible]
VAUX	15·1·18·		The Unit less Horse Transport moved to VAUX,Sheet 66 D·,F·2·c· 0·3· Hospital opened for the reception & treatment of sick· 437275 Cpl·GIBBS L·W· reported from detached duty with Brigade Schools·	[illegible]
"	16·1·18·		1805 Cpl·GEARY R· reported for duty from 2/3 S·M·Fld·Ambce· & taken on the strength· T4/248878 Dvr·ADAMS J·,No·4 Coy·A·S·C· attached reported for duty from 41 Stationary Hospital & taken on the strength·. 437517 Pte·HASSELL W·T· reported from detached duty with 2/6 R·Warwicks· 437464 Pte·BROADBENT G· having joined Cyclist Base Depot is struck off the strength to take effect from 4·1·18·. 437445 Pte·HERBERT V·H· having been discharged from Hospital to No·2 Con·Depot ROUEN 17·12·17 is struck off strength to take effect from that date·	[illegible]
"	17·1·18·		368313 Pte·MORGAN J· reported for duty from 61st·Division Main Dressing Station· Lieut· R·J·ERICKSON,M·O·R·C·,U·S·A· is posted to 2/5 R·Warwicks & struck off strength· 437478 Pte·WOODHEAD E·W· having been posted to 47th·Division from Base is struck off strength	[illegible]

A5834 Wt. W4973/M687 750,000 8/16 D. D. & L. Ltd. Forms/C.2118/13.

Instructions regarding War Diaries and Intelligence Summaries are contained in F. S. Regs., Part II. and the Staff Manual respectively. Title pages will be prepared in manuscript.

WAR DIARY
or
~~INTELLIGENCE SUMMARY.~~
(*Erase heading not required.*)

Army Form C. 2118.

Place	Date	Hour	Summary of Events and Information	Remarks and references to Appendices
VAUX	17·1·18·		to take effect from 9·1·18· O·C· accompanied by Sgt·Major JACKSON H·C· visited the A·D·S· & posts up the line·	
"	18·1·18·		437357 Pte·KEELING H· reported from detached duty with 2/6 R·Warwicks·	
"	19·1·18·		Car No·6 proceeded to Workshop· 437457 Pte·KIMBERLEY C·H·W· having joined Cyclist Base Depot is struck off strength to take effect from 15·1·18· T24201 Dvr·ENFIELD S·A·, No·4 Coy·A·S·C· attached reported for duty & taken on the strength· A·D·M·S· 61st·Division visited Headquarters·	
"	20·1·18·		Water cart with orderly sent to Workshop·	
"	21·1·18·		O·C· accompanied by Sgt·Major JACKSON H·C· visited the A·D·S· & posts up the line· 439538 Pte·BRAKE F·E· reported for duty from 41 Stationary Hospital & taken on the strength· T4/248410 Dvr·SMITH V·W· No·4 Coy·A·S·C· attached reported for duty & taken on the strength· 435530 Cpl·LUCAS J· having joined No·2 Con·Depot ROUEN,27·12·17 is struck off strength to take effect from that date·	
"	22·1·18·		The following Officer was recommended for the "Military Cross" 13·12·17·, was awarded the "Military Cross" 10·1·18·, & was presented by the G·O·C· 61st·Division with the ribbon for the Immediate Award of the "Military Cross" at GERMAINE today:- Captain REGINALD DEVEREUX MOORE R·A·M·C·(T·F·) 2/3 Sth·Mid·Fld·Ambce·R·A·M·C·F· " For courage and devotion to duty· " This Officer worked continuously from Dec·3rd·to Dec·10th· inclusive attending " to wounded at CHARING CROSS,Advanced Dressing Station,S·W· of BEAUCAMP (Map "reference Q·17·b·7·3· Sheet 57 c·)· During this period he attended to casual- " ties in the road which was frequently shelled,the only available shelter being " a galvanized iron shed· By his devotion & cheerfulness he inspired confid- " ence in all with whom he came in contact, & helped the men very considerably " in the performance of their duties· On Dec·7th· & 8th· he came out under " very heavy shell fire & would not seek cover until the patients had been put " in a place of safety· His general organisation of the work at this post was " excellent·	

A5834 Wt. W4973/M687 750,000 8/16 D. D. & L. Ltd. Forms/C.2118/13.

Instructions regarding War Diaries and Intelligence Summaries are contained in F. S. Regs., Part II. and the Staff Manual respectively. Title pages will be prepared in manuscript.

WAR DIARY
or
~~INTELLIGENCE SUMMARY.~~
(Erase heading not required.)

Army Form C. 2118.

Place	Date	Hour	Summary of Events and Information	Remarks and references to Appendices
VAUX	22·1·18·		The undermentioned men were awarded the Divisional Commander's Parchment on 10·1·18· No·437458 Private LEONARD WILSON·) 2/2 South Midland Field Ambulance No·437538 Private WILLIAM THOMAS HISCOCK·) R·A·M·C·T· "For conspicuous courage and devotion to duty· "On the 8th·December 1917 the Dressing Station at CHARING CROSS,S·W· of BEAUCAMP, "(Map reference Q·17·b·7·3· Sheet 57 c) was frequently heavily sheeled· "On two occasions this occurred when some wounded were lying outside· Pte·WILSON "& Pte·HISCOCK & another man,with great courage brought these cases in success- "fully in spite of the heavy fire to which they were exposed· No·M2/167360 Private ARTHUR BENNETT NETHERCOTT· 302 Coy·M·T·A·S·C·, attached 2/2 Sth·Mid·Fld·Ambce·R·A·M·C·T· "For personal courage and devotion to duty· "M2/167360 Pte·ARTHUR BENNETT NETHERCOTT,M·T·A·S·C· attached 2/2 South Midland "Field Ambulance as a driver of a Ford Ambulance has since Dec·2nd· to Dec·11th· "1917 made continuous journeys between CHARING CROSS,Advanced Dressing Station, "S·W·BEAUCAMP,(Map reference Q·17·b·7·3· Sheet 57 c) and VILLERS PLOUICH A·D·S· "(Map reference R·13·a·0·8· Sheet 57 c·) both by day and night· The road is a "very rough and exposed one and constantly swept by shell fire ·Capt·W·V·WOOD, "R·A·M·C·T· and others can personally vouch for numerous casualties occurring on "the road in question· It is largely ~~dne~~ owing to the devotion of this driver "that the speedy evacuation of seriously wounded men has been effected· A single "journey is hazardous but the continuous endurance of the strain is beyond all "praise· 5 men of the 2/6 R·Warwicks, 5 men of the 2/7 R·Warwicks & 5 men of the 2/8 R·Warwicks reported for instruction in Water Duties·	
"	23·1·18·		4 men & 1 Sergt of the 2/5 R·Warwicks reported for instruction in Water Duties·T/24201 Dvr·ENFIELD S·A· No·4 Coy·A·S·C· attached admitted to Hospital & evacuated to 61st· Division Main Dressing Station·	
"	24·1·18·		437101 Pte·LOVELESS W·H· proceeded for temporary duty to XVIII Corps Reinforcement Camp · Capt·D·F·DOBSON R·A·M·C·T·C· reported for duty & taken on the strength & proceeded for duty at SAVY A·D·S·	

A5834 Wt. W4973/M687 750,000 8/16 D. D. & L. Ltd. Forms/C.2118/13.

Army Form C. 2118.

Instructions regarding War Diaries and Intelligence Summaries are contained in F. S. Regs., Part II. and the Staff Manual respectively. Title pages will be prepared in manuscript.

WAR DIARY
or
INTELLIGENCE SUMMARY.
(Erase heading not required.)

Place	Date	Hour	Summary of Events and Information	Remarks and references to Appendices
VAUX	25·1·18·		O·C· visited A·D·S's and posts up the line· D·D·M·S· XV111 Corps visited SAVY A·D·S·	HRH
"	26·1·18·		40333 Pte·LLOYD D·O· reported for duty & taken on the strength· 493492 Pte·COCKRANE W·J· reported for duty from 41 Stationary Hospital & taken on the strength· T/24201 Dvr· ENFIELD S·A· No·4 Coy·A·S·C· attached evacuated from Divisional Main Dressing Station to C·C·S· & struck off strength·	HRH
"	27·1·18·		437523 Pte·STANWELL L·G· appointed Lance Corporal· 437360 Pte·FINDLAY F·L· having ~~xxxxx~~ been evacuated sick to England 11·1·18 is struck off strength to take effect from that date· 437507 Pte·HARRIS R·H·C· having been evacuated sick to England 5·1·18 is struck off strength to take effect from that date·	HRH
"	28·1·18·		6 men from Infantry Battalions of 182 & 183 Infantry Brigades reported for instruction in Chiropody· M2/079033 Pte·MORTON K·W·, M·T·A·S·C· attached proceeded for temporary duty to A·D·M·S· 61st·Division· 437523 L/Cpl·STANWELL L·G· proceeded to 16th·Divn· Hqrs as witness in trial of Pte·DALLON·	HRH
"	29·1·18·		3 men proceeded on leave to England· 437282 Pte·BANNISTER W·F· proceeded for temporary duty to 61st·Divn·Rest House· 21 Other Ranks proceeded for temporary duty to 172 Tunnelling Company	HRH
"	30·1·18·		Car No·A·19205 with driver & orderly sent to Workshop· 437523 L/Cpl· STANWELL L·G· reported back from 16th·Divn·Hqrs· 3 men proceeded on leave to England·	HRH
"	31·1·18·		Routine Work·	

H Burroughs
Lt Col. RAMC
Officer Commanding
2/2 Sth. Mid. Fld. Ambce. R.A.M.C., T.F.

A5834 Wt W4973/M687 750,000 8/16 D. D. & L. Ltd. Forms/C.2118/13.

14 Feb. 1918

14/2784

CONFIDENTIAL

Medical

Vol 22

"WAR DIARY"

2/2 Sth. Mid. Fld. Ambce.
R. A. M. C. (T. F.)

VOL. 22

February 1st. - 28 th. (inclusive)
1918

Instructions regarding War Diaries and Intelligence Summaries are contained in F. S. Regs., Part II. and the Staff Manual respectively. Title pages will be prepared in manuscript.

WAR DIARY
~~or~~
~~INTELLIGENCE SUMMARY.~~

(Erase heading not required.)

Army Form C. 2118.

Place	Date	Hour	Summary of Events and Information	Remarks and references to Appendices
VAUX.	1.2.18.		1 H.D.Horse No.768 evacuated to Base 29.1.18 & struck off strength. Car No.7 with driver & orderly reported from Workshop. No.437398 Pte.DUCKHOUSE H. reported from Base and taken on the strength. No.437326 Pte.RILEY A.H. transferred sick to 61st.Divn.Main Dressing Station. 18 Other Ranks attached for instruction in Water Duties returned to their various units fit to take over allotted duties.	
"	2.2.18.		435030 L/Sgt.BLUNN A., 435361 Pte.DAVIES L.,437428 Pte.TAYLOR L.,435355 Pte.HOLLIS H., 435367 Pte.HINKS J.,435256 Pte.WEST H.V., 435350 Pte.COTTRELL A., & 435372 Pte.BAUGHAN G.W. reported for duty,from detached duty as Water Duty men with Infantry Battalions of 182 Infantry Brigade,and taken on the strength.	
"	3.2.18.		No.322064 Pte.PATERSON H.F. having been discharged from Hospital to No.2 Con.Depot ROUEN 7.1.18 is struck off strength,to take effect from that date.	
"	4.2.18.		Lieut.E.V.WHITAKER,M.O.R.C.,U.S.A. reported for duty & taken on the strength. No.437274 Cpl.BARWELL F.,437082 Pte.DREWCOCK W.E.,437206 Pte.RICHARDSON F.L.,437116 Pte.STENT J., & 437298 Pte.WOODHALL H. reported from detached duty as Water duty men,& taken on the strength.	
"	5.2.18.		6 men attached for instruction in Chiropody returned to their various units fit to take over the duties as Battalion Chiropodists.	
"	6.2.18.		1 N.C.O & 1 man proceeded on leave to England. No.9 Car with driver & orderly reported from Workshop. No.437496 Pte.CHAPMAN F. having been evacuated sick to Base 17.12.17 is struck off strength to take effect from that date. Car No.24952 with driver and orderly sent to Workshop.	
"	7.2.18.		6 men from Units of the Brigade reported for course of Chiropody. No.437464 Pte.BROADBENT G.A.& No.437466 Pte.ROSCORIA A. reported from Base & taken on the strength.	
"	8.2.18.		M2/113089 Pte.MULGROVE S.,M.T.A.S.C. attached proceeded on leave to England. Ford Car proceeded for temporary duty to A.D.M.S. Office 61st.Division. Water Cart with orderly reported from Workshop. A party of 20 Other Ranks proceeded to ETREILLERS to clear out	

2353 Wt. W2544/1454 700,000 5/15 D. D. & L. A.D.S.S./Forms/C. 2118.

Instructions regarding War Diaries and Intelligence Summaries are contained in F. S. Regs., Part II. and the Staff Manual respectively. Title pages will be prepared in manuscript.

WAR DIARY
or
~~INTELLIGENCE SUMMARY~~

(*Erase heading not required.*)

Army Form C. 2118.

Place	Date	Hour	Summary of Events and Information	Remarks and references to Appendices
VAUX	8·2·18·		BASE MENT of a ruined building and to construct an underground Advanced Dressing Station·	HMB
"	9·2·18·		Routine Work·	HMB
"	10·2·18·		Capt·D·B·I·MALLETT,R·A·M·C·,on temporary duty with 2/4 Gloster Details,taken on the strength· Lieut·E·Q·NORTH,M·O·R·C·,U·S·A·,on temporary duty with 2/8 R·Warwicks Details, taken on the strength· Lieut·R·J·ERICKSON,M·O·R·C· ,U·S·A·,on temporary duty with 2/5 R·Warwicks Details,taken on the strength·	HMB
"	11·2·18·		Water cart with orderly proceeded to Workshop· Lieut·E·V·WHITAKER,M·O·R·C·,U·S·A· proceeded to XV111 Corps Headquarters to attend a series of lectures·	HMB
"	12·2·18·		No·437522 Pte·GORDON A·H· proceeded for temporary duty to 61st·Divn·Rest House to relieve Pte BANNISTER W·F· proceeding on leave· 1 man proceeded to A·D·M·S· Office for temporary water duty· No·437077 Cpl·STOKES F·S· proceeded for duty to 41 C·C·S· & struck off strength· Ford car with driver reported from detached duty at A·D·M·S· Office· Car No·24952 with driver & orderly reported from Workshop· Capt·R·D·MOORE,M·C·,R·A·M·C· T·F· with 6 Other Ranks proceeded as an advance party to HAM to take over XV111 Corps Officers Rest Station· Sgt·Major JACKSON H·C· visited A·D·Ss & posts up the line·	HMB
"	13·2·18·		7 Other Ranks proceeded for temporary duty to XV111 Corps Officers Rest Station HAM· D·D·M·S·XV111 Corps accompanied by D·A·D·M·S· 61st·Division inspected the Field Ambce· Headquarters·No·19241 Cpl·SHIPMAN S·C· reported for duty from 41 C·C·S· & taken on the strength·	HMB

H M Burroughes
Lt Col RAMC

Army Form C. 2118.

Instructions regarding War Diaries and Intelligence Summaries are contained in F. S. Regs., Part II. and the Staff Manual respectively. Title pages will be prepared in manuscript.

WAR DIARY

~~or~~

~~INTELLIGENCE SUMMARY.~~

(Erase heading not required.)

Place	Date	Hour	Summary of Events and Information	Remarks and references to Appendices
VAUX	14·2·18·		Lieut·Col·H·N·BURROUGHES,R·A·M·C·T·F· proceeded on leave to England & Major A·T·WATERHOUSE,R·A·M·C·T·F· assumed command of the unit· 4 Other ranks proceeded on leave to England· No·435081 Cpl·CLINTON C·H· reported for duty from detached duty with 2/7 R·Warwicks & taken on the strength· Lieut·R·J·ERICKSON,M·O·R·C·,U·S·A· reported for duty from 2/5 R·Warwicks Details· Capt·D·E·T·HALLETT,R·A·M·C·T·C· reported from detached duty with 2/4 Glosters & proceeded forthwith for temporary duty to 306 Bde·R·F·A· Water cart with orderly reported from Workshop·	
"	15·2·18·		Routine Work·	
"	16·2·18·		Ford Car with orderly proceeded to workshop· 5 Chiropodists returned to their various units qualified to take over duties as Chiropodists· 1 man attached for course of Chiropody evacuated sick·	
"	17·2·18·		T/27698 Dvr·BEAUCHAMP H· & T/309357 Dvr·WOOD C·H·No·4 Coy·A·S·C· attached reported for duty & taken on the strength· Lieut·E·V·WHITTAKER,M·O·R·C·,U·S·A· reported from Course of Lectures at XV111 Corps Schools & proceeded forthwith for temporary duty with 307 Bde·R·F·A· 2 L·D·Horses & 1 man driver attached for temporary duty to XV111 Corps Officers' Rest Station· No·437258 Sergt·MATHIAS J·K· proceeded for Course of Nursing at 61 C·C·S·	
"	18·2·18·		D·D·M·S· XV111 Corps inspected the work being done on the partly constructed A·D·S· at ETREILLERS· 12 men from various Infantry Battalions of the Division reported for Course in Chiropody· Capt·G·S·CLANCY,R·A·M·C·T·C· reported for temporary duty from 2/3 Sth·Mid·Fld·Ambce·	
"	19·2·18·		437326 Pte·RILEY A·M· evacuated sick to 61st·Divn·Main Dressing Station 2·2·18 & struck off strength,to take effect from that date· A·D·M·S·30th·Division visited Hqrs & A·D·Ss & posts up the line· Ford Car No·18 reported for duty from Workshop· Ford Car No·19 sent to Workshop· Capt·D·F·DOBSON, R·A·M·C·T·C· reported sick to Hqrs from HOLNON A·D·S· & evacuated to 61st·Divn·Main Dressing Station· Capt·CLANCY G·S·, R·A·M·C·T·C· proceeded for duty to HOLNON A·D·S·	

Army Form C. 2118.

WAR DIARY
or
INTELLIGENCE SUMMARY
(Erase heading not required.)

Instructions regarding War Diaries and Intelligence Summaries are contained in F. S. Regs., Part II. and the Staff Manual respectively. Title pages will be prepared in manuscript.

Place	Date	Hour	Summary of Events and Information	Remarks and references to Appendices
VAUX	20·2·18·		Lieut·R·J·ERICKSON,M·O·R·C·,U·S·A· proceeded to PARIS for duty with the American Red Cross & struck off strength· Lieut·T·S·WILLIAMS,M·O·R·C·,U·S·A· reported for temporary duty·	AFL
"	21·2·18·		Lieut·E·Q·NORTH,M·O·R·C·,U·S·A· evacuated sick to Base & struck off strength· 437270 Cpl·CIEAL C·A· & 437332 Pte·GREEN W·P· reported from detached water duty with 2/1 Bucks & taken on the strength· Personnel & Transport of the 98th·Field Ambulance arrived to relieve the unit·	AFL
" GERMAINE	22·2·18·		A·D·Ss·at SAVY and BOIS de SAVY and Headquarters at VAUX taken over by the 98th·Field Ambulance· The Unit with Transport complete moved from VAUX to GERMAINE · Headquarters Sheet 66D·E·17·a·2·9· and Transport Lines Sheet 66D·E·16 Central· 82417 Pte·CHESTER H·H 89938 Pte·CLARK S·,121936 Pte·COLESBY E·M·,124842 Pte·COLE C·J·,2888 Pte·DONALD J·, 376008 Pte·PROUDFOOT D·,44823 Pte·TAYLOR R·,374063 Pte·VERNON J·,68945 Pte·DAY D·W·, 121902 Pte·GREENHALGH L·,10396 Pte·CULLWICK G·, & 81952 Pte·CAMERON C· reported for duty from Base & taken on strength· Ford Car No·19 reported from Workshop· T/30751 Dvr· JARRETT No·4 Coy·A·S·C· attached reported for duty & taken on the strength·	AFL
"	23·2·18·		Lieut·T·S·WILLIAMS,M·O·R·C·,U·S·A· ceased to be attached for duty & proceeded for duty to 1/5 Gordons· No·368313 Pte·MORGAN J· evacuated sick to 61st·Divn·Main Dressing Station thence to C·C·S· & struck off strength· No·437258 Sergt·MATHIAS J·K· returned from Nursing Course held at 61 C·C·S· Capt·D·F·DOBSON,R·A·M·C·T·C· discharged from hospital & reported for duty·	AFL
"	24·2·18·		No·437255 Pte·WILLIAMS C· proceeded for course in Nursing at 61 C·C·S·	AFL
"	25·2·18·		No·437466 Pte·ROSCORLA A· proceeded to PERONNE for course in Sanitation·	AFL
FORESTE	26·2·18·		Unit R·A·M·C· personnel moved to FORESTE, Sheet 66D·E·Central·	AFL

Army Form C. 2118.

Instructions regarding War Diaries and Intelligence Summaries are contained in F. S. Regs., Part II. and the Staff Manual respectively. Title pages will be prepared in manuscript.

WAR DIARY
or
~~INTELLIGENCE SUMMARY~~

(Erase heading not required.)

Place	Date	Hour	Summary of Events and Information	Remarks and references to Appendices
FORESTE	27.2.18.		No.120662 Gnr.BRUNTON,R.G.A. attached ~~xxxxxx~~ & NO.27783 Gnr.HARRISON,R.F.A. attached reported for duty as I.B.Batmen & taken on the strength.	A57
"	28.2.18.		5 Other Ranks of 2/5 R.Warwicks,water duty men,ceased to be attached for duty & proceeded for duty to 1/8 Argyll & Sutherland Highlanders. 5 men attached for course in Chiropody returned to their units fit to take over the duties as Chiropodists. T/27698 Dvr.BEAUCHAMP H. & T/309357 Dvr.WOOD C.H.,No.4 Coy.A.S.C. attached returned for duty to No.4 Coy.A.S.C.,61st.Divisional Train & struck off strength. 1 H.D.Horse sent to 61st.Mobile Vet?Section.	

2353 Wt. W2544/1454 700,000 5/15 D. D. & L. A.D.S.S./Forms/C. 2118.

26 CONFIDENTIAL

Medical

Vol 23

140/2849.

Mar. 1918

WAR DIARY

2/2 Sth. Mid. Fd. Ambce.
R.A.M.C.T.

VOLUME 23

March 1st. - 31st. (inclusive)
1918

Instructions regarding War Diaries and Intelligence Summaries are contained in F. S. Regs., Part II. and the Staff Manual respectively. Title pages will be prepared in manuscript.

WAR DIARY
~~or~~
INTELLIGENCE ~~SUMMARY~~.
(Erase heading not required.)

Army Form C. 2118.

Place	Date	Hour	Summary of Events and Information	Remarks and references to Appendices
FORESTE	1.3.18		305180 Cpl. JONES W., 305220 Pte. HUNTER R., 305128 Pte. WILKINSON J., & 305257 Pte. TAYLOR G. reported for duty from 1/8 Argyll & Sutherland Highlanders & taken on the strength. 65971 Cpl. WILLMER G.A., 419113 Pte. HILL H., 495479 Pte. CLARETT G., 497145 Pte. MARTIN G., 11373 Pte. VINES V. & 437113 Pte. LANE J.W. reported for duty from Base & taken on the strength. 6 men attached for Course of instruction in Chiropody returned to their various units fit to take over the duties as battalion Chiropodists. 18 Other Ranks reported from detached duty with 173 Tunnelling Company. 439565 Pte. HECTOR H.J. admitted sick to 98 Field Ambulance. A Working Party was sent to VAUX to prepare selected site for an Advanced Dressing Station. 1 H.D. Horse evacuated sick from 61st. Mobile Vet. Sect. to Base & struck off strength.	
"	2.3.18.		435124 Pte. DENNY J. admitted sick to 2/3 S.M. Fld. Ambce. Lieut. Col. H.N. BURROUGHES, R.A.M.C. (T.F.) returned from leave & resumed command of the Unit. Work on A.D.S. at VAUX progressing.	
"	3.3.18.		No. 437255 Pte. WILLIAMS C returned from Course of Nursing held at 61 C.C.S. Capt. G.S. CLANCY, R.A.M.C. (T.C.) taken on the strength of the unit. Work on A.D.S. at VAUX progressing, two fatigue parties working in relays from dawn till dusk. 5 men reported from leave.	
"	4.3.18.		10 men from Infantry Battalions reported for course of instruction in Chiropody. Capt. D.B.T. HALLETT, R.A.M.C. (T.C.) reported from detached duty with 306 Bde. R.F.A.	
"	5.3.18.		Work on A.D.S. at VAUX progressing. 1 Nissen Hut sent to VAUX for erection. 4 men attached for training in Water Duties returned to their various units fit to take over allotted duties. 1 man of 2/7 R. Warwicks returned to his unit fit to take over the duties as battalion Chiropodistx. 437206 Pte. RICHARDSON F.L. proceeded for temporary ~~dx~~ water duty to 2/5 Glosters. Capt. D.B.T. HALLETT, R.A.M.C. (T.C.) proceeded for duty to 2/1 S.M. Fld. Amb. & struck off strength. 435124 Pte. DENNY J evacuated from 2/3 S.M. Fld. Amb. to C.C.S. & struck off strength. 303306 Pte. CONROY W. admitted sick to 2/3 S.M. Fld. Ambce. Capt. D.F. DOBSON, R.A.M.C. (T.C.) proceeded to HOLNON A.D.S. for duty vice Capt. G.S. CLANCY, R.A.M.C. (T.C.) who returned to Hqrs for duty.	

2353 Wt. W2544/1454 700,000 5/15 D. D. & L. A.D.S.S./Forms/C. 2118.

Army Form C. 2118.

WAR DIARY
or
INTELLIGENCE SUMMARY

(*Erase heading not required.*)

Instructions regarding War Diaries and Intelligence Summaries are contained in F. S. Regs., Part II. and the Staff Manual respectively. Title pages will be prepared in manuscript.

Place	Date	Hour	Summary of Events and Information	Remarks and references to Appendices
FORESTE	6·3·18		Work on A·D·S· at VAUX progressing· Capt·N·W·WALMSLEY,R·A·M·C·,(T·C·) reported for duty & taken on the strength· No·81953 Pte·CAMERON C· & NO·121936 Pte·COLESBY E·M· admitted sick to 2/3 S·M·Fld·Ambce· 1 N·C·O· & 4 men proceeded on leave to England· No·437371 Pte·HARRINGTON W· reported from detached water duty with 61st·Battn·M·G·C· & taken on the strength·	Hwd
"	7·3·18		Capt·G·S·CLANCY,R·A·M·C·(T·C·) proceeded for temporary duty to 2/6 R·Warwicks· 2 men sent for temporary duty to XVIII Corps Officers' Rest Station· 1 man proceeded on leave	Hwd
"	8·3·18		Work on A·D·S· at VAUX progressing· No·439365 Pte·HECTOR H·J· struck off strength in accordance with G·R·O No·3396·	Hwd
"	9·3·18		Work on A·D·S· at VAUX progressing· No·303306 Pte·CONROY W· evacuated from 2/3 S·M·Fld· Ambce· to C·C·S· & struck off strength· Hon·Lieut· & Q·Mr· O BASTABLE,R·A·M·C·(T·F·) granted extension of leave to the 14th·inst·	Hwd
"	10·3·18		No·437222 Pte·HIGGS C·R· admitted sick to 2/3 S·M·Fld·Ambce· Work on A·D·S· at VAUX progressing· No·437373 Pte·BUSBY F·W· proceeded for Course in Nursing at 61 C·C·S·	Hwd
"	11·3·18		MB/131222 Pte·ROGERS L·A·,M·T·A·S·C· attached evacuated to 41 Stationary Hospital & Struck off strength· No·100153 Cpl·BAGSHAW F·E· reported for duty from Base & taken on the strength·	Hwd
"	12·3·18		Capt·N·W·WALMSLEY,R·A·M·C·(T·C·) proceeded to England "Expiration of Contract" & struck off strength· T4/248865 Dvr·WHITE A·F·, No·4 Coy·A·S·C· attached, admitted sick to 2/3 S·M·Fld·Ambce·	Hwd

2353 Wt. W2544/1454 700,000 5/15 D. D. & L. A.D.S.S./Forms/C. 2118.

Army Form C. 2118.

WAR DIARY

or

~~INTELLIGENCE SUMMARY.~~

(*Erase heading not required.*)

Instructions regarding War Diaries and Intelligence Summaries are contained in F. S. Regs., Part II. and the Staff Manual respectively. Title pages will be prepared in manuscript.

Place	Date	Hour	Summary of Events and Information	Remarks and references to Appendices
FORESTE	13.3.18		437411 A/L/Sgt. OAKES R.T. promoted Acting Sergeant with pay to take effect from 14.11.17. Work at VAUX A.D.S. progressing.	
"	14.3.18		D.D.M.S. XVIII Corps accompanied by O.C. visited A.D.S. at HOLNON. 1 Nissen Hut drawn from EPPEVILLE & taken to VAUX for erection as extra accommodation at the A.D.S. 81952 Pte. CAMERON C & 121936 Pte. COLESBY E.M. struck off strength in accordance with G.R.O. 3396. T4/248865 Dvr. WHITE A.F., No.4 Coy. A.S.C. attached evacuated from 2/3 S. Mid. Fd. Ambce. to C.C.S. & struck off strength. 10 men attached for Course in Chiropody returned to their Units trained as Battalion Chiropodists. Car No. 10 with driver & orderly & Ford Car No 18 with driver sent to Workshop.	
"	15.3.18		437564 Pte. CHAMBERLAIN R. reported for duty from Base & taken on the strength. Work on A.D.S. at VAUX progressing.	
"	16.3.18		Ford Car No. 18 with driver reported for duty. 437222 Pte. HIGGS C.R. reported for duty from 2/3 S. M. Fd. Ambce. Work on A.D.S. at VAUX progressing.	
"	17.3.18		437480 Pte. BEDFORD E. proceeded to 61 C.C.S. for course of Instruction in nursing. 437373 Pte. BUSBY F.W. reported for duty from Course held at 61 C.C.S.	
"	18.3.18		8 N.C.O.'s & men from Infantry Battalions of Division reported for training in Chiropody. HON. Lieut. & Q.Mr. O. BASTABLE R.A.M.C. (T.F.) reported from leave.	

2353 Wt. W2544/1454 700,000 5/15 D. D. & L. A.D.S.S./Forms/C. 2118.

Instructions regarding War Diaries and Intelligence Summaries are contained in F. S. Regs., Part II. and the Staff Manual respectively. Title pages will be prepared in manuscript.

WAR DIARY
or
~~INTELLIGENCE SUMMARY.~~
(*Erase heading not required.*)

Army Form C. 2118.

Place	Date	Hour	Summary of Events and Information	Remarks and references to Appendices
FORESTE	19.3.18		7 O.Ranks with 2 H.D. horses, 1 G.S. wagon & 1 Daimler car proceeded for temporary duty to XVIII Corps Officers' Rest Station. 65971 Cpl. WILLMER C.A. & 100153 Cpl. BAGSHAW T.E. proceeded to A.D.M.S. 16th. Division for duty & struck off strength. 305150 Cpl. JONES H. proceeded to A.D.M.S. 24th. Division for duty & struck off strength. 1 man proceeded on leave.	[illegible]
"	21.3.18		437353 Pte. MILLER W.T. evacuated sick to 61 C.C.S. & struck off strength.	[illegible]
"	21.3.18		Enemy Bombardment opened at 4.30 am. Order to man Battle Stations was received at 5.20 am. The following dispositions were made at 7.0 am. 1 Sergeant & 5 men at Divisional Baths GERMAINE for the treatment of slightly Gassed cases. No cases were admitted during the day & the personnel were withdrawn at 6.0 pm. Major A.T. WATERHOUSE R.A.M.C.(T.F.) with party proceeded to VAUX to open Divisional Walking Wounded Station in conjunction with the 98th. Field Ambulance (30th. Divn.) Total number of personnel Other Ranks 18. Major A.T. WATERHOUSE R.A.M.C.(T.F.) was assisted by Capt. COLEMAN, M.O. [illegible] M.G. Battalion. 1 Sergeant & 5 men took over Divisional Rest Hut at Railhead FORESTE as an entraining centre (Light Railway) for Walking Wounded who were brought down from VAUX Walking Wounded Station by Red Cross Lorries. This service worked very well throughout the day & 254 patients were evacuated by this means to HAM up to 8.0 pm. For some hours after the Battle opened it was impossible for any traffic to proceed along the ETREILLERS - ATTILLY Road or the MARTEVILLE - ATTILLY Road owing to the extremely heavy & accurate barrage fire of the enemy.	[illegible]

2353 Wt. W2544/1454 700,000 5/15 D. D. & L. A.D.S.S./Forms/C. 2118.

Instructions regarding War Diaries and Intelligence Summaries are contained in F. S. Regs., Part II. and the Staff Manual respectively. Title pages will be prepared in manuscript.

WAR DIARY
or
~~INTELLIGENCE SUMMARY.~~
(Erase heading not required.)

Army Form C. 2118.

Place	Date	Hour	Summary of Events and Information	Remarks and references to Appendices
			At 11.0 am there was some lessening of the fire in intensity and 3 car loads of Stretcher Bearers were sent up along the ETREILLERS – ATTILLY Road to form a Bearer Post in a dugout at Sheet 62.C. X.10. b. Y. 2. The cars were unable to go the whole distance owing to the shelling – one car was hit & badly damaged – one bearer being wounded inside the car. The Bearers proceeded on foot to the dugout. The two undamaged cars returned.	
			As the ~~attacks~~ progressed VAUX village became untenable. The Walking Wounded Station was closed without casualty & re-opened at Y.M.C.A hut at FORESTE. Towards evening further efforts were made to get wounded down by car from ATTILLY. A few stretcher cases were evacuated but the shelling as a ~~rule~~ was too heavy to admit of a constant service. At 11.0 pm. there was a lull in the firing & 22 cases were evacuated from the Bearer dugout. One Daimler car was blown up and abandoned. There were no casualties.	
			At 8. opm. 1 Corpl. and 6 men with a small amount of medical equipment proceeded to DOUILLY to form the nucleus of a Dressing Station.	
FORESTE	22.3.18		At noon. Lieut SANFORD, MORC, USA, was sent up to 1/5 [illegible] dugout to act as O.C. Stretcher Bearers. Cases were evacuated by hand carry to the Car Loading Post, a distance of about 500 yards, whenever opportunity allowed. All cases that had been brought in were evacuated & the dugout was abandoned at the last possible moment. This took place at 12.8 (noon).	

2353 Wt. W2544/1454 700,000 5/15 D. D. & L. A.D.S.S./Forms/C. 2118.

Instructions regarding War Diaries and Intelligence Summaries are contained in F. S. Regs., Part II. and the Staff Manual respectively. Title pages will be prepared in manuscript.

WAR DIARY ~~or~~ ~~INTELLIGENCE~~ SUMMARY.

(*Erase heading not required.*)

Army Form C. 2118.

Place	Date	Hour	Summary of Events and Information	Remarks and references to Appendices
			The Medical Officer & Bearers all escaped through machine gun & shell fire without casualties. Meanwhile the Dressing Station at FORESTE continued to take in Stretcher cases & the Y.M.C.A. hut was in use as a walking wounded Station. At about 3.0pm. orders were received to move back to MATIGNY leaving an A.D.S. personnel & equipment at FORESTE. About 300 walking wounded cases & a few stretcher cases were treated here. All the cases were evacuated by train or by walking wounded lorries except 6 stretcher cases. The walking wounded Station in the Y.M.C.A. hut was closed. The Dressing Station was abandoned at about 6.0pm. on the near approach of the enemy. All walking wounded collected in lorries and ambulances were sent back across the SOMME Canal to VOYENNES where the ambulance established Headquarters. At. 10.30pm. the Unit was ordered to move back to GRUNY (Sheet 66D. M. 6.) All cases were evacuated from VOYENNES to C.C.S. at ROYE.	Hwh
GRUNY	23.3.18		The ambulance arrived at GRUNY at 3.0am. 23.3.18. Ptes Powell C, Carnell O.H, Sanders A.J, & Haines J.G. "wounded in action" evacuated to C.C.S. & struck off strength. The unit remained parked at GRUNY. Capt. D.F. DOBSON, R.A.M.C. (T.C) & 31 Other Ranks were now reported as missing. This represents the personnel of the A.D.S. at HOLNON & the R.A.P's in front of it. The whole of the equipment at this A.D.S. & posts was lost.	Hwh
LE QUESNOY	24.3.18		Unit moved to LE QUESNOY & remained parked.	Hwh
"	25.3.18		Orders were issued by A.D.M.S. 61st. Division that 2/2 5th. Mid. Fld. Ambulance would collect & evacuate wounded for 184 Infantry Brigade. The Division was	Hwh

Instructions regarding War Diaries and Intelligence Summaries are contained in F. S. Regs., Part II. and the Staff Manual respectively. Title pages will be prepared in manuscript.

WAR DIARY
or
~~INTELLIGENCE SUMMARY.~~
(Erase heading not required.)

Army Form C. 2118.

Place	Date	Hour	Summary of Events and Information	Remarks and references to Appendices
LE QUESNOY	25.3.18		acting under orders G.O.C. 20th. Division. The front occupied was roughly a point west of NESLE - LANGUEVOISIN - MOYENCOURT. A Dressing Station under Capt. R.D. MOORE, R.A.M.C.(T.F.) was opened at CARRE PUITS. An Advanced Dressing Station in conjunction with the 61st. Field Ambulance was established at BIARRE.	
"			Towards evening the troops fell back in order to evacuate the salient in which they were placed. At 10.30pm. the Dressing Station at CARRE PUITS was closed & was reopened in ROYE. Advanced posts had already been withdrawn.	[illegible]
"	26.3.18		At. 2.30am under orders from A.A.Q.M.G. 20th. Division the Dressing Station at ROYE was closed & the personnel proceeded by ambulances to BEAUCOURT reporting for instructions at 4.0am. to A.D.M.S. 61st. Division. The main body of the Ambulance moved at 8.0am. to LE QUESNEL & was rejoined by Capt. R.D. MOORE, R.A.M.C.(T.F.) & his party. At 1.0pm. the unit moved complete to VILLERS-aux-ERABLES. Here orders were received from A.D.M.S. 61st. Division to establish an A.D.S. and arrange evacuation from the Divisional front which included the LE QUESNEL - HANGEST line astride the ROYE - AMIENS road. The O.C. [illegible] the line & the route of evacuation - no instructions having been received from the A.D.M.S. 61st. Division where the Dressing Station or [illegible] should be placed.	
MOREUIL			At 5.30pm. a Dressing Station at the Boys' School MOREUIL was opened under Major A.T. WATERHOUSE, R.A.M.C.(T.F.). The Transport was sent back to a point on the MORISEL - AILLY Road about 1½ miles from MORISEL. [illegible] were established at VILLERS-aux-ERABLES at which point the motor ambulances were parked.	

Instructions regarding War Diaries and Intelligence Summaries are contained in F. S. Regs., Part II. and the Staff Manual respectively. Title pages will be prepared in manuscript.

WAR DIARY
or
~~INTELLIGENCE~~ SUMMARY.
(Erase heading not required.)

Army Form C. 2118.

Place	Date	Hour	Summary of Events and Information	Remarks and references to Appendices
MOREUIL	27·3·18		At 8·0 a.m. Capt. R. D. MOORE R.A.M.C.(T.F.) opened an A.D.S. at FRESNOY-en-CHAUSSÉE and one motor ambulance was stationed there. Many cases from 24th, 20th, 30th & 36th Divisions passed through & were evacuated to MOREUIL. At 9·0 p.m. notice that the 61st Division would be relieved by the French at midnight was received but the 2/2 S. Mid. Fd. Ambce. was ordered to keep the Dressing Station open at MOREUIL to receive French wounded & to await orders. The A.D.S. at FRESNOY and Advanced Headquarters at VILLERS aux ERABLES were closed and the Divisional Motor Ambulances were recalled. Ford Car No. A.A 9951 being considerably damaged by wear & tear was abandoned after it had been stripped of all valuable parts & tyres.	HM
"	28·3·18		The Dressing Station at MOREUIL remained open and received cases from all Divisions of the XVIII Corps and from the 8th, 24th, & 50th Divisions as well as from a portion of the French front. Several hundred cases were dealt with, including a large number of stretcher cases. The Evacuation Service to C.C.S. at NAMPS was well maintained by ambulance cars & motor lorries. At 6·0 p.m. the tactical situation was reported both by the Medecin General en Chef of the French & by D.D.M.S. XVIII Corps to demand the immediate closing of the Dressing Station. All cases were cleared and further arrivals were sent on to a dressing station established in JUMEL. Orders were sent at once to the Horse Transport to proceed to JUMEL & wait further instructions. The Dressing Station at MOREUIL being closed the personnel under O.C. marched to JUMEL. No orders as to destination were received from A.D.M.S. 61st Division, and in the absence of accurate news of the situation in front of MONTDIDIER the C.O. decided to	
CRESMAUX			march to ORESMAUX for the night. The complete ambulance arrived at ORESMAUX at 9·30 p.m. Billets were found, & the C.O. went to ST. SAUFLIEU to report his move to D.D.M.S. XVIII Corps.	HM

A5834 Wt. W4973/M687 750,000 8/16 D. D. & L. Ltd. Forms/C.2118/13.

WAR DIARY.

Place	Date	
ORESMAUX	29.3.18	In the absence of definite news as to the whereabouts of the 61st Division the C.O. decided to march North to DURY at the same time sending a motor cyclist forward to get in touch with the Division, & bring orders to DURY. The personnel with one G.S. waggon loaded with rations & materials for use in case it was necessary to open a Dressing Station marched at 9.0 am., reaching DURY at 11.30 am. The remainder of the Transport under Major A.T. WATERHOUSE, RAMC(T.F.) marched to CLAIRY to wait orders. On arrival at DURY a message was received from A.D.M.S. 61st Division to wait further instructions. The Divisional Headquarters were located at BOYES, & the C.O. accordingly proceeded thither where he received the order to billet in DURY. The unit therefore remained in reserve for the moment.
DURY "	30.3.18	The Transport was moved from CLAIRY to rejoin the unit at DURY. At 1.0 pm. orders were received to send all available motor ambulances to GENTELLES and report to O.C. 2/3 S. Mid. Fld. Ambce. at the A.D.S. Also all spare bearers were sent to report to A.D.M.S. 61st Division at BOYES for instructions, together with 3 horse ambulances. 3 Sergeants & 45 men were therefore sent.
"	31.3.18	The ambulance remained at DURY.

[illegible]
Lt. Col. RAMC(T)

9 CONFIDENTIAL MEDICAL

Vol 24

April/18

WAR DIARY

140/2900.

2/2 Sth. Mid. Fd. Ambce.
R.A.M.C.T.

VOLUME 24

April 1st. – 30th. (inclusive)
1918

Instructions regarding War Diaries and Intelligence Summaries are contained in F. S. Regs., Part II. and the Staff Manual respectively. Title pages will be prepared in manuscript.

WAR DIARY
or
INTELLIGENCE SUMMARY.
(Erase heading not required.)

Army Form C. 2118.

Place	Date	Hour	Summary of Events and Information	Remarks and references to Appendices
DURY	1·4·18·		The Ambulance remained stationed at DURY·	[illegible]
"	2·4·18·		Under orders from A·D·M·S·61st·Division a small Dressing Station was established in an operating tent & 2 bell tents on the North side of the AMIENS-ROYE Road about 300 yds· West of BOIS de GENTELLES· An advanced post consisting of 2 men was established across the river LUCE at HOURGES which is practically in the front line· These posts were established to help the 14th·Division whose Field Ambulances had not arrived in the area· Capt·R·D·MOORE,M·C·,R·A·M·C·T·F· & Lieut·W·A·S·MARRATT R·A·M·C·S·R· were stationed at the Dressing Station· Walking wounded were evacuated to BOVES & stretcher cases to ST ACHEUL on the S·E· outskirts of AMIENS·	[illegible]
"	3·4·18·		The 14th·Division was relieved & proceeded North & orders were received from A·D·M·S 14th·Division for Capt·R·D·MOORE,M·C·,R·A·M·C·T·F· & his party to return to DURY for duty· The ambulance remained stationed at DURY·	[illegible]
FLIXECOURT·	4·4·18·		Under orders received from A·D·M·S·61st·Division the Unit moved by march route to FLIXECOURT· Route,-HAIRY,ISSY,FLUY,BRIQUEMESNIL· Time of arrival 11·15·am· Hospital opened for treatment of sick of 183 Infantry Brigade·	[illegible]
"	5·4·18·		The Ambulance remained stationed at FLIXECOURT·	[illegible]
"	6·4·18·		The Ambulance remained stationed at FLIXECOURT·	[illegible]
"	7·4·18·		7 men attached for Course in Chiropody returned to their units trained as Battalion Chiropodists· No·437353 Pte·CURETON F·W· proceeded for temporary duty to XVIII Corps· No·435495 Pte·DOANE A·W· posted to A·D·M·S· 61st·Division· No·437003 Cpl·MARTYN S·S· reported for duty from 2/3 S·M·Fld·Ambce· & taken on the strength·T/309337 Dvr·WOOD H·W· No·4 Coy·A·S·C· attached,reported for duty & taken on the strength·	[illegible]
"	8·4·18·		Major A·T·WATERHOUSE,R·A·M·C·T·F· proceeded on special leave to England·	[illegible]
"	9·4·18·		Capt·R·D·MOORE,M·C·,R·A·M·C·T·F· promoted to ACTING MAJOR whilst commanding a Section of a Field Ambulance to take effect from 4·1·18·	[illegible]

Instructions regarding War Diaries and Intelligence Summaries are contained in F. S. Regs., Part II. and the Staff Manual respectively. Title pages will be prepared in manuscript.

WAR DIARY
or
INTELLIGENCE SUMMARY.

(Erase heading not required.)

Army Form C. [illegible]

Place	Date	Hour	Summary of Events and Information	Remarks and references to Appendices
FLOXICOURT	9·4·18·		No·437516 Pte·TAYLOR A·E· evacuated to C·C·S· & struck off strength· Lieut·W·A·S· MAGRATH, R·A·M·C·T·C· posted to 2/6 R·Warwicks & struck off strength· Lieut·C·H·AYLEN R·A·M·C·T·C· posted to 2/8 Worcesters & struck off strength· Lieut·E·V·WHITAKER, M·O·R·C·, U·S·A· evacuated sick to Base & struck off strength·	[illegible]
"	10·4·18·		Under orders received from 182 Infantry Brigade the Horse Transport moved by march route at 12·0 midnight to ST ROCH Station·	[illegible]
"	11·4·18·		The personnel moved by march route at 1·45·am· arriving at ST ROCH Station at 6·0·am; The whole Transport & personnel entrained & moved at 11·0·am·, arriving & detraining at BERGUETTE at 9·40·pm· The Unit with transport complete moved by march route &	[illegible]
PIERRIERE	12·4·18·		arrived at PIERRIERE at 1·30·am· & billeted for the night· 12·4·18·	
"	12·4·18·		The 61st·Division was ordered to take up a defensive line along the course of the Clarence River–roughly Q·3·c to P·23·d· sheet 36a· A·D·M·S· issued orders to 2/2 Field Ambulance to clear sick & wounded from 182 Infantry Brigade who were holding the middle sector of the Divisional Front· By 12·0·noon an Advanced Dressing Station was established at ST FLORIS, P·6·c·0·6· The Divisional Front was attacked by the enemy throughout the day· The A·D·S· at ST FLORIS was closed owing to the shell fire at 3·30·pm· & personnel moved back to the ASYLUM, P·9·d·1·9·, sharing the accommodation with 2/1 Field Ambulance· The Ambulance Hqrs were moved back to GUARBECQUE, O·17·b·5/6· & a Walking Wounded Station was established· Transport lines were	
GUARBECQUE			moved back to BERGUETTE· No·437483 Pte·SMITH F·E· "Killed in Action"· Ford Car No·17481 & Talbot Ambulance No·45689 with driver, No·M2/152965 Pte·SIMPSON H·, M·T· A·S·C· attached, reported for duty & taken on the strength·	[illegible]
"	13·4·18·		The neighbourhood of GUARBECQUE was shelled about 5·0·am· for half an hour· All surplus personnel were sent back to BERGUETTE, and thence to MOLINGHEM Schools where a Walking Wounded Station was perpared· GUARBECQUE was then closed & Hqrs	
MOLINGHEM			& transport removed to MOLINGHEM· Evacuation from A·D·S· was carried out by Divisional cars to M·D·S· at BERGUETTE (2/1 Field Ambulance) and Walking Wounded Station· Thence by M·A·C· cars & lorries to C·C·S· at AIRE and LILLERS· No·64936 Pte·OGDEN A·, 57189 Pte·HAIGH G·E·, 33896 Pte·WARD F·J·, 46892 Pte·HADLEY H·, 383343 Pte·AYRE C·G·, 6822 Pte·LAWLEY W·J· reported for duty from Base & taken on the strength·	[illegible]

Army Form C. 2118.

Instructions regarding War Diaries and Intelligence Summaries are contained in F. S. Regs., Part II. and the Staff Manual respectively. Title pages will be prepared in manuscript.

WAR DIARY
or
INTELLIGENCE SUMMARY.
(Erase heading not required.)

Place	Date	Hour	Summary of Events and Information	Remarks and references to Appendices
MOLINGHEM	14.4.18.		No further attack was made & the numberx of wounded was consequently much smaller. Lieut.J.C.THOMPSON,M.O.R.C.,U.S.A. reported for duty & taken on the strength. 76360 Pte.WEBSTER W.,87668 Pte.BARTON A.,87010 Pte.BAILEY N.G. reported for duty from Base & taken on the strength.	
"	15.4.18.		The situation remains quiet. Evacuation easily carried out. Few wounded coming in	
"	16.4.18.		The situation remains quiet.	
"	17.4.18.		A Walking Wounded Aid Post was established in the Schools at GUARBECQUE. Personnel 1 N.C.O. & 1 man.	
"	18.4.18.		No.437372 Cpl.OLDROYD J.R. transferred sick to 61st.Division Rest Station. Capt.J.R. RICHMOND RITCHIE,R.A.M.C.T.C. reported for duty & taken on the strength. 1 H.D.Horse drawn from Division & taken on the strength. The A.D.S. at the ASYLUM was closed and another established at P.14.b.9.3. Sheet 36a.	
"	19.4.18.		The situation remains quiet. Capt.J.R.RICHMOND RITCHIE,R.A.M.C.T.C. proceeded for temporary duty to A.D.S. vice Capt.R.C.COATSWORTH,R.A.M.C.T.C. who returned to Hqrs for duty.	
"	20.4.18.		The personnel at the Walking Wounded Aid Post at ~~XXX~~ GUARBECQUE was increased to 6. T/30751 Dvr.JARRETT F.,A.S.C. attached transferred sick to 61st.Divn.Rest Station. Capt. R.C.COATSWORTH,R.A.M.C.T.C. taken on the strength.	
"	21.4.18.		No.493492 Pte.COCKRANE W.J. evacuated sick to C.C.S. & struck off the strength. 437252 Pte.CURETON F.,reported from detached duty with XVIII Corps Hqrs. 493571 Pte.FREDERICKS A. "Wounded in Action" but remained on duty.	
"	22.4.18.		The situation remains quiet & all personnel was withdrawn from the line except 2 Bearer ~~Suadx~~ Squads at the R.A.P's & 2 Bearer Squads,2 Nursing Orderlies,& 2 runners at the A.D.S.	

Army Form C. 2118.

Instructions regarding War Diaries and Intelligence Summaries are contained in F. S. Regs., Part II. and the Staff Manual respectively. Title pages will be prepared in manuscript.

WAR DIARY
or
~~INTELLIGENCE SUMMARY~~
(Erase heading not required.)

Place	Date	Hour	Summary of Events and Information	Remarks and references to Appendices
MOLINGHEM	23·4·18·		303083 Cpl·BLACKHAIL D·,303081 A/Cpl·IRONSIDE D·B·,303244 Pte·ALLAN T·,303247 Pte·AITKEN J·D· & 395035 Pte·ROBINSON J·W· reported from detached duty with 1/5 Gordons & taken on the strength·	Hrd
"	24·4·18·		Major A·T·WATERHOUSE,R·A·M·C·T·F· reported from special leave· No·437161 Pte·PRITCHETT V·E·C· transferred sick to D·R·S· No·437372 Cpl·OLDROYD J·R· reported for duty from D·R·S·	Hrd
			The undermentioned N·C·Os& men were awarded " The Military Medal"	
			No·437412 L/CPL·A/SGT·FREDERICK HICKMAN,R·A·M·C·T·	
			"March 21 & 22 1918 at ATTILLY & HOLNON WOOD this N·C·O· was in charge of stretcher "bearers· In the absence of an officer he organised the bearers & superintended "their work in the open under extremely heavy shell fire· He also organised the "evacuation of stretcher cases from the bearer post in HOLNON WOOD to the motor "ambulances·Throughout the whole period from 11·0·am·on 21st·to 12·0·noon on 22nd· "he acted with the greatest gallantry & disregard of personal safety· He offered "a splendid example of courage & devotion to the bearers & by his efforts a large "number of cases were evacuated who would otherwise have fallen into the hands of "the enemy· No previous recommendation has been made·	
			No·M2/167360 PTE·ARTHUR BENNETT NETHERCOTT,M·T·A·S·C· attached·	
			"On March 21st·& 22nd· made repeated journeys in his ambulance under extremely heavy "shell fire·He displayed the utmost coolness throughout the period,& ultimately "drove his car under shell & machine gun fire to MARTEVILLE after that place had been "abandoned by R·A·M·C· Here he picked up 5 recently wounded men,& with the help of "his car orderly succeeded in getting them on to the car & back to safety· During "this operation the enemy was in view & advancing· He made this journey on his own "initiative against the advice of the Military Police,& thus saved 5 wounded men who "would otherwise inevitably have been captured· Previously to this he had taken his "car through ATTILLY & picked up 2 stretcher cases under extremely heavy shell fire "& brought them to safety· He displayed throughout the operations courage of a very "high order· This driver has been previously recommended for the M·M·(Dec·1917·)	
			No·437470 PTE·RICHARD COOPER,R·A·M·C·T·	
			"On the 21st·& 22nd·March in HOLNON WOOD for gallant conduct as a stretcher bearer· "He worked untiringly under heavy fire bringing in wounded,behaving with the greatest steadiness· After the bearer post was withdrawn on the 22nd March he established	

2353 Wt. W2544/1454 700,000 5/15 D. D. & L. A.D.S.S./Forms/C. 2118.

Army Form C. 2118.

Instructions regarding War Diaries and Intelligence Summaries are contained in F. S. Regs., Part II. and the Staff Manual respectively. Title pages will be prepared in manuscript.

WAR DIARY
or
INTELLIGENCE SUMMARY.

(Erase heading not required.)

Place	Date	Hour	Summary of Events and Information	Remarks and references to Appendices
MOLINGHEM	24·4·18·			

"an aid post in BEAUVOIS on his own initiative. Here he successfully attended many
"wounded men & evacuated two officers in a wheel-barrow who were unable to walk, thus
"enabling them to reach safety. By his action he showed himself possessed of a very
"high degree of courage & initiative, and offered a valuable example to other bearers
"of disregards of personal safety. No previous recommendation has been made.

No. M2/153302 PTE GERALD ALFRED ALEXANDER PACK M.T.A.S.C. attached.
"On 21 & 22 March Pte Gerald Alfred Alexander Pack drove his ambulance with
"remarkable coolness & judgement through very heavy shell fire, evacuating cases from
"HOLNON WOOD. He made repeated journeys by day & night, taking no rest. He continued
"driving his car through ATTILLY to pick up wounded until the last stretcher case
"was evacuated from the bearer post & drove off under the direct observation of the
"enemy who were approaching on either side. It was largely due to his magnificent
"devotion & high courage that no cases were left to fall into the hands of the enemy;
"No previous recommendation has been made.

No 405104 PTE OSCAR CARNELL R.A.M.C.T.
"No 405104 Pte Oscar Carnell on 21 & 22 March in HOLNON WOOD behaved with great
"coolness & gallantry while working as stretcher bearer. Exposed to the full
"violence of the bombardment he succeeded in guiding walking wounded to safety & in
"helping to bring in stretcher cases. He himself was wounded while carrying a
"stretcher. No previous recommendation has been made.

No 437509 PTE FRANK HAINES R.A.M.C.T.
"No 437509 Pte Frank Haines on the 21 & 22 March in ATTILLY & HOLNON WOOD displayed
"a high degree of steadfastness & courage during very heavy shell fire. He
"materially helped to clear stretcher cases from the Wood as far as the Bearer'
"Dugout repeatedly going out to bring in wounded and wasaffrally wounded & removed
"to safety by his comrades. He walked all the time with cheerfulness under violent
"shell fire. No previous recommendation has been made.

No 495479 PTE GOERGE PATRICK CIARRETT R.A.M.C.T.
"No 495479 Pte George Patrick Clarett on 22nd March in HIONON WOOD behaved with the
"utmost gallantry & courage while stretcher bearing under very heavy shell fire.
"While the road was subject to bombardment he helped to load stretcher cases on to
"the ambulances, working with dexterity & rapidity. He continued to work until the
"last case had been removed with no thought of his own safety. No previous
"recommendation has been made.

2353 Wt. W2544/1454 700,000 5/15 D. D. & L. A.D.S.S./Forms/C. 2118.

Instructions regarding War Diaries and Intelligence Summaries are contained in F. S. Regs., Part II. and the Staff Manual respectively. Title pages will be prepared in manuscript.

WAR DIARY
or
INTELLIGENCE SUMMARY.
(Erase heading not required.)

Army Form C. 2118.

Place	Date	Hour	Summary of Events and Information	Remarks and references to Appendices
MOLINGHEM	24·4·18·		No 437482 PTE FRANK SMITH R·A·M·C·T· "No 437492 Pte Frank Smith on 21 & 22 March while acting as car orderly showed great "coolness & courage· Everytime his car returned to HOLNON WOOD or ATTILLY he made "his way to the bearer post& helped to remove the stretcher cases,working all the "time along roads that were heavily shelled & proceeding to ATTILLY against the advic "of the Military Police· By his courage & devotion he materially helped to prevent "cases falling into the hands of the enemy· No previous recommendation has been made· No 437383 PTE (A/L/CPL GEORGE WILLIAM PLANT R·A·M·C·T· " No 437383 Pte (A/L/Cpl George William Plant on 22 March led his squad of bearers "in HOLNON WOOD with the greatest courage & gallantry· He was largely instrumental "in clearing the stretcher cases & by his good judgement & fine example showed "qualities of a high order· No previous recommendation has been made· No 439517 PTE REGINALD WILLIAM HANKS R·A·M·C·T· " No 439517 Pte Reginald William Hanks on 21 & 22 March at HOLNONWOOD -ATTILLY & "MARTEVILLE displayed great courage as a car orderly· On one occasion in HOLNON WOOD, "not finding any wounded ready to be removed he went out with the driver(Pte A·B· "Nethercott) & succeeded in finding two cases whom they brought back to the car & "so to safety· His conduct throughout was worthy of the highest praise,& he "maintained his coolness & cheerfulness under the heaviest shell fire· No previous "recommendation has been made·	H.W.S.
"	25·4·18·		The situation remains quiet·	H.W.S.
"	26·4·18·		Capt·R·LINTON RITCHIE,R·A·M·C· reported for duty & taken on the strength·	H.W.S.
"	27·4·18·		No·322051 Pte·HENDERSON H· transferred sick to D·R·S· The situation remains quiet·	H.W.S.
"	28·4·18·		No·439002 Cpl·PATTENT G·G· posted to 2/3 S·M·F·Amb· & struck off strength·	H.W.S.
"	29·4·18·		The situation remains quiet·	H.W.S.
"	30·4·18·		The situation remains quiet·	

H.W. [illegible]
Lt Col. RAMC.

14 CONFIDENTIAL

MEDICAL

Vol 25

May 1918

WAR DIARY

14

R.A.M.C.

VOLUME 25

Instructions regarding War Diaries and Intelligence Summaries are contained in F. S. Regs., Part II. and the Staff Manual respectively. Title pages will be prepared in manuscript.

WAR DIARY
or
INTELLIGENCE SUMMARY.
(*Erase heading not required.*)

Army Form C. 2118.

Place	Date	Hour	Summary of Events and Information	Remarks and references to Appendices
MOLINGHEM	1·5·18·		The situation remains quiet·	HNB
"	2·5·18·		No·437161 Pte·PRITCHETT V·E·C· reported for duty from Hospital· Cars Nos· 6, 9, & 18 sent to Workshop· No·112924 Pte·SMITH H·, 52051 Pte·SAMPSON M·, 43734 Pte·SMITH J·, 65628 Pte·SMITH C·, 45378 Pte·STEWARD D·C·, 20259 Pte·STILL A·, 73174 Pte·SMITH A·, 63217 Pte·SEABRIGHT T·, 20805 Pte·STONEHILL J·F·, 58776 Pte·SIMS C·, 64075 Pte·TURNBULL J·F·, 83292 Pte·SCOTTON E·, 18885 Pte·SHARP S·, 19229 Pte·SULLIVAN J·, 99684 Pte·SIDEBOTHAM S·, 1488 Pte·TAYLOR J·S·, 93658 Pte·THOMAS I·R·, 5652 Pte·TAYLOR R·, 91641 Pte·TINSLEY R·, 72199 Pte·TIBBLES J·D·, 51735 Pte·TAYLOR G·, & 11271 Pte·UNSWORTH R·, reported from Base via 61st·Divisional Depot Battalion & taken on the strength·	HNB
"	3·5·18·		Cars Nos· 6, 9, & 18 reported for duty from Workshop·	HNB
"	4·5·18·		Ford Car No·19 sent to Workshop· Capt·M·D·WOOD,R·A·M·C·T·F· reported for temporary duty from 2/3 S·M·Fld·Ambce· Major A·T·WATERHOUSE,R·A·M·C·T·F· with Capt·M·D·WOOD, & 36 Other Ranks proceeded for temporary duty to XI Corps Rest Station· Capt·J·R·RICHMOND RITCHIE,R·A·M·C·T·C· with 25 Other Ranks proceeded for temporary duty to O·C·,Detach·No·15 Field Ambulance for Constructional Work on XI Corps (New) Rest Station· Lieut·J·C·THOMPSON,M·O·R·C·,U·S·A· proceeded for temporary duty to King Edward's Horse· No·405262 Pte·ANTHONY J· evacuated sick to D·R·S·	HNB
"	5·5·18·		Car Loading Post re-established at P·14·b·9·3· (Sheet 36a·)· Routine Work· Situation remains quiet·	HNB
"	6·5·18·		No·322051 Pte·HENDERSON H· reported for duty from D·R·S· No·124802 Pte·COLE C·J· evacuated sick to C·C·S· & struck off strength·	HNB
"	7·5·18·		Ford Car No·18 proceeded for temporary duty to 61st·Division Rest Station·	HNB
"	8·5·18·		No·12432 Cpl·WARD A· reported for duty from Base via 61st·Divisional Depot Battalion & taken on the strength· Major A·T·WATERHOUSE,R·A·M·C·T·F· with Capt·M·D·WOOD,R·A·M·C·T·F & 35 Other Ranks returned from detached duty at XI Corps Rest Station· Capt·M·D·WOOD, R·A·M·C·T·F· ceased to be attached for duty & returned forthwith to 2/3 F·Amb· for duty· T/30751 Dvr·JARRETT F·,A·S·C· att· struck off strength in accordance with G·R·O· 3578·	HNB

A5834 Wt.W4973/M687 750,000 8/16 D. D. & L. Ltd. Forms/C.2118/13.

Instructions regarding War Diaries and Intelligence Summaries are contained in F. S. Regs., Part II. and the Staff Manual respectively. Title pages will be prepared in manuscript.

WAR DIARY
~~or~~
~~INTELLIGENCE SUMMARY.~~
(*Erase heading not required.*)

Army Form C. 2118.

Place	Date	Hour	Summary of Events and Information	Remarks and references to Appendices
MOLINGHEM	9.5.18		No.405362 Pte.ANTHONY J. evacuated from D.R.S. to C.C.S. & struck off strength. The u/m officer is awarded " THE MILITARY CROSS " . Captain RICHARD COLLIER COATSWORTH, R.A.M.C. (T.C.) " For conspicuous gallantry on March 21st. in HOLNON WOOD. At the beginning of " the battle he organized & led his regimental stretcher bearers through very " heavy shell fire, systematically removing all the wounded that could be found. " He organized the removal of all cases from a neighbouring aid post & by his " unfailing cheerfulness & coolness he set a very high standard to his men who " were inspired by his splendid disregard of safety & his untiring zeal on behalf " of the wounded. It was due to his efforts that so many cases were successfully. " evacuated. " Later at HOMBLEUX-CRESSY & BIARRE on March 24th. he again organized the regi- " mental bearers, working up ~~the line~~ to the battle line, directing the walking " wounded & managing the ambulance service . He acted throughout with a fine " disregard of danger & his whole bearing is worthy of the highest praise.	
"			Capt.J.R.RICHMOND RITCHIE, R.A.M.C.T.C. & party returned from temporary detached duty with O.C., Detach.No.15 Field Ambulance - Xl Corps (New) Rest Station.	
"	10.5.18.		Situation remains quiet. Routine Work. One large car proceeded for temporary duty to 61st.Division Main Dressing Station.	
"	11.5.18.		Routine Work .	
"	12.5.18.		Routine Work.	
"	13.5.18.		The Walking Wounded Dressing Station was inspected by the D.M.S., First Army attended by D.D.M.S., Xl Corps & A.D.M.S., 61st.Division. No.437212 L/Cpl.VIGURS E.N., 322076 Pte.HENDERSON H., & 495479 Pte.CLARETT P.G. transferred sick to 61st.D.R.S. Capt.J.R. RICHMOND RITCHIE, R.A.M.C.T.C. proceeded for temporary duty to 2/1 S.M.Fld.Ambulance.	

Instructions regarding War Diaries and Intelligence Summaries are contained in F. S. Regs., Part II. and the Staff Manual respectively. Title pages will be prepared in manuscript.

WAR DIARY
or
INTELLIGENCE SUMMARY.
(Erase heading not required.)

Army Form C. 2118.

Place	Date	Hour	Summary of Events and Information	Remarks and references to Appendices
MOLINGHEM	14·5·18·		Capt·R·C·COATSWORTH,R·A·M·C·T·C· evacuated sick to C·C·S· No·357310 Pte·DIXON W·E· evacuated sick to C·C·S· & struck off strength· No·322076 Pte·HENDERSON H· evacuated from D·R·S· to C·C·S· & struck off strength·	HML
"	15·5·18·		1 man proceeded on leave· One water cart with orderly proceeded for temporary duty to 2/3 S·M·Fld·Ambce·	HML
"	16·5·18·		No·87668 Pte·BARTON A· evacuated sick to C·C·S· & struck off strength· Car No·14419 with driver & orderly sent to Workshop·	HML
"	17·5·18·		No·388271 Pte·BARKER H· evacuated sick to C·C·S· & struck off strength· T4/248773 Dvr· HOWSE G·W· transferred sick to D·R·S· Capt·A·C·JEPSON,R·A·M·C·T·C· reported for duty & taken on the strength· Capt·J·R·RICHMOND RITCHIE,R·A·M·C·T·C· reported from detached temporary duty with 2/1 S·M·Fld·Ambce· No·437212 L/Cpl·VIGURS E·N· transferred from D·R·S· to C·R·S·	HML
"	18·5·18·		Car No·14419 with driver & orderly reported for duty from Workshop· T4/248773 Dvr· HOWSE G·W· evacuated from D·R·S· to 39 Stationary Hospital & struck off strength· No·495479 Pte·CLARETT G· (M·M·) evacuated from D·R·S· to C·R·S· No·437458 Private LEONARD WILSON,R·A·M·C·T· is awarded "THE MILITARY MEDAL" for gallantry and devotion to duty· " On Saturday 13th·April 1918 at a Regimental Aid Post (2/8th·Battn·Worcestershire " Regt·) Sheet 36a· Q·11·a·9·1· during a bombardment there was a direct hit on the " building, killing one man and seriously wounding five men· With complete dis- " regard of his personal safety Pte·Wilson remained with the wounded & dressed " their wounds during continuous heavy shell fire during which two more direct " hits were obtained on the building which had been evacuated by all men except " the wounded and Pte·Wilson· Pte·Wilson then fetched a stretcher squad & re- " moved all cases to safety· By his pluck & skill he not only was able to save the " life of at least one severely wounded man,but also set a fine example& by his " cheerfulness enabled the wounded to bear the continued shelling with fortitude " until they could be removed· His action throughout was worthy of the highest " praise· Pte·Wilson has been previously recommended for M·M· – VILLERS PLOUICH " December 1917·	HML

2353 Wt. W2544/1454 700,000 5/15 D. D. & L. A.D.S.S./Forms/C. 2118.

Instructions regarding War Diaries and Intelligence Summaries are contained in F. S. Regs., Part II. and the Staff Manual respectively. Title pages will be prepared in manuscript.

WAR DIARY
or
~~INTELLIGENCE SUMMARY.~~
(Erase heading not required.)

Army Form C. 2118.

Place	Date	Hour	Summary of Events and Information	Remarks and references to Appendices
MOLINGHEM	19·5·18·		Situation remains quiet· Routine Work ·	H.W.
"	20·5·18·		Routine Work· No·437212 L/Cpl·VIGURS E·N· & No·495479 Pte·CLARETT G·,(M·M) struck off strength in accordance with G·R·O· No·3578·	H.W.
"	21·5·18·		No·388342 Pte·AYRE C·D·,(D·C·M·) proceeded for duty to 2/2 Northumbrian Field Ambulance & struck off strength· Water cart with orderly reported from temporary detached duty with 2/3 S·M·Fld·Ambce· No·437299 Pte·YEOMANS A· evacuated to C·C·S· & struck off strength·	H.W.
"	22·5·18·		The C·O· presented the 61st·Divisional Commander's Parchment to M2/167360 Pte·HETHERCOTT A·(M·T·A·S·C· attached), No·437338 Pte·HISCOCK W·T·, & No·437458 Pte·WILSON L·(M·M·) · Ford Ambulance No·29119 evacuated from 61st·M·T·Company Workshops via XI Corps Workshops to 2nd·A·S·C· Repair Shop on 17·5·18 & struck off strength to take effect from that date No·437109 Pte·GREW C· evacuated to C·C·S· & struck off strength·	H.W.
"	23·5·18·		No·437212 L/Cpl·VIGURS E·N· & 437116 Pte·STENT J· taken on the strength but on temporary detached duty at 61st·Divn·Reinforcement Wing·	H.W.
"	24·5·18·		No·437212 L/Cpl·VIGURS E·N· & 437116 Pte·STENT J· reported for duty from 61st·Division Reinforcement Wing· Routine Work·	H.W.
"	25·5·18·		No·T4/248773 Dvr·HOWSE G·W·(A·S·C· attached) reported for duty from 39th·Stationary Hospital & taken on the strength·	H.W.
"	26·5·18·		Major R·D·MOORE,(M·C·),R·A·M·C·T·F· proceeded on special leave to England· Ford Ambce· No·14595 with driver reported for duty & taken on the strength· 2 N·C·O's & 5 men proceeded to 54 C·C·S· for instructional training·	H.W.
"	27·5·18·		2 Nursing Orderlies proceeded for temporary duty to XI Corps Schools· No·437509 Pte· HAINES F·G·(M·M·) reported for duty from Base & taken on the strength·	H.W.
"	28·5·18·		Horsed Ambulance with driver & orderly proceeded for temporary duty to 61st·Divn·Rest Station·	H.W.

Army Form C. 2118.

Instructions regarding War Diaries and Intelligence Summaries are contained in F. S. Regs., Part II. and the Staff Manual respectively. Title pages will be prepared in manuscript.

WAR DIARY
or
~~INTELLIGENCE~~ SUMMARY.
(Erase heading not required.)

Place	Date	Hour	Summary of Events and Information	Remarks and references to Appendices
MOLINGHEM	29·5·18·		Capt·A·C·JEPSON,R·A·M·C·T·C· proceeded for temporary duty to 2/1 S·M·Fld·Ambce· 5 men of 2/8 Worcesters & 4 men of 2/6 R·Warwicks reported for a course of Chiropody· 1 man of 2/8 Worcesters reported for instruction in Water Duties· No·437299 Pte· YEOMANS A· reported for duty from C·C·S· & taken on the strength· No·437373 Pte· BUSBY F·W· evacuated sick to C·C·S· & struck off strength·	HmB
"	30·5·18·		No·183768 Dvr·WOTHERSPOON L· (P·B·Batman) reported for duty & taken on the strength· Capt·R·C·COATSWORTH (M·C·),R·A·M·C·T·C· reported for duty from Hospital·	HmB
"	31·5·18·		Capt·R·L·RITCHIE,R·A·M·C· proceeded for temporary duty to 307th·Brigade R·F·A· No 495479 Pte CLARETT G·(M·M·) reported for duty from C·R·S· & taken on the strength·	HmB

HmBumphes
Lt Col Ramc
Officer Commanding
2/2 Sth. Mid. Fld. Ambce. R.A.M.C. T.F

2/2ND SOUTH MIDLAND FIELD AMBULANCE R.A.M.C. (T.F.) 31 MAY 1918

A5834 Wt. W4973/M687 750,000 8/16 D. D. & L. Ltd. Forms/C.2118/13.

16 CONFIDENTIAL **MEDICAL**

SB 26

140/3076.

June 1918.

WAR DIARY

2/2 [illegible]

R.A.M.C.T.

June 1st – 30th (inclusive)
1918.

VOLUME 26

Instructions regarding War Diaries and Intelligence Summaries are contained in F. S. Regs., Part II and the Staff Manual respectively. Title pages will be prepared in manuscript.

WAR DIARY
or
INTELLIGENCE SUMMARY.
(Erase heading not required.)

Army Form C. 2118.

Place	Date	Hour	Summary of Events and Information	Remarks and references to Appendices
MOLINGHEM	1·6·18·		Capt·A·C·JEPSON,R·A·M·C·,T·C· proceeded from 2/1 S·M·Fld·Ambce· for temporary duty to 61st·M·G·C· to relieve Capt·D·B·I·HALLETT,R·A·M·C·,T·C·	Initd
"	2·6·18·		Situation remains quiet· Routine Work·	Initd
"	3·6·18·		Routine Work·	Initd
"	4·6·18·		No·337290 Pte·HYETT G·A·, 437370 Pte·(L/Cpl·) WALKER H·J·, & 40333 Pte·LLOYD D·O· evacuated sick to C·C·S· & struck off strength· No·437447 Pte·BURTON W·, 500065 Pte·WANT A·G·, & 500151 Pte·SMITH C·H· reported for duty from Base & taken on the strength· Capt·D·B·I·HALLETT,R·A·M·C·,T·C· reported for duty· 4 men of 2/6 R·Warwicks returned to their unit trained as Battalion Chiropodists·	Initd
"	5·6·18·		5 men of 2/8 Worcesters returned to their unit trained as Battalion Chiropodists· 1 man of 2/8 Worcesters returned to his unit fit to takex over duties as Water Cart Orderly· ·Capt·J·R·Richmond Ritchie,R·A·M·C·,T·C· proceeded for temporary duty to 2/8 Worcesters· No·437250 Pte·HUNT A·E· & 437451 Pte·TRISTRAM B·J· evacuated sick to C·C·S· & struck off strength· No·437305 Pte·GOURLAY W·J· reported for duty from Base via 61st·Divn·Depot Battn· & taken on the strength·	Initd
"	6·6·18·		Routine Work·	Initd
"	7·6·18·		No·437101 Pte·LOVELESS W·H· attached for duty to 61st·Divn·Reception Camp and struck off strength· No·437297 Pte·ENGLISH W·J· & 437517 Pte·HASSELL W·T· evacuated sick to C·C·S· & struck off strength·	Initd
"	8·6·18·		Capt·D·B·I·HALLETT,R·A·M·C·,T·C· ceased to be attached for duty & proceeded to England "Expiration of Contract"· No·305188 Pte·MACFARLANE G·, 366025 Pte·MILLS A·C·, 372162 Pte·STEEL A·D·, 381012 Pte·SHADWELL C·, & 417310 Pte·THOMPSON E· reported for duty from Base & taken on the strength· No· 437285 Pte·KIMBERLEY J·C· taken on the strength but on temporary detached duty with No·523 Coy·A·S·C·	Initd
"	9·6·18·		No·437372 Cpl·OLDROYD J·R· proceeded for Gas Course at XI Corps Gas School· T4/040956 Dvr·CANNEY D· No·4 Coy·A·S·C· attached reported for duty & taken on the strength·	Initd

A5834 Wt. W4973/M687 750,000 8/16 D. D. & L. Ltd. Forms/C.2118/13.

Instructions regarding War Diaries and Intelligence Summaries are contained in F. S. Regs., Part II. and the Staff Manual respectively. Title pages will be prepared in manuscript.

WAR DIARY
or
INTELLIGENCE SUMMARY.
(Erase heading not required.)

Army Form C. 2118.

Place	Date	Hour	Summary of Events and Information	Remarks and references to Appendices
MOLINGHEM	9·6·18·		No·437441 Pte·O'LOUGHLIN P· reported for duty from 61st·Divn·Wing & taken on the strength· 1st·Lieut·R·HENSEL,M·O·R·C·,U·S·A· reported for duty & taken on the strength· No·543003 Sergt·DRYSDALE G·W· evacuated sick to C·C·S· & struck off the strength· No·437511 Pte·SEALES G·N· appointed Chiropodist with effect from 1·1·18·	[illegible]
"	10·6·18·		Routine Work·	[illegible]
"	11·6·18·		Capt·R·C·COATSWORTH,R·A·M·C·,T·C· admitted sick to 54 C·C·S·	[illegible]
"	12·6·18·		Major R·D·MOORE,M·C· reported from leave of absence· 1st·Lieut·R·HENSEL,M·O·R·C·, U·S·A·,No·437515 Pte·EVITTS T·L· & 495479 Pte·CLARETT G·P·(M·M·) proceeded for a course of instruction to No·1 C·C·S· WAVRANS·	[illegible]
"	13·6·18·		Lieut·C·H·AYLEN,R·A·M·C·,T·C· attached for temporary duty· No·437517 Pte·HASSELL W· reported for duty from C·C·S· & taken on the strength· No·437566 Pte·EVANS E·O· (attached 61st·Divn·Baths) evacuated sick to C·C·S· & struck off strength· Capt· R·C·COATSWORTH,(M·C·),R·A·M·C·T·C· evacuated to Base & struck off strength· Authority-A·D·M·S·61st·Division No·374 dated 13·6·18· No·439136 Pte·CRIDGE G· & 439152 Pte·ABBOTT A·W· taken on the strength but on temporary detached duty with 61st·Divn·Signals,R·E·	[illegible]
"	14·6·18·		No·364405 Pte·JONES J·,359387 Pte·HAMILTON R·,344074 Pte·CLEGG J·U·B·,481034 Pte· Bainbridge S·J·,499145 Pte·BEANEY H·, 437303 Pte·GRIFFITHS A·,421501 Pte·SHARMAN J·R·,437277 Pte·Littlewood H·G·, & 364343 Pte·JONES H·W· reported for duty from Base & taken on the strength·	[illegible]
"	15·6·18·		No·437275 Cpl·GIBBS J·W· & 437374 Pte·PORTMAN L· proceeded for temporary duty to 61st·Divn·Reception Camp· No·437250 Pte·HUNT A·E· & 437451 Pte·TRISTRAM B·J· reported for duty from C·C·S· & taken on the strength· Lieut·J·C·THOMPSON,M·O·R·C·, U·S·A· reported from detached duty with King Edward's Horse & proceeded forthwith for temporary duty with 9th·Northumberland Fusiliers· 1 N·C·O & 2 men reported from detached duty at 54 C·C·S· No·543003 Sergt·DRYSDALE G·W· reported from C·C·S & taken on the strength· No·439152 Pte·ABBOTT A·W·& 439136 Pte·CRIDGE reported for duty from 61st·Divn·Signals R·E·	[illegible]

A5834 Wt W4973/M687 750,000 8/16 D. D. & L. Ltd. Forms/C.2118/13.

Instructions regarding War Diaries and Intelligence Summaries are contained in F. S. Regs., Part II. and the Staff Manual respectively. Title pages will be prepared in manuscript.

WAR DIARY
or
INTELLIGENCE SUMMARY.
(Erase heading not required.)

Army Form C. 2118.

Place	Date	Hour	Summary of Events and Information	Remarks and references to Appendices
MOLINGHEM	16·6·18·		No·437270 Cpl·CLEAL C·A· proceeded for "Gas Course" at Xl Corps Schools· Capt·J·R· RICHMOND RITCHIE,R·A·M·C·,T·C· reported from temporary detached duty with 2/8 Worcesters vice Lieut·C·H·AYLEN,R·A·M·C·,T·C· who reported to 2/8 Worcesters for duty· No·437506 Pte·DEAN C·R·,437458 Pte·WILSON L;(M·M·), 437342 Pte·RUSSELL J·H·, & 437490 L/Cpl· EDGINGTON B·J· admitted to hospital & transferred to No·8 C·C·S· Rest Camp·	
"	17·6·18·		The following A·D·S· & Posts were taken over from the 2/3 Sth·Mid·Field Ambulance:- A·D·S·------ P·2·c·6·1·) Car Loading PostP·5·c·1·9·) Sheet 36a· R·A·P·------ P·5·c·8·5·) R·A·P·------ P·11·a·8·3·) One car reported for temporary duty from 2/1 S·M·Fld·Ambce· One car reported from temporary detached duty with 2/1 S·M·Fld·Ambce· Capt·J·R·RICHMOND RITCHIE,R·A·M·C·,T·C·, & party proceeded for duty at the A·D·S·	
"	18·6·18·		One car reported for temporary duty from 2/1 S·M·Fld·Ambce·	
"	19·6·18·		No·437506 Pte·DEAN C·R·, 437458 Pte·WILSON L·(M·M·),437342 Pte·RUSSELL J·H·,& 437490 L/Cpl·EDGINGTON B·J· reported for duty from No·8 C·C·S· Rest Camp· Owing to the large sick rate in the Division all available tents were pitched for the accommodation of "XXXXX "P·U·O·" patients· Three operating tents & 7 bell tents were borrowed from 2/3 S·M·Fld·Ambce· & 6 bell tents from 2/1 S·M·Fld·Ambce· These were all erected together with our own tents· The two schoolrooms occupied as billets were cleared and fitted as Hospital Wards· Accommodation was thus provided for 2 Officers and 153 Other Ranks·	
"	20·6·18·		One horsed ambulance with driver & orderly reported from detached duty at 61st·Divn· Rest Station· Capt·A·BLAKELEY (10th·Canadian Field Ambulance) reported for temporary duty· Capt;J·R·RICHMOND RITCHIE,R·A·M·C·,T·C· proceeded for temporary duty to 9th· Northumberland Fusiliers vice Lieut·J·C·Thompson,M·O·R·C·,U·S·A· admitted to Hospital sick·	
"	21·6·18·		No·437270 Cpl·CLEAL C·A· reported for duty from "Gas Course" held at Xl Corps Schools·	

A5834 Wt. W4973/M687 750,000 8/16 D. D. & L. Ltd. Forms/C.2118/13.

Instructions regarding War Diaries and Intelligence Summaries are contained in F. S. Regs., Part II. and the Staff Manual respectively. Title pages will be prepared in manuscript.

WAR DIARY
or
INTELLIGENCE SUMMARY.
(Erase heading not required.)

Army Form C. 2118.

Place	Date	Hour	Summary of Events and Information	Remarks and references to Appendices
MOLINGHEM	22·6·18·		Lieut·R·HENSEL,M·O·R·C·,U·S·A·,No·437515 Pte·EVETTS T·L·, & 495479 Pte·CLARETT G·P·(M·M) reported for duty from Course of Instruction at No·1 C·C·S· St·Sergt·CUMMINGS T· & 8 Other Ranks proceeded for temporary duty to 2/7 R·Warwicks to nurse the sick of the Battalion under M·O·i/c·	HmB
"	23·6·18·		No·303083 Cpl·BLACKALL D· proceeded for "Gas Course" to Xl Corps Gas Schools· Capt·A· BLAKELEY,(10 Canadian Field Ambce·) proceeded for duty with 2/3 S·M·Fld·Ambce· Lieut·J·C·THOMPSON,M·O·R·C·,U·S·A· discharged from Hospital·	HmB
"	24·6·18·		Motor Cycle sent to Workshop· Capt·J·R·RENNIE,M·C·, R·A·M·C· reported for duty & proceeded for duty forthwith to 2/7 R·Warwicks·	HmB
"	25·6·18·		Routine Work· Situation remains quiet·	HmB
"	26·6·18·		Capt·J·R·RENNIE,M·C·, R·A·M·C· & party on detached duty with 2/7 R·Warwicks proceeded for duty to the P·U·O·Camp (Aerodrome,TREIZENNE·)	HmB
"	27·6·18·		1 N·C·O· proceeded on leave· 1Car 2/1 S·M·Fld·Ambce· ceased to be attached for duty· 1 H·D·Horse No·785 sent to 61st·Mob·Vet·Section· No·437566 Pte·EVANS E·C· reported for duty at 61st·Divn·Baths from Hospital & taken on the strength to take effect from 19·6·18·	HmB
"	28·6·18·		No·85152 Pte·DUDENEY H·B·Y· reported for duty from Base & taken on the strength· 1 man proceeded on leave· No·303083 Cpl·BLACKALL D· reported for duty from "Gas Course" held at Xl Corps Gas School· Motor Cycle returned from Workshop·	HmB
"	29·6·18·		Lieut·J·C·Thompson,M·O·R·C·,U·S·A· proceeded for temporary duty to 36 Labour Group· The Divisional Commander accompanied by A·A·& Q·M·G·, & A·D·M·S· inspected the Hospital· 1 man reported from leave· Major G·SCOTT WILLIAMSON,R·A·M·C·T· reported for duty & proceeded to P·U·O·Camp as Officer i/c	HmB
"	30·6·18·		No·437283 L/Cpl·PLANT G·W· proceeded for "Gas Course" to Xl Corps Gas School·	

H Harrington [signature]
Officer Commanding
2/2 Sth. Mid. Fld. Ambce. R.A.M.C. T F

2353 Wt. W2544/1454 700,000 5/15 D. D. & L. A.D.S.S./Forms/C. 2118.

Instructions regarding War Diaries and Intelligence Summaries are contained in F. S. Regs., Part II. and the Staff Manual respectively. Title pages will be prepared in manuscript.

WAR DIARY
or
INTELLIGENCE SUMMARY.
(Erase heading not required.)

Army Form C. 2118.

Place	Date	Hour	Summary of Events and Information	Remarks and references to Appendices
MOLINGHEM	1·7·18·		Lieut·J·C·THOMPSON,M·O·R·C·,U·S·A· reported from temporary detached duty with 36 Labour Group· 1 Car with driver & orderly reported from temporary detached duty at 61st· D·R·S· No·437510 Pte·MORRIS H· "Wounded in Action" but remained on duty· Capt·A·C· JEPSON,R·A·M·C·,T·C· posted to 61st·Battn·M·G·C· & struck off strength· to take effect from 30·6·18· No·51735 Pte·TAYLOR G·W· admitted to hospital "Gassed-Wounded",evacuated to 54 C·C·S· & struck off strength· No·36131 Pte·KENNEDY J·,1/7 Mans· att· P·B·Batman, evacuated to C·C·S· & struck off strength·	HDL
"	2·7·18·		Routine Work· Situation remains quiet·	HDL
"	3·7·18·		Lieut·J·P·STOUT,M·O·R·C·,U·S·A· & Lieut·R·M·MacGuffie,M·O·R·C·,U·S·A· reported for duty & taken on the strength· T4/036273 Dvr·BLAND J· No·4 Coy·A·S·C· att· evacuated sick to C·C·S· & struck off the strength· No·32896 Pte·WARD F·J· admitted to Hospital·	HDL
"	4·7·18·		Lieut·R·HENSEL,M·O·R·C·,U·S·A· proceeded for temporary duty to 2/5 Glosters· No·437288 Sergt·UREN L·V· admitted to hospital & transferred to C·R·S·	HDL
"	5·7·18·		No·439143 Cpl·BERRY E·J· granted leave of absence to PARIS· No·D·14181 Pte·MALLINSON J –4 D·Guards reported for duty as P·B·Batman & taken on the strength· Ford Car No·19 with driver & orderly sent to Workshop· No·437283 L/Cpl·PLANT G·W·(M·M·) reported for duty from course held at XI Corps Gas School· 1 H·D·Horse evacuated from 61st·Mobile Veterinary Section to Base & struck off strength to take effect from 2·7·18·	HDL
"	6·7·18·		No·32896 Pte·WARD F·J· discharged from Hospital· Routine Work· Situation remains quiet·	HDL
"	7·7·18·		No·437424 Sergt·Birkby L· granted leave of absence to CHERBOURG·	HDL
"	8·7·18·		No·M2/099465 Pte·WEAVER J·,M·T·A·S·C· attached,granted leave of absence to England· Capt R·L·RITCHIE,R·A·M·C· reported from temporary detached duty with 307 Bde·R·F·A· Ford Car No·19 with driver & orderly reported from Workshop·	HDL
"	9·7·18·		No·64875 Pte·TURNBULL J·O· granted leave of absence to England· No·76570 Pte·WEBSTER W· evacuated sick to C·C·S· & struck off strength·	HDL

2353 Wt. W2544/1454 700,000 5/15 D. D. & L. A.D.S.S./Forms/C. 2118.

Instructions regarding War Diaries and Intelligence Summaries are contained in F. S. Regs., Part II. and the Staff Manual respectively. Title pages will be prepared in manuscript.

WAR DIARY
~~or~~
~~INTELLIGENCE SUMMARY~~.

(Erase heading not required.)

Army Form C. 2118.

Place	Date	Hour	Summary of Events and Information	Remarks and references to Appendices
MOLINGHEM	10·7·18·		No·82152 Pte·DUDENEY H·B·Y· transferred to Base Depot & struck off strength· Lieut· R·M·MacGUFFIE,M·O·R·C·,U·S·A· posted for duty with 2/7 R·Warwicks as Medical Officer & struck off strength· Advance Party of relieving Ambulance-231 Field Ambulance-arrived preparatory to taking over·	[initials]
FONTES·	11·7·18·		Headquarters, Advanced Dressing Station & posts up the line were taken over by the 231 Field Ambulance· Under orders received from A·D·M·S·61st·Division the Unit with Transport complete moved by march route at 2·0·pm· to FONTES (Sheet 36a·N·30·a·3·8·)· Hospital opened for the reception of sick· No·437288 Sergt·UREN L·V· evacuated from C·R·S· to C·C·S· & struck off strength· Two large motor ambulances reported for duty from 2/1 S·M·Fld·Ambce·	[initials]
"	12·7·18·		Capt·R·L·RITCHIE,R·A·M·C· proceeded for temporary duty to Fifth Army Headquarters· 1 N·C·O· proceeded on leave· 1 Car with driver & orderly proceeded for temporary duty to P·U·O·Detention Camp· No·52735 Pte·TAYLOR G·W· reported for duty from C·C·S· & taken on the strength·	[initials]
"	13·7·18·		1 N·C·O· reported from leave· No·437442 Pte·HARIUR S·J· evacuated sick to C·C·S· & struck off strength· Ford Car No·18 sent to Workshop·	[initials]
"	14·7·18·		No·437490 L/C EDGINGTON B·J· proceeded for "Gas Course" at XI Corps Gas School·	[initials]
"	15·7·18·		No·437288 L/Sergt·UREN L·V· reported for duty from Hospital & taken on the strength·	[initials]
"	16·7·18·		No·417210 Pte·THOMSON E· granted leave of absence to England· No·437233 Sgt·WHITE-HOUSE T·H· appointed unpaid Acting Staff Sergeant & No·437374 Cpl·BARWELL F· appointed unpaid acting Sergeant· No·437321 Cpl·WINDRIDGE L·J· evacuated sick to C·C·S· & struck off strength·	[initials]
"	17·7·18·		Lieut·J·C·THOMPSON,M·O·R·C·,U·S·A· posted to 9th·Northumberland Fusiliers as Medical Officer & struck off strength vice Capt·J·R·RICHMOND RITCHIE,R·A·M·C·T·C· who reported for duty· 3 large cars of 2/1 S·M·Fld·Ambce· ceased to be attached for duty· 9 men reported for a course of Chiropody· Ford Car No·18 returned from Workshop· 9 N·C·O's & men reported from detached duty at P·U·O· Detention Camp·	[initials]

Instructions regarding War Diaries and Intelligence Summaries are contained in F. S. Regs., Part II. and the Staff Manual respectively. Title pages will be prepared in manuscript.

WAR DIARY
~~or~~
~~INTELLIGENCE~~ SUMMARY.
(Erase heading not required.)

Army Form C. 2118.

Place	Date	Hour	Summary of Events and Information	Remarks and references to Appendices
FONTES.	18.7.18.		Ford Car No.19 sent to Workshop.	HW
"	19.7.18.		1 Car with driver & orderly reported for duty from 2/1 S.M.Fld.Ambce.	
"	20.7.18.		Ford Car No.16 reported for temporary duty from 2/1 S.M.Fld.Ambce.	
"	21.7.18.		2 Cars of 2/1 S.M.Fld.Ambce. ceased to be attached for duty. No.437247 u/a/Sgt.BARWELL F proceeded for Gas Course to X1 Corps Schools. No.437516 Pte.TAYLOR A.E. reported for duty from Base & taken on the strength.	HW
W. of RACQUINGHEM	22.7.18.		Under instructions received from 182 Infantry Brigade the unit with Transport complete moved by march route at 11.15.am. Route-MAZINGHEM,LAMBRES,AIRE,WITTES & RACQUINGHEM- Time of arrival 4.0.pm. -Location, Sheet 36a.B.13.c.1.2. Hospital opened for the reception of.sick of 182 Infantry Brigade, 1/5 D.C.L.I. & 61st.Battn.M.G.C. 1 Car reported from Workshop. No.93658 Pte.THOMAS J.R. evacuated sick to C.C.S. & struck off strength.	HW
"	23.7.18.		9 men ceased to be attached for Course of Chiropody. No.421501 Pte.SHARMAN J. granted leave of absence to England. Lieut.R.HENSEL,M.O.R.C., U.S.A. reported from temporary detached duty with 2/5 Glosters & posted forthwith ad Medical Officer to 2/8 Worcesters & struck off strength.	HW
"	24.7.18.		No.437101 Pte.LOVELESS W.H. reported for duty from 61st.Divn.Reception Camp & taken on the strength.	HW
"	25.7.18.		No.60376 Sergt.VAUGHAN H.W. & 71510 Pte.HARTLEY B.S. reported for duty from Base & taken on the strength.	HW
"	26.7.18.		No.499145 Pte.BEANEY H. evacuated sick to C.C.S. & struck off strength. 2 men reported from detached duty at X1 Corps Schools. No.437247 u/a/Sgt.BARWELL F. reported for duty from Gas Course.	HW
"	27.7.18.		Routine Work.	HW
"	28.7.18.		Routine Work.	HW

Army Form C. 2118.

Instructions regarding War Diaries and Intelligence Summaries are contained in F. S. Regs., Part II. and the Staff Manual respectively. Title pages will be prepared in manuscript.

WAR DIARY
or
INTELLIGENCE SUMMARY.
(Erase heading not required.)

Place	Date	Hour	Summary of Events and Information	Remarks and references to Appendices
W. of RACQUINGHEM.	29.7.18.		One car sent to Workshop. No.437206 Pte.RICHARDSON F.L., on temporary detached duty with 2/5 Glosters, transferred to 2/3 S.M.Fld.Ambce. & struck off strength with effect from 8.6.18. Capt;R.L.RITCHIE,R.A.M.C. struck off strength with effect from 25.7.18. One despatch rider proceeded for temporary duty to A.D.M.S. office.	
"	30.7.18.		Routine Work.	
"	31.7.18.		Routine Work.	

Lt.Col. RAMC

Officer Commanding
2/1 Sth. Mid. Fld. Ambce. R.A.M.C. T.F.

9 CONFIDENTIAL MEDICAL

WAR DIARY

WR 28

140/3200.

Aug. 1918.

2/2 Sth. Mid. Fd. Ambce. R.A.M.C.T.

VOLUME 28.

August 1st – 31st 1918 (inclusive).

Instructions regarding War Diaries and Intelligence Summaries are contained in F. S. Regs., Part II. and the Staff Manual respectively. Title pages will be prepared in manuscript.

WAR DIARY
or
INTELLIGENCE SUMMARY.
(Erase heading not required.)

Army Form C. 2118.

Place	Date	Hour	Summary of Events and Information	Remarks and references to Appendices
LAMBRES.	1.8.18.		Under orders received from 182 Infantry Brigade the unit with Transport complete moved by march route at 12.15.am. Route-WITTES, AIRE, LAMBRES; Time of arrival 3.15.am. Location-N.10.b.5.4.-Sheet 36a. All personnel billeted & transport parked. Hospital opened in village school for reception & treatment of sick. Ford Car No.18 with driver reported from detached duty with A.D.M.S.61st.Divn.	[initials]
"	2.8.18.		No.99684 Pte.SIDEBOTHAM S. proceeded on leave to England. Routine Work.	[initials]
"	3.8.18.		Routine Work. Despatch Rider reported from temporary detached duty at A.D.M.S.office. Ford Car No.19 sent to Workshop.	[initials]
"	4.8.18.		No.439517 Pte.HANKS R.W. evacuated sick to C.C.S. & struck off strength. Under orders received from A.D.M.S.61st.Division Major R.D.MOORE,M.C.,R.A.M.C.T. & party with "A" Section Equipment proceeded as an Advance Party to STEENBECQUE thence to A.D.S. at J.16.d.7.8.(Sheet 36a) preparatory to relieving 15th.Field Ambulance,5th.Division. No.437428 Pte.TAYLOR L. attached to 61st.Divisional Headquarters for duty & struck off strength. Car No.10 with driver & orderly sent to Workshop for inspection. Lieut.J.A.Mac.SWEENEY,M.O.R.C.,U.S.A. & Lieut.WOOD,M.O.R.C.,U.S.A. reported for temporary duty from 2/3 S.M.Fld.Ambce.	[initials]
"	5.8.18.		Lieut.J.P.STOUT,M.O.R.C,U.S.A. & party of bearers proceeded to STEENBECQUE to take over the following posts in the line from the 15th.Field Ambulance:- Drummond Post Sheet 36a, J.21.d.9.6. — Gunners' Post "A" — Sheet 36a.J.10.b.8.2. Gunners'Post "B" " " J. 4.b.6.2. — New Gunners'Post- Sheet 36a.D.28.b.6.6. Saw Mills " " J.18.c.4.5. — CAUDESCURE Station " " K.15.b.7.8. R.A.P. " " K.13.c.7.7. — Carrick Castle " " K.14.a.0.2. Station Post " " K.14.a.5.8. — Blank Farm " " L. 8.b.9.2. CAUDESCURE Post. " " K. 3.b.6.3. — Right R.A.P. " " K.19.c.3.0. Car Post taken over at J.23.a.3.6. Capt.J.R.RICHMOND RITCHIE,R.A.M.C.T.C. proceeded on leave to England. Car No.10 reported from Workshop.	[initials]

2353 Wt. W2544/1454 700,000 5/15 D. D. & L. A.D.S.S./Forms/C. 2118.

Army Form C. 2118.

WAR DIARY
or
INTELLIGENCE SUMMARY.
(Erase heading not required.)

Instructions regarding War Diaries and Intelligence Summaries are contained in F. S. Regs., Part II. and the Staff Manual respectively. Title pages will be prepared in manuscript.

Place	Date	Hour	Summary of Events and Information	Remarks and references to Appendices
	6·8·18·		Major A·T·WATERHOUSE,R·A·M·C·T· & party proceeded by ~~xxxxx~~ march route at 6·45·am· to STEENBECQUE to take over Headquarters of 15th·Field Ambulance· Remaining personnel & Transport moved by march route at 12·30·pm· under Capt·O'BASTABLE,R·A·M·C·T· Route-AIRE, BOESEGHEM,STEENBECQUE· Time of arrival 4·15·pm· Location-Sheet 36a·I·5·a·4·8·	
STEENBECQUE·			Hospital opened in village school for reception & treatment of sick· No·457279 Pte·MITCHELL A· "Died of Wounds"· No·457277 Pte·LITTLEWOOD H·G·, 43734 Pte· SMITH J·, & 65628 Pte·SMITH C· "Wounded in Action" & evacuated to C·C·S· & struck off strength· Lieut Col. A·N·BURROUGHES,R·A·M·C·T· proceeded on leave to England & Major A·T· WATERHOUSE, R·A·M·C·T· assumed command of the unit·	[initials]

2353 Wt. W2544/1454 700,000 5/15 D. D. & L. A.D.S.S./Forms/C. 2118.

Instructions regarding War Diaries and Intelligence Summaries are contained in F. S. Regs., Part II. and the Staff Manual respectively. Title pages will be prepared in manuscript.

WAR DIARY
or
INTELLIGENCE SUMMARY.
(Erase heading not required.)

Army Form C. 2118.

Place	Date	Hour	Summary of Events and Information	Remarks and references to Appendices
STEENBECQUE	7·8·18·		No·437305 Pte·GOURLAY W·J· proceeded on leave to England· Ambulance No·19205 reported for duty from Workshop·	AFL
"	8·8·18·		1 man reported from detached duty with 9th·Northumberland Fusiliers· A party of 25 Other Ranks reported for temporary duty from 2/1 S·M·Fld·Ambce·	AFL
"	9·8·18·		No·20259 Pte·STILL A·D· "Gassed Wounded" but remained on duty· No·72199 Pte·TIBBLES J·, 11271 Pte·UNSWORTH R·, 20805 Pte·STONEHILL J·F·W· & 53051 Pte·SAMPSON M· "GASSED" Wounded evacuated to C·C·S· & struck off strength· Motor Cycle returned from Workshop· No·439517 Pte·HANKS R·W· reported for duty from C·C·S & taken on the strength· 1 H·D·Horse drawn from No·4 Coy·,61 Divisional Train & taken on the strength· A party of 13 Other Ranks reported for Mosquito Guard·	AFL
"	10·8·18·		Car No·19 with driver reported for duty from Workshop· A party of 12 Other Ranks reported for temporary duty from 2/1 S·M·Fld·Ambce· Napier Motor Ambulances No·55128 & 55131 reported for duty from 61 M·T·Coy· & taken on the strength vice Siddeley Deasy No·14419 & Talbot No·45689 returned to 61 M·T·Coy· & struck off strength·	AFL
"	11·8·18·		M2/152965 Pte·SIMPSON H·, M·T·A·S·C· proceeded on leave to PARIS· No·364346 Pte·JONES H·W· proceeded on leave to England· No·437321 Cpl·WINDRIDGE L·C· reported for duty from C·C·S & taken on the strength·	AFL
"	12·8·18·		Motor Cycle sent to Workshop· Routine Work·	AFL
"	13·8·18·		Lieut·W·M·EDMONDS,M·O·R·C·,U·S·A·reported for duty & taken on the strength· A·D·M·S· 61 Division inspected hospital·	AFL
"	14·8·18·		No·64592 Pte·GOODMAN E· reported for duty from Base & taken on the strength· New Gunners' Post – Location,Sheet 36a·D·28·b·6·6· taken over at 12 noon by 31 Division·	AFL
"	15·8·18·		Motor Cycle returned from Workshop· 1 man proceeded on leave· D·D·M·S XI Corps inspected Hospital· G·O·C·,61 Division accompanied by D·A·D·M·S· 61 Divn·inspected Hospital·	AFL

2353 Wt. W2544/1454 700,000 5/15 D. D. & L. A.D.S.S./Forms/C. 2118.

Instructions regarding War Diaries and Intelligence Summaries are contained in F. S. Regs., Part II. and the Staff Manual respectively. Title pages will be prepared in manuscript.

WAR DIARY
or
INTELLIGENCE SUMMARY.
(Erase heading not required.)

Army Form C. 2118.

Place	Date	Hour	Summary of Events and Information	Remarks and references to Appendices
STEENBECQUE	15.8.18		No.437401 Pte.HARWOOD F. evacuated sick to C.C.S & struck off strength.	ATW
"	16.8.18		Lieut.W.M.EDMONDS,M.O.R.C.,U.S.A. proceeded for temporary duty to 2/3 S.M.Fld.Ambce. D.M.S. Fifth Army inspected Hospital. Major A.RADFORD,R.A.M.C. reported for temporary duty from 2/3 S.M.Fld.Ambce. & proceeded forthwith for duty to EDITH A.D.S. in place of MAJOR R.D.MOORE,M.C.,R.A.M.C.T. who returned to Hqrs. & assumed command of the Unit in place of MAJOR A.T.WATERHOUSE,R.A.M.C.T. ill. No.364264 Cpl.NEWNHAM C.H. reported for duty from Base & taken on the strength.	RDM
"	17.8.18		Napier Ambulance No.55128 Sent to Workshop. Lieut.J.P.STOUT,M.O.R.C.,U.S.A. proceeded for temporary duty to 2/6 R.Warwicks. One man proceeded on leave.	RDM
"	18.8.18		Major A.T.WATERHOUSE,R.A.M.C.T. re-assumed command of the unit & Major R.D.MOORE,M.C., R.A.M.C.T. proceeded for duty to A.D.S vice Major A.RADFORD,R.A.M.C. who returned to 2/3 S.M.Fld.Ambce. Lieut.W.M.EDMONDS,M.O.R.C.,U.S.A. reported from temporary detached duty with 2/3 S.M.Fld.Ambce. No.303081 Pte.IRONSIDE D.B. proceeded to XI Corps Gas School for Gas Course. No.60376 Sergt.VAUGHAN H.W. evacuated sick to C.C.S & struck off strength. DRUMMOND POST-Location-Sheet 36a.J.21.d.9.6. closed.	ATW
"	19.8.18		No.437401 Pte.HARWOOD F. reported for duty from C.C.S & taken on the strength. No.11273 Pte.VINES V.W. proceeded to England for transfer to R.A.F. & struck off strength. No.366025 Pte.MILLS A.C. & 64936 Pte.OGDEN A. transferred sick to C.R.S. No.439517 Pte.HANKS R.W. evacuated sick to C.C.S. & struck off strength.	ATW
"	20.8.18.		T/073197 Farrier/Dvr. SIMPSON H, No.4 Coy. ASC attached reported for duty & taken on the strength. MEREDITH POST-K.13 b.8.8. was opened as an A.D.S. and EDITH A.D.S. was closed as an A.D.S. leaving a small holding party there. The following posts were closed:- GUNNERS' POST-J.4.b.6.2: LE PARC J.10.b.2.2.: Car Post J.33.a.3.6.	ATW

Army Form C. 2118.

WAR DIARY
or
INTELLIGENCE SUMMARY.
(Erase heading not required.)

Instructions regarding War Diaries and Intelligence Summaries are contained in F. S. Regs., Part II. and the Staff Manual respectively. Title pages will be prepared in manuscript.

Place	Date	Hour	Summary of Events and Information	Remarks and references to Appendices
STEENBECQUE	21.8.18		Capt. J. R. RICHMOND RITCHIE, R.A.M.C.(T.C.) reported from leave and proceeded during the day for duty to A.D.S.. Saw Mills Post - J.18.C.4.5 closed.	AJW
"	22.8.18		Lieut J. A. McSWEENEY, M.O.R.C., U.S.A. proceeded for temporary duty to 2/4 R. Berks. The following posts were closed:- Right R.A.P. - K.19.C.2.0. and Left R.A.P. - K.13.C.7.7.	AJW
"	23.8.18.		Carrick Castle Post - K.14.a.0.2. closed. The 2/3 Sth. Mid. Fld. Ambce. took over the A.D.S. & all medical posts & became responsible for clearing the line of sick & wounded. Major R. D. MOORE, M.C. R.A.M.C.T. & party reported to Headquarters for duty. No. 64936 Pte. OGDEN A. transferred sick from C.R.S. to C.C.S. & struck off strength.	AJW
"	24.8.18		1 Large Car proceeded for temporary duty to 2/3 S. Mid. Fld. Ambce. Napier Ambulance No. 55128 reported for duty from Workshop. Napier Ambulance No. 55131 proceeded to Workshop. No. 500151 Pte. SMITH C.H. evacuated sick	AJW

2353 Wt. W2544/1454 700,000 5/15 D. D. & L. A.D.S.S./Forms/C. 2118.

Instructions regarding War Diaries and Intelligence Summaries are contained in F. S. Regs., Part II. and the Staff Manual respectively. Title pages will be prepared in manuscript.

WAR DIARY
or
INTELLIGENCE SUMMARY.
(Erase heading not required.)

Army Form C. 2118.

Place	Date	Hour	Summary of Events and Information	Remarks and references to Appendices
STEENBECQUE	24.8.18		to C.C.S. and struck off strength. No. 303081 Pte. IRONSIDE D.B. reported for duty from Gas Course. No 437447 Pte. BURTON W. proceeded on leave. Capt. J. R. RICHMOND RITCHIE, R.A.M.C.T.C. reported for duty from A.D.S. Part of the 61st. Division Reception Camp at WITTES was taken over as a Convalescent Camp. Capt. J.R. RICHMOND RITCHIE, RAMCTC & 31 Other Ranks proceeded to WITTES to take over 61st Division Convalescent Camp.	A.F.W.
"	25.8.18		Routine work.	A.F.W.
"	26.8.18		Routine work. No. 366025 Pte MILLS A.C. struck off strength in accordance with G.R.O. No. 3578.	A.F.W.
"	27.8.18		1 Despatch Rider proceeded for temporary duty to A.D.M.S. 61st. Division. No. 364343 Pte. JONES H.W. reported from Leave. No. 303247 Pte AITKEN J.D. "Gassed" 'wounded in action' evacuated to D.R.S.	A.F.W.

2353 Wt. W2544/1454 700,000 5/15 D. D. & L. A.D.S.S./Forms/C. 2118.

Instructions regarding War Diaries and Intelligence Summaries are contained in F. S. Regs., Part II. and the Staff Manual respectively. Title pages will be prepared in manuscript.

WAR DIARY
or
INTELLIGENCE SUMMARY.
(Erase heading not required.)

Army Form C. 2118.

Place	Date	Hour	Summary of Events and Information	Remarks and references to Appendices
STEENBECQUE	28.8.18		Motor Cycle sent to workshop. Daimler Ambulance No. 24952 sent to workshop. Ford Car No. 19 sent to workshop. No. 437470 Pte. COOPER R., (M.M.) evacuated sick to C.C.S. & struck off strength. 1 Ambulance returned from temporary detached duty with 2/3 S. Mid. Fld. Ambce.	[illegible]
"	29.8.18		Lieut J. P. STOUT, MORC, USA reported from temporary detached duty with 2/3 R. [illegible]. No 437106 Cpl. BENTON H.G. reported for duty from 307 Bde. R.F.A. and taken on the strength. T4/248876 Sergt. FOSS A.E. reported from leave. Lieut W. M. EDMONDS, MORC, USA proceeded for duty to WITTES Convalescent Camp. No 437365 Q.M. Sergt FOSS S.E. to be temporary Sergeant Major. Despatch Rider reported from A.D.M.S. 61st Division. 2 Ford Cars reported for duty from workshop & 1 of them proceeded forthwith to 2/3 S. M. Fd. Ambce for temporary duty. Lieut J. P. STOUT, MORC, USA, proceeded for temporary duty to 2/3 S. M. Fd. Ambce.	[illegible]
"	30.8.18		No 437365 T/Sergt. Major FOSS S.E. proceeded for duty to 2/3 [illegible] and struck off strength. T4/088798 Dvr. DAVIES T. reported for duty from [illegible] Coy. A.S.C. & taken on the strength.	[illegible]

2353 Wt. W2544/1454 700,000 5/15 D. D. & L. A.D.S.S./Forms/C. 2118.

Instructions regarding War Diaries and Intelligence Summaries are contained in F. S. Regs., Part II. and the Staff Manual respectively. Title pages will be prepared in manuscript.

WAR DIARY
or
INTELLIGENCE SUMMARY.
(Erase heading not required.)

Army Form C. 2118.

Place	Date	Hour	Summary of Events and Information	Remarks and references to Appendices
STEENBECQUE	30.8.18		Lieut J. A. McSWEENEY, M.O.R.C., U.S.A. rejoined 3/3 S. Mid. Fld. Ambce. No. 11271 Pte. UNSWORTH R., 53051 Pte. SAMPSON M., & 72199 Pte. TIBBLES J.G. reported for duty from C.C.S. & taken on the strength. No. 437365 T/Sergt. Major FOSS S.E. reported from 3/3 S. Mid. Fld. Ambce. & taken on the strength. Lieut. J. P. STOUT, M.O.R.C., U.S.A. reported from temporary detached duty with 3/3 S. M. Fld. Amb.	A.T.W.
"	31.8.18		Motor cycle returned from workshop. Routine work.	A.T.W.

A. T. Waterhouse Major RAMC
A/O.C. 2/2 S M Field Ambulance

2353 Wt. W2544/1454 700,000 5/15 D. D. & L. A.D.S.S./Forms/C. 2118.

21 Medicine

Sept. 1918.

CONFIDENTIAL

VM 29

14/32 9

WAR DIARY

2/2 S. M. Fd. Amba.
R.A.M.C.T.

VOLUME 29.

Sept. 1st – 30th. ( )
1918

Instructions regarding War Diaries and Intelligence Summaries are contained in F. S. Regs., Part II. and the Staff Manual respectively. Title pages will be prepared in manuscript.

WAR DIARY
or
INTELLIGENCE SUMMARY.
(Erase heading not required.)

Army Form C. 2118.

Place	Date	Hour	Summary of Events and Information	Remarks and references to Appendices
STEENBECQUE.	1.9.18.		No.344074 Pte.CLEGG J.H.,100916 Pte.GRIMSHAW T., & 437031 Pte.SHEPPARD H. proceeded on leave to England. Routine Work.	A.F.W.
"	2.9.18.		Lieut.S.A.WOOD,M.O.R.C.,U.S.A.proceeded for temporary duty as Medical Officer to Fifth Army School of Musketry. No.439517 Pte.HANKS R.W. reported for duty from C.C.S and taken on the strength.	A.F.W.
"	3.9.18.		Napier ambulance No.55131 reported for duty from Workshop. No.437520 Pte.SHEPLEY F. proceeded on leave. No.303247 Pte.AITKEN J.D. evacuated from D.R.S. to C.C.S. & struck off strength. The whole of the patients,personnel & stores at 61st.Divn. Convalescent Camp were moved to LA LACQUE Camp.	A.F.W.
"	4.9.18.		No.366025 Pte.MILLS A.C. reported for duty & taken on the strength. Lieut.J.P.STOUT, M.O.R.C.,U.S.A. & 8 other ranks proceeded to HAVERSKERQUE Brewery to make preparations for receiving patients.	A.F.W.
"	5.9.18.		Routine Work.	A.F.W.
"	6.9.18.		Hospital opened at HAVERSKERQUE Brewery for reception & treatment of sick. Daimler Ambulance No.24592 reported from Workshop. Lieut.W.M.EDMONDS,M.O.R.C.,U.S.A. proceeded for temporary duty to 51 C.C.S. Major R.D.MOORE,M.C.,R.A.M.C.T. proceeded for duty to HAVERSKERQUE Brewery by special order of the A.D.M.S.61st.Division vice Lieut.J.P.STOUT,M.O.R.C.,U.S.A. who reported to Headquarters for duty. No.437503 Pte CRIPPS W. proceeded on leave to England. The personnel at LA LACQUE Camp proceeded to HAVERSKERQUE Brewery for duty.	A.F.W.
"	7.9.18.		No.435355 Pte.HOLLIS H.proceeded on leave to England. Capt.J.R.RICHMOND RITCHIE, R.A.M.C.T.C. reported for duty from LA LACQUE Camp.	A.F.W.
"	8.9.18.		Lieut.J.P.STOUT,M.O.R.C.,U.S.A. & party proceeded for duty to HAVERSKERQUE Brewery.	A.F.W.

2353 Wt. W2544/1454 700,000 5/15 D. D. & L. A.D.S.S./Forms/C. 2118.

Army Form C. 2118.

Instructions regarding War Diaries and Intelligence Summaries are contained in F. S. Regs., Part II. and the Staff Manual respectively. Title pages will be prepared in manuscript.

WAR DIARY
or
INTELLIGENCE SUMMARY.
(Erase heading not required.)

Place	Date	Hour	Summary of Events and Information	Remarks and references to Appendices
STEENBECQUE.	9.9.18.		No.437358 Pte.BOOKER P.G. evacuated sick to C.C.S. for Dental Treatment & struck off the strength. No.437458 Pte.WILSON L.(M.M.) evacuated sick to C.C.S. & struck off strength.	AFL
"	10.9.18.		No.437414 Sergt.EDGINTON W.J. proceeded on leave to England. No.93658 Pte.THOMAS I.R. & 20805 Pte.STONEHILL J.F. reported for duty from C.C.S. & taken on the strength.	AFL
"	11.9.18.		20 Other Ranks of the 2/1 S.M.Fld.Ambce. attached for duty for Work at HAVERSKERQUE. T4/248896 Dvr.RUBERY C.J.,No.4 Coy.A.S.C. attached proceeded on Special Leave to England.	AFL
"	12.9.18.		One despatch rider proceeded for temporary duty to A.D.M.S. 61 Division? Daimler Ambulance No.44005 reported for duty from Workshop. No.435495 Pte.DOANE A.W. transferred to Corps of Military Police & struck off strength.	AFL
"	13.9.18.		No.82297 A/Cpl.WILSON F reported for duty from Base & taken on the strength. M2/167150 L/Cpl. BIGNELL A.,M.T.A.S.C. attached proceeded on leave to England.	AFL
"	14.9.18.		No.437485 Pte.WILSON L. "M.M." reported for duty from C.C.S. & taken on the strength. Lieut.W.M.EDMONDS,M.O.R.C.,U.S.A. reported from temporary detached duty at 51 C.C.S	AFL AFL
"	15.9.18.		No.376008 Pte.PROUDFOOT D. & No.20805 Pte.STONEHILL J.F. proceeded on leave to England. Routine Work.	
"	16.9.18.		Preparatory to Headquarters moving to HAVERSKERQUE, equipment & many of the personnel were sent there. Routine Work.	AFL
"	17.9.18.		More equipment & personnel sent to HAVERSKERQUE. One Ford Car sent to Workshop. Capt.A.L.AYMER,R.A.M.C. reported for duty & taken on the strength.	AFL

2353 Wt. W2544/1454 700,000 5/15 D. D. & L. A.D.S.S./Forms/C. 2118.

Army Form C. 2118.

Instructions regarding War Diaries and Intelligence Summaries are contained in F. S. Regs., Part II. and the Staff Manual respectively. Title pages will be prepared in manuscript.

WAR DIARY
or
INTELLIGENCE SUMMARY.
(Erase heading not required.)

Place	Date	Hour	Summary of Events and Information	Remarks and references to Appendices
HAVERSKERQUE	18.9.18.		Under instructions received from A.D.M.S. 61 Division, Headquarters, Q.M.Stores & Transport moved at 10.15.a.m. and arrived at HAVERSKERQUE at 12.0. noon. Location of Headquarters & Q.M.Stores, Sheet 36a. J.27.d.8.7. and Transport Lines - J.28.a.8.3. Construction work on Brewery & Convent continued, providing extra accommodation for patients. Lieut.S.A.Wood, M.O.R.C., U.S.A. reported for temporary detached duty at Fifth Army School of Musketry. No.46892 Pte.HADLEY H. proceeded on leave to PARIS & No.437252 Pte.CURETON F.H. proceeded on leave to England.	A.F.W.
"	19.9.18.		No.437352 Pte.BOOKER F.G. reported for duty from C.C.S. & taken on the strength. Ford Car reported for duty from Workshop. Lieut.J.P.STOUT, M.O.R.C., U.S.A. proceeded for temporary duty to 61 D.A.C.	A.F.W.
"	20.9.18.		No.2888 Pte.DONALD J. granted one month's leave in AUSTRALIA & struck off strength. 20 Other Ranks of 2/1 S.M.Fld.Ambce. ceased to be attached for duty. Lieut.S.A. WOOD, M.O.R.C., U.S.A. proceeded for temporary duty to 1st.E.Lancs. No.437269 Pte. MACFARLANE J.H. & 183768 Dvr.WOTHERSPOON L. (P.B.Batman) proceeded on leave to England.	A.F.W.
"	21.9.18.		No.437233 Sergt.WHITEHOUSE & T4/248901 Sergt.TRING R.J. (A.S.C. att.) proceeded on leave to England. T4/248895 Dvr.ROBINSON H.J. (A.S.C. att.) evacuated sick to C.C.S. & struck off strength. Lieut.Col.H.N.BURROUGHES, R.A.M.C.T. reported from leave and resumed command of the unit. No.64592 Pte.GOODMAN E. & T4/248885 Dvr.EARL A.E. (A.S.C. att.) proceeded on leave to England.	A.F.Whitehouse Major RAMC
"	22.9.18.		No.437365 T/Sgt.Major FOSS S.E. reverts to rank of Quartermaster Sergeant at his own request. No.439143 Cpl.BERRY E.J. proceeded for Gas Course to XI Corps Schools. No.437466 Pte.ROSCORLA A. & M2/167659 Pte.STEVENS H.C., (M.T.A.S.C. att.) proceeded on leave to England. Construction work continued.	HNB
"	23.9.18.		Napier Ambulance No.55131 sent to Workshop. Lieut.W.M.EDMONDS, M.O.R.C., U.S.A. proceeded for temporary duty to 28th.Bde.R.G.A.	HNB

2353 Wt. W2544/1454 700,000 5/15 D. D. & L. A.D.S.S./Forms/C. 2118.

Instructions regarding War Diaries and Intelligence Summaries are contained in F. S. Regs., Part II. and the Staff Manual respectively. Title pages will be prepared in manuscript.

WAR DIARY
or
INTELLIGENCE SUMMARY.
(Erase heading not required.)

Army Form C. 2118.

Place	Date	Hour	Summary of Events and Information	Remarks and references to Appendices
HAVERSKERQUE	23.9.18.		No.437212 L/C VIGURS E.N. evacuated sick to C.C.S. & struck off strength. No.419113 Pte.HILL R.T. transferred to 2/2 Nth.Mid.Fld.Amb. & struck off strength. Construction Work continued.	
"	24.9.18.		Routine Work. D.D.M.S. Xl Corps visited the Hospital.	
"	25.9.18.		Ford Car No.18 sent to Workshop. No.112924 Pte.SMITH H. proceeded on leave to England.	
"	26.9.18.		Construction Work continued. Ford Car No.18 reported from Workshop. No.303081 Pte. IRONSIDE D.B. & No.91641 Pte.TINSLEY R. proceeded on leave to England.	
"	27.9.18.		No.303083 Cpl.BLACKHALL D. proceeded on leave to England. Major A.T.WATERHOUSE, R.A.M.C.T. proceeded on leave in France. Construction Work.	
"	28.9.18.		Construction & Routine Work. No.437283 L/C PLANT G.W. appointed Lance Corporal with pay.	
"	29.9.18.		No.439143 Cpl.BERRY E.J. reported from Gas Course held at Xl Corps Schools. Motor Cycle sent to Workshop.	
"	30.9.18.		Construction & Routine Work.	

2353 Wt. W2544/1454 700,000 5/15 D. D. & L. A.D.S.S./Forms/C. 2118.

6.x.1916 16

MEDICAL

CONFIDENTIAL

Vol 30

16/33ry

WAR DIARY

2/2nd S. Midland F. A 2/2 Sth. Mid. Fld. Ambce.
R.A.M.C.T.

VOLUME. 30.

October 1st – 31st (inclusive) 1918.

Army Form C. 2118.

Instructions regarding War Diaries and Intelligence Summaries are contained in F. S. Regs., Part II. and the Staff Manual respectively. Title pages will be prepared in manuscript.

WAR DIARY
or
INTELLIGENCE SUMMARY.
(Erase heading not required.)

Place	Date	Hour	Summary of Events and Information	Remarks and references to Appendices
STEENBECQUE.	1-10-18		Ford Car proceeded to A.D.M.S. 61 Division for temporary duty.	
"	2-10-18		Advance Party 62/2 Nth.Mid.Fld.Amb. arrived preparatory to taking over. No.439143 Cpl. BERRY E.J. evacuated sick to C.C.S. & struck off strength.	
MOLINGHEM.	3-10-18		The Ambulance was relieved by 2/2 Nth.Mid.Fld.Amb. Under instructions received from 182 Infantry Brigade the unit with Transport complete moved at 2.30.pm. Route:- ST VENANT, GUARBECQUE, BERGUETTE, MOLINGHEM. Time of arrival 4.45.pm. Location, Sheet 36a. 0.13.b.8.7. Unit responsible for treatment of sick of 182 Infantry Brigade. No.437461 Pte.TURNER N.D. evacuated sick to C.C.S. & struck off strength. Ford Car & Despatch rider reported from temporary detached duty with A.D.M.S. 61 Division. One large car reported from temporary detached duty with 2/3 S.M.Fld.Amb. No.437323 Pte. LANE J.W. proceeded on leave. 1 Motor Cycle returned from Workshop.	
"	4-10-18		No.419115 Pte FLOOK H.J. reported for duty from 2/3 Nth.Mid.Fld.Amb. & taken on the strength.	
"	5-10-18		Lieut.W.M.EDMONDS, M.O.R.C.,U.S.A. reported from temporary detached duty with 38 Bde. R.G.A. No.49711 Pte.CAFFREY J.,1/7 Hans.att. Proceeded on leave to England. Under instructions received from 182 Infantry Brigade the Unit with transport complete moved by march route from MOLINGHEM at 8.0.pm. & entrained at BERGUETTE station at 9.30.pm. arriving at DOULLENS at 3.0.am. 6/10/18. The Unit personnel moved independ-	
FRESHEVILLERS	6-10-18		ently by march route & arrived at FRESHEVILLERS at 4.0.am. Transport arrived at 6.0.am Unit billeted & transport parked. Sick of 182 Infantry Brigade collected & treated.	
"	7-10-18		No.437021 Pte SHEPPARD H. proceeded for temporary duty to 61 Divn.Reception Camp vice No.437374 Pte PORTMAN L. who reported to H.Qrs.for duty. In accordance with instructions, surplus stores & equipment were dumped at DOULLENS with No.437553 Pte.OWEN G. placed in charge. Lieut J.F.STOUT,M.O.R.C.,U.S.A. reported from detached duty with 61 D.A.C. No.82146 Pte.CHESTER H.H. & 30805 Pte.STONEHILL J.F. evacuated sick to C.C.S. & struck off strength. Ford Car No.19 sent to Workshop.	

2353 Wt. W2544/1454 700,000 5/15 D. D. & L. A.D.S.S./Forms/C. 2118.

Instructions regarding War Diaries and Intelligence Summaries are contained in F. S. Regs., Part II. and the Staff Manual respectively. Title pages will be prepared in manuscript.

WAR DIARY
or
INTELLIGENCE SUMMARY.
(Erase heading not required.)

Army Form C. 2118.

Place	Date	Hour	Summary of Events and Information	Remarks and references to Appendices
FRESHEVILLERS	8-10-18		Under instruction received from 182 Infantry Brigade the Horse Transport under the command of Capt. A.L. AYMER, R.A.M.C. moved by march route at 9.30am. reaching BAILLEULVAL in the evening where they parked for the night. Unit personnel remained stationed at FRESHEVILLERS. No. 421516 Pte. COOK H., 437458 Pte. WILSON L. 'MM' & T4/248898 Dvr. STENBERG S. (A.S.C. att.) evacuated sick to C.C.S. & struck off strength.	H.W.B.
Sheet 57c. E. 28. c. 1. 9.	9-10-18		Under orders received from 182 Infantry Brigade the Unit less Horse Transport moved by march route at 8.25 am arriving at DOULLENS at 9.15 am where they entrained and moved at 11.30am. arriving & detraining at HAVRINCOURT at 5.30pm. The unit proceeded then by march route via HERMIES & DEMICOURT & arrived at E. 28. c. 1. 9. Sheet 57c. at 9.30pm. The unit became responsible for treatment of sick of 182 Infantry Brigade. The Horse Transport continued by march route arriving in the evening at BOISLEUX-AU-MONT where they parked for the night.	H.W.B.
"	10-10-18		The Horse Transport continued by march route and arrived at E. 28. c. 1. 9. Sheet 57c. at 5.30pm.	H.W.B.

2353 Wt. W2544/1454 700,000 5/15 D. D. & L. A.D.S.S./Forms/C. 2118.

Instructions regarding War Diaries and Intelligence Summaries are contained in F. S. Regs., Part II. and the Staff Manual respectively. Title pages will be prepared in manuscript.

WAR DIARY
or
INTELLIGENCE SUMMARY.
(Erase heading not required.)

Army Form C. 2118.

Place	Date	Hour	Summary of Events and Information	Remarks and references to Appendices
Sheet 57 C. E.28.c.1.9	11-10-18		Major A.T. WATERHOUSE, RAMC T & Lieut J.P. STOUT, MORC, USA, with 31 Other Ranks proceeded for temporary duty to XVII Corps Main Dressing Station. Capt. A.L. AYMER, RAMC proceeded on special leave to ENGLAND. The unit was transferred from 182 Infantry Brigade to 184 Infantry Brigade & came under orders of that Brigade.	[illegible]
"	12-10-18		Q.Mr. & Capt. O. BASTABLE, RAMC T proceeded on leave to England. Napier Ambulance No. 55138 sent to workshop.	[illegible]
"	13-10-18		Napier Ambulance No. 55138 reported for duty from workshop.	[illegible]
"	14-10-18		T4/043197 Dr. SIMPSON H. ASC att. evacuated sick to CCS & struck off strength.	[illegible]
"	15-10-18		One Despatch Rider proceeded for temporary duty to A.D.M.S. 58th Division.	[illegible]
"	16-10-18		Lieut W.M. EDMONDS, MORC USA, proceeded for temporary duty to 307 Bde R.F.A.	[illegible]

2353 Wt W2544/1454 700,000 5/15 D. D. & L. A.D.S.S./Forms/C. 2118.

Instructions regarding War Diaries and Intelligence Summaries are contained in F. S. Regs., Part II. and the Staff Manual respectively. Title pages will be prepared in manuscript.

WAR DIARY
or
INTELLIGENCE SUMMARY.
(*Erase heading not required.*)

Army Form C. 2118.

Place	Date	Hour	Summary of Events and Information	Remarks and references to Appendices
Sheet 57c. E. 28. c. 1. 9.	17.10.18		Routine work.	HNB
CANTAING.	18.10.18		18 Other Ranks proceeded for temporary duty to 45 C.C.S. Under orders received from 184 Infantry Brigade the Unit with transport complete moved by march route at 2.5 pm. Route - GRAINCOURT, LA JUSTICE, CANTAING. Time of arrival 4.30 pm. Location - Sheet 57c. F. 28. c. 3. 3.	HNB
" CAGNONCLES	19.10.18		Under orders received from 184 Infantry Brigade the unit with Transport complete moved by march route at 1.30 pm. Route - PROVILLE, CAMBRAI, thence by track across fields to CAGNONCLES. Time of arrival 6.15 pm. Location - Sheet 57 B. B. 4. 6. 8. Ford Ambulance No. 14364 reported for duty from Workshop & taken on the strength vice Ford Ambulance No. 14595 evacuated to Base & struck off strength. No. 20259 Pte. STILL A. evacuated to C.C.S. & struck off strength. No. 437222 Pte. HIGGS C.R. proceeded on leave to England.	HNB

2353 Wt W2544/1454 700,000 5/15 D. D. & L. A.D.S.S./Forms/C. 2118.

Army Form C. 2118.

WAR DIARY
or
INTELLIGENCE SUMMARY.
(Erase heading not required.)

Instructions regarding War Diaries and Intelligence Summaries are contained in F. S. Regs., Part II. and the Staff Manual respectively. Title pages will be prepared in manuscript.

Place	Date	Hour	Summary of Events and Information	Remarks and references to Appendices
CAGNONCLES.	20-10-18		Capt. J. R. RICHMOND RITCHIE, R.A.M.C. T.C. attached for temporary duty to 2/5 Glosters as Medical Officer. No. 437374 Pte. PORTMAN L. & 437234 L/Cpl. DAVIS E.N. proceeded on leave to PARIS.	[illegible]
"	20-10-18		439143 Cpl. BERRY E.J. reported for duty from C.C.S. & taken on the strength. No. 368046 Pte. FRENCH J.H. & 93658 Pte. THOMAS I.R. transferred sick to 2/3 S. Mid. Fld. Ambce.	[illegible]
"	22-10-18		T/370624 Dvr. NORMAN D.D. No. 4 Coy. A.S.C. reported for duty & taken on the strength. No. 437502 Pte. HAYES J.F. reported for duty from Div. Battn. M.G.C. & taken on the strength.	[illegible]
"	23-10-18		Under orders received from A.D.M.S. 61st Division the Unit with Transport complete moved by march route at 2.0pm. Route - along the CAMBRAI - SOLESMES Road, AVESNES-LEZ-AUBERT, ST. AUBERT. Time of arrival 4.30pm. Unit billeted & Transport parked. Location Sheet 51 A. U. 24. a. 6. 9. T4/226816 Dvr. PARSONS A, A.S.C. att. proceeded to [illegible]	
ST. AUBERT				

Army Form C. 2118.

Instructions regarding War Diaries and Intelligence Summaries are contained in F. S. Regs., Part II. and the Staff Manual respectively. Title pages will be prepared in manuscript.

WAR DIARY
or
INTELLIGENCE SUMMARY.
(Erase heading not required.)

Place	Date	Hour	Summary of Events and Information	Remarks and references to Appendices
ST. AUBERT	23.10.18		Reinforcement Training Camp & struck off strength. 3 Large Cars proceeded for temporary duty to 3/1 Sth. Mid. Fd. Ambce.	HMB
"	24.10.18		1 Large Car & 1 Motor Cyclist proceeded for temporary duty to 3/1 S. Mid. Fd. Ambce. No. 497143 Pte. MARTIN C.G. evacuated sick to C.C.S. & struck off strength. No. 437461 Pte. TURNER N.D. reported for duty from C.C.S. & taken on the strength. 13 O.Ranks attached for temporary duty to 2/1 S. Mid. Fd. Ambce.	HMB
"	25.10.18		No 437106 Cpl. BENTON H.G. proceeded on leave to England.	HMB
Sheet 51 A. P. 30. b.	26.10.18		Under orders received from A.D.M.S. 61st. Division the Unit with Transport complete moved at 1.0pm. – Route – MONTRÉCOURT, SAULZOIR, along the main CAMBRAI – BAVAI Road to Location – Sheet 51 A. P. 30. b. Time of arrival 4.0pm. Unit bivouaced in disused trenches & transport parked. No. 437502 Pte. HAYES J.F. proceeded for temporary duty with Camp Commandant 61st. Division. No. 112984 Pte. SMITH H. evacuated sick to 2/3 S. M. Fd. Ambce. 303083 Cpl. BLACKHALL D. admitted sick to 3rd. Can. Gen. Hospital, BOULOGNE & struck off strength.	HMB

Army Form C. 2118.

Instructions regarding War Diaries and Intelligence Summaries are contained in F. S. Regs., Part II. and the Staff Manual respectively. Title pages will be prepared in manuscript.

WAR DIARY
or
INTELLIGENCE SUMMARY.
(Erase heading not required.)

Place	Date	Hour	Summary of Events and Information	Remarks and references to Appendices
Sheet 51 A. P. 30. b.	27.10.18		Unit remained stationed at P. 30. b. Sheet 51 A. No. 437424 Sergt. BIRKBY L. transferred sick to 2/3 S. Mid. Fld. Ambce.	H.W.
"	28.10.18		71510 Cpl. HARTLEY B.S. evacuated sick to C.C.S. & struck off strength. No. 437424 Sergt. BIRKBY L. reported for duty from 2/3 S. Mid. Fld. Ambce. No. 366046 Pte. FRENCH J.H. reported for duty from 2/3 S. Mid. Fld. Ambce. One Despatch Rider reported from temporary detached duty with 2/1 S. Mid. Fld. Ambce.	H.W.
"	29.10.18		13 O.Ranks reported from temporary detached duty with 2/1 S. Mid. Fld. Ambce.	H.W.
"	30.10.18		437352 Pte. CURETON F.W. & 437515 Pte. EVETTS T.L. proceeded for temporary duty to 61st D.A.Q. No. 435595 Pte. TAYLOR E.F. & 437364 Pte. SMITH E. proceeded on leave to England. T/264777 Dvr. SPRIGGS J.F., & T4/246610 Dvr. VALENTINE E, No 4 Coy. A.S.C. reported for duty & taken on the strength. Capt. A.L. AYMER, R.A.M.C. reported from leave.	H.W.
"	31.10.18		Routine Work.	

H. W. ... Lt. Col. R.A.M.C.

2353 Wt. W2514/1454 700,000 5/15 D. D. & L. A.D.S.S./Forms/C. 2118.

17
Nov. 1918

MEDICAL
VR 31

140/3401.

CONFIDENTIAL.

WAR DIARY

2/2. 5th. Mid. Fld. Amb. R.A.M.C.T.

VOLUME - 31

Nov 1st - 30th (inclusive)
1918

Instructions regarding War Diaries and Intelligence Summaries are contained in F. S. Regs., Part II. and the Staff Manual respectively. Title pages will be prepared in manuscript.

WAR DIARY
or
INTELLIGENCE SUMMARY.
(Erase heading not required.)

Army Form C. 2118.

Place	Date	Hour	Summary of Events and Information	Remarks and references to Appendices
Sheet 51 A. P. 30. b.	1.11.18		437234 L/Cpl DAVIS E.N. & 437374 Pte. PORTMAN L. reported from leave in FRANCE. No. 73174 Pte. SMITH A. transferred sick to 72 Field Ambulance. No. 437455 Pte. STANFORD G.A.C. proceeded for temporary duty to A.D.M.S. office 61st. Division. T4/248709 Dvr. PORTSMOUTH J. A.S.C. att. proceeded on leave.	HWS
AVESNES-LEZ-AUBERT	2.11.18		Under orders received from 184 Infantry Brigade the Unit with transport complete moved by march route at 1.30pm. Route - SAULZOIR, ST AUBERT, AVESNES-LEZ-AUBERT. Time of arrival 5.0pm. Location - Sheet 51 A. U. 28. a. 3. 7. Unit responsible for collection & evacuation of sick in ST. AUBERT Area. No 437516 Pte. TAYLOR A.E., 437501 Pte. EKINS A.A. & 19229 Pte. SULLIVAN J. proceeded on leave to England. No. 73174 Pte. SMITH A. transferred sick from 72 Fld. Ambce to 2/3 S. Mid. Fld. Ambce. M2/156597 Pte WILLIAMS W.J., M.T.A.S.C. att. transferred sick to 2/3 S. Mid. Fld. Ambce.	HWS
"	3.11.18		No. 49743 Pte. MARTIN C.G. reported for duty from C.C.S. & taken on the strength. 437113 Pte. LANE J.W. admitted sick to 2/3 S. Mid. Fld. Ambce.	HWS

2353 Wt. W2544/1454 700,000 5/15 D. D. & L. A.D.S.S./Forms/C. 2118.

Army Form C. 2118.

Instructions regarding War Diaries and Intelligence Summaries are contained in F. S. Regs., Part II. and the Staff Manual respectively. Title pages will be prepared in manuscript.

WAR DIARY
or
INTELLIGENCE SUMMARY.
(Erase heading not required.)

Place	Date	Hour	Summary of Events and Information	Remarks and references to Appendices
AVESNES-LES-AUBERT.	4.11.18		437334 Pte. TAYLOR A.G. proceeded on leave to England. Capt. A. L. AYMER, R.A.M.C. proceeded for temporary duty to 2/6 R. Warwicks. 1 Horsed ambulance proceeded for temporary duty to 2/3 S. Mid. Fld. Ambce. No. 112924 Pte. SMITH H. & No. 93658 Pte. THOMAS I.R. reported for duty from Hospital. 4 Cars reported from temporary detached duty with 2/1 S. Mid. Fld. Ambce. No. 372162 Pte. STEEL A.D. evacuated sick to C.C.S. & struck off strength.	HWB
BERMERAIN	5.11.18		Under orders received from 184 Infantry Brigade the Unit with transport complete moved by march route at 12.30pm. Route - ST. AUBERT, MONTRÉCOURT, SAULZOIR, BERMERAIN. Time of arrival 4.30pm. Location Sheet 51 A. Q. 22. a. 2. 2. Unit responsible for treatment & evacuation of sick of 184 Infantry Brigade. 73174 Pte SMITH A. reported for duty from Hospital. No. 112924 Pte SMITH H. evacuated sick to C.C.S. & struck off strength. Lieut J.A. MacSweeney, M.O.R.C. U.S.A. attached for temporary duty. No 437107 Pte. NICHOLLS F.W. proceeded on leave to England.	HWB
"	6.11.18		437161 Pte. PRITCHETT V.E.C. evacuated sick to C.C.S. & struck off strength.	HWB

Instructions regarding War Diaries and Intelligence Summaries are contained in F. S. Regs., Part II. and the Staff Manual respectively. Title pages will be prepared in manuscript.

WAR DIARY
or
INTELLIGENCE SUMMARY.
(Erase heading not required.)

Army Form C. 2118.

Place	Date	Hour	Summary of Events and Information	Remarks and references to Appendices
BERMERAIN.	6.11.18		T4/248887 Dvr: GUEST V.N. A.S.C attached proceeded to A.S.C Base Depot HAVRE & struck off strength. No. 82297 P/acting/Cpl. WILSON F. to be acting Sergeant from 19 8/18 – assumed duty as such 13 9/18. Capt. O. BASTABLE, R.A.M.C.T. reported from leave. No. 437352 Pte. BOOKER P.G. & M2/077033 Pte. MORTON K.W. M.T.A.S.C attached proceeded on leave to England. Major A.T. WATERHOUSE, R.A.M.C.T. & Lieut J.P. STOUT, M.O.R.C. U.S.A. & party reported from temporary detached duty at XVII Corps Main Dressing Station.	[illegible]
"	7.11.18		437487 Pte. BURROWS W.M. proceeded on leave. Lieut W.M. EDMONDS, M.O.R.C. U.S.A. reported from temporary detached duty with 307 Bde. R.F.A.	[illegible]
SEPMERIES	8.11.18		Under orders received from 184 Infantry Brigade the Unit with transport complete moved by march route at 1.30 pm. arriving at SEPMERIES at 3.0 pm. Location, Sheet 51 A. K. 36. c. 7. 2. No. 305188 Pte MACFARLANE G. transferred to 1/3 Highland Field Ambulance & struck off strength. No. 364264 Cpl. NEWNHAM C.H. transferred to R.A.M.C. Base Depot & struck off strength. Lieut W.M. EDMONDS, M.O.R.C. U.S.A	[illegible]

Instructions regarding War Diaries and Intelligence Summaries are contained in F. S. Regs., Part II. and the Staff Manual respectively. Title pages will be prepared in manuscript.

WAR DIARY
or
INTELLIGENCE SUMMARY.
(Erase heading not required.)

Army Form C. 2118.

Place	Date	Hour	Summary of Events and Information	Remarks and references to Appendices
SEPMERIES	8.11.18		proceeded for temporary duty to 2/4 Ox. & Bucks. L. I. Lieut E. P. NEARY, M.O.R.C.U.S.A. attached for temporary duty. T4/248894 Dvr. ROBERTS S. L., A.S.C. att. proceeded on leave.	HWB
"	9.11.18		Lieut J. A. MACSWEENEY, M.O.R.C. U.S.A. proceeded for duty to 61st Divisional Reception Camp & ceased to be attached. T4/040074 Far/Dvr. BURDETT W., No 4 Coy. A.S.C. reported for duty & taken on the strength. No 437480 Pte. BEDFORD E & 437441 Pte. O'LOUGHLIN P. proceeded on leave to England.	HWB
"	10.11.18		Napier Ambulance No. A. 55128 sent to Workshop. Lieut J. A. MACSWEENEY, M.O.R.C. U.S.A. reported from detached duty at 61st Divisional Reception Camp & proceeded forthwith for temporary duty to 1/5 D.C.L.I.	HWB
"	11.11.18		No 437006 Sgt. Major JACKSON H. C. proceeded on leave to England & No. 437365 Q. M. Sgt. FOSS S.E. assumed duties as Sergeant Major. Major A. T. WATERHOUSE, R.A.M.C.T. proceeded on leave to England. XVII Corps Wire received that "Hostilities will cease at 1100 hours today". Daimler Ambulance No. A. 55128 reported from workshops.	HWB

Instructions regarding War Diaries and Intelligence Summaries are contained in F. S. Regs., Part II. and the Staff Manual respectively. Title pages will be prepared in manuscript.

WAR DIARY
or
INTELLIGENCE SUMMARY.
(Erase heading not required.)

Army Form C. 2118.

Place	Date	Hour	Summary of Events and Information	Remarks and references to Appendices
SEPMERIES	12-11-18		No 437387 Pte. GREEN A.C. & 439126 Pte. CRIDGE G. proceeded on leave to England.	HmL
"	13-11-18		437113 Pte. LANE J.W. reported for duty from Hospital. D/14181 Pte. MALLINSON J. 4th Dragoon Guards att. & 437394 Pte. DINGLEY J.W. proceeded on leave to England. One Motor Cycle sent to Workshop. One Motor Cycle returned from temporary detached duty at A.D.M.S. Office Divl. Division & sent to Workshop. Horsed Ambulance returned from temporary detached duty with 2/3 S. Mid. Fld. Ambce.	HmL
"	14-11-18		Daimler Ambulance No. 24952 sent to Workshop. No. 45378 Pte. STEWARD G.C. admitted sick to 2/3 S. Mid. Fld. Ambce. No 437482 Pte. OSLAND H.J., 437309 Pte. TONKS J. & 437398 Pte. DUCKHOUSE H. proceeded on leave to PARIS. No. 437331 Pte. RIDOUT C.V. & M2/153802 Pte PACK G.A.A., M.T. A.S.C. att. proceeded on leave to England. Under orders received from 184 Infantry Brigade the Unit with transport complete moved by march route at 11.30 a.m. Route -	
ST. AUBERT			BERMERAIN, ST. MARTIN, HAUSSY, ST. AUBERT. Time of arrival 3.30 p.m. Location Sheet 51 A. V.13. C.8.5 Unit came under the orders of 183 Infantry Brigade.	HmL

2353 Wt. W2514/1454 700,000 5/15 D. D. & L. A.D.S.S./Forms/C. 2118.

Army Form C. 2118.

Instructions regarding War Diaries and Intelligence Summaries are contained in F. S. Regs., Part II. and the Staff Manual respectively. Title pages will be prepared in manuscript.

WAR DIARY
or
INTELLIGENCE SUMMARY.
(*Erase heading not required.*)

Place	Date	Hour	Summary of Events and Information	Remarks and references to Appendices
ST. AUBERT CAMBRAI	15.11.18		Under orders received from 183 Infantry Brigade the Unit with transport complete moved by march route at 11.30 am. Route - AVESNES-LEZ-AUBERT, thence along the main SOLESMES - CAMBRAI Road to CAMBRAI. Time of arrival 4.0 pm. Location - Sheet 57 b. A. 12. c. 2. 2. Unit responsible for treatment & evacuation of sick of 183 & 184 Infantry Brigades. No. 45378 Pte STEWARD G. C. evacuated sick from 3/3 S. Mid. Fld. Ambce. to C.C.S. & struck off strength. No. 437350 Pte. ALDIS E. taken on the strength but on temporary detached duty with 851 Employment Company. 437517 Pte HASSELL W. T. & 495479 Pte. CLARETT G. P. proceeded on leave to England.	HDB
"	16.11.18		Lieut E. P. NEARY M.O.R.C.U.S.A. proceeded for duty to 3/4 Ox. & Bucks. L. I. & ceased to be attached. 2 Daimler Ambulances, Nos. 44005 & 19303 with Drivers - No M2/152965 Pte SIMPSON H. & M2/113059 Pte MULGROVE S. M.T.A.S.C. att. proceeded for duty to VI Corps M.T. Column & struck off strength. Motor Cycle reported for duty from Workshop & taken on the strength. 1 R. Horse handed over to 24 th. Divn. & struck off strength.	HDB

2353 Wt. W2544/1454 700,000 5/15 D. D. & L. A.D.S.S./Forms/C. 2118.

Army Form C. 2118.

Instructions regarding War Diaries and Intelligence Summaries are contained in F. S. Regs., Part II. and the Staff Manual respectively. Title pages will be prepared in manuscript.

WAR DIARY
or
INTELLIGENCE SUMMARY.
(Erase heading not required.)

Place	Date	Hour	Summary of Events and Information	Remarks and references to Appendices
CAMBRAI	17.11.18		1. H.D. sent to 24th Division & struck off strength. 435361 Pte Davis L reported from detached duty at 184 Inf. Bde. Hqrs. Capt. A. LAYMER - R.A.M.C. reported from detached duty with 2/6 R. WARWICKS. 437401 L/Cpl HARWOOD. F & 437479 Pte TIMMS B. proceeded on leave to England. Lieut W.M. EDMONDS. U.S.M.C reported for duty from detached duty with 2/4. Oxf BUCKS. L.I.	H.M.S.
CAMBRAI	18.11.18		437502 Pte. HAYES J.F. posted to 61st Div H.Q. & struck off strength. No 437451 Pte TRISTRAM. B.J. & No 11271 Pte UNSWORTH. R. granted leave of absence to England. No M2/150236 Cpl MOSS. C.E.T. M.T.A.S.C att. granted leave in FRANCE. No 437448 Pte BROOKHOUSE. A. awarded the Military Medal "For conspicuous gallantry & devotion to duty." [illegible] D.R.O. No 3263 dated 13.11.18. "This man was in charge of Stretcher Bearers working" "from the R.A.P. in SEPMERIES to the Car Loading" "Post on the SEPMERIES - LA JUSTICE ROAD. "During the whole of the day & night of October [illegible] he" "worked incessantly under very heavy shell fire & was"	H.M.S.

T2134. Wt. W708-776. 500000. 4/15. Sir J. C. & S.

Instructions regarding War Diaries and Intelligence Summaries are contained in F. S. Regs., Part II. and the Staff Manual respectively. Title pages will be prepared in manuscript.

WAR DIARY
or
INTELLIGENCE SUMMARY.
(Erase heading not required.)

Army Form C. 2118.

Place	Date	Hour	Summary of Events and Information	Remarks and references to Appendices
			"responsible for the successful evacuation of a large" 'number of wounded'. 'In particularly trying circumstances he showed a' 'fine example of courage & stedfastness"	HmB
CAMBRAI	19-11-18		No82297 SGT. WILSON F. & No435361 PTE DAVIS L. proceeded on leave to England.	HmB
"	20-11-18		No437506 PTE DEAN C.R. & No437321 CPL WINDRIDGE L.C. proceeded on leave to England No366025 PTE MILLS. A.C. proceeded on leave to PARIS.	HmB
"	21-11-18		No439143 CPL BERRY E.J. & T4/248878 DR ADAMS J. A.S.C att proceeded on leave to England.	HmB
"	22-11-18		MAJOR R.D. MOORE. R.A.M.C.T. (M.C.) No437492 PTE READ S.O, No437488 PTE. BROCKHOUSE A. (MM) & No435281 PTE DUDLEY. J. proceeded on leave to England. No303247 PTE AITKEN. J.D. reported for duty from C.C.S. & taken on the strength.	HmB

2353 Wt W2544/1454 700,000 5/15 D. D. & L. A.D.S.S./Forms/C. 2118.

Instructions regarding War Diaries and Intelligence Summaries are contained in F. S. Regs., Part II. and the Staff Manual respectively. Title pages will be prepared in manuscript.

WAR DIARY
or
INTELLIGENCE SUMMARY.
(Erase heading not required.)

Army Form C. 2118.

Place	Date	Hour	Summary of Events and Information	Remarks and references to Appendices
CAMBRAI	23.11.18.		Under orders received from the 183rd Infantry Brigade the Horse Transport less 1. Water Cart & 1 Limber, under command of Capt. A. L. AYMER. R.A.M.C. moved by march route at 0815 to HAPLINCOURT. No 437495 Pte BEDFORD A.R & No 437481 Pte CLARKE J.K. proceeded on leave to England. No 437334. Pte TAYLOR A.G. & No 437107 Pte NICHOLLS. F.W. reported from leave.	HM
"	24.11.18.		Horse Transport moved by march route at 0840 to ALBERT STATION Area. No 437509 Pte HAINES F.G. No 437357 Pte KEELING H & No 450020 Pte FLOOK H.G. proceeded on leave to England. No 437352 Pte BOOKER P.G. reported from leave.	HM
"	25.11.18.		Horse Transport moved by march route at 0615 to BERNAVILLE Area. No 439571 Sgt. DERRICK. C. proceeded on course of Physical & Recreational Training at HARDELOT PLAGE. No 437258 Sgt. MATHIAS L.J.K. proceeded by Train conveying 11th SUFFOLKS. 9th NORTH. FUSLRS.	HM

2353 Wt. W2544/1454 700,000 5/15 D. D. & L. A.D.S.S./Forms/C. 2118.

Instructions regarding War Diaries and Intelligence Summaries are contained in F. S. Regs., Part II. and the Staff Manual respectively. Title pages will be prepared in manuscript.

WAR DIARY
or
INTELLIGENCE SUMMARY.
(Erase heading not required.)

Army Form C. 2118.

Place	Date	Hour	Summary of Events and Information	Remarks and references to Appendices
MESNIL-DOMQUEUR.	26-11-18.		Unit entrained at 0300 at CAMBRAI VILLE for New Area. Detrained at CONTEVILLE at 2000 hours & proceeded by march route to MESNIL-DOMQUEUR & established Headquarters at 2200 hours. No 437462 PTE OSLAND H.J., 437209 PTE TONKS. J, No 437398 PTE DUCKHOUSE H reported from leave in France. No 437364 PTE SMITH E reported from leave. No M2/167360 PTE NETHERCOTT A. - M.T. A.S.C att & No T4/248838 Dr GEORGE A - A.S.C att proceeded on leave to England. 1. H.D. died from Colic. No 437468 Cpl WARD. R.W, 437494 Pte HUNT L.V, & No 437294 PTE COX G proceeded on leave to England.	HRS
MESNIL DOMQUEUR	27.11.18.		Hospital opened for reception of Sick of 183 & 184 Infantry Brigades. Napier Ambulance No 55131 proceeded to Workshop. No 437487 PTE BURROWS W.M. reported from leave.	HRS
	28.11.18		437372 CPL OLDROYD. J.R, 543003 SGT. DRYSDALE G.W., No 32896 PTE WARD. F.J. & No 27783 GNR. HARRISON R.W. R.F.A att proceeded on leave to England. MAJOR. A.T. WATERHOUSE - R.A.M.C.T. reported from leave. No 437161 PTE PRITCHETT V.G.C. reported for duty from Base & taken on the strength.	HRS

2353 Wt W2544/1454 700,000 5/15 D. D. & L. A.D.S.S./Forms/C. 2118.

Army Form C. 2118.

Instructions regarding War Diaries and Intelligence Summaries are contained in F. S. Regs., Part II. and the Staff Manual respectively. Title pages will be prepared in manuscript.

WAR DIARY
or
INTELLIGENCE SUMMARY.
(Erase heading not required.)

Place	Date	Hour	Summary of Events and Information	Remarks and references to Appendices
MESNIL DOMQUEUR	29.11.18		Ford Car No 19 & Motor Cycle proceeded to Workshop. No M/08192 PTE LANGRIDGE W & No T4/248410 DR. SMITH V W. proceeded on leave to England. No T4/248894 DR ROBERTS S L reported from leave.	HmB
	30.11.18		No 439150 PTE ABBOTT A.W., No T4/088798 DR DAVIS T & No 437218 PTE JONES L proceeded on leave to England. No 24592 Daimler ambulance proceeded to workshops with back broken axle shaft.	

H. M. Murghe Lt. Col. R.A.M.C.

Officer Commanding
2/2 Sth. Mid. Fd. Ambce. R.A.M.C. T.F.

2353 Wt W2544/1454 700,000 5/15 D. D. & L. A.D.S.S./Forms/C. 2118.

Dec. 1918.

CONFIDENTIAL

4

MEDICAL.

140/3490

VR 33

WAR DIARY

2/2 S. Mid. Field Ambce. R.A.M.C.T.

VOLUME. 32.

Decr 1st – 31st (inclusive)
1918.

Instructions regarding War Diaries and Intelligence Summaries are contained in F. S. Regs., Part II. and the Staff Manual respectively. Title pages will be prepared in manuscript.

WAR DIARY
or
INTELLIGENCE SUMMARY.
(Erase heading not required.)

Army Form C. 2118.

Place	Date	Hour	Summary of Events and Information	Remarks and references to Appendices
MESNIL-COMBUEUR	1.12.18	—	435350 PTE COTTRELL A, 437490 L/CPL EDGINGTON B.J. proceeded on leave to England. 2 Cars reported for temporary duty from 15 A A C. 437006 SGT. MAJOR JACKSON H.S. reported from leave. M2/150553 CPL MOSS C.E.T. - M.T. A.S.C. att. R 36605 PTE MILLS A.S. reported from leave in France. 437372 PTE GREEN W.P. R 437218 CPL GIBBS L.W. att to Div. Reception Camp. proceeded on leave to England.	[initials]
	2.12.18		93174 PTE SMITH A. R 437464 PTE BROADBENT G.A. proceeded on leave to England. 437274 L/C. DAVIS E.N. R 437480 PTE BEDFORD E R 19229 PTE SULLIVAN J. reported from leave. No 19 Ford Car reported from Workshops. 52034 PTE SHERRINGTON G.T, 403030 PTE PYCOCK H, 339297 PTE ROBINSON C.T, 92697 PTE PROLE S. 92677 PTE EARES B, 93815 PTE RUTTER M, R 20198 PTE TOMLINSON H.W. reported for duty from the Base & taken on the strength.	[initials]
	3.12.18		T4/124557 DR STEVENS C. R T4/124587 DR WHEELER A.H. A S C att. proceeded on leave to England. 437403 PTE ASTON J.J. R M2/110700 SGT. COLLIER E - M.T. A.S.C. att. proceeded on leave to England. 15555 PTE SHARPE S reported from [illegible]	[initials]

2353 Wt. W2544/1454 700,000 5/15 D. D. & L. A.D.S.S./Forms/C. 2118.

Army Form C. 2118.

Instructions regarding War Diaries and Intelligence Summaries are contained in F. S. Regs., Part II. and the Staff Manual respectively. Title pages will be prepared in manuscript.

WAR DIARY
or
INTELLIGENCE SUMMARY.
(Erase heading not required.)

Place	Date	Hour	Summary of Events and Information	Remarks and references to Appendices
			detached duty with 1/5. D.C.L.I. T4/364777 DR SPRIGGS. J.T. evacuated to C.C.S. & struck off the strength.	HmB
MESNIL-DOMQUEUR.	4-12-18		437332 PTE MORTON. C.A. & 437374 PTE PORTMAN L. proceeded on leave to England. 24952 Daimler Ambulance & Motor Cycle reported from Workshop. 437401 L/CPL HARWOOD F, 437479 PTE TIMMS. B, 437517 PTE HASSELL W.J. 437394 PTE DINGLEY J & M2/153802 PTE PACK G.A.H. - M.T. A.S.C. all reported from leave. 91641 PTE TINSLEY R admitted to Hospital & evacuated to C.C.S. & struck off the strength	HmB
"	5-12-18		14781 Ford Car proceeded to Workshop. 437273 PTE SYMES H.G, 51735 PTE TAYLOR G.W. T4/248881 DR BRYAN J. & T4/248893 DR OAKLEY C.J. proceeded on leave to England. LIEUT W.M. EDMONDS - M.C. USA. & Batman proceeded for temporary duty to 2/5. GLOSTERS. 66376 SGT VAUGHAN H.W. reported for duty from Base & taken on the strength. T4/040956 DR CANNEY D - ASC att proceeded on leave to England. 437451 PTE TRISTRAM B.J. reported from leave.	HmB

Instructions regarding War Diaries and Intelligence Summaries are contained in F. S. Regs., Part II. and the Staff Manual respectively. Title pages will be prepared in manuscript.

WAR DIARY
or
INTELLIGENCE SUMMARY.
(Erase heading not required.)

Army Form C. 2118.

Place	Date	Hour	Summary of Events and Information	Remarks and references to Appendices
MESNIL-DOMQUEUR.	6.12.18		437299 PTE YEOMANS A, 437461 PTE TURNER N.D, 5652 PTE TAYLOR. [illegible] T4/243940 DR [illegible] T4/248897 DR STANLEY L.B. proceeded on leave to England. 52297 SGT WILSON.F. reported from leave	[initials]
MESNIL-DOMQUEUR.	7.12.18		437116 Pte STENT J. [illegible]73815 PTE ROTTER M. proceeded on leave to England. A party proceeded to HEIRMONT to collect R.E. material [illegible].	[initials]
AGENVILLE	8.12.18		Under orders of 182 Infantry Brigade the Unit proceeded by march route at 0930 hours to AGENVILLE arriving at 1100 hours. [illegible] Ritchie & Bateman reported from detached duty with [illegible]. Lieut A.M. Edmonds & Bateman proceeded for [illegible] duty with 2/5. Glosters. Sub Division reported for duty from [illegible].	[initials]
	[illegible].12.18		[illegible] Pte Hadley H., [illegible] Pte [illegible] proceeded on leave to England. 437492 Pte Read S.[illegible] T4/24[illegible] [illegible] reported from leave.	[initials]

2353 Wt. W2544/1454 700,000 5/15 D. D. & L. A.D.S.S./Forms/C. 2118.

Instructions regarding War Diaries and Intelligence Summaries are contained in F. S. Regs., Part II. and the Staff Manual respectively. Title pages will be prepared in manuscript.

WAR DIARY
or
INTELLIGENCE SUMMARY.
(Erase heading not required.)

Army Form C. 2118.

Place	Date	Hour	Summary of Events and Information	Remarks and references to Appendices
AGENVILLE.	10-12-18		437444 PTE BUCK J., 437213 PTE SMITH A.L., 439455 PTE DIKE H.J., 395035 PTE ROBINSON G.W., 437283 L/Cpl PLANT G.W. (M.M.) proceeded on leave to England. 439571 SGT. DERRICK C. A.M. reported from course. 435231 PTE DUDLEY J. & 437481 PTE CLARK T.K. reported from leave. Lieut J. P. STOUT & Batman reported from detached duty with 2/8 Worcesters.	HWB
"	11.12.18		437495 Pte. BEDFORD A.R. reported for duty from leave. 437521 Pte. FRANKUM J.W., 437288 Sgt. UREN L.V. & 303248 Pte. AITKEN J.D. proceeded on leave to England. 1 Large car proceeded for temporary duty to A.D.M.S. 61st Division.	HWB
"	12.12.18		439571 Sgt. DERRICK C. & 437515 Pte. EVETTS T.L. proceeded on leave to England. 437468 L/Cpl. WARD P.W., 437394 Pte. COX G., 437357 Pte. KEELING H., 450020 Pte. FLOOK H.J., & 437448 Pte. BROCKHOUSE A. reported for duty from leave.	HWB
"	13.12.18		T4/248888 Dvr. GEORGE A, A.S.C. attached & M2/167360 Pte. NETHERCOTT A, M.T.A.S.C. attached reported from leave. 437312 L/Cpl. VIGURS E.N. reported for duty from C.C.S. and	HWB

Instructions regarding War Diaries and Intelligence Summaries are contained in F. S. Regs., Part II. and the Staff Manual respectively. Title pages will be prepared in manuscript.

WAR DIARY
or
INTELLIGENCE SUMMARY.
(Erase heading not required.)

Army Form C. 2118.

Place	Date	Hour	Summary of Events and Information	Remarks and references to Appendices
AGENVILLE	13.12.18		taken on the strength. 53034 Pte. SHERRINGTON G.T. & 437455 Pte. STANFORD G. proceeded on leave to England.	[initials]
"	14.12.18		Lieut J. P. STOUT, MORC USA, proceeded on leave to England. No. 417210 Pte. THOMPSON E. admitted to Hospital & evacuated to CCS & struck off strength. No 437372 Cpl. OLDROYD J.R., 543003 Sgt. DRYSDALE G.W., 437494 Pte. HUNT L.V. & 27783 Gnr. HARRISON R.W., R.G.A attached reported from leave. Capt. (Acting Major) R. D. MOORE, M.C., RAMC(T) transferred to Home Establishment & struck off strength with effect from 8/10/18. T4/248670 Dvr. GEORGE K & T4/248779 Dvr. SPRINGHAM S, No 4 Coy ASC attached proceeded on leave to England.	[initials]
"	15.12.18		Douglas Motor Cycle sent to Workshop. T4/246596 Dvr. RUBERY C.T. ASC attached with 2 L.D. Horses & Limber proceeded for temporary duty to 48 Sanitary Section. 417210 Pte. THOMPSON E reported for duty from CCS & taken on the strength. 437365 Q.M. Sgt. FOSS S.E. & 10113 Pte FARRINGTON. J., 24 Manc. att. proceeded on leave to England.	[initials]

2353 Wt. W2534/1454 700,000 5/15 D. D. & L. A.D.S.S./Forms/C. 2118.

Army Form C. 2118.

Instructions regarding War Diaries and Intelligence Summaries are contained in F. S. Regs., Part II. and the Staff Manual respectively. Title pages will be prepared in manuscript.

WAR DIARY
or
INTELLIGENCE SUMMARY.
(Erase heading not required.)

Place	Date	Hour	Summary of Events and Information	Remarks and references to Appendices
AGENVILLE.	16.12.18		Napier Ambulance No. A 55131 sent to Workshop. Stude Baker Ambulance attached unfit to take the road & sent back to No. 15 M.A.C. No. 435256 Pte. WEST H.V. & 435540 Pte. LUMLEY H. proceeded on leave to England.	HWB
"	17.12.18		Sunbeam Ambulance No. A 54821 reported for temporary duty from No. 15 M.A.C. T4/246839 S/Sgt. Major PLAISTOW T., A.S.C. att. & 18885 Pte. SHARPE S. proceeded on leave to England. Large car reported from temporary detached duty at A.D.M.S. Office [illegible] Div.	HWB
"	18.12.18		437398 Pte. WOODHALL H. proceeded on leave to England. 437018 Pte. JONES L. reported for duty from leave.	HWB
"	19.12.18		437372 L/Cpl. VIBURS E.N. & 305830 Pte. HUNTER B. proceeded on leave to England. 435350 Pte. COTTERELL A reported for duty from leave. Capt J. R. RICHMOND RITCHIE, R.A.M.C.T.C. proceeded on leave to England.	HWB
"	20.12.18		T4/248896 Dvr. RUBERY C.J., A.S.C. att. with 2 L.D. Horses & limber returned from	HWB

Instructions regarding War Diaries and Intelligence Summaries are contained in F. S. Regs., Part II. and the Staff Manual respectively. Title pages will be prepared in manuscript.

WAR DIARY
or
INTELLIGENCE SUMMARY.
(Erase heading not required.)

Army Form C. 2118.

Place	Date	Hour	Summary of Events and Information	Remarks and references to Appendices
AGENVILLE	20-12-18		temporary detached duty with 48 Sanitary Section. M2/099465 Pte. WEAVER J., M.T.A.S.C. reported for duty from Hospital & taken on the strength.	HRL
"	21-12-18		1 Large Car with driver & orderly proceeded for temporary duty to C.R.A. 61st Division. No. 303744 Pte. ALLAN T., 58776 Pte SIMS C. & 1458 Pte. TAYLOR J.S. proceeded on leave to England.	HRL
"	22-12-18		T4/247839 Dvr. TAYLOR W. A.S.C. reported for duty. T4/309357 Dvr. Wood C.H., A.S.C. att. evacuated sick to C.C.S. & struck off strength. M2/150236 Cpl. MOSS C.E. M.T.A.S.C. att., T4/248882 Dvr. BURLING E.T., A.S.C. att. & 437582 Pte. GORDON A.H. proceeded on leave to England.	HRL
"	23-12-18		437032 S/Sgt. CUMMINGS T., 437342 Pte. RUSSELL H., & 439517 Pte. HANKS R.W. proceeded on leave to England. No 435372 Pte. BAUGHAN G.W., 437484 Pte. BROADBENT G.A., 437332 Pte. GREEN W.P., 437273 Pte. SYMES H.G., 51735 Pte. TAYLOR G.W. & M1/08192 Pte LANGRIDGE W.T., M.T.A.S.C. att. reported from leave.	HRL

2353 Wt W2544/1454 700,000 5/15 D. D. & L. A.D.S.S./Forms/C. 2118.

Army Form C. 2118.

Instructions regarding War Diaries and Intelligence Summaries are contained in F. S. Regs., Part II. and the Staff Manual respectively. Title pages will be prepared in manuscript.

WAR DIARY
or
INTELLIGENCE SUMMARY.
(Erase heading not required.)

Place	Date	Hour	Summary of Events and Information	Remarks and references to Appendices
AGENVILLE	24.12.18		Lieut W. M. EDMONDS, MORC USA reported from temporary detached duty with 2/5 Glosters. 87010 Pte. BAILEY N. T., 435030 SGT. BLUNN A., & 437270 Cpl. CLEAL C.A. proceeded on leave to England. T4/040956 Dvr. CANNEY D, A.S.C. att. reported from leave. 83292 Pte SCOTTON E., & 344074 Pte. CLEGG J. proceeded on leave to BOULOGNE.	HMS
"	25.12.18		53051 Pte. SAMPSON M, 421032 Pte. GUEST W. H., & 301105 Pte. NICOL C. proceeded on leave to England.	HMS
"	26.12.18		303257 Pte. TAYLOR G., 437284 Pte. WADEY E. & 439546 Pte. KING C.E proceeded on leave to England. 437461 Pte. TURNER N.D. reported from leave. T4/248999 Dvr. POPE P, A.S.C. reported for duty.	HMS
"	27.12.18		543003 Sgt. Drysdale G.W., & 99684 Pte. SIDEBOTHAM S. proceeded to XVII Corps Educational Establishment for a Commercial Course. 435007 Pte MOSELEY A.J., 374063 Pte VERNON J & 44822 Pte. TAYLOR ROBT. proceeded on leave to England.	HMS

2353 Wt. W2544/1454 700,000 5/15 D. D. & L. A.D.S.S./Forms/C. 2118.

Instructions regarding War Diaries and Intelligence Summaries are contained in F. S. Regs., Part II. and the Staff Manual respectively. Title pages will be prepared in manuscript.

WAR DIARY
or
INTELLIGENCE SUMMARY.
(Erase heading not required.)

Army Form C. 2118.

Place	Date	Hour	Summary of Events and Information	Remarks and references to Appendices
AGENVILLE.	28·12·18		11271 Pte. UNSWORTH J.R. - despatched to Third Army Miners' Reception Camp and struck off strength. 'C' Section watercart sent to workshop. Lieut W. M. EDMONDS, M.O.R.C. U.S.A. proceeded for temporary duty to 6th. Bn. Tank Corps. 437215 Sgt. RAMSEY J.B. T4/97145 Pte MARTIN C.G. proceeded on leave to England.	[illegible]
	29·12·18		Lt Col. H. N. BURROUGHES, RAMC proceeded on leave to PARIS and Major A. [illegible] assumed command of the Unit. 437511 Pte. SEALES B.N. [illegible] proceeded on leave to ENGLAND. 437283 Pte. PLANT B.W. [illegible] 437510 Pte. TURNER W. 437510 Pte MORRIS H. [illegible] Pte. [illegible] 439426. Pte CRIDGE C. [illegible] Pte DIKE A.J. [illegible] T4/248881 Dr BRYAN J. [illegible] R.A.S.C. [illegible] reported from leave. 1 M.A.C. car returned to 15 M.A.C.	ATW.
	30·12·18		57189 Pte HAIGH B.E. despatched to Third Army Miners' Reception Camp and struck off strength. Lieut EDWARDS M.O.R.C. U.S.A. [illegible] Capt. J. P. STOUT M.O.R.C.U.S.A. reported from leave	ATW

2353 Wt. W2544/1454 700,000 5/15 D. D. & L. A.D.S.S./Forms/C. 2118.

Army Form C. 2118.

WAR DIARY
or
INTELLIGENCE SUMMARY.
(Erase heading not required.)

Instructions regarding War Diaries and Intelligence Summaries are contained in F. S. Regs., Part II. and the Staff Manual respectively. Title pages will be prepared in manuscript.

Place	Date	Hour	Summary of Events and Information	Remarks and references to Appendices
Agenville	31.12.18		T/309357 Dr Wood C.H. R.A.S.C. att. proceeded on leave to ENGLAND M2/116711 Sgt. COLLIER E. M.T. A.S.C. att. rejoined from leave	

A.F. Waterhouse
Major RAMC T
for Officer Commanding
2/2 Sth. Mid. Fld. Ambce. R.A.M.C. T.F.

2/2nd SOUTH MIDLAND FIELD AMBULANCE R.A.M.C. (T.F.)
No.
Date

D. D. & L., London, E.C.
(10340) Wt W5300/P713 750,000 3/18 Forms/C2118/16.

17 (61st DN Box 2929 MEDICAL

Jan 1919

CONFIDENTIAL

98 34

14/24.90

WAR DIARY

2/2 S^th^ Midland Field Ambulance

R.A.M.C. T.

VOLUME 33.

January 1st - 31st inclusive

1919.

Instructions regarding War Diaries and Intelligence Summaries are contained in F. S. Regs., Part II. and the Staff Manual respectively. Title pages will be prepared in manuscript.

WAR DIARY
or
INTELLIGENCE SUMMARY.
(Erase heading not required.)

Army Form C. 2118.

Place	Date	Hour	Summary of Events and Information	Remarks and references to Appendices
AGENVILLE.	1/1/19.		Daimler Ambulance No 25542, with driver, MT/133594 PTE CAMPLIN. H. reported for duty & taken on the strength. T4/247239, DR. TAYLOR. W. R.A.S.C. taken on the strength with effect from 23 12/18. T4/245999, DVR. POPE. P. R.A.S.C taken on the strength with effect from 26 12/18. MT/079033, PTE. MORTON K.W. M.T. A.S.C admitted sick to 1st Southern General Hospital, whilst on leave, in England, & struck off the strength with effect from 28 11/18. 437412, SGT. HICKMAN F. proceeded on leave to England.	AFW
"	2/1/19		437441, PTE O'LOUGHLIN. P. proceeded for temp. duty to 61st DIVN. HQRS.	AFW
	3/1/19		LIEUT. J. P. STOUT M.O.R.C. U.S.A. posted to 307 BRIGADE. R.F.A. for duty & struck off strength. 60376 SGT. VAUGHAN, H. W. proceeded on leave to England.	AFW

D. D. & L., London, E.C.
(10340) Wt W5300/P713 750,000 3/18 E 2688 Forms/C2118/16.

Instructions regarding War Diaries and Intelligence Summaries are contained in F. S. Regs., Part II. and the Staff Manual respectively. Title pages will be prepared in manuscript.

WAR DIARY
or
INTELLIGENCE SUMMARY.
(Erase heading not required.)

Army Form C. 2118.

Place	Date	Hour	Summary of Events and Information	Remarks and references to Appendices
AGENVILLE	4/1/19		Routine work. Ford Ambulance No 14364 sent to Workshops. D/14151 PTE MALLINSON. J. 4th DRAGOON GUARDS attached reported for duty from leave & placed under [illegible] arrest from 1400 hours.	[illegible]
	5/1/19		LIEUT. COL. H. N. BURROUGHES, R.A.M.C.(T) returned from leave & resumed command of the unit. 43[illegible], PTE [illegible] attached 523 Co. R.A.S.C. proceeded on leave to England. 6344 PTE SEABRIGHT. E.R reported for duty from hospital.	[illegible]
	6/1/19		437400 PTE APP. H 437490 L/C EDGINGTON. D.J. & 3[illegible] PTE ROBINSON C.F. proceeded to XVII Corps [illegible] for demobilization, & struck off strength.	[illegible]
	7/1/19		500665 PTE NANT. A.G. proceeded on leave to [illegible] 20197 PTE TOMLINSON. H.H. reported from temp. duty with 307 [illegible] R.F.A.	

D. D. & L., London, E.C.
(10340) Wt W5300/P713 750,000 3/18 E 2688 Forms/C2118/16.

Army Form C. 2118.

WAR DIARY
or
INTELLIGENCE SUMMARY.
(*Erase heading not required.*)

Instructions regarding War Diaries and Intelligence Summaries are contained in F. S. Regs., Part II. and the Staff Manual respectively. Title pages will be prepared in manuscript.

Place	Date	Hour	Summary of Events and Information	Remarks and references to Appendices
AGENVILLE.	8/1/19		91641 PTE. TINSLEY. R. reported for duty from Hospital & taken on the strength. 437250, PTE. HUNT. A.E. reported for duty from Hospital. 437408, L/C. BROWN. J.L. proceeded on leave to England.	HMB
"	9/1/19		437493. PTE. DUFFILL. A.J. evac sick to C.C.S. & struck off strength. Douglas Motor Cycle W.D. No R.S. 25978, reported for duty from Workshops, & taken on the strength. MT/133594 PTE CAMPLIN. H. M.T. R.A.S.C attached, proceeded on leave to England.	HMB
"	10/1/19		T4/247239, DR. TAYLOR. W. No 4. Co. R.A.S.C. attached, evac sick to C.C.S. & struck off strength.	HMB
"	11/1/19		437515. PTE. EVETTS. T.L. despatched to XVII Corps Concentration Camp, for Demobilization, & struck off strength. 437258. SGT. MATHIAS. L.J.K. Granted special leave of absence to England.	HMB

D. D. & L., London, E.C.
(10340) Wt W5300/P713 750,000 3/18 E 2688 Forms/C2118/16.

Army Form C. 2118.

WAR DIARY
or
INTELLIGENCE SUMMARY.
(Erase heading not required.)

Instructions regarding War Diaries and Intelligence Summaries are contained in F. S. Regs., Part II. and the Staff Manual respectively. Title pages will be prepared in manuscript.

Place	Date	Hour	Summary of Events and Information	Remarks and references to Appendices
AGENVILLE.	12/1/19		437517 PTE. HASSELL W.T. and 51[illegible]5 PTE. TAYLOR G.H. despatched to XVII Corps Concentration Camp for demobilization & struck off strength.	[illegible]
	13/1/19		Routine Work.	[illegible]
	14/1/19		CAPT. [illegible] R. RICHMOND RITCHIE [illegible] reported for duty from leave. 437334. PTE. TAYLOR A.J. despatched to XVII Corps Concentration Camp for demobilization & struck off the strength.	[illegible]
	15/1/19		43[illegible]5. PTE. ADAWAY G. evacuated sick to C.C.S. & struck off strength. CAPT. H. G. DODD, R.A.M.C.T. reported for duty from 315 Army Brigade, R.F.A. & taken on the strength.	[illegible]
	16/1/19		232051 PTE. HENDERSON C.G. proceeded on leave to [illegible]. T4/24[illegible]30 DRV TAYLOR W. R.A.S.C. reported for duty from Hospital & taken on the strength.	[illegible]

D. D. & L., London, E.C.
(10340) Wt W5300/P713 750,000 3/18 E 2688 Forms/C2118/16.

Army Form C. 2118.

Instructions regarding War Diaries and Intelligence Summaries are contained in F. S. Regs., Part II. and the Staff Manual respectively. Title pages will be prepared in manuscript.

WAR DIARY
or
INTELLIGENCE SUMMARY.
(Erase heading not required.)

Place	Date	Hour	Summary of Events and Information	Remarks and references to Appendices
AGENVILLE.	17/1/19		CAPT. H. G. DODD, R.A.M.C. (T) proceeded for temporary duty to D.M.S. Second Army. 437522 PTE GORDON A.H. proceeded whilst on leave in England to No 1. Dispersal Centre OSWESTRY, for demobilization, 6/1/19, & struck off strength with effect from that date.	[illegible]
"	18/1/19		437564 PTE CHAMBERLAIN R despatched to XVII Corps Concentration Camp, for demobilization, & struck off strength.	[illegible]
"	19/1/19		437270. CPL. CLEAL. C. A. joined No 1. Dispersal Unit, Oswestry, while on leave in U.K. for demobilization & struck off strength 15/1/19. 374063 PTE VERNON J A joined No 1. Dispersal Unit, Shorncliffe, 10/1/19, for demobilization, while on leave in U.K. & struck off the strength. 58776. PTE SIMS C joined No 1. Dispersal Unit, Shorncliffe, 4-1-19, for demobilization, while on leave in U.K. & struck off the strength.	[illegible]

D. D. & L., London, E.C.
(10340) Wt W5300/P713 750,000 3/18 Sch. 2688 Forms/C2118/16.

Army Form C. 2118.

Instructions regarding War Diaries and Intelligence Summaries are contained in F. S. Regs., Part II. and the Staff Manual respectively. Title pages will be prepared in manuscript.

WAR DIARY
or
INTELLIGENCE SUMMARY.
(Erase heading not required.)

Place	Date	Hour	Summary of Events and Information	Remarks and references to Appendices
AGENVILLE	9/1/19		CAPT. R. C. COATSWORTH, R.A.M.C. T.F. reported for duty from Hospital; 74/248576. SGT. FOSS. A. E. [illegible] leave of absence to U.K.	
	10/1/19		[illegible] PTE. BORROWS N.M. [illegible] PTE SULLIVAN J. [illegible] DR. WOTHERSPOON, L. (3rd RES. BDE. R.F.A. [illegible]) [illegible] to XVII Corps Concentration Camp for demobilization [illegible] struck off the strength.	
	11/1/19		[illegible] PTE OSBAND H.J. 437218 PTE. JONES [illegible] PTE. PYCOCK A. [illegible] to XVII Corps Camp [illegible] for demobilization [illegible]	
	[illegible]/1/19		[illegible] PTE JONES A.H. 437443 PTE TURNER W. [illegible] DR. GEORGE [illegible] No. 4 Co. R.A.S.C. attached) [illegible] XVII Corps Concentration Camp for demobilization [illegible] struck off the strength. [illegible] reported for duty to 61st DIV. HQRS. [illegible]	

D. D. & L., London, E.C.
(10340) Wt W5300/P713 750,000 3/18 2688 Forms/C2118/16.

Instructions regarding War Diaries and Intelligence Summaries are contained in F. S. Regs., Part II. and the Staff Manual respectively. Title pages will be prepared in manuscript.

WAR DIARY
or
INTELLIGENCE SUMMARY.
(Erase heading not required.)

Army Form C. 2118.

Place	Date	Hour	Summary of Events and Information	Remarks and references to Appendices
AGENVILLE.	23/1/19		1. H.D. sent to 61. DIV. MOBILE VET. SEC. & evacuated to Base 24/1/19. 437284 Pte HARDEY E. joined No 1. Dispersal Unit, Oswestry, 11-1-19, for demobilization whilst on leave in U.K. and struck off the strength. 12066 GNR BRUNTON G. (265 Siege Bty. R.G.A. attached) reported from detached duty at Fifth Army Headquarters.	[illegible]
"	24/1/19		CAPT. R. C. COLESWORTH R.A.M.C. T.C. proceeded for temporary duty to 1/5th D.C.L.I. CAPT. J. R. RICHMOND RITCHIE, R.A.M.C. & batman proceeded for temporary duty to "R" Corps [illegible]. Grey Gelding, H.D. evacuated to Base & struck off strength.	[illegible]
"	25/1/19		CAPT. A. L. HYMER R.A.M.C. Granted leave to ROUEN. LT. A. R. EDWARDS. M.R.C. U.S.R. admitted sick to Hospital. 457424 SGT. BIRKBY – proceeded for temporary duty to XVII Corps Concentration Camp.	[illegible]

D. D. & L., London, E.C.
(10340) Wt W5300/P713 750,000 3/18 2688 Forms/C2118/16.

Instructions regarding War Diaries and Intelligence Summaries are contained in F. S. Regs., Part II. and the Staff Manual respectively. Title pages will be prepared in manuscript.

WAR DIARY
or
INTELLIGENCE SUMMARY.
(Erase heading not required.)

Army Form C. 2118.

Place	Date	Hour	Summary of Events and Information	Remarks and references to Appendices
AGENVILLE [illegible]	[illegible]		Capt. [illegible] AYMER R.A.M.C. to be acting Major, while commanding a section of a Field Ambulance, with effect from [illegible] authority: appointments, promotions, etc. [illegible] F. Marshall C. in C. list No. [illegible], dated [illegible]	
	[illegible]		LIEUT. A. R. EDWARDS, M.R.C. U.S.A. [illegible] effect from 20/1/19. LIEUT. H. M. EDMONDS [illegible] off the strength [illegible] 6th Bn. Lanc. Corps. 300105 PTE. NICHOL C. reported from [illegible]	
	25/1/19		Routine Work.	[illegible]
	29/1/19		LIEUT. A. R. EDWARDS, M.R.C. U.S.A. reported [illegible] [illegible] PTE. THOMPSON E. reported from detached [illegible] 6th Bn. Lanc. Corps.	[illegible]

D. D. & L., London, E.C.
(10340) Wt W5300/P713 750,000 3/18 E 2688 Forms/C2118/18.

Army Form C. 2118.

Instructions regarding War Diaries and Intelligence Summaries are contained in F. S. Regs., Part II, and the Staff Manual respectively. Title pages will be prepared in manuscript.

WAR DIARY
or
INTELLIGENCE SUMMARY.
(Erase heading not required.)

Place	Date	Hour	Summary of Events and Information	Remarks and references to Appendices
AGENVILLE	30/1/19		437106. CPL. BENTON H. G. (M.M.) 450020. PTE. FLOOK H. G. 495479 PTE CLARETT G. F. (M.M.) 435350 PTE COTTRELL A. 437299 PTE YEOMANS A. 100196 PTE GRIMSHAW T. and 339387 PTE HAMILTON. R. proceeded for duty to O.C. 59th Field Ambulance, under orders of A.D.M.S. 19th Division, thence to D.D.M.S. ROUEN, and struck off the strength. 437275. CPL. GIBBS. L. W. 407143 PTE. MARTIN C. G. 73815 PTE. RUTTER M. 437431 PTE CLARKE. J.R. 63317. PTE SEABRIGHT E. L. 437322. PTE HIGGS C. R. and 303247 PTE AITKE. J. D. proceeded for duty to A.D.M.S. ABBEVILLE, under orders of A.D.M.S. 20th Division, + struck off strength. 543003. SGT. DRYSDALE G. N. and 99684 PTE SIDEBOTHAM S. reported for duty from XVII Corps Education Establishment. 437215 SGT. RAMSEY. J. B. joined No1. Dispersal Unit, Oswestry, for demobilization, whilst on leave in U.K. 18/1/19; and struck off strength. 437342. PTE RUSSELL H. joined No1. Dispersal Unit, Oswestry, for demobilization, whilst on leave in U.K. 18/1/19 and struck off the strength.	HDS.

D. D. & L., London, E.C.
(10340) Wt W5300/P713 750,000 3/18 E 2688 Forms/C2118/16.

Instructions regarding War Diaries and Intelligence Summaries are contained in F. S. Regs., Part II. and the Staff Manual respectively. Title pages will be prepared in manuscript.

Army Form C. 2118.

WAR DIARY
or
INTELLIGENCE SUMMARY.

(Erase heading not required.)

Place	Date	Hour	Summary of Events and Information	Remarks and references to Appendices
ABENVILLE	20/1/19		457412. SGT. HICKMAN F. joined No 1 Dispersal Unit, [illegible] for demobilization, 17-1-19 and struck off strength.	[illegible]
"	31/1/19		D/14181. TROOPER MALLINSON. J. 4th Dragoon Guards attached, tried by "F.G.C.M." 24/1/19, for offence "When on active service absenting himself without leave from 4/1/19 to [illegible]" A.A. 15(1a) and awarded "56 days F.P. No 1."	[illegible]

H. [illegible] Lt Col. RAMC.

Officer Commanding
2/2 Sth. Mid. Fd. Ambce. R.A.M.C. T.F.

D. D. & L., London, E.C.
(10340) Wt W5300/P713 750,000 3/18 E 2688 Forms/C2118/16.

Feb. 1919 9

MEDICAL

CONFIDENTIAL

V 834

140/3524

WAR DIARY

2/2nd Sth. Midland Field Ambulance.

R. A. M. C. T.

VOLUME 34.

February 1st to 28th inclusive
1919.

Army Form C. 2118.

Instructions regarding War Diaries and Intelligence Summaries are contained in F. S. Regs., Part II. and the Staff Manual respectively. Title pages will be prepared in manuscript.

WAR DIARY
or
~~INTELLIGENCE SUMMARY~~.
(Erase heading not required.)

Place	Date	Hour	Summary of Events and Information	Remarks and references to Appendices
AGENVILLE	1/2/19.		6 H.D. Horses & 4 L.D. Horses despatched to No. 4 Veterinary Hospital, ABBEVILLE, for transfer to Base, & struck off strength.	[illegible]
"	2/2/19.		LIEUT. A. R. EDWARDS. M.R.C. U.S.A. proceeded on leave to England. 27783 GNR. HARRISON R.W. R.F.A. attached, 50920. PTE. [illegible] A. 18th MANCHESTERS attached, and 120662 GNR BRONTON G. R.G.A. attached proceeded to XVII Corps Concentration Camp, for demobilization, & struck off strength.	[illegible]
"	[illegible]		MAJOR A. L. HYMER R.A.M.C. reported from leave.	[illegible]
"	[illegible]		MAJOR A. L. HYMER R.A.M.C. proceeded to A.D.M.S. [illegible] Division for temporary duty as D.A.D.M.S. No. 437250. PTE HUNT A.E. [illegible] to C.C.S. & struck off strength.	
	[illegible]		No. 313257. PTE. TAYLOR G. and 437303. PTE. GRIFFITHS A. proceeded on temporary duty to O.C. 70th Sanitary Section. 437520. PTE. SHEPPEY. F. proceeded for temporary duty to A.D.M.S. 61st Division, vice 437252. PTE. CURETON. F. who returned to [illegible] for duty.	

D. D. & L., London, E.C.
(10340) Wt W5300/P713 750,000 3/18 E 2688 Forms/C2118/16.

Instructions regarding War Diaries and Intelligence Summaries are contained in F. S. Regs., Part II. and the Staff Manual respectively. Title pages will be prepared in manuscript.

WAR DIARY
or
~~INTELLIGENCE SUMMARY~~.
(Erase heading not required.)

Army Form C. 2118.

Place	Date	Hour	Summary of Events and Information	Remarks and references to Appendices
AGENVILLE.	6/2/19		493571. PTE. FREDERICKS. A. proceeded for temporary duty to 70th Sanitary Section. T4/247259, DVR. TAYLOR W. R.A.S.C. attached, proceeded on leave to England. 437365 Q.M.Sgt. FOSS. S.E. demobilized whilst on short leave in U.K. & struck off strength, with effect from 27/1/19. 87010 PTE BAILEY. N.J. demobilized whilst on short leave in U.K. & struck off strength with effect from 26/12/18.	[initials]
"	7/2/19.		437364 PTE SMITH E. & 437252 PTE. CURETON F.H. proceeded to XVII Corps Concentration Camp for demobilization & struck off strength. 368046. PTE FRENCH. J.H. proceeded on leave to England. 305220. PTE. HUNTER B. demobilized whilst on leave in U.K. & struck off strength with effect from 4/1/19. 93658. PTE THOMAS. I.R demobilized whilst on leave in U.K. & struck off strength with effect from 5/2/19. 5652 PTE. TAYLOR RICHARD demobilized whilst on leave in U.K. & struck off strength with effect from 22/12/18.	[initials]
"	8/2/19.		366025. PTE MILLS. A. C. proceeded on leave to England.	[initials]

D. D. & L., London, E.C.
(10340) Wt W5300/P713 750,000 3/18 E 2688 Forms/C2118/16.

Army Form C. 2118.

Instructions regarding War Diaries and Intelligence Summaries are contained in F. S. Regs., Part II. and the Staff Manual respectively. Title pages will be prepared in manuscript.

WAR DIARY

or

~~INTELLIGENCE SUMMARY~~.

(Erase heading not required.)

Place	Date	Hour	Summary of Events and Information	Remarks and references to Appendices
AGENVILLE	[illegible]		Lt Col. H.N. BURROUGHES. RAMC [illegible] Major H.T. WATERHOUSE, R.A.M.C. [illegible] [illegible] 65% Sgt [illegible] [illegible] PTE WEST H.V. [illegible] U.K. [illegible]	ATW
	10/2/19		[illegible] PTE BAINBRIDGE S.T. [illegible] PTE TIMMS B. [illegible] PTE [illegible] [illegible]	ATW
	11/2/19		437372 CPL OLDROYD J.R. proceeded on special leave of absence to ENGLAND.	ATW
	12/2/19		T4/248885 Dr EARL A.E. evacuated sick to C.C.S. and struck off the strength	ATW

D. D. & L., London, E.C.
(10340) Wt W5300/P713 750,000 3/18 E 2688 Forms/C2118/16.

Instructions regarding War Diaries and Intelligence Summaries are contained in F. S. Regs., Part II. and the Staff Manual respectively. Title pages will be prepared in manuscript.

WAR DIARY
or
~~INTELLIGENCE SUMMARY~~.
(Erase heading not required.)

Army Form C. 2118.

Place	Date	Hour	Summary of Events and Information	Remarks and references to Appendices
AGENVILLE	13/2/19		Under orders received from A.D.M.S. 61st Divn the Hqrs and most of personnel and transport moved by march route at 0945 hours. Route - DOMLEGER, MESNIL-DOMQUEUR, DOMQUEUR, LE PLOUY, BUSSUS-BUSSUEL, YAUCOURT-BUSSUS. Time of arrival 1300 hours. All men billetted and transport parked.	A.T.W.
YAUCOURT-BUSSUS	14/2/19		Most of personnel and transport left at AGENVILLE arrived YAUCOURT-BUSSUS at 1600 hours. 437285 PTE KIMBERLEY J.C. demobilized whilst on leave in U.K. and struck off strength 21-1-19. 303244 PTE ALLAN T. demobilized whilst on leave in UK and struck off strength 6-1-19. 437258 SGT MATHIAS L.J.K demobilized whilst on leave in UK and struck off strength 27-1-19. 437408 PTE BROWN J.L. demobilized whilst on leave in UK and struck off strength 27-1-19.	A.T.W.
"	15/2/19		Remainder of personnel and transport reported for duty from AGENVILLE. M2/156597, PTE. WILLIAMS W.J. Granted leave of absence to U.K.	A.T.W.
"	16/2/19		T4/088798 DR. DAVIS. T. Granted special leave of absence to U.K.	A.T.W.
	17/2/19		MAJOR. A.L. AYMER. R.A.M.C. & Batman, reported from detached duty at 61st DIVNL. HDQRS.. 437234, L/Cpl. DAVIS. E.N. & No 437021,	

D. D. & L., London, E.C.
(10340) Wt W5300/P713 750,000 3/18 E 2688 Forms/C2118/16.

Army Form C. 2118.

Instructions regarding War Diaries and Intelligence Summaries are contained in F. S. Regs., Part II. and the Staff Manual respectively. Title pages will be prepared in manuscript.

WAR DIARY
or
~~INTELLIGENCE SUMMARY.~~
(Erase heading not required.)

Place	Date	Hour	Summary of Events and Information	Remarks and references to Appendices
	17/2/19.	Contd		
YAUCOURT-BUSSUS.			PTE SHEPPARD H. reported from detached duty at the 61st Divl. Reception Camp.	ASW
	19/2/19		M/08192. PTE LANGRIDGE W.T. evacuated sick to C.C.S. and struck off strength.	ASW
	20/2/19		LT. A. R. EDWARDS. M.C. U.S.A., and batman, proceeded for duty to 2/6 Bn. R. Warwicks. LT. A. R. EDWARDS. M.C. U.S.A. struck off the strength in accordance with instructions from A.D.M.S. 61st DIVISION. No 20195, PTE TOMLINSON. A.A. reported from temp. detached duty at "R" Corps Siege Park. 431374 PTE PORTMAN L. proceeded to Concentration Camp for demobilization.	ASW
	21/2/19.		CAPT (A/MAJOR) A. L. AYMER R.A.M.C. proceeded for duty to No1. Stationary Hospital ROUEN, & struck off the strength. Auth. D.G.M.S. No D.G. 6/654. Dated 8/2/19. T4/248881 DVR. BRYAN. J. R.A.S.C. attached, proceeded to Concentration Camp, ABBEVILLE, for demobilization.	ASW
	22/2/19		Routine Work.	ASW

D. D. & L., London, E.C.
(10340) Wt W3,500/P713 750,000 3/18 E 2688 Forms/C2118/16.

Army Form C. 2118.

Instructions regarding War Diaries and Intelligence Summaries are contained in F. S. Regs., Part II. and the Staff Manual respectively. Title pages will be prepared in manuscript.

WAR DIARY

or

~~INTELLIGENCE SUMMARY.~~

(Erase heading not required.)

Place	Date	Hour	Summary of Events and Information	Remarks and references to Appendices
YAUCOURT BUSSUS.	23/2/19.		303281 PTE. IRONSIDE. D. B. 437338. PTE HISCOCK. W. T. + 6822 PTE. LAWLEY. W. T. proceeded to Concentration Camp, Abbeville, for demobilization.	A.T.W.
"	24/2/19		CAPT. O. BASTABLE R.A.M.C. T. granted leave of absence to U.K.	A.T.W.
"	25/2/19		LT.-COL. H. N. BURROUGHES, R.A.M.C. T. reported from leave + re-assumed command of the Unit.	H.N.B.
"	26/2/19.		99684 PTE. SIDEBOTHAM S. + T/370264 DVR. NORMAN D. D. proceeded on leave to U.K. 437468 L/CPL. WARD F. W. 439143 CPL. BERRY E. J. 437466 PTE. ROSCORLA A. 32267 PTE COATES. A. (24th Manchesters attached) proceeded to Concentration Camp ABBEVILLE, for demobilization.	H.N.B.
"	29/2/19.		T4/248878 DVR. ADAMS. J. proceeded on leave to U.K. 437013. S. SGT. MARTIN R. P. proceeded to Concentration Camp for demobilization.	H.N.B.

D. D. & L., London, E.C.
(10340) Wt W5300/P713 750,000 3/18 E 2688 Forms/C2118/16.

Army Form C. 2118.

Instructions regarding War Diaries and Intelligence Summaries are contained in F. S. Regs., Part II. and the Staff Manual respectively. Title pages will be prepared in manuscript.

WAR DIARY
or
~~INTELLIGENCE SUMMARY~~.
(Erase heading not required.)

Place	Date	Hour	Summary of Events and Information	Remarks and references to Appendices
YAUCOURT BUSSUS	28/2/19	—	Routine Work.	

2/2nd SOUTH MIDLAND FIELD AMBULANCE R.A.M.C. (T.F.)
No. ✓
Date 28/2/19

[illegible]
Lt. Col. R.A.M.C.
Officer Commanding
2/2 Sth. Mid. Fld. Ambce. R.A.M.C. T.F.

D. D. & L., London, E.C.
(10340) Wt W5300/P713 750,000 3/18 E 2688 Forms/C2118/10.

2

Mar. 1919

Vol 35
144/3557

CONFIDENTIAL.

2/2nd SOUTH MIDLAND FIELD AMBULANCE R.A.M.C. (T.F.)
No.________
Date________

WAR DIARY

VOLUME 35.

for March 1919.

2/2 South Mid Field Amb

Army Form C. 2118.

WAR DIARY

~~INTELLIGENCE SUMMARY~~.

(*Erase heading not required.*)

Instructions regarding War Diaries and Intelligence Summaries are contained in F. S. Regs., Part II. and the Staff Manual respectively. Title pages will be prepared in manuscript.

Place	Date	Hour	Summary of Events and Information	Remarks and references to Appendices
YAUCOURT-BUSSUS.	1/3/19		437424. SGT. BIRKBY. L. reported from detached duty at XVII Corps Concentration Camp. 437495. PTE BEDFORD A.T. 437521. PTE. FRANKUM J.W. + 437209 PTE TONKS J. proceeded to Concentration Camp. Abbeville, for demobilization.	
	2/3/19		Routine Work.	
	3/3/19		Routine Work.	
	4/3/19		437414 SGT. EDGINGTON W.J. 395055 PTE. ROBINSON G.W. [illegible] 344074 PTE. CLEGG J.H.B. proceeded to Concentration Camp. Abbeville, for demobilization. 4/3/19.	
	6/3/19		PTE. BROCKHOUSE A. (M.M.) proceeded on French Leave.	
	7/3/19		CAPT J. P. STOUT M.C. U.S.A. reported for duty & taken on the strength. 437207 PTE MOSELEY A.J. demobilized whilst on leave & struck off strength 10/2/1919.	

(10340) Wt W5300/P713 750,000 3/18 E 2688 Forms/C2118/16. D. D. & L., London, E.C.

Instructions regarding War Diaries and Intelligence Summaries are contained in F. S. Regs., Part II. and the Staff Manual respectively. Title pages will be prepared in manuscript.

WAR DIARY
or
~~INTELLIGENCE SUMMARY~~.
(Erase heading not required.)

Army Form C. 2118.

Place	Date	Hour	Summary of Events and Information	Remarks and references to Appendices
YAUCOURT -BUSSUS.	7/3/19.		437350 PTE ALDIS E, Demobilized & struck off strength 18/2/19. 43734 PTE PORTMAN L. Demobilized & struck off strength 23/2/19. 57171 PTE SMITH R, 20198 PTE TOMLINSON H. & 437461 PTE TURNER N.D. Proceeded to Concentration Camp, Abbeville, for demobilization. M2/099465 PTE WEAVER J. proceeded for temp. duty to 61st Div M.T. Coy.	[illegible]
"	8/3/19.		M2/099465 PTE WEAVER J. reported for duty from 61st Div. M.T. Coy 63446. Ford Ambulance, reported for duty & taken on strength 8/3/19.	[illegible]
"	9/3/19.		12432. CPL WARD A. Granted leave of absence to U.K.	[illegible]
"	10/3/19.		437404 PTE BROADBENT G, 437403 PTE ASTON J.J. and 437116 PTE STENT J. Proceeded to Concentration Camp, Abbeville, for demobilization; Ford Car proceeded for temp. duty with A.D.M.S. 61st Div.	[illegible]

D. D. & L., London, E.C.
(10340) Wt W5300/P715 750,000 3/18 E 2688 Forms/C2118/16.

Instructions regarding War Diaries and Intelligence Summaries are contained in F. S. Regs., Part II. and the Staff Manual respectively. Title pages will be prepared in manuscript.

WAR DIARY

or

~~INTELLIGENCE SUMMARY.~~

(Erase heading not required.)

Army Form C. 2118.

Place	Date	Hour	Summary of Events and Information	Remarks and references to Appendices
[illegible]	[illegible]		Routine Work	[illegible]
	[illegible]		Routine Work [illegible] Pte Evans E.O. reported [illegible] duty with 61st Div [illegible]	[illegible]
	[illegible]		[illegible] Pte Stanford [illegible] Pte Cox [illegible] Pte Evans E.O. [illegible]	[illegible]
	[illegible]		437126. Pte. Cridge G reported from temp duty with 2/6 R. Warwicks.	
			437460. Pte. Davies. H.F. Demobilized & struck off strength 5/5/19.	
			437333. " Hiscock W.T. " " " " 5/5/19.	
			437013 St. Sgt. Martin. R.P. " " " " 5/5/19	
			437495 Pte. Bedford A.R. " " " " 5/5/19	
			437521 Pte Frankum J.W. " " " " 5/5/19	
			437201 Pte Tonks. J " " " " 5/5/19	[illegible]

A5834 Wt W4973/M687 750,000 8/16 D. D. & L. Ltd. Forms/C.2118/13

Instructions regarding War Diaries and Intelligence Summaries are contained in F. S. Regs., Part II. and the Staff Manual respectively. Title pages will be prepared in manuscript.

WAR DIARY
or
~~INTELLIGENCE SUMMARY.~~
(Erase heading not required.)

Army Form C. 2118.

Place	Date	Hour	Summary of Events and Information	Remarks and references to Appendices
YAUCOURT -BUSSUS.	14/3/19.		437298 PTE. WOODHALL H. Admitted to Hospital in England 31/12/18, + struck off strength from that date. 1 Ford Car + 1 Driver reported for temp. duty to 2/3. S.M. Fld. Amb. LT-COL H. N. BURROUGHES R.A.M.C.T. Embarked for England, for demobilization + struck off strength 14/3/19. AUTH. "Deborted" Wire, No. S.M. 509/3. A.M.D. 1. Dated 9/3/19. MAJOR A. T. WATERHOUSE, R.A.M.C.T. assumes command of the Unit.	ATW
"	15/3/19.		1 Ford Car + Driver proceeded for temp. duty with Headquarters, 182 Infantry Brigade; DIEPPE. 437572. CPL. OLDROYD J. R. posted to 1st Eastern General Hospital, Brighton, + struck off strength, 14/3/19. Auth. O i/c R.A.M.C. Section G.H.Q. No. 2620/19. D/13/3/19.	ATW
"	16/3/19.		437212 L/CPL. E. N. VIGURS proceeded on French Leave 16/3/19 to 25/3/19.	ATW
	17/3/19.		437[illegible] PTE BUCK. J. proceeded on French Leave 18/3/19 to 26/3/19.	ATW

Instructions regarding War Diaries and Intelligence Summaries are contained in F. S. Regs., Part II. and the Staff Manual respectively. Title pages will be prepared in manuscript.

WAR DIARY
or
~~INTELLIGENCE SUMMARY.~~
(Erase heading not required.)

Army Form C. 2118.

Place	Date	Hour	Summary of Events and Information	Remarks and references to Appendices
YAUCOURT-BUSSUS	17/3/19		91641 PTE TINSLEY R. Granted leave of absence to England 19/3/19 to 2/4/19. 303081 PTE IRONSIDE D.B. demobilised & struck off strength 26/3/19. 424424 SGT BIRKBY L Granted leave of absence in France. 20/3/19 to 29/3/19.	[illegible]
	15/3/19		1 W.O. 2 N.C.Os + 22 MEN proceeded to A.D.V.S. [illegible] on duty & struck off the strength 15/3/19. Auth. [illegible] No. [illegible] Dated 15/3/19.	
			305035 PTE ROBINSON G.N. demobilised & struck off strength 9/3/19.	
			431461 " TURNER N.D " " " " 9/3/19.	
			344094 " CLEGG J.H.B. " " " " 8/3/19.	
			431404 " BROADBENT G. " " " " [illegible]	
			431402 " [illegible]YON. J.T. " " " " [illegible]	
			316065 " PROUDFOOT D. " " " " 4/3/19.	
			439143 CPL. BERRY. E.T. " " " " [illegible]	
			431414 SGT EDGINTON W.T. " " " " [illegible]	
	19/3/19		[illegible]	

2353 Wt. W2544/1454 700,000 5/15 D. D. & L. A.D.S.S./Forms/C. 2118.

Instructions regarding War Diaries and Intelligence Summaries are contained in F. S. Regs., Part II. and the Staff Manual respectively. Title pages will be prepared in manuscript.

WAR DIARY
or
~~INTELLIGENCE SUMMARY.~~
(Erase heading not required.)

Army Form C. 2118.

Place	Date	Hour	Summary of Events and Information	Remarks and references to Appendices
YAUCOURT - BUSSUS	20/3/19.		64875 PTE. TURNBULL J.O. 72199 PTE TIBBLES J.G. 439447 PTE. HAWKS R.W. 439447. PTE. BURTON W. and 439316 PTE. DIKE A.J. proceeded for temporary duty to No 2. Stationary Hospital, ABBEVILLE 20/3/19.	A.P.W.
"	21/3/19.		M2/116702 SGT COLLIER E. (M.T. R.A.S.C. attd) returned to 61 Div. M.T. Co for demobilization.	A.P.W.
"	22/3/19.		10113 PTE. FARRINGTON J. (24th Manchesters - P.B. Batman attached) whilst on leave in England, transferred to Class "Z" Army Reserve, with effect from 4/3/19, & struck off the strength. 32267 PTE. COATES A. (24th Manchesters - P.B. Batman attached) demobilized 28/3/19 & struck off the strength. 20198 PTE. TOMLINSON H. A. and 73174 PTE. SMITH A. demobilized & struck off strength.	A.P.W.
"	23/3/19		431234 L/CPL. DAVIS E.H. Granted leave of absence in France, 24/3/19 to 4/4/19.	A.P.W.

2353 Wt. W2544/1454 700,000 5/15 D. D. & L. A.D.S.S./Forms/C. 2118.

Instructions regarding War Diaries and Intelligence Summaries are contained in F. S. Regs., Part II. and the Staff Manual respectively. Title pages will be prepared in manuscript.

WAR DIARY

or

~~INTELLIGENCE SUMMARY~~.

(Erase heading not required.)

Army Form C. 2118.

Place	Date	Hour	Summary of Events and Information	Remarks and references to Appendices
[illegible]OCOURT -BOSSUS	23/3/19.		53391 CPL WILSON F promoted to rank of Sergeant with pay to take effect from 16/1/1919. 1 Ford Ambulance & 1 Driver reported from temp. duty with 1/3 S.M.F.A. D[illegible] TROOPER MALLINSON J (4th Dragoon Guards [illegible] attached) evacuated sick to 6 C.C.S. & struck off the strength 23/3/19. 1 Ford Ambulance & 1 Driver proceeded for temp. duty with Adqrs 18th [illegible]	
	24/3/19.		40351 PTE FREDERICKS H. 30351 PTE TAYLOR [illegible] PTE GRIFFITHS A. reported for duty from [illegible] & taken on the strength 24/3/19. [illegible] XIII Corps [illegible]	
	25/3/19.		[illegible] with 1/3 S.M.F. AMB. 4 men [illegible] 5 [illegible] for temp. duty with [illegible]	

D. D. & L., London, E.C.
(10340) Wt W5300/P713 750,000 3/18 E 2688 Forms/C2118/16.

Instructions regarding War Diaries and Intelligence Summaries are contained in F. S. Regs., Part II. and the Staff Manual respectively. Title pages will be prepared in manuscript.

WAR DIARY
or
~~INTELLIGENCE SUMMARY~~.
(Erase heading not required.)

Army Form C. 2118.

Place	Date	Hour	Summary of Events and Information	Remarks and references to Appendices
VAUCOURT-BUSSUS.	26/3/19.		MAJOR A. T. WATERHOUSE R.A.M.C.T. promoted Acting-Lieut-Colonel, from 18-3-19 whilst in command of the 2/2 S. M. FLD. AMBULANCE. Auth. 61st Division. R.O. A.R. 14/5. Dated 18/3/19.	
			437566. PTE. EVANS E. O. demobilized + struck off strength, 16/3/19.	
			M2/167150 PTE. BIGNELL A. (M.T. R.A.S.C. attd) Granted leave to England, from 28/3/1919 to 11/4/1919.	
			LIEUT-COLONEL A. T. WATERHOUSE R.A.M.C.T. proceeded to England on leave, from 28/3/1919 to 10/4/1919. During his absence, CAPT. R. C. COATSWORTH. (M.C.) R.A.M.C. assumes command of the unit.	RCC
"	27/3/19.		437523. L/CPL. STANWELL L. G. + 437448 PTE. BROCKHOUSE A. demobilized + struck off the strength. 20/3/19.	RCC
"	28/3/19.		2 N.C.Os. 6 MEN + 10 Horses (R.A.S.C. attd) reported from temp. duty with 2/3 S. M. F. AMB.. 4 Men + 8 Horses (R.A.S.C. attd) reported from temp. duty with 2/1 S. M. F. AMB.	RCC
"	29/3/19		92699. PTE. PROLE G. demobilized + struck off strength. 20/3/19.	RCC

D. D. & L., London, E.C.
(10340) Wt W5300/P713 750,000 3/18 E 2688 Forms/C2118/16.

Instructions regarding War Diaries and Intelligence Summaries are contained in F. S. Regs. Part II. and the Staff Manual respectively. The pages will be prepared in manuscript.

WAR DIARY

or

~~INTELLIGENCE SUMMARY~~.

(Erase heading not required.)

Army Form C. 2118.

Place	Date	Hour	Summary of Events and Information	Remarks and references to Appendices
VAUCOURT BUSSUS.	29/3/19.		One Ford Ambulance & One Driver reported for temp. duty with Headquarters 185th Inf. Brigade.	RCC
"	30/3/19.		Routine Work.	RCC
"	31/3/19.		Routine Work. 12432. Cpl. WARD A. proceeded to No 2 Stationary Hospital, Abbeville, for duty, & struck off strength. 31/3/19.	RCC

R.C. Coatsworth
Captain. R.A.M.C.
A/O.C. 2nd South Mid. Field Ambulance.

SOUTH MIDLAND FIELD AMBULANCE R.A.M.C. (T.F.)
No. K 35.
Date 31/3/19.

D. D. & L., London, E.C.
(A7301) Wt W5300/P713 750,000 3/18 E 2688 Forms/C2118/16.

Apr. 1919

CONFIDENTIAL Vol 36

140/3550.

WAR DIARY

VOLUME. 36. for April. 1919.

2/2 South Mid Field Ambulance.

Army Form C. 2118.

Instructions regarding War Diaries and Intelligence Summaries are contained in F. S. Regs., Part II. and the Staff Manual respectively. Title pages will be prepared in manuscript.

WAR DIARY
or
~~INTELLIGENCE SUMMARY~~.
(Erase heading not required.)

Place	Date	Hour	Summary of Events and Information	Remarks and references to Appendices
YAUCOURT - BUSSUS.	1/4/19.		Routine Work.	[illegible]
"	2/4/19.		1/11067. Co. Sgt. Major. OLIVER G.H. (522 Co. R.A.S.C.) reported for duty & taken on the strength, 2/4/1919.	[illegible]
"	3/4/19.		437455 Pte. STANFORD G.A.C. & 437294 Pte. COX G. demobilized & struck off the strength 23/3/1919. M2/150236. Cpl. Moss. C. (61st Div. M.T. Co. attached) was severely reprimanded, for the offence, "When on active service, conduct to the prejudice of good order & military discipline, in that he (1) Took out a motor ambulance on an unauthorized journey & (2) Disobeyed Commanding Officer's Order No. 3117 dated 29/3/1919. 437233. Sgt. WHITEHOUSE T. promoted to rank of Quartermaster-Sergeant, with effect from 27-1-1919.	[illegible]

D. D. & L., London, E.C.
(10340) Wt W5300/P713 750,000 3/18 Z 2688 Forms/C2118/16.

Army Form C. 2118.

WAR DIARY
or
~~INTELLIGENCE SUMMARY.~~
(Erase heading not required.)

Instructions regarding War Diaries and Intelligence Summaries are contained in F. S. Regs., Part II. and the Staff Manual respectively. Title pages will be prepared in manuscript.

Place	Date	Hour	Summary of Events and Information	Remarks and references to Appendices
VAUCOURT-BUSSUS.	4/4/19.		49711 PTE CAFFREY J. (1/7 Manchesters. D.D. Batman attached) Granted leave to England, 6 4/19 to 20 4/19. 493571. PTE. FREDERICKS A, 303257 PTE TAYLOR G, and 437303 PTE GRIFFITHS A. proceeded to Concentration Camp Abbeville, for demobilization. 4/4/19. 437520. PTE SHEPPEY. F reported from temp. duty with 61st Div. Headquarters	RCC
	5/4/19.		421032. PTE GUEST N. Struck off strength of B.E.F. Demobilized off leave in U.K from 10/1/19. Auth. O i/c R.A.M.C. Records, Woking, L/219/16/T.F. Dated 21/2/19. 437520 PTE SHEPPEY F, 99634 PTE SIDEBOTHAM S, and 91641 PTE TINSLEY R, reported for duty to No 2 Stationary Hospital, Abbeville, & struck off strength 5/4/19. CAPT. J. P. STOUT, M.C. U.S.A. reported to Commanding General, 1st Replacement Dept, for demobilization, in accordance with	RCC

D. D. & L., London, E.C.
(10340) Wt W5300/P713 750,000 3/18 E 2688 Forms/C2118/16.

Instructions regarding War Diaries and Intelligence Summaries are contained in F. S. Regs., Part II. and the Staff Manual respectively. Title pages will be prepared in manuscript.

WAR DIARY
or
~~INTELLIGENCE SUMMARY.~~
(Erase heading not required.)

Army Form C. 2118.

Place	Date	Hour	Summary of Events and Information	Remarks and references to Appendices
YAUCOURT - BUSSUS.	5/4/19. contd		orders received from the American Exp. Force, G.H.Q. Special Orders No 79. Extract 57. Dated 20/3/1919, and is struck off the strength accordingly. 5/4/19.	[illegible]
	6/4/19.		M2/116702 SGT. COLLIER. E. (61st M.T. Co attd.) Demobilised & struck off the strength from 23/3/19.	[illegible]
	7/4/19.		Routine Work.	[illegible]
	8/4/19		T4/248839. STAFF-SGT. MAJOR PLAISTOWE T. Proceeded to [illegible] Concentration Camp, Abbeville, for demobilisation, 5/4/19.	[illegible]
	9/4/19.		M2/031732 PTE. CHURCHMAN H. and [illegible] relieved for temp. duty from [illegible] S.N.F. [illegible] 8/4/19.	[illegible]
	10/4/19		T4/248719. DR. SPRINGHEM. S. R. evacuated to [illegible] off strength 10/4/19.	[illegible]

D. D. & L., London, E.C.
(10340) Wt W5300/P713 750,000 3/18 E 2688 Forms/C2118/16.

Instructions regarding War Diaries and Intelligence Summaries are contained in F. S. Regs., Part II. and the Staff Manual respectively. Title pages will be prepared in manuscript.

WAR DIARY
or
~~INTELLIGENCE SUMMARY.~~
(Erase heading not required.)

Army Form C. 2118.

Place	Date	Hour	Summary of Events and Information	Remarks and references to Appendices
~~VAUCOURT-BUSSUS~~	10/4/19.		64875 PTE TURNBULL J. O. 72199 PTE TIBBLES J. G. 439517 PTE HANKS R. W. 437447 PTE BURTON W. 439816 PTE DIKE A. J. reported from temp duty with No. Stationary Hpl. Abbeville. R C Coatsworth Captain. R.A.M.C.	
"	11/4/19.		M2/031732. PTE H. CHURCHMAN, and Daimler Ambulance No. A.1293, (2/3 S. M. FLD. AMB. ATTd) proceeded to 61st Div. Workshops for repairs. Stores and Vehicles rendered surplus to Establishment of the New Mobilization Store Table, returned to C. O. O. Abbeville, 10/4/19.	
"	12/4/19.		LIEUT-COL. A. T WATERHOUSE. R.A.M.C.T. having reported from leave, re-assumes command of the unit.	
"	13/4/19.		M2/153802. PTE PACK G. A. A. (M.T. R.A.S.C. attd) returned to the 61st Div. M. T. Coy. for demobilization, & struck off strength. 13/4/19.	

D. D. & L., London, E.C.
(10340) Wt W5300/P713 750,000 3/18 E 2688 Forms/C2118/15.

Army Form C. 2118.

WAR DIARY
or
~~INTELLIGENCE SUMMARY~~.
(Erase heading not required.)

Instructions regarding War Diaries and Intelligence Summaries are contained in F. S. Regs., Part II. and the Staff Manual respectively. Title pages will be prepared in manuscript.

Place	Date	Hour	Summary of Events and Information	Remarks and references to Appendices
YAUCOURT -BUSSUS.	14/4/19.		14/248709. Dr. PORTSMOUTH J. Granted leave of absence to England. 16/4/19 to 30/4/19. M2/099465. PTE. WEAVER J. (M.T. R.A.S.C. ~~A.H.S.~~) & Napier Ambulance, proceeded to workshops.	
"	15/4/19.		CAPT. R. C. COATSWORTH. R.A.M.C. proceeded for duty, to 2/5 Gloucesters, & struck off strength 15/4/19. Authority A.D.M.S. ABBEVILLE. P/3/780. dated 14.4.19.	
"	16/4/19.		Routine Work.	
"	17/4/19.		Routine Work.	
"	18/4/19.		493571. PTE FREDERICKS A. and 303257 PTE. TAYLOR G. demobilized & struck off strength 8/4/19. 457303 PTE. GRIFFITHS A. demobilized & struck off strength 9/4/1919.	
"	19/4/19.		Routine Work.	

D. D. & L., London, E.C.
(10340) Wt W5300/P713 750,000 3/18 E 2688 Forms/C2118/16.

Army Form C. 2118.

WAR DIARY
or
~~INTELLIGENCE SUMMARY~~.
(Erase heading not required.)

Instructions regarding War Diaries and Intelligence Summaries are contained in F. S. Regs., Part II. and the Staff Manual respectively. Title pages will be prepared in manuscript.

Place	Date	Hour	Summary of Events and Information	Remarks and references to Appendices
~~YAUCOURT~~ BUSSUS.	20/4/19.		Routine Work.	[illegible]
"	21/4/19.		1 Light Draught Horse evacuated sick to No. 14. Vety. Hospital, & struck off the Strength.	[illegible]
"	22/4/19.		14/ 248901. SGT. TRING R. J. (524 Co R.A.S.C. attd) proceeded to Concentration Camp, Abbeville, for demobilization. 22/4/19.	[illegible]
"	23/4/19.		Routine Work.	[illegible]
"	24/4/19.		Routine Work.	[illegible]
"	25/4/19		Routine Work	[illegible]
"	26/4/19.		M2/099465. PTE. WEAVER J. and "Napier" Ambulance No. A. 55128, reported for duty from workshops.	[illegible]

D. D. & L., London, E.C.
(10340) Wt W5300/P713 750,000 3/18 E 2688 Forms/C2118/16.

Instructions regarding War Diaries and Intelligence Summaries are contained in F. S. Regs., Part II. and the Staff Manual respectively. Title pages will be prepared in manuscript.

WAR DIARY

or

~~INTELLIGENCE SUMMARY.~~

(Erase heading not required.)

Army Form C. 2118.

Place	Date	Hour	Summary of Events and Information	Remarks and references to Appendices
YAUCOURT BUSSUS.	27/4/19.		Routine Work.	[illegible]
"	28/4/19.		Routine Work.	[illegible]
"	29/4/19.		Routine Work.	[illegible]
"	30/4/19.		Routine Work.	[illegible]

2/2ND SOUTH MIDLAND [FIELD] AMBULANCE R.A.M.C. (T.F.) 30 APR 1919

[illegible signature]
Commanding 2/2 South Mid. Field Amb.

2353 Wt. W2544/1454 700,000 5/15 D. D. & L. A.D.S.S./Forms/C. 2118.

Aug. 1919.

2/2 SM Fd Amb

Vol 37

140/35-60

CONFIDENTIAL.

2/2nd. S. Mid. Field Amb.

WAR DIARY.

VOLUME 37.

for MAY 1919

Instructions regarding War Diaries and Intelligence Summaries are contained in F. S. Regs., Part II. and the Staff Manual respectively. Title pages will be prepared in manuscript.

WAR DIARY
or
~~INTELLIGENCE SUMMARY~~.
(Erase heading not required.)

Army Form C. 2118.

Place	Date	Hour	Summary of Events and Information	Remarks and references to Appendices
YAUCOURT -BUSSUS.	1/5/19.		Routine work.	[illegible]
"	2/5/19.		Routine work.	[illegible]
"	3/5/19.		1 Light Draught Horse (Man "Y") evacuated sick to [illegible] Vety. Hospital, Abbeville & struck off strength [illegible].	[illegible]
"	4/5/19.		T4/248999. DVR. POPE. P. (524 Co. R. A. S. C. Attd.) Evacuated sick to C. C. S. & struck off the strength. 4/5/19. 437553 PTE. OWEN G. Granted leave to U.K. } 4/5/19 to 15/5/19. 53292 PTE. SCOTTEN E. Granted leave to U.K. } 4/5/19 to 15/5/19. T4/245801. CPL. CREFFIELD F. W. (524 Co. R. A. S. C. attd.) Granted leave to U.K. 6/5/19 - 20/5/19. 72199. PTE. TIBBLES. J. G. Granted leave to U.K. 6/5/19 - 20/5/19.	
"	5/5/19.		Routine Work.	[illegible]

2353 Wt. W2544/1454 700,000 5/15 D. D. & L. A.D.S.S./Forms/C. 2118.

Army Form C. 2118.

Instructions regarding War Diaries and Intelligence Summaries are contained in F. S. Regs., Part II. and the Staff Manual respectively. Title pages will be prepared in manuscript.

WAR DIARY
or
~~INTELLIGENCE SUMMARY.~~
(Erase heading not required.)

Place	Date	Hour	Summary of Events and Information	Remarks and references to Appendices
YAUCOURT -BUSSUS	6/5/19.		Routine Work	A.T.W.
"	7/5/19		Routine Work.	A.T.W.
"	8/5/19.		M2/099465, PTE. WEAVER J. (61st M.T. Co) and 417210 PTE. THOMPSON E, granted leave to U.K. 10/5/19 - 24/5/19.	A.T.W.
"	9/5/19.		M2/150236. CPL. MOSS. C.E, M2/33594 PTE. CAMPLIN H, M2/167346. PTE. SCOTT E.R, M2/099465, PTE. WEAVER J, M2/167150. PTE. BIGNELL A, M2/167360, PTE. NETHERCOTT. A, M2/167659 PTE STEVENS H, and M2/156597 PTE. WILLIAMS J. (M.T. R.A.S.C. att'd) struck off strength as from 1/5/19 & posted to 61st Div. M.T. Coy under G.R.O. No 6685. Para 2. (d) M2/150236 CPL. MOSS C.E, M2/167346 PTE SCOTT E.R, M2/099465 PTE WEAVER J, M2/167150 PTE BIGNELL A, M2/167360 PTE. NETHERCOTT. A, and M2/156597 PTE WILLIAMS J, (61st M.T. Co) attached for temp duty 1/5/19.	A.T.W.
"	10/5/19		Routine Work.	A.T.W.

Army Form C. 2118.

WAR DIARY

or

~~INTELLIGENCE SUMMARY~~.

(Erase heading not required.)

Instructions regarding War Diaries and Intelligence Summaries are contained in F. S. Regs., Part II. and the Staff Manual respectively. Title pages will be prepared in manuscript.

Place	Date	Hour	Summary of Events and Information	Remarks and references to Appendices
HAUCOURT - BUSSUS.	11/5/19.		CAPT. O. BASTABLE. R.A.M.C.T. Granted leave to Paris, 11-5-19 to 15-5-19. 366025 PTE. MILLS A.C. Granted leave to Paris, 12-5-19 to 22-5-19. 437321. CPL. HINDRIDGE. L.C. Granted leave to Hollingham, 12/5/19 to 22/5/19. 437305 PTE GOURLAY W.J. } 421501 PTE SHARMAN J.R. } Granted leave to England from 13/5/19 to 24/5/19.	
"	12/5/19		Routine Work.	
"	13/5/19		Routine Work.	
"	14/5/19		1458. PTE. TAYLOR. J.S. R.A.M.C. Proceeded to A.D.M.S. ABBEVILLE AREA, for reposting, & struck off the strength. 14/5/19. T4/246610. DVR. VALENTINE E. (524 Co. R.A.S.C. (A.H.)) Granted leave to U.K. 16/5/19 – 20/5/1919. 437274 SGT. BARWELL F. and 437447 PTE. BURTON W. Granted leave to U.K. 16/5/19 to 30/5/1919.	

2353 Wt. W2544/1454 700,000 5/15 D. D. & L. A.D.S.S./Forms/C. 2118.

Army Form C. 2118.

Instructions regarding War Diaries and Intelligence Summaries are contained in F. S. Regs., Part II. and the Staff Manual respectively. Title pages will be prepared in manuscript.

WAR DIARY
or
~~INTELLIGENCE SUMMARY~~.
(Erase heading not required.)

Place	Date	Hour	Summary of Events and Information	Remarks and references to Appendices
YAUCOURT-BUSSUS.	15/5/19.		14/248999. DVR. POPE P. (524 Co. R.A.S.C.) reported from C.C.S. & taken on the strength 15/5/19.	ATW
"	16/5/19.		Routine Work.	ATW
"	17/5/19.		435290. PTE SMITH. T. and 437503 PTE CRIPPS. W. Granted leave to U.K. 19/5/19 to 2/6/19.	ATW
"	18/5/19.		Routine Work. A.T. Waterhouse Lieut-Colonel. R.A.M.C.T. Commanding 2/1st South Midland Field Ambulance.	
"	19/5/19.		LIEUT-COLONEL A.T. WATERHOUSE. R.A.M.C.T. proceeded to U.K. for demobilization, 19/5/19, and is struck off the strength accordingly. Auth. "Deported wire" D.M/29558, A.M.D.1. CAPTAIN. O. BASTABLE, R.A.M.C.T. assumes command of this Field Ambulance, 19/5/19.	[illegible]

D. D. & L., London, E.C.
(10340) Wt W5300/P713 750,000 3/18 E 2688 Forms/C2118/16.

Instructions regarding War Diaries and Intelligence Summaries are contained in F. S. Regs., Part II. and the Staff Manual respectively. Title pages will be prepared in manuscript.

WAR DIARY

or

~~INTELLIGENCE SUMMARY.~~

(Erase heading not required.)

Army Form C. 2118.

Place	Date	Hour	Summary of Events and Information	Remarks and references to Appendices
HAUCOURT – BOSW.	20/5/19.		T4/248897. Dr RUBERY C.J. (524 Co R.A.S.C. (AH)) Granted leave to U.K. 22/5/19 to 5/6/19.	R
	21/5/19.		Routine Work.	R
	22/5/19		4 Riding, 9 Light Draught & 9 Heavy Draught Horses, returned to to No 2 Remount Depot, Abbeville, & struck off strength in accordance with H.Q. L of C. No Q.L. 428/A.F. 42 D/14 5/19.	R
	23/5/19.		No 83294. PTE SCOTTON E. Reported to A.D.M.S. Abbeville Area for reposting in accordance with A.D.M.S. No 960. dated 21/5/19, & struck off strength 23/5/19. M2/150236. CPL. MOSS. C. (61st M.T. Co R.A.S.C. attd) Granted leave to Paris, 23/5/19 to 29/5/19.	R
	24/5/19.		T4/040074 DR. BURDETT. W (524 Co R.A.S.C.) Granted leave to U.K. 25/5/19 to 6/6/19.	R

D. D. & L., London, E.C.
(10340) Wt W5300/P713 750,000 3/18 E 2688 Forms/C2118/16.

Army Form C. 2118.

Instructions regarding War Diaries and Intelligence Summaries are contained in F. S. Regs., Part II. and the Staff Manual respectively. Title pages will be prepared in manuscript.

WAR DIARY

or

~~INTELLIGENCE SUMMARY.~~

(Erase heading not required.)

Place	Date	Hour	Summary of Events and Information	Remarks and references to Appendices
YAUCOURT -BUSSUS.	25/5/19		500065. PTE. WANT. A. G. Demobilized off leave in U.K. & struck off strength with effect from 24/1/19. 32896. PTE. WARD. F. J. Demobilized off leave in U.K. & struck off strength with effect from 31/1/19.	
"	26/5/19		2 Riding, 2 L.D. & 4 H.D. Horses handed in to No 2 Remount Depot, Abbeville, & struck off the strength 26/5/19. Auth. H.Q. L. of C. No Q.L. 428/A.F./42, dated 14/5/19.	
	27/5/19		437233. SGT. BIRKBY. L. Granted leave to U.K. from 28/5/19 to 11/6/19.	
	28/5/19		Routine Work.	
	29/5/19		1 W.O. 1 N.C.O. & 10 DRIVERS, R.A.S.C. attached, returned to No 524 Co R.A.S.C. & struck off strength 29/5/19.	

D. D. & L., London, E.C.
(10340) W1 W5300/P713 750,000 3/18 Sch. 2688 Forms/C2118/16.

Army Form C. 2118.

Instructions regarding War Diaries and Intelligence Summaries are contained in F. S. Regs., Part II. and the Staff Manual respectively. Title pages will be prepared in manuscript.

WAR DIARY

or

~~INTELLIGENCE SUMMARY~~.

(Erase heading not required.)

Place	Date	Hour	Summary of Events and Information	Remarks and references to Appendices
YAUCOURT-BUSSUS.	30/5/19.		437305. PTE. GOURLAY W. J. proceeded to Concentration Camp Abbeville, for demobilization & repatriation to Melbourne, Australia. 30/5/19.	R
	31/5/19.		Routine Work	R
			[signature] Captain R.A.M.C.T. Commanding 2/2 S. Mid. Fd. Amb.	

3RD SOUTH MIDLAND FIELD AMBULANCE R.A.M.C. (T.F.) 31 MAY 1919

D. D. & L., London, E.C.
(10340) Wt W5300/P713 750,000 3/18 E 2688 Forms/C2118/16.

19

2/2 S M Fd Amb.

Vol 38

140/35-85

June 1919

WAR DIARY

CONFIDENTIAL

VOLUME 38.

for JUNE 1919

Army Form C. 2118.

WAR DIARY
or
~~INTELLIGENCE SUMMARY.~~
(Erase heading not required.)

Instructions regarding War Diaries and Intelligence Summaries are contained in F. S. Regs., Part II. and the Staff Manual respectively. Title pages will be prepared in manuscript.

Place	Date	Hour	Summary of Events and Information	Remarks and references to Appendices
YAUCOURT -BUSSUS.	1/6/19.		14/248839. St-Sgt-Major. PLAISTOWE T. (524 Co R.A.S.C. attached) demobilized 12/5/19 and struck off strength. 14/248901 SGT. TRING R.J. (524 Co. R.A.S.C. Attd) demobilized 25/5/19 + struck off strength.	
			437357. PTE. KEELING H. Granted leave to England from 3/6/19 to 17/6/19.	
"	2/6/19		Routine Work.	
	3/6/19		Routine Work.	
	4/6/19.		Routine Work.	
	5/6/19		437480. PTE. BEDFORD E. Granted leave to U.K. via Calais, from 7/6/19 to 21/6/19.	

D. D. & L., London, E.C.
(10340) Wt W5300/P713 750,000 3/18 E 2688 Forms/C2118/16.

Army Form C. 2118.

Instructions regarding War Diaries and Intelligence Summaries are contained in F. S. Regs., Part II. and the Staff Manual respectively. Title pages will be prepared in manuscript.

WAR DIARY

or

~~INTELLIGENCE SUMMARY.~~

(Erase heading not required.)

Place	Date	Hour	Summary of Events and Information	Remarks and references to Appendices
YAUCOURT -BUSSUS.	6/6/19.		14/248410 Dr SMITH V. N. (524 Co. R.a S. C. ANd) Granted leave to U.K via Calais from 8/6/19 to 22/6/19. M2/150236. Cpl MOSS C.E (61st M.T. Co. ANd) Granted leave to U.K. via Calais, from 8/6/19 to 22/6/19.	B
ABBEVILLE	7/6/19		Under orders from 61st Div Headquarters, No. A/184/15/1. this Field Ambulance moved from YAUCOURT BUSSUS, to the Signal Depot. ABBEVILLE, arriving at 1230 Hours. 437441. PTE. O'LOUGHLIN. P. reported from duty with 61st. Div. Headquarters.	B
"	8/6/19.		437331. PTE. RIDOUT C. reported from detached duty with 61st Div. Baths.	B
"	9/6/19.		437506. PTE. DEAN C.R. Granted leave to U.K. via CALAIS from 11/6/19 to 25/6/19.	B

D. D. & L., London, E.C.
(10340) Wt W5300/P713 750,000 3/18 E 2688 Forms/C2118/16.

Army Form C. 2118.

WAR DIARY

or

~~INTELLIGENCE SUMMARY.~~

(Erase heading not required.)

Instructions regarding War Diaries and Intelligence Summaries are contained in F. S. Regs., Part II. and the Staff Manual respectively. Title pages will be prepared in manuscript.

Place	Date	Hour	Summary of Events and Information	Remarks and references to Appendices
ABBEVILLE	10/6/19.		28 O.R. R.A.S.C. & 6 O.Rs. (524 Co. R.A.S.C. AHS) proceeded to Concentration Camp, Abbeville, for demobilization.	
	11/6/19 to 15/6/19.		Routine Work.	
	16/6/19.		M2/169346. PTE. SCOTT E. R. (61 M.T. Co. AHS) Granted leave to the U.K. from 17/6/19 to 1/7/19.	
	17/6/19.		CAPT. J. R. RICHMOND RITCHIE, R.A.M.C. Demobilized & struck off strength with effect from [illegible] 19. Authy. War Office, No. 24/R/364, (A.M.D. 1.) dated [illegible] 19. T4/248897. DR. RUBERY. C. J. (524 Co. R.A.S.C. AHS) despatched to Concentration Camp, for demobilization. 431424. SGT. BIRKBY. L. despatched to Concentration Camp for demobilization.	
	18/6/19		431496. PTE. NICHOLLS. W. A. despatched to Concentration Camp for demobilization.	

D. D. & L., London, E.C.
(20340) Wt W5300/P713 750,000 3/18 E 2688 Forms/C2118/10.

Army Fo[illegible]C. 2118.

WAR DIARY

or

~~INTELLIGENCE SUMMARY~~.

(Erase heading not required.)

Instructions regarding War Diaries and Intelligence Summaries are contained in F. S. Regs., Part II. and the Staff Manual respectively. Title pages will be prepared in manuscript.

Place	Date	Hour	Summary of Events and Information	Remarks and references to Appendices
ABBEVILLE.	19/6/19	to	22/6/19. Routine Work.	R/
"	23/6/19.		437305 PTE GOURLAY W. J. Demobilized & struck off strength with effect from 3/6/19.	R/
	24/6/19.		437231. Cpl WINDRIDGE L. C. despatched to Concentration Camp for demobilization.	R/
	25/6/19	to	27/6/19. Routine Work.	R/
"	28/6/19		2199 PTE TIBBLES J. G. evacuated sick to C.C.S. & struck off strength 28/6/19.	R/
	29/6/19		Routine Work.	R/
"	30/6/19.		Routine Work.	R/

[signature]
Captain R.A.M.C. T.

Officer Commanding
2/2 Sth. Mid. Fld. Ambce. R.A.M.C. T.F.

D. D. & L., London, E.C.
(10340) Wt W5300/P713 750,000 3/18 E 2688 Forms/C2118/16.

Army Form C. 2118.

Instructions regarding War Diaries and Intelligence Summaries are contained in F. S. Regs., Part II. and the Staff Manual respectively. Title pages will be prepared in manuscript.

WAR DIARY
or
INTELLIGENCE SUMMARY.

(Erase heading not required.)

Place	Date	Hour	Summary of Events and Information	Remarks and references to Appendices

D. D. & L., London, E.C.
(10340) Wt W5300/P713 750,000 3/18 E 2588 Forms/C2118/16.

July 1919.

CONFIDENTIAL.

Vol 39

140/3605

WAR DIARY

VOLUME 39.

for JULY 1919

Army Form C. 2118.

Instructions regarding War Diaries and Intelligence Summaries are contained in F. S. Regs., Part II. and the Staff Manual respectively. Title pages will be prepared in manuscript.

WAR DIARY
or
~~INTELLIGENCE SUMMARY.~~
(Erase heading not required.)

Place	Date	Hour	Summary of Events and Information	Remarks and references to Appendices
ABBEVILLE	1/7/19		No 167659 PTE. STEVENS. H. C. & Ford Ambulance (61st M. T. Coy) reported for temp. duty.	R/
	2/7/19.		64875 PTE. TURNBULL J. O. Demobilized & struck off strength 4/6/19.	R/
	3/7/19		Routine Work.	R/
	4/7/19		49711 PTE. CAFFREY J. (1/7 Manchesters. [illegible] attd) Transferred to No 523 Coy R.A.S.C. under 61 Div. letter No 4/37/9, dated [illegible] — struck off strength from 4/7/19. M2/150236 Cpl MOSS. C, M2/167150. PTE BIGNELL A. M2/167659 PTE STEVENS H. C. M2/167360, PTE NETHERCOTT A, & M2/156597 PTE WILLIAMS W. J. & Ford Ambulances Nos 63446 & 63456 Motor Cycle No 9301 on completion of temp. duty with the Ambulances returned to 61st Div. M. T. Company. 417210 PTE THOMPSON E, 421501 PTE SHARMAN J & 366025 PTE WILL[illegible] demobilized 14/6/19 & struck off strength.	R/

D. D. & L., London, E.C.
(10340) Wt W5300/P713 750,000 3/18 E 2688 Forms

Instructions regarding War Diaries and Intelligence Summaries are contained in F. S. Regs., Part II. and the Staff Manual respectively. Title pages will be prepared in manuscript.

WAR DIARY

or

~~INTELLIGENCE SUMMARY.~~

(Erase heading not required.)

Army Form C. 2118.

Place	Date	Hour	Summary of Events and Information	Remarks and references to Appendices
ABBEVILLE.	5/7/19	to 8/7/19.	Routine Work.	[illegible]
"	9/7/19.		23 O.R. R.A.M.C. demobilized 14/6/19, 1 O.R. R.A.M.C. demobilized 21/6/19, 1 O.R. R.A.M.C. demobilized 22/6/19 + 1 O.R. R.A.M.C. demobilized 28/6/19, & struck off strength.	[illegible]
"	10/7/19	to 12/7/19	Routine Work.	[illegible]
"	13/7/19.		52034 PTE. SHERRINGTON G. Demobilized off leave in U.K. + struck off strength with effect from 28/5/1919.	[illegible]
"	14/7/19.		82297 A/SGT. WILSON F. Granted acting rank of Staff-Sergeant with effect from 14/6/19. Vice 43032 St.-Sgt. CUMMINGS T. demobilized 14/6/19.	[illegible]
"	15/7/19	to 31/7/19.	Routine Work.	[illegible]

[signature]
Captain R.A.M.C. T.
Officer Commanding
2/2 5th. Mid. Fld. Ambce. R.A.M.C. T.F.

D. D. & L., London, E.
(10340) Wt W5300/P713 750,000 3/18 E 268

www.ingramcontent.com/pod-product-compliance
Lightning Source LLC
Chambersburg PA
CBHW080805010526
44113CB00013B/2327
9781474533027